Money Politics, Globalisation, and Crisis

The Case of Thailand

John Laird

CREDIT PAGE

Published by:
Graham Brash Pte Ltd
Reg. Address: 144 Upper Bukit Timah
Singapore 588177
Mailing Add.: Jurong Point Post Office
P.O. Box 884, Singapore 916430
Tel: 65-7372311 Fax: 65-7372285
E-mail: <u>oses@pacific.net.sg</u>

ISBN: 9812180761

Printed in Singapore.

Contents

Money Politics, Globalisation, and Crisis

Thai people are happy that the International Monetary Fund came in and took over our economic sovereignty, because we do not trust our government. At least we hope the IMF would be as incorruptible as we think, and see to it that the people in power here would manage the IMF fund with integrity and honesty. . . .

Anand Panyarachun, former prime minister, at the Foreign Correspondents Club of Thailand in August 1997, following Thailand's financial crash.

Politics in Thailand is so backward that it cannot follow economic development, and even tries to pull down the economic achievements.

Dr. Arthit Ourairat, former speaker of the House of Representatives and former minister of health, at the Foreign Correspondents Club of Thailand, August 1992.

In high-rise apartments, kids have no place to play. It is very bad for their development. Playing is very important. They need exercise. We don't think about this, only about making money. . . . Now, school children spend their time in supermarkets — they don't understand nature and society.

Dr. Prawase Wasi, quality-of-life advocate and pro-democracy campaigner, interviewed in January 1995.

The representatives who are elected into the Parliament are not of a high quality. . . . Political decisions are not made on a scientific basis. They are made . . . out of consideration for profits or personal benefits or group benefits. That is why our urban health is poor, because of political power plays.

Dr. Hatai Chitanondh, director of the Thailand Health Research Institute, interviewed in November 1994.

Foreword

Can Thailand, following the disastrous financial crash of 1997 and the ensuing economic recession extending into 1999, create a new vision of a satisfying, harmonious, and stable society for its citizens? This book seeks avenues towards such a society by reflecting on what has gone wrong in Thailand's quest for development, and by offering prescriptions for a sustainable quality of life for the 21st Century.

This book presupposes a certain degree of familiarity with Thailand among its readers; for example, with its political system, social structure, economy, and society. However, readers not so familiar with Thailand will still find this work valuable for the pattern of unsustainable development that it describes, elements of which are present in various shapes and forms in other developing and developed countries.

I have not attempted to be exhaustive in research, but rather have tried to draw linkages between aspects of the quality of life, environmental preservation, sustainability, and politics—while showing how false and destructive values promoted by Thailand's materialistic, status-seeking culture and its political culture have severely undermined the first three, and have ushered Thailand into economic crisis. Thailand's unsustainable politics, mired in patronage and corruption, have wrought havoc on the environment, distorted the economy, and lowered the quality of life for all Thais. These questions have become very important for Thailand as it seeks a new vision of society for the 21st Century.

The discourse offered here illustrates these themes through a journalistic approach, and proposes constructive policy suggestions for balanced and sustainable development in Thailand and globally, within the broader objective of achieving a sustainable global society. They include an analysis of Thailand's Crash of 97, an inquiry into the increasingly unstable global economy, an assessment of Thailand's 1997 "people's power" Constitution, further proposals for political reform, and an examination of an emerging and encouraging political trend: the involvement of civil society in political decision making.

My interest in compiling this book grew from my research as a journalist in Thailand, from my commitment as a United Nations official dealing with the environment, and from my academic studies in political science. During the 1990s, I had written a number of articles about environment and quality of life, published in Bangkok. I had also written about political and constitutional reform in Thailand, and delivered a lecture at Thammasat University entitled *Money Politics and the Survival of Thai Democracy*. Reflecting on those writings, I realised that there was a consistent theme running through all of them: the need to move from the present conceit in economics and politics to a genuine development that would be sustainable far into the future. It required just one more leap to link these themes together in the present book, elaborating on my previous writings and adding new material.

Finally, I wish to acknowledge my indebtedness in drawing considerably on information published in *The Nation*, with which I have had a long association. *The Nation* has not shied away from reporting on corruption and related issues, but has adopted a cautious policy in such reporting, in contrast to some sensationalist Thai-language newspapers. Thanks are also due to Tulsathit Taptim, the deputy editor of *The Nation*, who kindly read through and commented upon the manuscript for this book.

John Laird
Hua Hin, Thailand
January 2000

INTRODUCTION

Chapter 1

Thailand Discovers the Meaning of Sustainability

It was in 1997 that Thailand discovered the meaning of sustainability.

The economic bubble that had grown since the early 1990s finally burst, taking both Thais and foreigners by surprise. The grand illusion that Thailand's high-growth economic boom could go on "forever"—fuelled by debt-driven consumption, ill-advised mega-projects, fiscal mismanagement, and political cronyism—came back to earth with a crash: the crash of the property market and the plunge in the value of the baht. The baht was cut loose from its fixed exchange rate on 2 July 1997 and steadily lost value, ending the year about 45 per cent lower against the US dollar. Fifty-six of the country's finance companies had gone broke under massive bad debts, many other companies were facing bankruptcy, and unemployment was increasing. The situation had not improved at year-end 1998.

By then, the crisis, by one estimate, had pushed the number of unemployed up to 1.31 million,[1] compared with 623,000 unemployed in 1997 and 486,000 in 1996; other estimates, however, placed unemployment somewhat higher. GDP declined by 9.4 per cent in 1998.[2] Thailand's total foreign debt stood at around 70 to 80 billion dollars by year-end, according to various calculations.

The poor, or nearly-poor, were being hit the hardest by unemployment. In addition, wages for the less-educated were falling. Between 1996 (the beginning of the economic downturn) and 1998, about one million additional Thais were forced below the poverty line, defined as living on less than US$1 per day. In 1997, the total figure stood at 14.7 million people out of a population of 60 million. These figures were published in January 1999 in a World Bank report, *Thailand Social Monitor: Challenge for Social Reform*. The report warned of a possible breakdown of society, and called for a redoubling of efforts to mitigate the short term impacts of the economic crisis on the poor. It called for drastic reforms to be introduced.[3]

As 1999 began, a social crisis was apparent, driven by business failures, increasing unemployement, and a fall in household incomes. There were fears (which later proved to be unfounded) that the economic downturn would cause a dramatic upsurge in the number of children suffering from low-level malnutrition and in the number of children dropping out of school around the country. Thailand had achieved good indicators for health in pre-Crash days, but had not put into place an effective *social safety net*, largely because rapid economic growth had diverted attention from the need for such a measure to cope with social adversity.

The World Bank, in assessing the East Asian crisis as a whole, noted in January that:

> Inefficiencies in the public health and education systems which existed prior to the crisis are now being exposed, as demand for low-cost social services increases. Over the long-term, declining health and malnutrition will affect worker productivity, reducing future growth, and delaying the recovery. The impact of malnutrition and the removal from schools will be especially hard on children, who may suffer from stunting and poor cognitive development as a result.[4]

However, by July 1999, the World Bank had modified its January assessment, in its subsequent issue of *Thailand Social Monitor,* noting that new data showed that Thai families and Thai policy makers had cushioned and in some cases eliminated expected negative consequences of the crisis in health and education. The report asked:

> Did education and health outcomes decline during the crisis, as predicted? Did use of services, such as school enrollments and visits to public health facilities, go down during the crisis, as was expected? Did families cut back on vital social expenditures so they could spend their reduced incomes on other priorities?

> Did the Government cut back on education and health budgets and thus reduce the quality and availability of education and health services? The answer to those questions is encouraging: overall, on a national scale, the expectations of dire consequences have not materialised. . . . [However,] the positive results seen in the aggregate data could change substantially if another year of economic contraction or stagnation follows in 1999-2000.

The World Bank noted that Thai families, including the poor, were more resilient and responsible than many anticipated; and that government and local officials in particular had proven more adept at crisis response than many had predicted. In the year following the onset of the crisis, overall enrollments in education actually increased. In spite of declining incomes and rising costs, households made optimal reallocation decisions—reducing expenditures on tobacco and alcohol, clothing and footwear, and on household goods while increasing expenditures on education. Some students shifted from private to public schools to reduce expenditures, and families used savings, or borrowed, to help meet the higher costs of education. There was an upsurge in utilisation of the student loan programme.

In addition, the government succeeded in maintaining real expenditures on education and sensible allocations within the aggregate budget, said the World Bank. In sum, between 1996 and 1998, per capita expenditures on education in real terms increased.

Regarding health, the bank noted that two years after the onset of the 1997 economic crisis, there was little if any evidence of its impact on health outcomes. Maternal and child health outputs and outcomes were stable or improving. Routine data as well as surveys showed no increase in the number of cases of malnutrition reported.

Said the World Bank:

> Two years after the onset of the 1997 economic crisis, most of the pessimistic expectations did not materialise. There is little if any evidence of a crisis impact on health needs and outcomes. The growth of public health budget was interrupted, but budget cuts have been limited. When adjusted for inflation, the 1998 post-crisis expenditures are at a similar level to the pre-crisis 1996 level, and operating budgets have increased. The crisis

halted the trend of sustained high level capital investment. Overall, household health expenditures declined, but poor people were less affected than the non-poor. . . .

The expected drop in utilisation of public services was not realised during the crisis. On the contrary, there was increased use of public services, particularly for outpatient services. The government has enlarged its health safety net by increasing the coverage of public health insurance.

A continuing problem, into the second half of 1999, was what to do with new graduates who were facing unemployment, and with the urban migrants returning to the countryside, many of whom had been unskilled labourers employed in the construction sector. International organisations were working with the Thai government to create community development projects for the graduates, and to support rural investment schemes for skills training and for small enterprises development for the returning migrants. The urban returnees faced a dramatic change in their lifestyles as low-paid landless labourers; it was thought that the agricultural sector could not absorb many of them.

Analysts scurried to discover the reasons behind Thailand's fall. They looked at the performance of the Bank of Thailand, with its secretiveness and apparent lack of accountability in spending huge sums of money to prop up an overvalued currency and failing finance companies. By the end of 1997, many Thais were blaming errors by the central bank for Thailand's economic collapse, and the bank was subject to an investigation in 1998. But that was only part of the story. It was becoming apparent that economic and political practices which underlay Thailand's boom were unsustainable.

Thailand was pursuing the global trend of financial liberalisation; following the establishment of the Bangkok International Banking Facility in March 1993, tens of billions of dollars of foreign money flowed into the country—the much sought-after foreign "investment" that has been seen conventionally as a necessity for Thailand's development. But, with hindsight, it became very apparent that the Thai business and financial community lacked the capacity, the maturity, or the vision to use it wisely. Much of the huge borrowings in US dollars found their way into unproductive investment such as property and stock market speculation.

Other money went into grandiose schemes. Unbridled ambition linked with carefree management practices and lack of foresight, served to further inflate the growing economic bubble.

The huge amount of foreign money flowing into Thailand had an intoxicating effect. The attitude seemed to be, "The money is there, you had better grab it"—whether or not carefully-thought-out investment plans existed for it. Thai banks and finance companies had a field day as long as the baht was closely pegged to the US dollar: borrowing dollars at 6–7 per cent interest and lending at 13–14 per cent interest in baht. Such was the intoxication that many beneficiaries of the loans seemed to forget that loans have to be repaid, and that repaying them depends on sound investment decisions.

Something like a cult mentality prevailed: a self-reinforcing, euphoric "cult of growth". Foreign bankers and investors, likewise, seemed intoxicated by the prospect that by throwing money into a high-growth economy, they would inevitably gain high returns—while apparently pushing concerns about sustainability, transparency, and accountability into the background. Indeed, there was a belief (commonly cited by foreign investors) that high economic growth could somehow excuse or at least bypass these shortcomings in financial integrity. This "cult of growth" and "grab the money" mentality affected not only Thailand, but many of its Asian neighbours as well.

Who would want to be troubled about sustainability in such circumstances? Indeed, what was it?

Nobody wanted to pay attention to elements such as macro-economic fundamentals, market capacity, or prudent regulation of the property market. Government ministers, it seems, hardly understood the implications of a current account deficit of eight per cent of GDP, and of overlending to the property market. The Bank of Thailand made some weak noises about it, but did not insist on measures to discourage it. After all, who would presume to tell Thailand's high-flying, high-status tycoons that they were taking too many risks with carefree property investment and were threatening the country's financial stability? Those who should have been regulating and guiding such investment—the cabinet, the Finance Ministry, and the Bank of Thailand—seemed eager to go along with it, or at least to disregard the risks. After all, under the Thai patronage system, those who smooth the way for big projects and big transactions routinely expect rewards in return. Big money changing hands, big towers going up in Bangkok's central business district (of course, adding to big families' so-important prestige) looked something like a money-making dream world that could go on forever.

Then came the forced devaluation of the baht and the suspension of the 58 near-bankrupt finance companies (56 would later be closed permanently). The extent of the huge debt liabilities of the financial system and big companies was finally revealed. The Bank of Thailand, trying to defend the value of the baht, had committed almost all its foreign reserves in forward currency contracts. Other financial institutions and banks looked very shaky as shock waves from macro-economic mismanagement reverberated throughout the economy. Thailand was forced to seek a 17-billion-dollar rescue package from the International Monetary Fund, accompanied by requirements to cut government spending and to reform the financial system.

The hard lesson of 1997 is that sustainable development—in its many dimensions—is the first and all-important requirement of economy and society. But how many people understand its implications?

> Very few people even know what sustainable development is; they don't pay attention to it.

That was the comment of Thailand's senior official in charge of the environment, Kasem Snidvongs, in July 1996.[5] Twelve months later, Thailand was veering on the brink of national bankruptcy.

Of course, much of this crisis could be explained by the fact that Thailand is a developing country. Its institutions, therefore, were not developed enough to fully understand and cope with the shock of these new, momentous events. Following that observation, however, we must also ask, why was the political system incapable of producing leadership which could provide rational guidance to economic decision making, and pursue fiscal prudence?

In fact, Thailand's political culture has produced few party politicians who have had the intellectual ability or the inclination to act in the interest of Thailand's sustainable development, or as regulators of the financial and economic system; the governments of prime ministers Banharn Silpa-archa (July 1995–September 1996) and Chavalit Yongchaiyudh (November 1996–November 1997) generally lacked such expertise or commitment. "Technocrats" brought into the Chavalit cabinet from outside politics encountered many political obstacles to the introduction of rational guidance into economic policy.

Rather, Thailand's pervasive money politics, lubricated by patronage and corruption, served to encourage the bubble economy throughout the 1990s through a proliferation of money-making projects and schemes. Politics feasted off the huge influx of "hot money" into the country, a substantial amount of which seems to have found its way into politicians' bank accounts or to have been spent on elections. This is apparent when we consider reports that money spent on vote-buying reached an all-time high during campaigning for the November 1996 general election, which preceded Thailand's economic crash by about eight months. Political analysts estimated that at least 20 billion baht was spent on the election as a whole. At the prevailing exchange rate, that amounted to an astonishing US$800 million.[6] By comparison, in Britain, a country with a similar-sized population to Thailand, an estimated US$75 million was spent by the two main political parties on the 1997 general election.[7] Thailand's political and financial systems, deeply entangled in an incestuous relationship, had both failed the development needs of the country.

The Scourge of Money Politics

Money politics is anti-democratic and unsustainable in the long run, as well as unlawful. We can see that money politics is unsustainable because, in a competitive political atmosphere, it must grow in order to reach its objective: attainment of political power. Thus, the growth of money politics (and its chief accessory, patronage politics) must increasingly infiltrate institutions of governance, seeking higher rewards. Patronage and money politics increasingly undermine the rule of law and fiscal responsibility. That is one of the lessons of Thailand's financial meltdown. In the end, if strong countermeasures are not forthcoming, politicians of the patronage/corruption system will even attempt the large-scale transfer of state financial assets into private bank accounts.

In a lecture at Thammasat University in August 1992, I raised the prospect of the Thai patronage/corruption system ever growing and ever expanding the methods by which it extracted wealth from the state. I compared it to the Marcos dictatorship in the Philippines, where Marcos completely corrupted the system of government and set up a massive patronage system of cronies (the famous Marcos cronies) who were granted monopolies and favours in order to control the economy, with "royalties" flowing back to the centre. This arrangement made a complete mockery of law and economics. The Philippines subsequently suffered a political crisis, an economic collapse, and 10 years of stagnation.

Many analysts in 1992 thought that the same thing could not happen in Thailand because it was impossible for one man to centre such power on himself in Thailand's multi-party, coalition politics. Yet we have witnessed a version of Marcos-style cronyism, the politics of *kleptocracy*,[8] asserting itself through temporary alliances of big political players within the cabinet-quota system of coalition government. Following the collapse of Thailand's financial system in 1997, there were strong suspicions that politicians, through more complex and deceptive practices than Marcos's, had achieved a *de facto*, large-scale transfer of state finances into private bank accounts.

The scandal and court cases surrounding the 1996 collapse of the Bangkok Bank of Commerce may eventually provide interesting information showing how politicians benefited financially from dubious practices which led to the collapse. The Bank of Thailand poured in billions of baht to prop up the failing, apparently fraud-ridden bank, without revealing to the public the dire condition of the bank. Some analysts now pinpoint this scandal and cover-up as the beginning of Thailand's financial crisis. (Circumstances surrounding this case are examined in more detail in Chapters 4 and 7.)

The unrestrained growth of money politics can undermine the sustainability of the financial system and even of the economy—because money politics abhors the rule of law, transparency, and accountability; and because it fails utterly to promote high standards of decision making. These are all requirements for good governance, sustainable development, and the pursuit of a genuine quality of life—the major themes of this book. Under money politics, decision making on the basis of merit, employing rational criteria, can hardly take place. Sustainability in the economy and in national development ceases to have any meaning, and the door is opened to widespread graft and large-scale financial fraud. Witness all the grand schemes for a new capital city, a new airport, mass transit systems, etc., that have changed, been relocated, or been renegotiated every time a new government has come to power. The needs of patronage and money politics take precedence over the needs for continuity of policy and for rational development of infrastructure.

And then there is the illegal economy, accounting for something like 20 per cent of the country's gross domestic product. Businesses of gambling, drug smuggling, prostitution, smuggling of illegal foreign labour, oil smuggling, and sales of illegal weapons, are almost all owned by politicians, according to researchers, and are worth more than 400 billion baht per year (see Chapter 7). Under the patronage system, the law cannot touch these politicians.

How much did politicians of the political patronage system contribute to the downfall of Thailand's high-flying economy? The demise of the Banharn government in September 1996 offered a graphic clue. As the government came to a sudden end, ministers scrambled during the final few cabinet meetings to approve their pet projects and get their chunk of the 1997 budget committed before losing their posts. The *Bangkok Post* wrote about the scramble:

> Only three working days before the general election, the government has approved a record budget of 211.6 billion baht for 2,661 projects, forcing the new administration to commit on-going funding for at least the next three fiscal years. No details of the approvals were submitted to cabinet. Documents tabled before cabinet members on Tuesday only categorised the projects. Prime Minister Banharn Silpa-archa also ordered that details not be publicised. . . .[9]

Spend, spend, spend was the order of the day. Forget about feasibility studies, public debate, or the priorities of sustainable development. (The pervasive, destructive nature of the political patronage system in Thailand is examined in Chapter 8.)

Former prime minister, Anand Panyarachun, promoting the draft of Thailand's new, anti-corruption Constitution in August 1997, opined that corrupt cabinet ministers bore the greatest share of responsibility for Thailand's economic collapse.[10] It was obvious years earlier that money politics would one day drag down Thailand's economy. It had already ravaged the rural environment and contributed to the wretched pollution and overcrowding in the cities, particularly Bangkok. University academics and journalists came closest to recognising that the parasites of patronage/money politics were feasting on the flesh of the Thai nation. The business community in general did not actively oppose money politics, although some individual businessmen spoke out against corruption. The big, well-connected players of the business community (particularly in the construction and communications sectors) were rather indulging in large-scale purchasing of political influence to serve their interests.

The Eighth Development Plan

Thailand's Eighth National Economic and Social Development Plan (1997–2001) reflects many of the concerns arising from Thailand's rapidly changing society, and shifts emphasis for the first time from a mainly economic perspective to the emerging perspective of people-centred development. While the plan sets out a vision of a sane and sustainable society, many doubts hang over its implementation. The financial and economic crisis which struck in mid-1997 required severe cuts in the national budget, giving rise to calls for a revision of the plan. By 1998, emphasis was rather shifting back to old formulas of economic stimulation. Moreover, recent, elected governments had shown little inclination to follow provisions of past development plans, although at election time most political parties borrow their electoral platforms more or less directly from the plan. Another constraint to the plan's implementation is Thailand's lethargic, under-motivated bureaucracy.

The introduction to the Eighth Plan (written before the July 1997 plunge of the baht precipitated Thailand's economic crisis) states:

> As we enter the 21st Century, which will happen within the period of the Eighth Plan, Thailand is facing one of the most crucial transitions in its development history. During the past two decades advances in information technology have greatly contributed to rapid globalisation, dictating the need for new world orders—economic, social, and in international relations. . . .

> The influx of foreign culture and information through the existing media in forms such as advertising and entertainment, is already creating undesirable values based on materialism, consumerism, and extravagance among the younger generation, and allowing cultural domination. Globalisation has also brought with it new international values regarding democracy, human rights, gender

equality, and environmental protection. From these has arisen a wider belief that the type of development which has prevailed to date, focusing on economic growth without due consideration for the individual, the family, the community, and social and environmental issues, cannot be sustained in the long run. If no action is taken to redirect the development process, the chance for the people to co-exist harmoniously with Nature may be lost forever.[11]

Human development is thus the theme of the plan, especially focusing on the need to reform the education system and curriculum, and to make 12 years of compulsory education available to all Thai children. Educational reform has now become urgent for Thailand, not only to keep up with economic competitors in a globalising economy, but also for improvement of the quality of life and achievement of democratic aspirations. Past indifference to reform of the education system is now seen as a bottleneck hampering the quest for sustainable development and achievement of a sustainable quality of life; the political indifference to educational reform, largely a by-product of money politics, has made a tragedy out of this quest. However, by mid-1999, Thailand finally seemed ready to seriously tackle this deficiency following the passage of the National Education Act. (The question of educational reform is discussed in Chapter 9.)

It is the growing need for social and personal development—arising in the first place from educational reform—that is now being recognised, following decades of economic growth that has increased material wealth and improved basic infrastructure of the countryside, but which has left many problems in its wake. The Eighth Plan summary notes that

> . . . fiercer competition for income and wealth in Thailand has brought with it greater materialism. This in turn has had a negative impact on people's behaviour, bringing about a lack of discipline, declining ethical and moral standards, and the rise of practices which centre around self-interest and the exploitation of others. These unfavourable trends are threatening the traditional Thai values and ways of life, and they have contributed to the collapse of families, communities, and local cultures. In addition, the social stresses that accompany economic prosperity have started to alter

the patterns of sickness and mortality, bringing the diseases of modern life, such as cancer, heart disease, and high-blood pressure. The number of reported tragedies and deaths resulting from accidents and natural disasters has likewise increased.[12]

(These issues are examined more closely in Section 3 of this book, Quality of Life or Growth Without Development.)

In brief, the Eighth Plan states its objectives as:

1. To foster and develop the potentials of all Thais, in terms of health, physical wellbeing, intellect, vocational skills, and ability to adapt to changing social and economic conditions.
2. To develop a stable society, strengthen family and community, support human development, improve quality of life, and promote increased community participation in national development.
3. To promote stable and sustainable economic growth, and to empower the people to play a greater role in the development process and receive a fair share of the benefits of growth.
4. To utilise, preserve, and rehabilitate the environment and natural resources in such a way that they can play a major role in economic and social development and contribute to better quality of life for the Thai people.
5. To reform the system of public administration so as to allow greater participation of non-governmental organisations, the private sector, communities, and the general public in the process of national development.[13]

It can be seen from the above points that people's empowerment has emerged as a major goal in the sustainable development of Thai society. This goal is also apparent in Thailand's people's power Constitution which was passed by Parliament on 27 September 1997. The time has come for Thais to become participants in development rather than subjects of development. This long-overdue concern to define and promote such a democratic dimension in Thailand gained a great boost, both in the Eighth Plan and the Constitution, by taking the drafting process to the people.

People from all walks of life were encouraged for the first time to participate in the national development planning process for the Eighth

Plan. Ten brainstorming meetings were arranged to elicit ideas from intellectuals all over the country; ideas were also sought from members of different professions; and finally, ten sub-regional seminars were held to gather comments and recommendations from people at the grassroots level. The actual drafting then took place in three planning sub-committees.

A similar approach was taken for the first time with the 1997 Constitution, Thailand's sixteenth charter since the overthrow of absolute monarchy in 1932. Comments were elicited from the public on a large scale: some 198,600 questionnaires and nearly 15,000 letters were reportedly received by the Constitutional Drafting Assembly's public hearing committee. Public hearings were organised in every province, and finally, seminars to discuss and explain the draft were organised on a regional basis.

These processes of the Eighth Plan and the sixteenth Constitution have given a new meaning to public participation and planning. In 1998–99, the same process was again employed to get much-needed educational reform on the right track. This momentum should be applied in other ways: Thailand's woefully unplanned urban development needs to benefit from such participatory planning (and this question is discussed in Section 5, The Urban Challenge, particularly in Chapter 18).

Additionally, as Thailand's industrialising economy has suffered from the financial collapse and a shortage of educated personnel, renewed attention is turning towards agriculture as Thailand's solid foundation on which to rebuild the economy. Agriculture has been neglected in the recent past as sectors such as textiles and tourism became big money-earners. Also neglected have been millions of Thailand's low-income population dependent on agriculture. Policy makers, rather than seeing these people as a resource to be educated to uplift agriculture, saw them as cheap labour to fuel Thailand's bid for industrialisation. The psychology of the influential business sector was, "Why educate the poor if they are required only to work in factories?" This imbalance in social and economic development became more apparent after the Crash of 97 and the dissipation of the wealth that had been extracted from the rural economy. Thailand's profligate rich ploughed money into the property bubble and into fostering a consumer economy, leaving the agricultural economy deprived of investment, and the financial system bankrupt when the Crash came.

Now it is time for a second wave of agricultural development to further strengthen Thailand's economy in the 21st Century. But it must be sustainable agricultural development which protects the resource base and which is aimed at uplifting the rural poor as much as at gaining export revenue. (These needs, which have been severely neglected in the past rush for industrialisation and profits, are discussed in Chapter 14.)

Sustainability or Another Bubble?

As Thailand's economy lingered in recession at the start of 1999, with the possibility of further shocks from a volatile global economy, many educated Thais were asking, what had the country's years of rapid growth achieved in the final analysis? The high-growth, high-profit, high-consumption mentality had further devastated the environment; many business tycoons and middle-class investors who gambled on an unsustainable economy were broke; and the country had incurred massive private and public debt. Additionally, the country faced the daunting task of reconstructing its economy within the context of a much more competitive global economy. Would Thais continue to dream of the get-rich-quick days and try to restore the bubble economy, or would wiser leaders motivate Thais to construct a sustainable economy that would reduce inequalities in society and begin to remedy Thailand's massive environmental problems?

In 1999, whether or not Thailand could follow a sustainable course of development depended on whether or not politics could become more mature and rise above the abusive practices of the past. Could politicians discover a new sense of responsibility to the nation and people? Much hinged on new rights and anti-corruption measures included in the 1997 Constitution, and particularly how new enabling laws would be implemented. A general election due by November 2000 promised to be a major test of these new measures and laws. Would the old, money-hungry patronage system reassert itself and seek ways to neutralise the new laws? The main question was still whether or not many, or any, "big" politicians, whose massive corruption earlier helped to drag down the country, could be prosecuted and jailed.

Thailand has the intellectual, technical, and entrepreneurial resources to become a sustainable society, enjoying a satisfying quality of life in harmony with Nature. Note that I have deliberately omitted to say that Thailand has the resources to become a developed country with a high per capita income and a high level of material consumption. I regard these as obsolete concepts in a world which urgently needs to rethink economic priorities and establish global ecological and social stability. (This question is discussed more fully in the next introductory chapter.)

In fact, Thailand's economic crisis should now be seen as an opportunity: old-style politicians and self-absorbed business leaders are on the defensive over their mistakes which impoverished the country. The weak, the corrupt, and the venal deserve to perish, as do companies that relied on deceptive and dishonest practices. Economic recessions present opportunities for a clean-out of non-performing companies and government offices.

For consumers, drawing back from the high life may give them time to reflect on what are the really important ingredients of their lives. And the heresies of the discredited real estate and property developers will give fuel to those officials and activists who value well-planned urban development which gives the highest priority to environment. The (previous) quest for high economic growth rates—which in the past also included the unproductive growth of inflated land and property prices—should now be put into its proper perspective.

Thailand has now entered a necessary period of soul-searching and redefinition, coinciding with the dawn of the new millennium. The kingdom's new people's power Constitution gives fresh opportunities for concerned groups to bring quality-of-life issues into the public arena, through all the provisions of transparency and public participation it guarantees. It is time for quality-of-life advocates to mount their offensive. Will there thus be an upsurge of public demand, sensitively mobilised and channeled, to put these issues on the political agenda? (Such questions are discussed in the next chapter and in Chapters 3 and 9.)

While Thailand's quest for a sustainable society depends on the enlightened development and use of its own resources, the country is more than ever influenced by global trends:

- the forming of a super-competitive global economy where efficient "value" creators are rewarded, and the less efficient often severely punished;
- the internationalisation of consumerism, and its attendant cultural and spiritual degradation; and

- the continuing inability of governments in an international context to protect the global resource base from pollution and destructive exploitation.

All of these are encompassed by what I call the global ideology of *economism*. At the end of 1998, this global ideology was showing signs of unravelling (see Chapter 3). The major question hanging over it was, can *economism* evolve and incorporate sound ecological principles for all economic activities, and thus guarantee a sustainable quality of life for the Earth's future generations?

This question has largely been ignored by ruling elites in developing countries, in their rush to "catch up" with and emulate the development mistakes of the industrialised countries. Countries such as Thailand need to reflect more upon how the goal of sustainability applies globally, and how they can reorder national priorities and accept their responsibility to resist unsustainable trends on a global basis. (This global perspective and the ideology of *economism* are discussed in the next introductory chapter.)

Chapter 2

Stepping Back From Global Disaster

As we experience the dawning of a new millennium, we look back on the conclusion of the 20th Century with a certain awe. This was the century when the first humans travelled in outer space, when technology asserted its mastery over Nature and held out the vision of a life of wealth and ease for humankind, when the "look good, feel good" culture of mass consumption bade to dominate global consciousness.

It was also the century when an awesome truth about the nature of this newly technologised humanity became evident, a truth that people wanted rather to forget: the 20th Century was the century when humankind gained the ability to destroy itself.

This chilling realisation occurred in the last quarter of the 20th Century, as the nuclear arms race reached a frenzy, and ideological foes confronted each other with thousands of nuclear weapons, each capable of destroying a mega-city. Just a limited detonation of such weapons would be enough to send huge dust clouds into the atmosphere which would shroud the earth for years, shutting out sunlight and bringing on nuclear winter leading to a global failure of food crops and the fall of high civilisation as we know it.[1]

The possibility of nuclear winter is still with us, although political leaders of the major powers, finally understanding where their predecessors had led the world, have now stepped back from such a disaster, made peace, and are gradually eliminating weapons of mass destruction. In May 1998, however, as India and Pakistan tested nuclear weapons, the world was reminded that nuclear dangers still exist in politically unstable parts of the world.

But nuclear winter is not the only potential global disaster that we can foresee as we enter the new millennium. The 21st Century must be a

19

century of reflection, when all human beings are educated to take into their hearts the fact that humankind may still wreak devastation on the planet through a more subtle and less obvious process: the accumulated effects of unsustainable consumption—with its attendant pollution and destruction of natural resources—on the Earth's ecological balance. Human-induced climate change leading to global warming—the so-called greenhouse effect—became recognised by many in the closing years of the 20th Century as the biggest potential environmental disaster of the 21st Century.

If humankind cannot drastically reduce air pollution from carbon dioxide and other greenhouse gases, the climate will heat up significantly in the latter half of the 21st Century, with predicted catastrophic results. Expanding oceans would threaten to inundate low-lying coastal cities (where a majority of the world's urban population lives); increased temperatures would wreak havoc on agriculture in many countries through droughts and invasions of pests; and there would be an upsurge in disease throughout the world. In 1999, new evidence indicated that higher temperatures at the South Pole were causing an increasingly rapid melting and erosion of the Antarctic ice shelf.

It took about 40 years after the first nuclear weapon was used in warfare for leaders of the big powers to realise that the path of nuclear confrontation had taken the world to the brink of devastation. The global warming phenomenon—as a long-term effect of the still-growing industrial revolution—has been predicted for perhaps a century. But it is only since the 1980s that scientists have felt confident enough about the data they had collected to call on political leaders to change the course of basic, consumptive economics that now fuels the growth of global gross domestic product (GDP). By 1999, that scientific confidence had grown into virtual certainty. Nations made a serious attempt to come to grips with global warming at climate change negotiations at Kyoto in December 1997 with mixed results. (More about this crucial issue later in the chapter.)

But, unlike the efforts which defused big-power nuclear confrontation, major changes in the assumptions and practices of the new competitive, globalised economics—which promote unsustainable mass consumption—will take much longer. Such changes require major shifts, on a global basis, in human behaviour, expectations, and civil organisation. The challenge is to introduce and foster these changes and to place ecological sustainability at the centre of economics, so that all economic and consumptive activities adopt ecological principles as first, inviolable principles. These principles cannot be traded off against other high-minded ideas such as free-market, liberal economics, or the human freedoms taken for granted as natural rights—since a stable ecology is the foundation of human societies in the first place, from which all other notions of human rights and freedoms arise. This point has been utterly overlooked in philosophy and history up to the mid-20th Century, when the devastating impacts of man's economic activities on the global ecology became widely apparent. The need to put ecological principles at the heart of every human endeavour is what I call the *ecological imperative*.

It is all too obvious to scholars of ecology that present global economic assumptions and practices are not sustainable in the long term. The great majority of conventional economists, however, trapped within the closed logic of prevailing economic theory, cannot see this. But a major ideological change is on the way. The compelling logic of having to deal with global warming (among other emerging environmental crises) in the 21st Century will bring this about: political leaders will be compelled to repudiate the assumption of limitless growth and limitless consumption, and define a new quality of life which integrates global ecological concerns into the foundations of economic life. For the first time in economic history, a sustainable balance will have to be found, new equations formed. The *ecological imperative* calls for a reassessment of human endeavour and human aspirations, both at the individual level and that of society.

One important requirement is becoming more widely discussed in this growing global debate: in order to strive for global sustainability, the basic needs of the poor must be met. Recently, as economic globalisation has increased in pace, it has created greater gaps between rich and poor, both within countries and among countries. This is potentially destabilising and dangerous. The present glorification of self-indulgent, high-consumption levels of the rich provides an unsustainable model for the middle class—and, indeed, for society as a whole. It is towards that sector of society possessing disposable income that we must look to redefine the concept of quality of life.

Moving to Sustainable Development

Sustainable development—it sounds like a jargon phrase, buzzwords out of a dull, bureaucratic United Nations report. But it is crucial to the favourable evolution of our global civilisation, and its implications touch everyone. Whether our populations can take it to heart or not will determine the quality of life for future generations of humankind.

What is sustainable development? It is often easier to say what it is not, as in the case of the financial and economic collapse in Thailand which began in 1997. It has everything to do with humankind's impact on global ecology. When human activities fall out of balance with what Nature can support, terrible accidents arise. Consider this example:

The ethnically-based genocide in Rwanda in 1994 was largely the result of rapid, unsustainable population growth within a small area of land. That small, Central African country is one of the most overcrowded on the planet, with one of the world's highest population growth rates. The fact that two rival tribes, one pastoral and the other agricultural, shared and depended upon a relatively diminishing resource—land— added the extra spark to make the crisis of overpopulation manifest itself in a horrific genocide, in which perhaps half a million people died.[2]

There are many time-bombs of unsustainability ticking away towards crisis. Again, look at the conflict in 1995 between Spain and Canada over fish catches allowed in the North Atlantic off the coast of Newfoundland. Many countries are trying to boost their economies and feed their growing populations by catching more fish, even as major fishing grounds around the world are becoming overexploited, threatening the viability of species. The spread of new, "more efficient" fishing technology threatens to further deplete fish stocks, leading to more crises between nations competing for a diminishing resource.

Of course, the answer to such dilemmas is enlightened management on a global basis for sustainable use of resources. This has proved to be a difficult proposition at a time when free-market, exploitative economic theory talks mainly about winners and losers in the global economic race. Current economic theory does not preach reduced expectations of individuals and nations; it preaches growth. There is no shortage of businessmen who oppose environmental regulations because such rules limit the growth and profits of their businesses. There are many significant disputes in which exploitation of natural resources threatens the environment, but where business interests continue to hold sway over sustainability. Forest destruction is one; the burning of fossil fuels, leading to global warming, is another.

The question of sustainable development must be placed firmly on national political agendas. People must recognise the diverse implications that this term has for their lives and their activities, and for their grandchildren's future. Sustainable development is a theory, a process, and an imperative.

As a theory, sustainable development recognises that we are living on a finite planet with finite resources. It recognises that the Earth's natural systems have achieved a certain equilibrium over millions of years that has allowed the human species to grow and prosper to a level of some six billion individuals, and to dominate the life of the planet. It recognises that the finite nature of the Earth imposes limits that human economic activity cannot exceed.

As a process, sustainable development tries to identify all the ecologically destructive activities of humankind, and to minimise or eliminate them. At the same time, it strives to promote activities that will preserve and enhance our natural living environment and that will enhance the lives of all the Earth's people.

Sustainable development is an imperative (arising from the *ecological imperative*) because it has now been acknowledged that humankind, through population growth and economic growth, is making excessive demands on the world's natural systems. If these are seriously destabilised—as we are now beginning to experience with the world's climate system, through human-induced global warming—ecological disaster and social strife will be the likely result.

Measures to bring about sustainable development are presently the subject of continuing global negotiations that were initiated or given momentum by the historic Rio de Janeiro Earth Summit. It may be some time before significant measures emerge, but the next 25 years promise major changes in how economies are run, and in how the mass media reflect the new imperatives of sustainable development.

Here is a quote from James Gustave Speth, then the administrator of the United Nations Development Programme (UNDP), speaking in Seoul at a 1995 policy workshop, Towards the Goals of a Sustainable Society:[3]

23

Our current patterns of production and consumption are not sustainable. With reckless abandon, we are rapidly depleting our natural resources and polluting our air and water. As a result, skies once blue are now brown. Water once pure is now unsafe, often, even for industrial purposes. Deforestation and desertification continue to spread, and species continue to disappear at alarming rates.

But the downward environmental spiral stemming from current production and consumption patterns can be reversed. Change is possible. It's feasible. And it's necessary. Indeed, some form of change is inevitable. So we can either choose to take the high road and manage the change now, or we can pursue business as usual and have the change forced upon us later as our natural resources become depleted and Earth's fragile balance is permanently disrupted.

Here is an observation from Claude Fussler, a senior executive in the transnational Dow Chemical Company, in a 1996 interview with London-based environmental journalist Geoffrey Lean:[4]

Developed countries will have to cut their use of energy and other raw materials—and their impact on the environment—more than 10 times over in little more than a generation, if the needs of the world's growing population are to be met without destroying the planet.

Lean comments:

This stark conclusion might seem radical enough coming from a deep green environmental group. Remarkably, it comes from a report by a business-led group of leading industrialists, government officials, and academics from the world's richest countries [The World Business Council for Sustainable Development.[5]]

Fussler continues:

> The technology and consumption models of developed countries have become the problem rather than the solution. . . . The individual today needs an absurd share of natural resources for residence, mobility, infrastructure, and cleaning or flushing everything he makes or owns.

The concept of sustainable development is quite new in economic and historical terms, but marks a momentous turning point, even though it is still little understood by the general population, and still awaits serious, coordinated efforts to apply it. The year 1972 was perhaps the first major landmark in the quest for sustainable development and global environmental awareness, as the Stockholm Conference on the Human Environment became a focus for global action on environmental problems. According to the United Nations Environment Programme (UNEP):

> In the preparations for the conference, the links between environment and development were comprehensively drawn for the first time. [The conference] established that certain environmental problems needed to be studied globally or regionally. It was generally assumed that the world's system of national governments, regional groupings, and international agencies had the power to take effective action, and that the limiting factors were scientific and economic.[6]

Also in 1972, the Club of Rome published *The Limits to Growth*, in which the world's continuing ability to deal with the waste resulting from development was questioned.

Fifteen years later, in 1987, the World Commission on Environment and Development (also known as the Brundtland Commission) published *Our Common Future*, in which sustainable development was defined as development which meets the needs of the present generation without compromising the ability of future generations to meet their own needs. This is presently the most popular short definition of sustainable development.

Then came the most significant global meeti g on the environment of the 20th Century, the 1992 Earth Summi (the United Nations

Conference on Environment and Development, or UNCED) held in Rio de Janeiro. It was the zenith of the rising global concern about the environment. It touched all major environmental issues, and—although its many compromises could not please everyone—it produced a comprehensive blueprint, *Agenda 21*, to achieve global sustainable development in the 21st Century.

The major fault accompanying *Agenda 21* was that the countries that negotiated it lacked the imagination and the political will to devise a global mechanism to pay for all the activities that they recommended, leaving an enormous vacuum surrounding all their lofty intentions. Much of the financing for tackling global environmental problems was left up to the developing countries themselves (where most of the problems occurred) and to the generosity of donors in the "developed" world. Such a system of voluntary generosity has failed the needs of sustainable development: donors' commitment was weak in 1992, and has since suffered from further attrition. (This point is expanded below.) At the time of the Earth Summit, it was estimated that $600 billion was needed to implement *Agenda 21*, of which around 80 per cent would be mobilised by the developing countries themselves.

However, *Agenda 21* did provide a much-needed, comprehensive vision of a future Earth, around which concerned individuals and groups could rally. It legitimised the role of the NGO movement in environmental action, and thus gave impetus to a vibrant and growing approach to boost public consciousness. And it created expectations and a momentum towards integrating environmental concerns into governmental activities, and into education, around the world.

The spirit of Rio also boosted efforts to create a body of binding international law governing the environment. In the 25 years since 1972, some 200 legal instruments[7] have been created to target environmental issues, making a huge contribution to the body of international law. This painstaking legalistic process—taking place, with a few exceptions, within the United Nations system—has become perhaps the major achievement to date in tackling global environmental issues. It has resulted in such globally-negotiated treaties such as the Framework Convention on Climate Change (under which global warming is being tackled) and the Treaty on Biodiversity. This body of international law is perhaps also the greatest testament to the necessity for the United Nations system itself. But some crucial issues unfortunately still remain outside this process of negotiating legally-binding international agreements; for example, global deforestation.

Meanwhile, the efforts at clarifying and promoting sustainable development go on. Following are some additional observations about its nature and requirements. The report, *State of the Environment in Asia and the Pacific, 1995* gives an overview of the progress towards sustainable development.[8] Some excerpts:

> The concept of sustainable development, as proposed by the Brundtland Commission's report, *Our Common Future*, and elaborated by *Agenda 21*, is universally accepted as the basis of all future development-environment relationships. The world community recognised that sustainability of the quality of human life is inextricably linked to the quality of life of the environment. However, it very much depends on a global effort to operationalise the concept of sustainability. There is still uncertainty on when this would start producing results. . . .

> Viewed pessimistically, the burden of poverty and environmental degradation accumulated by all the generations of the 20th Century may look overwhelming and beyond the future carrying capacity of the planet Earth. But there is also room for optimism. The process initiated during this decade to minimise the burden of the past still offers not only hope but also provides possibilities of meeting this challenge effectively, if not totally, with the development of new political will and the vast array of resources and tools that humankind has developed during the current century.

So says the *State of the Environment* report. But where will this political will come from? Sustainability has been recognised as a necessity mainly by the scientific and intellectual community. Governments and the business sector up to now have proven reluctant or incapable of coming to grips with the fundamental requirements of sustainable development. Governments are mostly preoccupied with being re-elected every four or five years within the liberal-democratic political model, or merely with holding on to power in the case of non-elected governments. Their horizons encompass short-term objectives, not long-term planetary survival. Business corporations have an even more limited, profit-oriented horizon than governments. While some have donned a green mantle, or are profiting from selling anti-pollution technology, business as a whole is still not looking at environmental protection as a long-term investment, nor at sustainability as a long-term necessity.

Another observation: UNDP, taking up the dimension of inter-generational equity propounded by the Brundtland Commission, notes that

> . . . what needs to be passed on is not so much a specific stock of productive wealth, as the potential for a particular level of human development. What should this level be? Basically, it must involve the absence of poverty and deprivation. What needs to be sustained are people's opportunities to freely exercise their basic capabilities. . . . Good economic growth is growth that promotes human development in all its dimensions.[9]

An observation of the global NGO, Greenpeace International, adds another dimension to sustainable development. Its executive director, Thilo Bode, met Thai NGOs and journalists in Bangkok in March 1996 where he explained Greenpeace's focus in Asia on making technology cleaner. He also offered this comment:

> Clean technology is necessary but not sufficient for sustainability. We have to fight against the big lie: unlimited belief in unlimited growth, which is not possible in a limited world. We can't solve environmental destruction through economic growth. The economies of the future will have to live with a steady throughput of energy and resources.[10]

Thus, a broader picture of sustainability is beginning to emerge. In fact, the perspective of sustainability can be applied across the whole range of human activities, from the macro-level to the micro-level. Here are a few more analytical observations regarding sustainability.

When we call an activity unsustainable, we may mean one of two things:

1. Its growth will sooner or later exceed the capacity of its foundations (the system) to support it, causing the collapse of the

activity. This collapse may even spread to other components of the system to which the activity is fundamentally linked (for example, the property market crash in Thailand, which caused a crash of the financial system, which then contributed to a general economic recession, and so on).

2. The growth, or merely the continuation, of such an activity will cause severe side-effects to individuals, to society, or to the ecology, that are unacceptable (for example, undermining health, infringing human rights or welfare, or destroying living species).

The key to avoiding collapse or severe negative consequences is management for sustainability. Such management is guided by an awareness of all the factors necessary to nurture the continuation or expansion of an activity, and seeks to remove or limit its negative consequences.

In a business context, for example, management for sustainability means knowing your market, and knowing how much investment it can absorb and still provide a reasonable rate of return. It means embracing financial rectitude, prudent financial practices, and transparency. It means employing sound decision making which is socially responsible and in accordance with law. That is one kind of sustainability, within the context of fiscal discipline and market supply and demand, that governs the viability or bankruptcy of a business, or indeed, of a whole sector such as property.

In an environmental context, management for sustainability means assessing the threats to health and environment—locally, nationally, and globally—of all business and development activities, and halting those activities which have a negative impact. This has proven difficult up to now, especially at the higher levels of government decision making, which are most susceptible to the influence of big money. Management for environmental sustainability requires foresight in leadership and an understanding of how small-scale activities such as the ownership of fossil-fuel powered vehicles, for example, when magnified millions or billions of times, can have a severe and destabilising impact on global ecology.

One of the concerns of this book is to emphasise the broadest concept of sustainability, the big picture: whether the totality of humankind's economic activities can avoid undermining the viability of the planet's ecological balance and diversity, and thus avoid global environmental bankruptcy and instability.

To conclude this topic of moving to sustainable development, we may ask, what is now necessary, since the awareness of, and commitment to, sustainable development seems weak and fragmented?

Perhaps what is missing is an ideological approach. Ideologies encompass economics and politics, and provide a world view. They establish basic principles to govern societies' functions and set societies' goals. At the level of the individual, ideologies, similar to religions, provide a system of beliefs and a moral code to define and motivate responsible behaviour. The purpose of ideologies, historically, has usually been to foster a viable, cohesive and contented society. Often, ideologies, as with religions, arise to remedy perceived destructive or barbaric trends.

Free-wheeling, free-market economics which lacks responsibility to global ecology is the present culprit, along with notions of individual freedom that are not accompanied by duties and responsibilities. The remedy in this context may be the creation of a new, ecologically-based ideology that will redefine economics and the individual's place in it. Such an ideology must be based on sustainable economics.

Sustainable Economics

What have been the major issues within the realm of economics in the last decade of the 20th Century? Within the globalising, free-market model that has become dominant, the major concerns have been the expansion of the global free trade regime to include free movement of all kinds of goods, services and capital, now the subject of global negotiations within the World Trade Organisation. The familiar concepts of this model are the removal of trade barriers, gaining access to markets, maximisation of market share, maximisation of profit—all within the overall assumption of ever-increasing economic growth and consumption. Thus, within national economies, and globally, the notion of competitiveness has recently taken on a new urgency. The perceived needs are to perfect corporate management systems, to refine skills of product positioning and marketing, to rationalise production methods and product delivery, and to develop new products aimed at global mass-markets and specialised consumer groups. Company mergers and consolidations to create larger "more competitive" entities are part of this logic.

Commentators have characterised many of these new competitive machines as the "lean and mean" corporations, readier than ever to "downsize" to increase efficiency and cut costs by cutting unwanted personnel. Export or perish might be seen as the catch-cry of this globalising economic trend, and it has profound impacts for developing countries such as Thailand which are struggling to upgrade education and development of the workforce, to streamline government bureaucracies, and to define policies to meet the increasingly competitive requirements of globalisation.

Thus, we see the evolution of what has become—under the capitalist system—the most efficient, productive, and "wealth"-generating economic model the world has seen. It has delivered the goods. The free-wheeling, free-market, resource-exploiting economy has raised production levels quickly in many developed and developing countries. It has been somewhat indispensable in providing the more affluent segments of the world society with an adequate level of material comfort, and in helping to lift large numbers of people out of poverty. Capitalist production linked to free markets and free trade, and—more recently— to the free allocation of capital, has been the industrial age's global engine of growth; and it has been very successful in its unfettered form in transforming societies.

Thus, if we look at capitalism in a vacuum, as a pure concept, as an integral system, it looks beautiful. The late-1980s collapse of communism with its planned economies gave the capitalist model increased impetus. Its "penetration" became more pervasive; capitalism demanded and achieved more liberal access to previously protected national markets. Capitalism is dynamic. As innovations in technology continue to be absorbed by it, and as global market liberalisation progresses, its dynamism increases.

But now, capitalism's philosophy of growth-at-all-costs is looking dangerous, in view of the deepening ecological crisis. The economic system is so geared to money-making on a short-term basis—with politicians expected to support the competitiveness of their national industries—that it cannot deal effectively with long-term threats to the global environment. The limits of growth-at-all-costs have been reached.

As the 21st Century dawns, this global system is also being seen as increasingly more brutal—as the Asian meltdown taught us in 1997 when a massive amount of "globalised" money suddenly fled East Asian economies, seeking a safer and more profitable haven and leaving chaos in its wake. The increasing "need" for competitiveness in a globalised market, spurred on by technological advance and the consolidation of transnational corporations into ever-larger entities, can wreak havoc on whole industries within a country that loses its competitive edge. The collapse of industries, and the attrition of technological advance on the size of the workforce, can lead to large-scale surges in unemployment. This emerging global system presupposes that there will be winners and losers in the global economic race; it may eventuate that there will be many more losers than winners.

Competitiveness and excellence in management and innovation are all spurred by monetary reward. Governments, including their officials and ministers, have been co-opted into this system—which espouses enrichment as the highest goal—on a national as well as personal basis. After all, money is power, and it wields enormous influence in government and political affairs.

The wealth-generating economy is seen as all-important, at least by the current crop of political decision makers groomed under current economic assumptions. This is the background to the failure of governments around the world to fulfil their promises of sustainable development following the Rio conference.

The above economic assumptions, concerns, and practices are encompassed within what I have called the ideology of *economism*, in which development is largely equated with functions that will serve the wealth-generating economy. Whole schools of monetarism, marketing, and management have grown up within *economism* in an attempt to refine its mechanisms to lend it stability and to promote consumption (i.e., economic growth). But it is more or less a closed system. Its internal mechanisms and theories cannot take into account that the whole system may be unsustainable when placed in the wider context of the need for enduring stability of the global ecology.

So much for economics based on assumptions of individual indulgence and consumption rather than ecological sustainability. But what of politics? How does political theory fit into this scenario?

Politics in modern times has become the bedfellow of economics. For some eight decades of the 20th Century, a fierce ideological struggle raged across the global stage between Marxist economics and Leninist politics on the one hand, and free-enterprise economics and liberal-democratic politics on the other. It gave proof to the maxim that economics is politics. That ideological struggle has now been more or less resolved. The imperative of ecological stability never entered into it. But this new perspective has emerged to challenge political and economic assumptions and add a new edge to the development debate: humankind is living in a finite world, and humans' growing economic impacts upon it are disrupting global ecological stability.

Social systems, assumptions about rights and duties, economic theories and ideologies—all come and go. Ideologies—including both free-market capitalism and Marxism—become popular when they offer credible remedies to perceived obstacles impeding the human compulsion to develop and evolve. Capitalism came and has thrived on the need to efficiently organise human and financial resources towards the creation of wealth, towards meeting the material needs of people, and in the exploitation of natural resources. Marxism (communism) gained currency when it became clear that 19th Century capitalism lacked humanitarian values and compassion, and placed value on human lives only so far as members of the working class could contribute to higher productivity and profits. Communism did not challenge the assumed purpose of economics: the utilisation of human and natural resources to produce material goods and services. It rather questioned how such goods and services would be distributed and who would benefit from their production. Thus, communism and capitalism in their theoretical form are both materialistic ideologies—in fact, we can even say that they are opposite sides of the coin of *economism*, since they both stress the fundamental nature of economic rights above all others.

Communism (based on Marxism-Leninism) as an ideology has faded. Capitalism is the dominant ideology for economic organisation, creation of wealth, and distribution. Communism lost its currency when it proved inefficient in organising resources and meeting material needs of people (not to mention their spiritual needs). It also proved to be stifling of individual creativity, choice, self-determination, and notions of human rights. But, while capitalism has triumphed over communism on the global political stage, it has at the same time absorbed certain human-itarian values associated with the socialist philosophy underlying communism, since those values have answered many of the needs created by the crude model of exploitative capitalism. These absorbed values often reside in modified socialist parties (and even to some degree in

33

centrist and conservative parties) which have adapted to the framework of democracy and capitalism. For example, the principle that the state should provide a basic safety net for the unemployed, the sick and the underprivileged is now hardly questioned in the "developed" countries, except for a very small minority among the extreme right. The evolution of the welfare state, especially in Europe and New Zealand, carried these humanitarian values further, to provide free education, free or inexpensive medical treatment, and other benefits as a matter of right—although, during the 1990s, many governments have stepped back from the welfare state, finding that it had grown too big to sustain financially, and that it was sometimes abused by its beneficiaries.

Thus, the ideology of capitalism has proved to be flexible and, unlike that of its former communist rival, able to adapt to new challenges. This may be its saving grace. Now the challenge of sustainability is posed to capitalism by the environmental movement (what we might call the green movement, or *ecologism*) which has sprung up as a force on the global scene since the landmark Stockholm Conference of 1972. Will capitalism genuinely (not superficially) be able to take on board the ideals of the green movement and thus survive by transforming itself? Unlike communism, the green movement by and large does not seek to overthrow capitalism, but seeks to introduce and integrate a new moral and survivalist perspective into economy and government—what I have already termed the *ecological imperative*, in which all economic and consumptive activities must submit to ecological principles as first, inviolable principles. These principles, in the first place, can be defined as advocating:

- living in harmony with Nature;
- ensuring environmental equity (equal rights for all to environmental benefits, and equal duties towards environmental protection);
- preserving the stability of natural systems, including the Earth's climate; and
- choosing alternatives in our daily lives that minimise impact on the environment (the *minimalist principle*).

At the beginning of the new millennium, capitalism (or *economism*) has reached the stage of seeking to green itself, but finds itself falling far short of embracing the wholesale reassessments and remedies necessary to abate the pollution and destruction of the global environment.

This is evident in the decline of global commitment following the 1992 Rio Earth Summit. The follow-up assessment to Rio, the June 1997 special session of United Nations General Assembly (UNGA), showed that governments were hardly able to begin substantially to redirect their economies or to provide finance to tackle pressing global environmental problems. This occurred during a time of unprecedented growth of the global economy. Apparently, the seductiveness of consumerism, fuelled by mass media and accompanied by illusions of "progress" generated by the veneration of global economic growth, has made people more selfish to the extent that they have become more reluctant to scale down their consumerist aspirations in order to address global environmental problems. One is reminded here of the terse observation of Maurice Strong, the chief organiser of the 1992 Earth Summit. He expressed his frustration during the concluding press conference in Rio about the lack of commitment among world economic powers on measures to finance *Agenda 21*. He said:

> Never have the rich felt so poor.

People (and governments) will always feel poor when their goal is to constantly raise the level of their consumption, especially in pursuit of the vacuous purpose of "looking better" than someone else. In 1997, the wealthy countries (and many developing countries) were considerably richer in monetary terms than in 1992, but their enthusiasm for creating durable, global mechanisms to finance environmental protection was considerably less than in 1992. The 1997 special session of the UNGA brought together many heads of state and government, as at Rio, but the amount of discord (or unwillingness to make sacrifices) among the delegations, in discussing how to further sustainable development, was so great that they were unable to agree on a political statement to end the session. Instead, following frantic, eleventh-hour diplomacy, they substituted a watered-down Statement of Commitment. Among its conclusions was the observation that

> . . . the overall trends for sustainable development are worse today than they were in 1992. . . .

There were some positives amid the generally negative trends, however. The International Institute for Sustainable Development reported:

Speakers generally agreed that in the five years since UNCED, the concept of sustainable development has come to inform economic planning worldwide. The principles of *Agenda 21* are being codified into national legislation, and major new conventions on climate change and biodiversity are being applied. . . .

But:

Despite commitments made at Rio, consumption and production patterns remain unsustainably high, official development assistance (ODA) has actually declined, deforestation continues, and developing countries lack essential "green technologies". Several speakers pointed out that one third of the world's population did not have access to clean drinking water.[11]

The Institute noted that the state of the global environment has continued to deteriorate, as also noted in the United Nations Environment Programme's *Global Environment Outlook* report:

Some progress has been made in terms of institutional development, international consensus-building, public participation, and private sector actions and, as a result, a number of countries have succeeded in curbing pollution and slowing the rate of resource degradation. Population growth rates have been declining globally, largely as a result of expanded basic education and health care. Overall, however, trends are worsening. Increasing levels of pollution threaten to exceed the capacity of the global environment to absorb them, increasing the potential obstacles to economic and social development in developing countries.

But, at least, the International Institute for Sustainable Development noted, governments were now actually discussing indicators for sustainable development, reproductive health care, and production and consumption patterns.

In 1998, the United Nations Children's Fund (UNICEF) quantified the declining commitment to foreign aid, reporting that:

> For the fifth straight year, aid for development provided by
> industrialised countries has declined, slipping to $55.5 billion in
> 1996, a decrease of 4 per cent in real terms from 1995, and down
> by 16 per cent from the highest aid level, in 1992. . . . Official
> development assistance as a proportion of donor countries' GNPs,
> a measure of their ability to provide aid, fell to an average of
> 0.25 per cent in 1996, compared to 0.34 per cent in 1990. That is
> the lowest proportion since 1970, when the aid target of 0.7 per
> cent of donors' GNPs was agreed upon.[12]

But, given the decline of commitment since the early 1990s, could the talked-about need for the greening of capitalism actually take place to the extent that such pressing new-millennium needs as the abatement of global warming could be seriously addressed in a spirit of sacrifice? The greening of capitalism may prove to be more problematic than capitalism's previous taking-on-board of the humanitarian ideals espoused by Marx's original description of socialism. Such things as the "freedom to consume" and the primacy of financial influence within the democratic process assumed by big business, are central to capitalism but in many ways incompatible with *ecologism*.

Capitalism cannot remain stagnant, but must grow. Even when it is forced to retreat, as during a recession, it must rebuild its base and create new fundamentals in order to grow again. And it relies on "stimulating consumer demand" for this growth. This dynamic has spurred the drive towards globalisation. The transnational corporations of the developed countries find it hard to grow much in their own countries, due to the intense competition there and the fact that the societies have "matured", are closely regulated, and are already somewhat saturated by consumerism. Thus, global expansion into the developing world, fuelled by the perceived need for corporations to continually expand their revenues, has become the major thrust of global economic growth and an objective of money politics in the developed world.

The problem with capitalism, leading into the third millennium, is not its efficient allocation of resources to meet human needs, nor its ability to create jobs. The problem is its pursuit of "growth" through the artificial creation of "needs" according to capitalism's imperative of ever-expanding consumption focused on the consuming individual. This imperative relentlessly appeals to people's vanity, greed, and impulses of self-indulgence—negative values that are a threat to global environmental stability, as well as to the mental health of individuals and to social cohesion; but which are trumpeted as "progress" every day through the mass media. I am reminded here of a quotation of Mahatma Gandhi regarding the limits of global ecology:

> The Earth provides enough to satisfy every man's need but not every man's greed.[13]

I have already noted that the promotion of consumerism, through capitalism's "magic of the marketplace" and through the assumed desirability of accumulating wealth, has, in the 20th Century, apparently become elevated to the highest goal of human attainment, as far as the mass adherents of *economism* are concerned.

Consumerism has insinuated its way into such basic ideals as human freedom, where some aspects of freedom are equated with self-indulgent individualism. Those who live by fuelling the superfluity of consumerism arrogantly declare it to be the defining essence of the individual: you are only as good as what you buy. Consumerism has, in addition, presumed itself to be a prime motivator of technological advance. The Washington-based Worldwatch Institute has researched the phenomenon of consumerism and points out:

> Measured in constant dollars, the world's people have consumed as many goods and services since 1950 as all previous generations put together. . . . Yet this historical epoch of titanic consumption appears to have failed to make the consumer class any happier. . . . The happiness that people derive from consumption is based on whether they consume more than their neighbours and more than they did in the past. . . . Thus, individual happiness is more a function of rising consumption than of high consumption as such. The reason, argues Stanford University economist Tibor Scitovsky, is that consumption is addictive: each luxury quickly becomes a necessity, and a new luxury must be found. This is as true for the young Chinese factory worker exchanging a radio for a black-and-white television as it is for the German junior executive trading in a VW for a Mercedes. . . .

Luxuries become necessities between generations as well. People measure their current material comforts against the benchmark set in their own childhood. So each generation needs more than the previous did to be satisfied. Over a few generations, this process can redefine prosperity as poverty. . . . With consumption standards perpetually rising, society is literally insatiable. The definition of a "decent" standard of living—the necessities of life for a member in good standing in the consumer society—endlessly shifts upward. . . .[14]

Now, as consciousness rises about the need for global ecological preservation and for harmony with Nature and within society, this preoccupation with materialism and self satisfaction seems quite inadequate as a guiding ideology for the third millennium.

We have to draw a new baseline against which all human activities and relationships are measured. In an age where the prevailing economic ideology calls for less government regulation and intervention, the *ecological imperative* calls for positive interventions to create momentum towards sustainability. If human relationships and the mental and physical health of the people can be improved by this process, so much the better. It does not mean replacing notions of freedom with authoritarianism; it means that idealistic notions of freedom, particularly so-called "economic freedoms" and the acceptable limits of media freedom, must be closely measured against the *ecological imperative*. Freedom will exist within a new, ecologically sound framework.

Sustainability, additionally, depends on the principle of universality: if one person is allowed to do something, or to be prevented from doing something, then the action must apply to everyone. The accepted rule in democratic politics and in sustainable development, among individuals and among nations, is that all have equal rights. Thus, the final goal of global sustainability requires that environmental equity will prevail.

Asian Bubble, Global Bubble?

How can we best understand the prospect that the global economy is unsustainable, as asserted in this treatise? A look at the East Asian economic bubble which burst in 1997 may be instructive. From the perspective available in the early months of 1999, we can see that the Asian bubble economies—Indonesia, South Korea, Thailand, and Malaysia—were constructed on overleveraged foundations and an accumulation of malpractices, some overt, others covert. This, in spite of the fact that the IMF and the World Bank just months earlier were praising the economic policies and growth of these Asian economies as strong and dynamic. Those global institutions, along with the national institutions of the affected economies, did not see the bubble forming.

Is the global economy forming into just another big bubble, built on deteriorating ecological foundations (comparable to the overleveraged foundations of those East Asian economies) and exacerbated by unsustainable global competition—a process that "optimistic" national and global economic institutions cannot see, or would rather not see? Let's examine this notion more closely.

The formation of a bubble economy has a lot to do with unsustainable practices which look like a good way to make money in the first place, but which become dangerously untenable as more and more speculators and profiteers jump on the bandwagon. These are often practices of carefree abandon, in which speculators ignore the economic health of the system and focus only on personal, large-scale, and often immediate gains. Deception, concealment, and high-risk, highly-leveraged financial practices may be employed.

Economics is an imprecise discipline involving many interacting variables in complex relationships; its uncertainties are compounded by the often irrational behaviour of human beings, especially where a "herd-mentality" reinforced by instantaneous communications comes into play. Hence, economics often produces big surprises. Many economists saw negative trends growing in Asia, such as the formation of high current account deficits, the undesirable appreciation of Asian currencies tied to the US dollar, the unhealthy distortions of crony capitalism; but no one (with a few notable exceptions) predicted the combined effect of the interaction of these variables. Hence the widespread surprise when the East Asian bubbles successively began to burst.

National economic bubbles typically take ten to twenty years to form, as in the case of Thailand and the earlier case of Japan (still unresolved after a decade). It seems that the bigger the bubble, the harder it is to recognise by those that operate within it and benefit from it. Denial of reality plays a large part in this. Generally, it is mostly those analysts taking an objective standpoint outside the bubble who can actually see it forming.

A global bubble would be much bigger and broader than national bubbles, taking many more decades to form. This writer is inclined to believe that such a bubble is forming. The best of our traditional economists within the prevailing ideology of *economism* cannot see it, just as the International Monetary Fund, the World Bank and the US treasury secretary, among others, were unable to see the bubbles forming in East Asia.

The Asian bubbles burst with disastrous consequences in the short term. But those consequences could be repaired with a readjusted focus on financial sustainability, including a redefinition of economic and fiscal responsibility, a purging of national economies and institutions of bad policies and practices, and a large-scale injection of fresh capital. Importantly, those bubbles formed within the broader, global system of *economism* whose agencies—the IMF, the World Bank and their main backers—already contained the means to provide rescue packages comprising financial bail-outs, structural reforms, and expertise to assist with their implementation. But who could come to the rescue if the whole system of *economism*—encompassing the globalised economy— eventually proves to be a giant, global bubble? This warning is not far-fetched, and is already being taken seriously by major global development agencies. Let us recall again the observation of James Gustave Speth, the administrator of the UNDP, mentioned above:

> We can either choose to take the high road and manage the change now, or we can pursue business as usual and have the change forced upon us later as our natural resources become depleted and Earth's fragile balance is permanently disrupted.

The Worldwatch Institute makes a similar observation:

> If we attempt to preserve the consumer economy indefinitely, ecological forces will dismantle it savagely. If we proceed to dismantle it gradually ourselves, we will have the opportunity of replacing it with a low-consumption economy that can endure— an economy of permanence.[15]

There is no supreme bail-out agency external to a global bubble that we might call upon to rescue the global system, unlike national bubbles within the system of *economism*. The only alternative is to avoid such a global bubble—even though many doubt that such a bubble is forming— by generating a decisive political consciousness which will ultimately compel political institutions to re-evaluate the fundamental assumptions of *economism* that they have taken for granted for so long. The task is to establish the *ecological imperative* as the basic principle with which all other principles and liberal assumptions of economics must conform. The required political consciousness will have to arise among concerned and educated people and diffuse to the grassroots through the education system, media, and information technology.

And if this fails to happen? There could likely be global havoc worse than that caused by the Great Depression which began in the late 1920s: after all, the Great Depression arose from the widespread and unforeseen collapse of national financial systems caused by the "get-rich" mentality of free-market capitalism and the inability of governments to avoid its boom-and-bust cycles in an increasingly complex global economy. It led to a severe and devastating worldwide economic contraction. But, occurring at a relatively early stage of global industrialisation, that depression left the global resource base relatively unscathed. The feared global bubble of *economism* will be one that results from overexploitation of the resource base of the planet and from destabilisation of natural systems, perhaps worsened by other unsustainable economic practices. The ensuing havoc would have a much more fundamental impact than the Great Depression—and a certain potential for man's rational use and enjoyment of Nature's bounty may be lost forever. Worse still, destabilisation of natural systems such as the climate may cause a chain effect leading to a progressive degeneration of other systems within the biosphere's web of life.

At stake here is the stability of the global ecosystem, the vastly complex relationship between the organic elements which make up the biological web of life and the non-organic elements which constitute the atmosphere, the oceans, and the land. This dynamic relationship has given rise to a life-supporting, global ecology over millions of years. This relatively stable global ecology—constituting the ecological baseline, as I have called it—has allowed human beings to evolve. It forms the foundation which has allowed civilisations and their economies to emerge.

The initial evidence of human-induced destabilisation of the global ecosystem is now clear. Can we afford to be complacent?

The austerity measures imposed in 1997 to rescue the deflated Asian bubble economies seemed extreme and unwarranted to many analysts, and proved very painful to ordinary citizens. How much more extreme and radical will measures to avoid a global economic bubble prove to be? An early indication, moving into the new millennium, will be governments' response to global warming. For the first time, the ethos of global consumerism is being seriously challenged as nations are being asked to make radical cuts in fossil fuel consumption—but very wealthy corporate vested interests in such consumption continue to resist significant cuts by bringing financial leverage to bear on political decision makers.

Global Warming and Political Impasse

As of 1999, the scientific consensus on the validity of the greenhouse effect was more certain than ever.[16] The World Resources Institute reported that 1998 set yet another new record for the warmest year since records began in the last century. Since 1979, the world has experienced its 14 warmest years, it said.[17]

But the political posturing leading up to the important December 1997 Kyoto conference on global warming showed that the political leadership—operating under obsolete economic and political assumptions, both in the developed and developing nations—were not equipped intellectually, nor in terms of popular sentiment, to expedite a major winding-down of consumption of fossil fuels to halt the human-induced change in the global climate.

We can see that while leaders make all kinds of rhetorical statements about protecting the environment, in actual fact they find it hard to escape from *economism* and economic nationalism. Proposals for the negotiation of global conventions—such as a global forestry convention—often fail to take off because most governments' first priority is the protection of their nationals' money-making industries. We see the same psychology over climate change. Governments, particularly in the third world, habitually make the preservation of economic advantage, or the "catching up" with other nations' economic advantage, their major condition in such negotiations.

The magnitude of the need for reduction of fossil fuel consumption was estimated by Greenpeace, with the release of its report, *The Carbon Logic*, in October 1997. It reported that

> . . . even with major curbs on deforestation, no more than 225 billion tonnes of carbon can be released from the burning of fossil fuels over the next century to keep global warming in check. This translates to about a quarter of the world's known reserves of coal, oil, and gas, and just a fraction, around five per cent, of estimated reserves. If no action is taken, carbon emissions from fossil fuels are projected to reach 1,415 billion tonnes by 2100. This "business as usual" scenario would lead to a temperature increase of $2.5^{\circ}C$ to $2.9^{\circ}C$ above pre-industrial levels, resulting in longer term increases of over $4^{\circ}C$. Just half this emission level would lead to a dangerous doubling of carbon dioxide concentrations.

With the burning of just 70 per cent of the world's existing reserves of fossil fuels enough to cause such damage, Greenpeace said the report justifies its call for an end to oil exploration.[18] The deputy executive director of Greenpeace UK, Chris Rose, said the report spelled out the unavoidable logic for an intergovernmental phase-out of fossil fuels.

The Kyoto conference of December 1997 (officially known as the third conference of the parties to the Framework Convention on Climate Change) marked a serious attempt to make commitments and to begin the process of neutralising the greenhouse effect. It will take many more such conferences and commitments, and the raising of global consciousness to a critical mass regarding sustainable development, before its objectives can be achieved.

Nevertheless, Kyoto was a turning point of sorts, as the developed countries among some 160 nations present agreed, for the first time, to commit themselves to mandatory target figures for the reduction of greenhouse gases. The bad news was that the United States Senate had already declared, by a 95–0 vote, that it would not ratify a treaty that did not also require emission cutbacks in the developing world. As it turned out, the developing countries, particularly China, declined to make any such commitment. This raised worries that, if the United States did not sign and ratify the treaty, commitments of other developed countries would also unravel. But the possibility lay open that the US Administration could still initiate activities to begin to fulfil the target, despite a non-ratification of the Kyoto Protocol.

The US Administration agreed to cuts of seven per cent (but did not sign the protocol), the European Union agreed to cuts of eight per cent, and Japan to cuts of six per cent from 1990 emission levels over the next 15 years.

How would they actually reduce emissions? That was not clear, and awaited policy initiatives of the various parties. However—under a major new development—proposed market-based mechanisms would act as an incentive for countries to meet and exceed their targets, or to assist other countries in doing so. *The Nation's* environment editor, James Fahn, wrote about the most significant of the market-based proposals:

> The agreement in principle to set up a greenhouse gas (GHG) emissions trading system may eventually stand as the most important achievement of the Kyoto Protocol. . . . Under the most basic form of emissions trading, one country which finds it difficult to lower its GHG emissions to meet its target, could pay another party to reduce its own emissions by a suitable amount instead. . . .[19]

Fahn expounded on other similar mechanisms under the Kyoto Protocol:

- Joint Implementation (JI), where a company or country would help carry out a project to reduce GHG emissions or store carbon in another country, and receive "carbon credits" in return. Typically, a JI project would use money and technology from a developed country, but would be carried out in developing countries, where costs are usually cheaper;

- the Clean Development Mechanism to finance climate-friendly development, a refinement of a Brazilian proposal to funnel fines paid by developed countries into GHG reduction projects in the developing world.

Other commentators, however, feared that making commodities out of carbon emissions would not go far enough to ensure that emissions reductions would be achieved, for the most part, at home. Instead there would be a drift towards off-shore fulfillment of commitments. Some commentators were sceptical of the whole process. For example, the *Seattle Times* editorialised that

> . . . a clear-eyed assessment of the Kyoto pact shows that negotiators merely produced more of what they set out to contain in the first place: hot air. The United States and other industrialised nations agreed to unprecedented binding limits on so-called greenhouse gases. The pact also includes endorsement of market-based mechanisms by which companies in wealthier nations can provide technology and funding to help cut power-plant emissions and other polluting sites in poorer nations. But the crucial issue of whether the world's underdeveloped nations must abide by emission limits was left unaddressed. As long as more than 130 developing nations [led by China and India] are exempt from emission reductions, neither the economy nor the environment is better off.[20]

The conservative magazine, *The Economist*, noted:

> For all its imperfections, the treaty marks the most ambitious feat of environmental diplomacy ever attempted. Some of the language incorporated in the text—for example, the acceptance at least in principle of untried market mechanisms such as tradable emissions permits—represents a great leap forward in global environmental thinking. The 11-day conference has also helped to educate public opinion, putting the fears of pessimists into some perspective, and pricking the insouciance of those who refuse to believe that global warming is any sort of problem at all. . . . One of the conference's biggest failures was its failure to win even theoretical agreement from the 136 countries that are not yet required to reduce emissions that they ought, in principle, to be ready to do so at some unspecified point in the future. . . .[21]

The developing countries were justified, to some extent, in refusing at Kyoto to make any commitment on emissions reductions because a previous negotiation in Berlin in 1995 agreed to exclude developing countries from any new commitments until after the Kyoto meeting. Just the same, the United States tried a final ploy to encourage the developing countries to accept a revised Article 10 of the Kyoto Protocol, under which they would eventually agree to binding emission limits without at that time having to specify when they would join up. However, it was rejected by China and India, who are respectively the world's second-largest and fifth-largest producers of carbon dioxide. They argued that developing countries could not afford such expenses while their economies were at an early stage of growth.

At the Buenos Aires follow-up to Kyoto, held in November 1998, negotiations continued on how to put pledges into operation. But little progress was made, and it may take years before agreement can be reached.

Meanwhile, environmentalists continued to protest that the Kyoto targets are much too modest. In November 1998, an international gathering of Green politicians in London cited an "authoritative assessment", saying that a worldwide carbon dioxide reduction of 50 to 70 per cent was necessary to contain climate change.[22] On the other hand, world energy demand is forecast to grow by some 65 per cent from 1995 to 2020, according to data presented to the Buenos Aires meeting. Without action by leading economies to limit air pollution levels, global output of carbon dioxide emissions would climb 70 per cent.[23]

The Clinton Administration signed the Kyoto Protocol shortly after the Buenos Aires meeting, but the US Senate was still threatening to reject it. Reuters news agency reported:

> US Senator Jesse Helms, chairman of the Senate Foreign Relations Committee and a staunch opponent of many UN-sponsored treaties, called on Secretary of State Madeleine Albright in a letter to submit the pact quickly "so that the Senate may reject the treaty and scrap the Kyoto Protocol process altogether. . . ." The European Union and many developing countries have complained that the US is pushing plans to let it meet its Kyoto target of a 7 per cent reduction in emissions below 1990 levels by buying allowances to pollute from other countries. They say the US must make more domestic sacrifices.[24]

This leads to the question of whether or not developing countries are presently following a realistic development model, given that the path taken during the 20th Century by the developed countries has now been revealed as unsustainable. Both developing and developed countries still seem more intent on jockeying for economic advantage within this unsustainable system rather than in addressing the more crucial, long-term issue of climate change. American businessmen, for example, in lobbying against the emissions-reduction treaty, cite the likelihood that energy-intensive industries will move to developing countries where, under current treaty provisions, they would escape carbon-limitation requirements. The leading North American trade union grouping, the AFL-CIO, argued in Kyoto along similar lines, saying that while big labour groups supported measures aimed at protecting the environment, current plans to cut rich nations' emissions of climate-changing gases, and to transfer technology to the developing world, would lead to a huge exodus of business and jobs from developed countries.[25]

Could China refocus its industrial and consumer policies to place abatement of climate change at their centre? After all, under the business-as-usual scenario, rising sea levels caused by global warming threaten to inundate major Chinese cities such as Shanghai and Guangzhou by 2050, displacing up to 76 million people.[26]

The London newspaper, *Daily Express*, editorialised on global warming:

> Global warming is real. And it is happening now. If present trends continue over the next 20 years, temperatures will go up by 1.2°C—double the rise over the last 130 years. The world population is growing too fast: by 2010, one billion more people will be living on our planet. This is the conclusion of a report drawn up by Sir Robert May, the British government's chief adviser. . . . Without an environmental future, there is no economic, political, or social future worth speaking of. We all know in our hearts that we are in a desperately serious situation. What we need is action, now.[27]

Government attitudes in countries such as the United States and China will be crucial in abating global warming, as will attitudes towards certain pollution-producing industrial sectors worldwide. Take production and marketing of the venerated automobile, for instance.

The production and sales of cars have become indicators of the "health" of an economy. In countries such as Malaysia, India, and

Indonesia, the production of a "national car" became an economic status symbol. Attainment of a large-scale ownership of cars in developing countries has come to be regarded as an indicator of development. Transnational auto-makers have been rushing to set up plants in countries such as China and Thailand, in anticipation of the one-car-per-family dream that originated with Henry Ford and the invention of the mass-production assembly line in America. The emerging middle class of the third world, in slavish emulation of the now-apparent mistakes of the rich (overdeveloped) countries, place the ownership of private vehicles at the centre of their aspirations. Such dreams must now be seen as spelling disaster for the environment. Cars and other petrol-burning vehicles are one of the major sources of CO_2 emissions.

If we are to take global warming seriously, humanity really has to reassess its love affair with the automobile. After all, vanity and self-indulgence (often masked as convenience) are prime motivators in owning automobiles. They are much less necessary than status-conscious consumers want to believe, and much less healthy than available alternative transportation. (These themes are explored in the Thai context in Chapter 12.)

Again, who will take the lead? Will it be Americans, the world's biggest consumers and polluters? Could American society, wedded to conspicuous high-consumption and veneration of the automobile, turn to embrace a spirit of sacrifice for a global ideal? Consciousness can grow through education, but there are other ways. *The Economist* magazine had this to say about fossil fuel consumption:

> Nine-tenths of the world's commercial energy comes from fossil fuels, such as oil, coal, and gas, which give off greenhouse gases. Alternative sources of energy, such as solar power, are still more expensive. . . . On one estimate, energy subsidies worldwide are worth over $600 billion a year. Many of these subsidies force down the price of fossil fuels, encouraging consumers to burn them wastefully. . . . Naturally, governments prefer to avoid the political flak which comes with slashing subsidies: but how better to promote an economically sensible reform than as an attempt to save the Earth too? A full-scale assault on fossil-fuel subsidies in rich countries would salvage the global-warming negotiations.

> Only then will governments be able to discuss more costly attempts to cut greenhouse gas emissions with any credibility.[28]

Projections for American CO_2 emissions by the turn of the century put them about 13 per cent above 1990 levels,[29] accounting for about one quarter of total global emissions. China, by 1995, was responsible for 10 per cent of global CO_2 emissions.

Redefining a Sustainable Quality of Life

Many people who are familiar with global environmental issues and the many-sided crisis that the Earth is now facing, have already concluded that the Earth's children who will be born around the middle of the 21st Century will experience a quality of life somewhat inferior to that which we have taken for granted in the 20th Century. This statement may come as a shock to people who have never had cause to reflect upon where industrialisation, overpopulation, the mania to increase personal consumption, and the continuing degradation of Nature, are leading humankind.

Its pessimism arises from trying to visualise where the globe will stand by 2050 if the negative trends of the late 20th Century continue. Fresh, clean water will be somewhat more scarce. Food also may be scarce if degradation of soil and loss of farmland continues. Problems of waste disposal and natural resources depletion are predicted to worsen, at least in the short term. People (especially in Asia) will be packed into ever more crowded mega-cities as global population expands from the six billion reached in October 1999, to between 7.3 and 10.7 billion people by 2050, when the population should be close to stabilising.[30] The potential nightmares of huge Asian mega-cities, when half of the Asian population lives in them, are already beginning to be felt. The greed and insensitivity of influential sections of the urban community who regard open space as a commercial commodity rather than as a vital human need, and the inability of political leaders to address this problem, do not bode well for the future. (This is the theme of Section 5 of this book, The Urban Challenge.)

Global warming, if not mitigated early in the 21st Century, will mean trillions of dollars will have to be spent just to repair damage and to relocate or protect populations threatened by rising sea levels.

Environmental emergencies may increase social tensions, both within and between countries, and may lead to mass migrations of environmental refugees.

Of course, it may be said that these fears are merely extrapolations of negative trends detected globally at present. But, the reality is that the major changes that need to be embraced and carried out by governments and their people in general, are still severely lacking.

By mid-1999, the reality of global warming was gaining increasing recognition. But governments had not yet felt able to tell their peoples that big changes in their consumption patterns were necessary: the concept of quality of life had become so thoroughly equated with the self-indulgent individual as a consuming unit requiring high consumption of energy, and with individual reliance on automobiles or motorcycles for transportation. The salesmen—the purveyors of goods, services, and sensual distractions—had usurped the meaning of quality of life. Political leaders were committed to economic growth through ever-increasing mass consumption—and politics in many countries had become little more than a courtship of vested interests for financial support during elections, with a consequent need to offset pressing ecological concerns against those interests.

The pervasion of materialistic *economism* in people's minds had palpably led to spiritual impoverishment and to a noticeable degree of alienation, particularly amongst the world's consumptive middle class and would-be middle class. The single-minded pursuit of economic globalisation through increased competition had contributed to occupational stress: demands for corporate excellence were intensifying, to be rewarded only by bigger pay cheques and expectations of higher rates of personal consumption. Symptoms of personal and societal stress were evident globally in increasing rates of suicide and mental illness.

Counter-trends to this phenomenon were emerging, such as Buy Nothing Day. This idea sprang up in Canada in 1991, and by 1996 had spread to the USA and beyond, promoted by a loose coalition of international groups. The day after American Thanksgiving (the unofficial start of the Christmas and Chanukah gift-buying rush), shoppers were urged by the campaigners to buy nothing for 24 hours, and to discover

> . . . the joys of buying less and living more simply with less environmental damage, less stress, more happiness and personal

> fulfillment. . . . People who try it gain an awareness about their
> lifestyle and our consumer culture that encourages us to buy,
> buy, buy. Buying is like an addiction for us in the West.[31]

Thus, we are starting to come to a more clear-minded view of what the quality of life is about.

Quality of life, of course, is a broad concept which may mean vastly different things to different people. It can take in practically every grievance that a group or individual may hold: poverty, violation of human rights, exploitation (of various kinds). It would certainly mean one thing to a landless agricultural labourer struggling to provide for his family; something else to a member of the jet-setting, consumptive elite; and something else again to an individual dedicated to an ecological cause.

I define quality of life in its basics as being the health of the individual, the family, and the community—which in turn depends on maintaining a diverse and healthy natural environment, including harmony between humankind and Nature. I have avoided the usual, materialistic approach in defining quality of life. This approach has been thoroughly articulated already through the prevailing materialistic ideology of *economism*, whose excesses, as indicated above, must now be seen as a major contributor to the deepening, global ecological crisis.

Additionally, it is well accepted that poverty is a major impediment to the quality of life; to be sure, a certain level of material attainment is necessary to one's physical and mental security. Thus, as a new body of international law and new mechanisms emerge through the re-evaluation of the fundamental assumptions of *economism* and recognition of the primacy of the global ecology, special attention will need to be given to meeting the real needs of the absolute poor.

A quality of life for the third millennium will increasingly discourage self-indulgent, consumptive behaviour that degrades the environment. Thus, the notion of human satisfaction will need remoulding. Self-fulfilment will still be a major psychological and social goal, but in a context of redefined spiritual, intellectual, creative, artistic, and physical/recreational development. Community life—a greater degree of commitment to the community, and satisfaction from community activity—will become a more appropriate alternative to self-indulgent individualism as the prime source of self-fulfilment.

In this new world, we might ask, what will happen to the notion of *choice*—a notion that has become a cherished principle of the individualistic, liberal philosophy of freedom and self-satisfaction which is a major legacy of Western civilisation? The notion of choice is something of a double-edged sword in this era of ecological crisis, desirable in its own right, but not often occurring within the bounds of a carefully-defined responsibility. Choice, in the commercial context, has become a degraded concept. In the minds of the unenlightened, it has become synonymous with "show off, enjoy, consume." Do what you want. . . . Do what feels good. . . . If we have learned anything from the approaching ecological crisis of planet Earth, it is that personal responsibility to ecological goals must replace such self-centred "feel good" sentiments. Choice must be put in its proper place.

Does all this sound incredible in a world that has become too comfortable—a world of fast food, fast entertainment, and fast technological fixes to save one from labour, boredom, and even the need to think for oneself? Actually, the major, relevant question regarding all of this has already been asked a few thousand years ago by the ancient Greek philosopher Socrates:

How should one live one's life?

This question has persisted through the ages. It is a potent reminder that things can be different; that the human being, or human society, can remould itself; that what is taken for granted as "normal" or routine can be rethought according to changing circumstances; that assumptions about the quality of one's life can be redefined. (Socrates's celebrated question is asked once again, in the Thai context, in Chapter 11.)

Again, this issue of quality of life comes back to politics: perhaps the single most important factor in creating the conditions to realise a sustainable quality of life. If the political culture is seriously flawed, attempts to improve the quality of life of the population will suffer. When politicians and political parties become obsessed with personal gain, employing deceit and manipulation, it becomes impossible even to pose questions about the quality of life to them. The answer to this is an active civil society with access to decision-making processes, transparency in government, and freedom of information. In an international context, political diplomacy to save the environment through negotiations has achieved only mixed results, leaving many key issues untouched. Now, a more grassroots approach is needed: through media, NGOs, education, and political organising to generate the necessary, decisive, political consciousness at an international level.

The Worldwatch Institute poses this question in calling for a transition to a culture of permanence:

> The future of life on Earth depends on whether we among the richest fifth of the world's people, having fully met our material needs, can turn to non-material sources of fulfillment. Whether we—who have defined the tangible goals of world development—can now craft a new way of life, at once simpler and more satisfying. Having invented the automobile and airplane, can we return to bicycles, buses, and trains? Having pioneered sprawl and malls, can we recreate human-scale settlements where commerce is an adjunct to civic life rather than its purpose? Having introduced the high fat, junk-food diet, can we instead nourish ourselves on wholesome fare that is locally produced? Having devised disposable plastics, packaging without end, and instantaneous obsolescence, can we design objects that endure, and a materials economy that takes care of things?[32]

In summary, one thing should be clear: the concept of quality of life must be redefined in terms of sustainability—in terms of human lifestyles and material aspirations that can be accommodated and fulfilled within the limits of global ecological stability. As the world's population grows, pressures on remaining natural resources will grow even more, and the quality of life will increasingly focus on people's ability to enjoy clean, natural surroundings and good mental and physical health.

SECTION 1

STRIVING FOR
SUSTAINABLE ECONOMICS

Chapter 3

Global Ecology and the Crisis of Free-market Economics

What is the most important lesson to be learned from the financial and economic crisis which was sparked off in Thailand in 1997, spread to Asia, and in the latter half of 1998 was threatening to become global?

In trying to make sense of it all, we have heard the economic experts expound upon the failures of the so-called free market; upon the destructive power of huge, unregulated financial flows, reckless bank lending, Asian cronyism, non-transparency, industrial overcapacity, consumers living beyond their means, etc. . . . We have heard them expound upon the virtues of free markets (regardless of their aberrance); the assumed benefits of greater economic openness, globalisation, deregulation, stimulation of personal consumption. . . . Both lists could be considerably longer.

Many of the supposed virtues mentioned above are politically-loaded, double-edged prescriptions which could just as well be seen as culprits for the market failures than as cures. Such is the dissention and disarray that prevailed at the end of the 20th Century within the discipline called economics.

A series of international economic meetings in October and November 1998—including the International Monetary Fund and World Bank annual conferences, the meeting of the Group of Seven industrialised countries (G-7), and the recently firmed-up Group of 22 developed and developing countries (G-22)—provided opportunities to face the growing dangers, but merely revealed a lack of leadership and an apparent apathy towards placing bold, new initiatives on the table. Likewise, another international meeting, the Buenos Aires session of the Framework Convention on

Climate Change, which dealt with the economics-related global warming phenomenon, was short on initiatives. Following the IMF and World Bank meetings, the remarks of Indian finance minister, Yashwant Sinha gained global media circulation:

> The brute fact is that after five days of intense discussion and debate we are still at a loss as to why the contagion has continued to spread. . . . Nor do we seem to have achieved clear, agreed, and effective measures to contain the crisis. . . .[1]

The G-22 decided to forward three reports on making the world financial system more effective to international lending institutions and to countries, so they could put them into practice. US Treasury Secretary, Robert Rubin commented:

> We must ensure that the international financial architecture is prepared for the new challenges of our time, especially the challenge of building a system that will lessen and manage the risks in the global market to allow countries to reap the benefits of free-flowing capital in a way that is safe and sustainable. . . .[2]

The reports recommended making hedge funds and other institutions show what exposure they had in markets, making countries meet all debt commitments in full and on time, and creating a framework for debt problems to be resolved. Additionally, the US proposed a new lending facility be set up within the IMF for "structurally-sound" economies facing speculative attacks against their currencies. But, in terms of new initiatives, that was it.

One international monetary official said little momentum had been given to redesigning the architecture of the world's financial system, or reshaping the institutions (the IMF and the World Bank) set up at Bretton Woods after World War II. Experts disagreed over macro-economic policy, and such things as the pace of devaluation, or the liberalisation of capital flows in developing countries.[3]

The global fraternity of free-market economists fell back on well-worn formulas by calling for cuts in taxes and interest rates to stimulate consumption worldwide and particularly in Asia. This was the best that the world's economic leaders could come up with. The call for all countries to meet their debt commitments, even at a time of adversity related to system failure, strangely echoed the IMF's bail-out requirements for Indonesia, Thailand, and South Korea. One leading investment-bank strategist, Kenneth Courtis of the Deutsche Bank Group, compared the lack of leadership in the global emerging market crisis to the situation of 1920 leading up to the Great Depression: there were competitive devaluations, financial collapse, bank failures, high current account deficits, and financial volatility. . . . and no exercise of leadership to halt the inevitable. . . . [4] As for the market failures seen as largely responsible for the crisis, I will presently suggest that they are glimpses of a greater and growing malaise of which the 1997–99 crisis is merely a symptom.

The Buenos Aires meeting was reminded of the great dangers to environment and societies posed by the present unsustainable consumption of fossil fuels in the global economy. But, mirroring the apathy of the other forums, the big players argued amongst themselves about what measures should be taken to implement the Kyoto Protocol, which in 1997 set targets for the developed economies to reduce their production of carbon dioxide (and other greenhouse gases) to abate global warming. The tough decisions were deferred until late 1999, and may take many more years before they come to fruition.

There was a certain irony arising from these gatherings (the seeds of disaster, we might call it) that was largely missed by many conventional economic analysts: the economic meetings called for increased consumption (including automobile sales), while the environmental meeting called for decreased consumption of energy that created greenhouse gases. Both groups, represented by government-level negotiators, were quite earnest—but between them they spawned an appalling contradiction. However, that is not the worst of it. . . .

What is the most important lesson to be learned from the financial and economic crisis, the question asked at the beginning of this chapter? My candidate for the most important—even alarming—lesson of this crisis up to now is: that despite scores of prestigious universities turning out hordes of macro-economists, that despite all their sophisticated computer-driven economic models and monetary theories, only a few could see the crisis coming. The consequences in terms of human suffering, particularly in East Asia, have been great. The World Bank estimated that absolute poverty in the crisis-hit countries there grew from

40 million to an estimated 60 million in 1998, with the prospect of it growing to 80 million or more by 2002.[5] In view of the culpability of current economics and its adherents, and of its dominance in global affairs, can we expect further failures in the future with even worse consequences?

A General Failure of Economics?

Are we therefore looking at the early signs of a general failure of an economic model—the technology-driven, consumption-driven, debt-driven model of endless growth based on the simple, time-honoured principles of free trade and free-market capitalism? Environmentalists up to now have been the greatest critics of the assumption that infinite economic growth can take place feeding upon a finite natural resource base. The movement to promote zero growth came and went in the 1970s; perhaps it was premature in the present phase of global development. But other stresses which the primacy-of-growth model has built up over the past few decades became clearly evident in 1998:

- Unemployment has risen even at a time of high global growth. High unemployment is the rule in Europe, even as their economies are regarded as "sound". In crisis-hit Thailand, unemployment rose from 486,000 in 1996 to an estimated 1.31 million[6] people at end-1998.
- Gaps between the rich and poor continue to grow, both within and among nations. Capital mobility and competition among countries for jobs also make it harder for governments to tax their businesses and richer citizens to maintain policies that promote equality, or cushion the shocks of trade, such as minimum wages or social safety nets.[7]
- Despite a decline, until recently, in the percentage of the poor globally, there still remains, through a current global population increase of 78 million people per year, a core of some 1.2 billion people living at the poverty line or in absolute poverty.
- The march of technological excellence allows fewer workers to saturate global markets to the point of overproduction. The industrial world has built a capacity to produce far more than it can sell. *The Economist* surveyed the situation at the end of 1998 and wrote:

Thanks to enormous overinvestment, especially in Asia, the world is awash with excess capacity in computer chips, steel, cars, textiles, ships, and chemicals. The car industry, for instance, is already reckoned to have at least 30 per cent unused capacity worldwide—yet new factories in Asia are still coming on stream.[8]

- As a corollary to the above, commercially-induced stress is becoming a major health problem in both industrialised and newly-industrialising countries, arising from intensified competition, the pressure to "perform" at work, fear of losing one's job through corporate "downsizing" to reduce labour costs, and stress from peer pressure to keep up appearances of materialistic prosperity. The International Labour Organisation, in urging control over global markets, warns that intensified competition could tear societies apart.[9]

- Within the global financial system, a huge "industry" has grown up that seeks riches without creating value: the "money-for-nothing" syndrome. Big profits are to be made by players who can leverage huge amounts of short-term credit to force upward or downward movements in currency exchange rates, often creating devastating consequences in the process. For example, international hedge funds and investment banks forced the devaluation of the Thai baht in July 1997, allowing the "players" to pocket some $12 billion in profits. (UBS Global Research estimated that Thailand lost that amount as the final cost of the failed attempt to defend the baht's fixed exchange rate).[10] In October 1998, the Japanese yen suddenly appreciated against the US dollar by an unprecedented 16 per cent or so, over three trading days. The explanation at the time was that some big hedge funds suddenly moved massive amounts of dollars into yen.

There is so much loose, unproductive money—estimated at 1.5–2 trillion dollars—swashing around the world every trading day seeking a new home. This money derives mainly from the surplus savings generated by the industrialised economies, and placed in the hands of the managers of pension funds, money funds, hedge funds, and the like. It is continually on the move, seeking a slightly more profitable parking place than the day before or the month before. In an overborrowed, goods-saturated economy, conventional economics finds it difficult to employ this "loose money" to create genuine value. It goes to create property bubbles, for example. Or it ends up preying on the financial system itself, attempting to extract "profit" by such things as speculating on currency movements.

Whenever there are big winners, there are many losers—and often instability. These movements of enormous amounts of capital have, in the 1990s, brought shocks and instability to no less than the global financial system, which was not created to support such a pattern of massive capital flows. They far exceeded the daily value of transactions of goods and services, the "real" economy. Only a small proportion of these flows is involved in trade financing: some three to four per cent, a figure offered by Thai deputy prime minister, Suphachai Panichpakdi.[11] Other evident stresses of the primacy-of-growth model are:

- Because of financial liberalisation, questionable and corrupt bank lending practices, and foolhardy investment decisions which ignored the principle of sustainability, the global banking system going into 1998 had accumulated very high levels of non-performing loans. In Asia, bad debts amounted to more than one trillion dollars.[12] There had been a major destruction of bank capital, banks had failed and massive support operations were necessary. Globally, this represented the greatest failure rate amongst banks than at any time since the Great Depression.[13]
- And perhaps worst of all, the commercially-oriented economic system is failing to cope with global environmental destruction and contamination of natural resources, and rather is resisting solutions to these growing problems. The liberalisation of global trade and investment has allowed transnational corporations to use their growing power to pressure investment-hungry developing countries to lower, or not to raise, their national environmental standards. The failure of the commercial system to ensure ecological sustainability threatens to cause serious global consequences in the 21st Century. (That theme is the subject of a major discussion, below.)

A main conclusion of all this is that greed has become institutionalised, and its voracious appetite is now attacking the system that spawned it. What do cronyism and hedge funds have in common? They have both been blamed for starting the crisis in Asia, and they are both manifestations of the money-by-all-means syndrome. This greed—wanting to acquire more money, wanting to accumulate more assets, or wanting to "enjoy" ever higher levels of "luxury" consumption—has led to societies being enticed and encouraged to live beyond their means, on credit, in effect drawing on their future income for present-day material gratification. This situation is certainly not sustainable, and cries out for rational solution.

Capitalism cannot continue growing in terms of resource exploitation and despoliation, and through the overproduction of goods that no one really needs. The simplistic, compelling logic of capitalism has outgrown its economic purpose. That purpose needs to be brought back into focus: it is to enable the global citizenry to achieve a certain sustainable quality of life, within a stable and vibrant society, while enjoying a healthy and diverse natural environment.

Societies in these days of competitive frenzy and self-gratifying excesses do not seem so stable and vibrant; the health and diversity of the natural environment has declined considerably in the second half of the 20th Century through the relentless pressure of exploitative economics.

As outlined in Chapter 2 of the Introduction to this book, we must enter a new phase of global economy in which primacy will shift from relentless economic growth propelled by consumerism, to achieving social and environmental stability on a global basis. This means incorporating into economic theory what I have already called the *ecological imperative*. We can afford to move into this new phase. Capitalism has already generated trillions of loose dollars that can be put to better use. Capitalist markets will continue to serve their wealth-generating functions, but they will do so within the framework of a managed global economy, with a new set of societal and ecological goals that will receive the primacy that unrelenting growth previously enjoyed.

The contradiction apparent between the Washington and the Buenos Aires meetings must be resolved: global economic growth must be tempered by ecological goals, and must serve them through the transfer of tax revenues, on a global scale, to ecological programmes, and to strengthened global institutions. (More about that later.)

A New Era of Managed Economy

After two decades of "freeing up the markets", arguably begun in earnest in the 1980s with the Ronald Reagan - Margaret Thatcher era of economic deregulation and hands-off government, the pendulum is now swinging back the other way. In the wake of the speculative frenzy and severe volatility on globalised financial markets in 1997, and amid ensuing fears in the latter part of 1998 of a global economic meltdown, a realisation has dawned that the global economy has become dysfunctional and must be managed.

Underlying the perceived need to manage the global market is a subtle change in perception about what markets can and cannot do. It was assumed until recently (before the Asian crisis) that economic growth alone would eliminate poverty in the developing world, that "market forces" would somehow correct imbalances that arose. But it has now become apparent that the marketplace alone cannot achieve a stable global economic system, nor can it alone eliminate global poverty. The thrust towards globalisation is creating new marketing opportunities, but it has also widened previous inequalities and compounded financial and economic uncertainties.

The inadequacies, even dangers, of the global capitalist system have been revealed in the events of 1997–98. There had been a kind of smug complacency among economists and proponents of *laissez-faire* market economics in the modern era (say, 1970 to the present) that economists had become too wise—with their accumulated experience, advanced technologies, research models, and information databases—to ever allow a Great Depression like that of the 1930s to recur. But, there is evidently a self-destructive potential within the system, as seen by the previous financial bubbles, boom and bust cycles. Now—in a globalised world, with integrated financial systems and instant telecommunications—the hurricane force of herd-like, electronic money-flows have globalised the potential of the boom and bust cycle, taking us dangerously close to a global meltdown.

Volatility and upheavals have occurred so quickly that they have perplexed economists, businessmen, and officials, who require predictability in the markets in order to make economic and business decisions. Thus, if the global economy is to be managed, it must be managed according to a vision, not merely with a "patch and stitch" approach accompanying a blind faith in market forces. The first step towards gaining a new vision is to examine the inadequacies of the ideology of "freedom" in economics.

Free Markets Are Never "Free"

Free markets are never "free". The myth of free markets is propagated by transnational corporations and their parent governments which seek economic advantage by breaking down barriers to markets. If market forces were left completely alone to do their work, greed and exploitative chaos would dominate global markets.

In 1998, the "free-market" workings of the global financial system, by many accounts, were on the point of plunging the world into a depression. The hands-off, Friedmanite doctrine of "take the risks, take the failures" would have seen the collapse of major financial institutions on a global scale, as it became obvious that unregulated hedge funds, operating in an untransparent, highly-leveraged, casino-like environment, could cause a chain reaction of failures that could imperil the whole globalised banking and financial system. That was the rationale of the bail-out in September 1998 of the American hedge fund Long-Term Capital Management (LTCM), which received $3.5 billion in rescue funds from 14 American and European investment banks, brokered by the Federal Reserve of New York. LTCM had lost some 90 per cent of its $4.8 billion capital on bond trading and the Russian currency collapse.

The lesson is that the "carefree" free market had to have responsibility imposed on it from outside, by a government agency, to avoid self-destruction. The LTCM episode was probably the one that convinced the sceptics that regulation and management of the global economy was indeed necessary; freedom must exist within a framework.

So much for the Friedmanite doctrine and the Reagan-Thatcher philosophy that business knows what's best for the world and that the best government is hands-off government.

The savings and loan crisis in the United States in the 1980s resulted from deregulation under Reagan-Thatcher economic ideology, empowering small-scale, deposit-taking enterprises to extend loans. The executives of thousands of these small enterprises were not equipped to make prudent lending decisions, and the deregulated climate of freedom without responsibility led to massive insolvencies and failures of these enterprises. More than 1,000 had to be liquidated. Yes, deregulation brought freedom to those enterprises and to their customers who got the loans, but this freedom ultimately cost American taxpayers $300 billion in bail-out funds. Free markets are never "free".

Ironically, this event repeated itself on a much larger scale with the financial collapse in East Asia. This time, lax regulation, lack of transparency, and a strange, hysteria-like suspension of prudence led to so many bad lending decisions by big international (and local) banks. Now, taxpayers of Japan, Malaysia, South Korea, and Thailand pay the very high price of bank bail-outs. Curiously, almost none of this responsibility for imprudent loans involved in East Asia's collapse has been passed on to the taxpayers of the United States or Europe, whose banks were all too willing to fuel Asia's bubble mentality. Free markets are never "free"; somebody ends up paying, and it is often not the wealthy.

The free-market ideology of "getting rich" from business savvy and shrewd investment has its costs, which capitalists have ever been loath to pay: the costs of environmental destruction, of cultural degradation, of social disintegration. Technology (especially new electronic technology) has vastly amplified the capitalist system's propensity for destruction, whether it is the destabilising effects of massive financial flows, the large-scale destruction of forests by machinery, or overexploitation of fisheries by technologies that require few personnel but can scoop up large quantities of fish and threaten whole species with depletion or even extinction.

As I noted in the Introduction to this book, the capitalist system has become the most efficient, productive, and "wealth"-generating economic model the world has seen. It has delivered the goods. But, we need to recognise that capitalism contains no inherent moral code; it requires only that business follows market principles, that national laws are obeyed, and that contracts are honoured. Whatever falls outside established laws and contracts is of no inherent concern to it, and there is a lot that falls outside established laws and contracts.

The free market ignores social and environmental dimensions until regulators impose laws upon it, or until national governments (or, as seen recently, international institutions) dispense financial resources to mitigate damage caused: an indirect way of making capitalists pay for the negative consequences they create. Still, the free market is first and foremost concerned about the most efficient use of money to make more money.

The free market rewards those whose management of resources (human, technological, and natural) is most efficient, and whose perception of risk and what the market "wants" (or can be persuaded to "want") is the most cogent.

Thus, the history of capitalism (the pursuit of affluence through free-market economics) embodies a major sub-theme: that governments must constantly scramble to rectify the undesirable side-effects of capitalist enterprise. That is true at the national level; it is becoming increasingly evident at a global level, too.

A sustainable economic globalisation calls for global institutions and arrangements that mirror effective national ones, actively promoting such things as stability, equity, humanitarianism, compassion, and environmental protection and rehabilitation. It demands a rethink of current global institutions such as the United Nations and the Bretton Woods institutions (the IMF and World Bank), which have proved to be weak and subject to manipulation by the wealthy powers for their own national interests. In September 1998, British prime minister, Tony Blair made such a call for a comprehensive overhaul of the IMF and World Bank. It remains to be seen whether or not these institutions can be refashioned into a system not only to maintain global financial stability and redress imbalances that hit individual countries, but also to rectify the destruction and disharmony occurring globally—just as we expect governments to do automatically at the national level.

Thus, if the liberalisation and globalisation of trade and investment are regarded as "unstoppable", international regulatory and revenue-generating arrangements will sooner or later be seen as desirable or inevitable.

Yes, globalisation requires action beyond merely the trade and investment spheres, but here is the hard part: effective global regulation requires governments to give up portions of their national sovereignty, and to embody that surrendered sovereignty (with the required resources) in international conventions and institutions. As the 21st Century dawns, nations are groping for such relevant arrangements, creating a gradually growing body of international law at the same time. But such global accords are never easily achieved.

The opening of markets and the freeing up of investment and capital movements globally have already diminished the sovereignty and authority of national governments in favour of, especially, the large transnational corporations. Now, a leap is required to systems of global regulation, including global taxation, with the aim of redressing imbalances and bringing stability to the international arena—just as advanced nations have more or less stabilised their societies through juxtaposing legal systems, embodying the principles of fairness and humanitarianism, against the raw power and abuses of money.

Now, for the all-important environmental perspective. Since the first global environmental conference (the 1972 Stockholm Conference on the Human Environment), it has become more and more clear that we all share a global environment, and that nation-to-nation conflicts over resources and environmental quality will become ever more acute if comprehensive international arrangements are not put into place to resolve them. Note the "Suharto smog", the clouds of smoke from Indonesian forest fires that affected five Southeast Asian nations in 1997 damaging health and economies, and causing diplomatic protests. Other ecology-based conflicts—such as competition for fresh water—are predicted to become more acute as the global demand for increasingly-scarce fresh water rises sharply in the coming century. A new global system of "redress and balance" is surely needed.

Just as a new "financial architecture" is needed for global economic stability, so imaginative and potent new measures are needed to bring about stability of the global ecology through a new "ecological architecture". Times of crisis often prompt leaders to embark on radical change. Financial and ecological needs can be linked—and the time to start is now.

The international economic and financial system, as a system, is closed off from ecology. There are no binding links between the two, only voluntary governmental arrangements to fund global environmental programmes, mostly through the United Nations system. And nothing is more closed off than the global capital markets, with their daily 1.5-trillion-dollar, yield-hungry transfers. If free markets and free trade are the engines of global economic growth, and if a healthy global environment is necessary to the sustainability of both the global ecological system and the global economic system, then global trade and financial flows must be tapped for the sake of managing and protecting the global environment.

When we gaze with a critical eye at the functioning of the global system—in all its dimensions—we find considerable ironies. There is more monetised wealth in the world today than ever before, yet the global environment is facing its biggest (man-made) threats ever. There is a growing gap between rich and poor, with some 1.2 billion people in poverty. Yet, those consumers in the so-called advanced and advancing countries who already lead lifestyles of "luxurious" consumption are being urged to consume more, to "progress" to a "higher level" of consumption.

The global financial crisis has spurred calls for action because of its suddenness and the immediacy of its consequences. The global ecological crisis is broad-based and complex, and is advancing incrementally. There is no immediacy about it, so leaders do not call for urgent global measures. But it is a potentially more devastating crisis, and potentially much harder to deal with when its impact unfolds, than even the collapse of a dysfunctional global financial system. The unfolding global ecological crisis touches every human being, and has implications for every human being's freedom—now taken for granted—to degrade the global environment.

What can we then say about freedom?

We are discovering the limits of individual economic freedom as the third millennium begins. In fact, we have come to the end of an era which may be best described as one of *naïve liberalism*.

Freedom has been an exhilarating impulse of the human spirit for centuries, as the development of civilisation liberated greater segments of humanity from mere subsistence. Advancing technology enhanced the freedom to create, and the freedom to benefit from one's creations. Freedom from ignorance through knowledge and education became a spiritually-uplifting kind of freedom. In the liberal Western tradition, freedom became embodied in the high-minded ideals of human rights, freedom of expression, and freedom through the ballot box to elect one's government. Theories of economic freedom to create and expand one's wealth advanced; those theories included the supposition that individuals were free to exploit, and to profit from, the natural environment. The concept of mass consumption as a wealth-generating system grew up, promoting its own supposed "freedom of choice" of the consumer—a kind of intoxicating freedom that knows little responsibility.

It is in the realm of these latter, supposed economic freedoms that a great potential for destruction has arisen, and thus where the notion of individual freedom is now under scrutiny. The freedom to destroy—now that we are beginning to know the full impact of humankind's exploitative and consumptive activities on the ecology—is not a high-minded ideal.

The new awareness emerging from the 1997–99 financial crisis teaches us that economic freedom must exist within a regulatory framework of financial sustainability. So, too, the nature of personal freedom within a context of ecological responsibility must be redefined. At the centre of this redefinition must be a new and universal appreciation of the notion of human dignity: that dignity arises through individuals' contribution to a new harmony, embracing humankind, Nature, and society—not from the accumulation of material things.

The Dilemma of Consumption

What is the most common prescription, under the current monetarist and consumer-driven economic model, for the present global financial and economic ills? "Everybody, spend more money on buying things!" is the commonly heard chorus. Can these appeals of economists for governments to "stimulate" global consumption provide the magic that will reverse the present downturn in the global economy? After all, the purpose of striving to get more money is to consume more, isn't it?

In Thailand, on 20 October 1998, the governor of the Bank of Thailand, Chatu Mongol Sonakul, urged Thais to spend more to help battered businesses, in order to help pull Thailand out of its economic crisis. But how many Thais would want to spend their savings on non-essential consumption when they were unsure if they would still have their jobs next year?

Japan was in a similar dilemma (as were many other countries). Conventional economic wisdom said that ordinary Japanese must increase their consumption (especially of foreign goods) to lead a recovery in Asia, and perhaps even to save the global economy from further meltdown. But, like Thais, ordinary Japanese were experiencing job losses at the fastest rate since World War II.

Is this imperative to consume the answer to economic wellbeing? Ironically for Thailand and Japan, both Buddhist countries, the teachings of the Buddha say no to materialistic consumption as a way of life. In addition, unsustainable consumption (including much of what we take for granted in our daily lives) is seen by environmental authorities as posing increased danger to ecological stability in the future. Japan's

Environment Agency declared in a 1995 publication that current economic assumptions, coupled with a growing global population, would continue to increase natural resource consumption, and to worsen pressure on the environment. The agency noted:

> To avoid this situation, we must strictly curtail further increases in environmental load, and we must form a sustainable society.[14]

The agency offered the following prescription:

> It is necessary to review the concepts that underlie modern civilisation—mass production, mass consumption, mass disposal. We must change our civilisation into a sustainable one which has its economic/social system based on the concept of circulation, and where Nature and people live in harmony.

Even more ironically, American and European economists of the free-trade school subsequently pressured the Japanese government to cut taxes in order to spur consumption. Yet the Environment Agency—along with environmental experts from many countries and from the United Nations—are calling for taxes on consumption that has a negative impact on the environment. The Environment Agency noted:

> By utilising economic measures such as taxes and charges, environmental costs could be reflected in the trade prices of services and products. This, in turn, would make it possible to utilise inherent market mechanisms in an environmentally positive way.

Thus, we face the dilemma that the call for increased consumption in Asia, stimulated by government-sponsored credit to consumers, by tax cuts, and by government spending programmes, may lead us out of the current deflationary crisis, only to usher us eventually into a broader and more severe, ecologically-based crisis.

It is folly to believe that the major, global priority of human endeavour will always be to increase production, leading to the ever increasing generation of wealth, with the ultimate goal and reward of a life of ever increasing consumption. Wealth generation may be a priority now for countries with an impoverished population, but even in those countries, redistribution of wealth, and emphasis on public infrastructure, shared resources, and universal access to a clean and healthy natural environment, can do a lot to bring the society into a satisfying balance.

As alluded to earlier, the current preoccupation with increasing industrialisation, production, and consumption should be seen as a phase that the global economy is passing through. In the next phase, the priorities will be balance, harmony with Nature, and sustainability of the global ecology. Sustainable growth and consumption, however, will not be precluded.

What, then, can supercede ever increasing consumption as a global economic force, at least leading into this next phase of global development based on sustainability? The huge financial surpluses generated from a consumption-based economy can, in a large part, be redirected on a global basis to massive-scale environmental projects. Large-scale employment generated through these projects, especially in the impoverished countries, will put money in the hands of the unemployed, which will be a boost to economies in general. The overall aim of this new priority may be described as nothing less than a *stewardship of the global environment*. If the global environment becomes severely destabilised, there can be no economic stability or security. Yet, humankind is presently advancing rapidly along the road to such destabilisation.

Environmental Warning

Super-hurricane Mitch, which tore through five countries of Central America creating enormous devastation in October 1998, is already being cited as an example of the extreme climatic events predicted by scientists to become more common and more severe as global warming advances.

Winds from Mitch reached almost 300 km per hour and dumped huge amounts of driving rain on the region over several days, causing extensive flooding and mudslides. *The Economist* said it was Central America's worst natural disaster in its modern history; Cable Network News reported it was the worst disaster in 200 years. The death toll was in the region of 10,000 people. More than one million people in worst-hit Honduras and Nicaragua were left without shelter, and the massive devastation to infrastructure and agriculture was estimated to have set both countries' development back by as much as one generation.

Global warming, spurred by human-induced pollution of the atmosphere, is already happening. It raises serious questions about an economic system based on energy-intensive consumption, and about such a system's ability to change. (These issues were outlined in Chapter 2.)

Another emerging environmental crisis is the impending global scarcity of fresh water—with all the social dislocations, human misery, and international tensions that it could cause. At the International Conference on World Water Resources, earlier in 1998, UNESCO director-general Federico Mayor warned that the present usage of fresh water was not sustainable, as population growth, changing consumption patterns, and increasing urbanisation have put a greater demand on water supplies with a parallel increase in waste-water. Said Mayor:

> To secure an adequate food supply, more water is required for irrigation, but at the same time the use of fertilisers produces more pollution which drains into our rivers and infiltrates our ground water systems. Industry is also a large water consumer, and produces pollutants that are disposed of in our waterways.

There are other ongoing crises of ecology that demand attention: the increasing loss of biodiversity (the whole range of species from plants to animals to micro-organisms), deforestation, loss of agricultural land through soil erosion and desertification. . . . Many of these problems are interlinked. Also to be tackled are the many forms of human-induced pollution of land, sea, and air. Awareness of these problems has grown throughout the second half of the 20th Century, and many positive responses have resulted. But the overall declining situation has yet to be reversed. Unless major changes in economic assumptions are made, could these negative trends combine into a mega-crisis of the ecology?

It is becoming apparent now that current economic assumptions are part of this gathering crisis, and not part of the solution. If the vast majority of conventional economists—those whose concerns are confined to lubricating the workings of the free-market, consumptive model of *economism*—could not see the 1997–99 financial crisis coming, would anyone be surprised that they are also failing to acknowledge a much broader, more pervasive crisis brewing?

This, then, is the challenge to economic and political policy makers: *Any solution to further global financial malaise must contain the seeds of a solution to the looming ecological crisis.* It is a truism that economics must serve ecology, because the free-enterprise, value-creating sector is really the only source of funds to protect the ecological baseline.

Let us not forget the broken promise of consumption-driven, market economics, and the rich countries' game plan to expand it to the so-called emerging economies through deregulation and freeing up of their markets. Two or more decades ago, the fraternity of free-market economists offered their vision for solving global poverty: produce, trade, and sell. "Forget about the environment and the destruction that extractive economics brings," was the refrain taken up by the vision's protagonists in the developing world. "We will get rich, then we can solve the environmental problems."

Now, the world is richer than ever before, but the number of impoverished remains the same, while environmental problems are worse than ever—and growing. That is why ecologists wince when market-oriented economists, who have seldom foreseen disaster approaching, say that increased consumption is the answer to improve presently ailing economies.

Meanwhile, economics, ever seeking to unfetter itself through deregulation, serves itself. To be sure, free enterprise has accomplished a wealth-creating miracle in this century, and remains a major hope of poverty-stricken nations (and regions within nations). But now, it is time for the adherents of free enterprise to recognise that they must operate within—and contribute to—an overriding framework of higher responsibility.

Environmental Spending to Boost Global Economy

Free-market economics must be tapped to serve global ecological goals. Judiciously engineered taxes to fund ecological programmes and to strengthen global institutions are the way to build the needed global ecological architecture. Enter the Tobin tax.

This measure was proposed more than two decades ago by the economist James Tobin—the winner of a Nobel Prize—to avert short-term currency speculation and its destabilising effects. Its proponents note that a tax of just 0.1 per cent on all foreign-currency trades would deter speculators from moving massive amounts of "hot money" in and out of currencies on a short-term basis, while such a tax would be too small to affect genuine, long-term investors. It was recently dusted off and thrown into the arena once again following the financial crisis in East Asia.

Revenues from such an instrument as the Tobin tax could be used to mount large-scale activities to rehabilitate degraded environments, through such institutions as the Global Environment Facility (GEF), which is jointly run by the World Bank, the UN Development Programme and the UN Environment Programme. The GEF was set up in 1991, but as of 1998 had programmed only US$1.9 billion in grant funding spread across more than 500 projects in 119 countries—far short of the large-scale funding needed to make a real impact on major global environmental problems. Grants and concessional funds of the GEF are provided in four areas: biodiversity, climate change, international waters, and ozone layer depletion. Funding for desertification and deforestation can be provided only in relation to those four areas, thus severely limiting GEF funding for those two acute problems. The GEF also operates the financial mechanism for the Convention on Biological Diversity, and the United Nations Framework Convention on Climate Change. The GEF's scope could be greatly expanded to transform it into a major global financing agency.

For example, another possibility for channeling of major international funding is the UN Convention to Combat Desertification, which came into effect in 1996 as a beginning towards returning the world's drylands to economic and environmental health. Back in the 1980s, it was estimated that at least $100 billion per year was needed to stop the spread of deserts worldwide and to rehabilitate previously productive land; about 35 per cent of the Earth's land surface was seen as at risk of desertification. As of 1998, parties to the convention were struggling to give it meaning, in the absence of any major funding. They had agreed on a mechanism to share information globally among affected countries, including information about multilateral and bilateral sources of help.

Once the misplaced priorities of the international commercial system are remedied and large-scale financing becomes available for the global environment, effective ways to programme spending will be needed. The concept of "joint implementation" could be employed on a large scale. This concept had, by the mid-1990s, gained currency within United Nations forums discussing approaches to global problems, especially climate change. It could allow teams of international officials to work with nationals of recipient countries on specific projects that will benefit the global ecology.

But difficulties with international taxation schemes such as James Tobin's have been pointed out: that they would be difficult to administer, and perhaps easy to avoid, in the labyrinthine world of international finance. Additionally, some critics fear that difficulties would arise in deciding how the money should be spent, and in deciding who should make spending decisions. The United States has consistently opposed suggestions to introduce international taxation schemes for funding even such worthy enterprises as UN peacekeeping operations.

Efforts to expand and institutionalise economic globalisation have taken place, particularly through the creation of the World Trade Organisation in 1995, and through other institutions such as the International Monetary Fund and the World Bank. But the movement to institutionalise protection of the global environment, and thus safeguard humankind's future quality of life, is making much less progress than promotion of global money-making efforts.

If not a Tobin tax, eventually other means will be found for raising international revenue so that international programmes do not have to rely on the fickle generosity and manipulative influence of voluntary donations. All UN specialised programmes—from peacekeeping to health and to environment—are currently dependent on this voluntarism.

At the 19th UN General Assembly Special Session to Review Implementation of *Agenda 21* in June 1997, the European Union proposed an international tax on airline fuel, to raise some two to three billion dollars annually for sustainable development.[15] The proposal failed to take off because it lacked American support.

I would further like to suggest a modest tax on international trade flows. Set even-handedly on the flow of goods internationally, such a tax would not be felt by consumers, as new efficiencies and market openings generated through globalisation of free trade will lower the prices of goods worldwide. Additionally, such a tax would not discriminate against any particular country or product. It would not constitute a barrier to trade and would not inhibit its growth. Of course, we can expect some quarters to complain vigorously about this. Nobody likes taxes, but people are willing to pay them at the national level because they want an education system, water supplies, roads, a police force, an army, a legal system, and so on.

As the third millennium begins, the big question is, who will pay now to prevent our grandchildren and great-grandchildren inheriting a miserable, degraded planet?

Another alternative method of fund raising is the levying of environmental taxes on a global basis. Proposals for such taxes at the national level—on fossil fuels, for example—are gaining adherents, particularly in European countries. Globally, a proposal for a fossil-fuels tax has gained increasing prominence as the global warming negotiations have progressed—both to lower the economic attractiveness of burning such fuels, and to create funds to subsidise clean alternative fuels. The proposed fossil-fuels tax is one example of the polluter-pays principle— a proposal which many people agree with in principle, but want to avoid when it affects them.

A wide range of taxes that make polluters pay need to be proposed and promoted. Polluting technology can be rendered obsolete gradually, causing less economic pain, by increasing tax on its products year by year, say a 10 per cent, 20 per cent, or 50 per cent increase per year, until the product becomes priced out of the market and environmentally-friendly (perhaps subsidised) alternatives to it become attractive. Eventually, all commercial products—including goods traded internationally—should be priced to include the full environmental costs that their production, packaging, and transportation incur.

The role of the media in promoting unsustainable consumption needs to be considered along with a redirection of the media to support environmental sustainability. For example, goods which are subject to environmental taxes should not be allowed to be advertised through the mass media. The whole culture of consumerism, as portrayed by the entertainment media, needs to be rethought. Financial mechanisms and incentives need to be devised to get creative, well-produced, and persuasive messages promoting sustainable lifestyles on to the airwaves. The principle of environmental taxation can be applied to the media: place a hefty tax on advertising and use the money to promote culturally-sensitive and environmentally-friendly programming.

A new global system of "redress and balance" is surely needed, and the challenge is to transfer a meaningful amount of the surplus wealth generated by a rapidly growing and globalising consumer economy, through new global institutional arrangements, for massive spending to stabilise an increasingly destabilised global ecology. Yes, by all means let us start a huge, worldwide programme incorporating joint implementation to oversee and guide the huge sums of money that the task requires.

The potential to create jobs through environmental management, especially in the poorer countries, is great. One major aim will be to convert degraded land into usefulness—for economic purposes and for environmental enhancement purposes. Much can be done, particularly in the arid countries threatened by advancing desertification, as well as in countries where man-made degradation has created wastelands. The massive planting of trees can serve many purposes: stabilising the climate both locally and globally, enhancing water catchment, preserving wildlife habitats, acting as windbreaks, contributing to the reclamation of desert lands. Land can be terraced for increased agricultural output, programmes can be mounted to stabilise eroding land, and intensive water management for agricultural rehabilitation can be achieved.

These are some of the important and necessary actions (other worthy and neglected objectives will surely be found) that may be tackled through labour-intensive programmes, producing long-term environmental and social benefits. Permanent task forces may be created to protect the environment and particularly endangered species. Through the power of taxation and subsidies, pollution-creating technology may be retired and replaced by environmentally-friendly technology: for example, through small-scale industry for renewable energy generation.

The concept of joint implementation may help to counteract the do-nothing inertia of corrupt third world governments. The much-needed transfer of clean technology from the industrialised world to the developing world might just be included into the bargain, as environmental regeneration within individual nations becomes a global objective through the elaboration of a new global ecological architecture.

International Law and Money Politics

Where will the leadership come from for this new global ecological architecture? The world's only superpower in the 1990s was preoccupied with extending its global economic advantage through a comprehensive strategy of forcing open global markets for all kinds of trade and services, particularly in finance and investment. The noted American economist Jeffrey Sachs, who is director of the Harvard Institute for International

Development, had this to say about American leadership in a 1998 essay on global capitalism:

> America has wanted global leadership on the cheap. It was desperate for the developing world and post-communist economics to buy into its vision, in which globalisation, private capital flows, and Washington advice would overcome the obstacles to shared prosperity, so that pressures on the rich countries to do more for the poorer countries could be contained by the dream of universal economic growth. In this way, the United States would not have to shell out real money to help peaceful reconstruction of Russia, or to ameliorate the desperate impoverishment and illness in Africa. In essence, America has tried to sell its social ethos: the rich need not help the poor, since the poor can enjoy rising living standards and someday become rich themselves. . . .

Sachs called for the global financial crisis to be used creatively, to engineer a sounder basis for globalisation, to avoid a highly dangerous new period of confusion and confrontation.[16]

Since 1980, under successive presidents (Reagan, Bush, and Clinton), the United States' primary international objective was to use every multilateral negotiating forum available, from the World Trade Organisation (and its predecessor, GATT) to the Asia Pacific Economic Cooperation, to spread the American economic gospel. At the same time, it resisted making binding commitments in multilateral negotiations for the financing of global social and environmental goals. The United States would not pay its United Nations dues (accumulating to some $1.5 billion by 1998) and would not entertain proposals to devise a global taxation system as an alternative to individual country assessments in financing multilateral institutions. Two common arguments were regularly cited in opposing such taxation:

- that commitments to global taxation schemes would infringe upon US sovereignty, since only Congress could levy taxes on Americans or American entities; and
- that binding commitments—for example, to lower emission rates—would damage the competitiveness of American business.

This policy was evidently an abdication of global leadership in the face of a deepening global ecological crisis. An opportunity to champion high-minded ideals in a spirit of sacrifice was eclipsed by the "need" to protect American corporate enterprises from an imagined loss of profit or competitive advantage, and to actively promote that advantage. Another reason for not favouring global taxation is perhaps a feared loss of political leverage that comes with being the United Nations' biggest source of funds.

Hence, we see how money politics within the American political system has held back attempts to achieve ecological sustainability on a global scale. Big business's financial alliance with politicians, arising from its large-scale financing of political candidates, applies to both major political parties. Many individual Americans do care about the environment, and are modifying their lifestyles to have less impact upon it; there are many organisations in the United States attempting to promote sustainable lifestyles and sustainable economics. But money politics has ruled out decisive American leadership in the international arena.

What remains of US leadership in the world? The United States gained its global leadership through the fight against communism, when it built up an awesome military machine, and through the size of its economy. When security fears are raised either in Europe or Asia, liberal-democratic countries still turn to the United States, as a superpower, to guarantee their security. Associated with the fight against communism, the United States' promotion of democracy and human rights became a centrepiece of its diplomacy. However, in the early 1990s, when US business interests intensified their bid to gain access to closed markets (particularly the Chinese market) the Clinton Administration downgraded the non-profit-making issue of human rights in favour of economic cooperation and market opening: joint venture contracts would not be forthcoming to large American transnational corporations in an atmosphere of China-bashing on human rights.

American global leadership has eroded, or is non-existent, in another field: the development of international law. Ever since its inception, the United States has gained the admiration of the world in the development of its own national legal system, which regards every individual as equal before the law. The system's striving for unbiased application of the rule of law in protecting the weak and in holding the rich and powerful accountable, has been more consistent than in most other countries.

But, American legislators are failing to extend this same legalistic tradition to the international arena at a time when such leadership is most needed. Rather the opposite is happening: in global attempts to extend the international rule of law for social, environmental, and other purposes, American support is lukewarm or absent. Rather, American money politics often places impediments in the way of other countries' initiatives to create new international legal instruments that attempt to lower global pollution or to institute principles of environmental equity, for example.

The United States seems more concerned with protecting the privileges that flow from its size and power rather than shaping a global system that will lead to ecological sustainability and offer protection for all countries. The rest of the developed world is far ahead of the United States in attempts to enlist every nation's commitment to a body of international law.

It is becoming increasingly repugnant that the world's largest and richest economy—which is also the world's largest polluter and consumer of natural resources—should consistently resist moves towards the transfer of portions of its national sovereignty to global organisations and legal instruments, merely because its corporations are the biggest, most powerful, and most pervasive in the international arena, and thus have the most to gain from operating in an unregulated global environment. Some examples of American recalcitrance:

- The US, for a decade, resisted signing the United Nations Convention on the Law of the Sea (finalised in December 1982 and entered into force in November 1994) because it would limit the profit-making abilities of US corporations which monopolised the technology for extracting minerals from the international seabed.
- At the 1992 Earth Summit in Rio de Janeiro, the US led the opposition to the creation of a binding financial mechanism to fund *Agenda 21*, the 800-page, comprehensive blueprint for achieving global, sustainable development in the 21st Century. Some $125 billion for *Agenda 21* was supposed to come from donor nations and international financial institutions, but no deadline was set for this amount to materialise. US President George Bush was the only leader not to sign the Convention on Biological Diversity. The treaty was widely supported by the developing nations to protect them from the exploitation of their natural

resources vital to their own future development. The US was against provisions in the treaty that it believed could hurt its dominant biotechnology industry by threatening the industry's move to gain intellectual property rights and patents on products gleaned from natural resources such as forests in developing nations.

- The US has yet to accept binding targets for the reduction of carbon dioxide emissions under the Framework Convention on Climate Change. This was true during the treaty's adoption in Rio in 1992, and at the Kyoto session in 1997, in which the Kyoto Protocol set out negotiated targets for emission reductions by industrialised countries. The Clinton Administration signed the Kyoto Protocol following the Buenos Aires meeting in November 1998, but the US Senate was threatening to reject it.

- The US refused to back the creation of the International Criminal Court (which was created on 17 July 1998 when 120 countries voted for it and 7 against) apparently because it feared US military action might be fettered by it. The court was proposed to hold individuals personally accountable for charges of genocide, crimes against humanity, war crimes, and crimes of aggression. Ironically, the United States entered negotiations on creating the court saying it supported a permanent court. Then it manoeuvred to weaken the court's powers and independence. The final product is a court which can investigate only with the agreement of the country (of which the accused is a citizen) where the crime took place. And the United Nations Security Council can stop any investigation or trial. In an analysis of US manoeuvrings, Phyllis Bennis, a fellow of the US-based Institute for Policy Studies, wrote:

So, with all those safeguards, what made Washington so afraid. . . ? The real fear in Washington is that the court could become a tool for global opponents of future US military interventions that other countries would view as illegal. . . . In reality, the US wanted a court for everyone in the world accept Americans. It wanted a full immunity guarantee for American troops, American generals, and American policy makers. . . .[17]

Again, the United States was seen to be lacking in leadership towards the development an effective and binding system of international law.

How often do we hear official US spokespersons cite "US interests" as their reason for opposing or supporting a particular measure? We seldom or never hear US spokespersons invoking "national self-denial" or "the interests of the international community" as a factor in decision making.

It is difficult for the powerful to give up portions of their power or sovereignty for the common good. Power is addictive. When a nation can use the influence arising from its powerful economic base to gain further economic advantage, why would it want to give up its disproportionate share of benefits? Thus, an underlying reason why the United States resists instituting taxation on a global basis (such as the Tobin tax) is because it would lose the leverage and influence over even a small amount of revenue that would migrate from US investment banks and hedge funds to an international body.

The United States, as the world's leading financial power, can exercise great influence over the direction of international institutions merely by withholding or providing large sums of money. Particularly, the US supports institutions such as the World Trade Organisation and the IMF, whose commitments to opening markets stand to benefit corporate America. The United States is the biggest contributor to the IMF, which has become in many ways an appendage of US economic policy in the global arena. Indeed, many analysts had come to believe, in the late 1990s, that the US had an undeclared strategy to emasculate the United Nations and to invest the WTO and IMF with the UN's previous mandate for promoting global development.

During the onset of the Asian financial crisis, the first reaction of the IMF was to protect the investments of the G-7 banks, which had lent billions of dollars to private companies in Thailand, Indonesia, and the Republic of Korea, despite the fact that many of those investments were not properly evaluated and were imprudent. The agency's second objective was to continue to open up segments of developing economies to participation and ownership by the Western corporate world. Thirdly, it imposed high interest rates and fiscal austerity on the economies it was called in to help. This prescription, by the end of 1998, became widely regarded as a mistake which had led to deflation and large-scale job losses; at the same time it allowed American and European companies to buy up cheaply the assets of faltering Asian companies.

The financial crisis in Asia, with its dislocations and sufferings, has led many in the South to question whether globalisation is really worth it. This is particularly so when powerful corporations and financial institutions of the North get shielded from their bad investment decisions through the political power of their parent nations, while at the same time stricken enterprises of the South are asked to pay the full price for their folly. There is more than a grain of truth in the observation of Malaysian prime minister Mahathir Mohamad that pressure for the opening of markets and promotion by the North of free flows of capital and investment represents a creeping form of neo-colonialism.

The process of globalisation apparently cannot be stopped, although there is still room for vulnerable countries of the South to develop a national ethic of self-sufficiency, as King Bhumibol of Thailand has advocated for Thais. But it is worth stressing that globalism is an emerging system whose workings and responsibilities are still in the process of being defined and developed.

As discussed previously in this chapter, a sustainable economic globalisation calls for global institutions and arrangements that mirror effective national ones, actively promoting such things as stability, equity, humanitarianism, compassion, and environmental protection and rehabilitation. If the liberalisation and globalisation of trade and investment are regarded as "unstoppable", international regulatory and revenue-generating arrangements will sooner or later be seen as desirable or inevitable.

Countries, particularly in the South, have already seen their national sovereignty diminished in economic and financial matters through market opening and unrestricted financial flows. It remains for the developed countries of the North to accept that they, in turn, must surrender some of the sovereignty enjoyed by their corporate and financial entities so that greater financial stability can be achieved through international regulation and taxation.

The continued development and refinement of international law is the way forward. By financing the strengthening of international institutions and programmes, and the creation of new ones, international taxation can begin in a major way to remedy global financial turbulence and to solve the pervasive and growing global ecological crisis.

Chapter 4

Politics and Thailand's Financial Crisis

Two years after Thailand's financial and economic collapse, people were still seeking the meaning of it all. The euphoria of the high-growth, high-consumption bubble economy had given way to a grim acceptance of the hardship and difficult choices that had come in its wake. Was the acquisitive lifestyle of the bubble economy just an illusion? Could it be recreated in future years? Or, if it was just an illusion, should it be taken as a warning that something was fundamentally wrong—on a massive scale—with Thai society's expectations?

The technical causes of the collapse have been well analysed, and can be summarised as a compendium of inadequacies in Thai politics, culture, and administration. But the questions can still be asked: What were Thais seeking, as a nation and as a culture, that led them to pursue the illusions that led to the bubble? What were the deeper causes underlying the apparent technical blunders and institutional short-comings?

An Overview

There are two contexts that need examining to place the Nineties Bubble into perspective: the context of Thai development; and the context of the global economy and its development. (This latter context was dealt with at length in the previous chapter.)

Firstly, a point that often seems to be overlooked is that Thailand remains a developing country. Foreign fund managers and investment bankers, the ones who provided the massive inflow of foreign money which fuelled the bubble economy during the mid-1990s, were not very interested in this perspective. Being a developing country can mean many things. Some major characteristics are: a lack of financial resources, low-level development of human resources, inadequate institutional development, and an inadequate appreciation of the importance of professional standards in the various spheres of government and business. The notion of responsibility among senior government officials, politicians, and many corporate leaders is also often severely lacking. These latter two points are also a question of the maturity of a society. These are basic issues of development, not fundamentally economic issues, although they have an impact on economics as the Crash of 97 proved.

Rather than seeing developing societies as lacking maturity in several spheres—political, legal, social, administrative—in which investment is needed, the foreign fund managers and investment bankers characterise the developing societies as *emerging markets*—in other words, under-developed countries with rising affluence that are ready for various kinds of business and financial investment where risks may be high, but where high GDP growth can mean high profits. Their impulse, along with the transnational corporations, is to influence their own governments to bring pressure to break down barriers to their participation in such economies through liberalisation of trade, capital flows, and services.

Because the funds, the banks, and the corporations have grown large and powerful in the so-called developed world through attaining higher standards of organisation, they have an inherent advantage in participating in developing societies. And, by characterising such societies as *markets*, they conveniently avoid responsibility for aspects such as balanced and sustainable development, environmental protection, economic equity, improved education, and poverty alleviation.

Transnational corporations may argue that they are creating employment and paying tax revenues to governments, but in many (not all) cases, such corporations' negative impact on the cultural values of underdeveloped societies, and their aggressive fostering of a self-centred (and ultimately unsustainable) culture of vanity consumption, appear in many cases to far outweigh the advantages.

The making of profits subscribes to a narrow set of rules that are applicable everywhere, and do not necessarily take into account whether a society is developing or developed. What matters is the seeking of commercial advantage, immediate or gradual, which can be converted into profits. Investors and creditors were not so much interested in whether Thailand (and the rest of Asia) was "underdeveloped" or not. They were more conscious of risk, and whether or not their expected high rewards justified perceived risks that might undermine their operations. But, the opportunity to create consumer "needs" in a virgin market, by applying a marketing machinery that had already been well tuned in the transnationals' developed markets, was too compelling to ignore.

As outlined in the previous chapter, when the Crash of 97 came, the first reaction of governments of the so-called developed countries, acting through international agencies they control, such as the IMF, was to protect their nationals' investment—the large, often dubious loans made by their bankers and investors to Thai institutions and companies. Never mind that those bankers and investors seldom closely scrutinised the institutions they were dealing with, nor examined their clients' motives, morals, or capabilities for rational decision making. Their mission was to get their money back, with profit. Hence, the austerity demands of the IMF leading to the generation of current account surpluses, which could subsequently be used to pay foreign creditors, irrespective of the prolonged hardships resulting in the host country. And hence the pressure placed on Thailand by the IMF and the World Bank in the first instance for the Thai government to guarantee repayment of the bad loans of the Thai private sector to foreign lenders.

The American view of Thailand's crisis was that it was self-inflicted; that the "markets" punished Thailand for its excesses and failures. This was expressed by US Treasury deputy secretary, Lawrence Summers in a speech about the World Trade Organisation's financial services negotiations, in which the US was pressing for opening of countries' financial sectors to outside competition:

> With hindsight, the lesson of Thailand is . . . that relatively open capital markets, independent monetary policy, a fixed exchange rate, and a current account deficit of eight per cent of GDP do not mix. The speculative activity we saw in the weeks leading to the crisis was the result—not the cause—of Thailand's problems. The unsustainable macro-economic policy mix, combined with highly inefficient domestic intermediation and a poorly equipped regulatory regime, had given banks the freedom—and incentive—

to become heavily overextended. The lack of transparent and timely balance sheets and other information meant there was little early warning that this was taking place.[1]

Thus, the US government did not entertain the notion that its bankers and investment funds should share the responsibility—and losses—arising from bad investment decisions. In its view, the fault lay completely with Thailand.

Secondly, the above system, where developing and developed countries meet in the arena of the global "free market", is based largely on a major—but flawed—supposition: that ever-increasing consumption is the goal and the reward of modern economic development. This supposition attempts to ignore the imperative of global environmental sustainability (a major theme of this book). It ignores the mental health and other problems that accompany poorly-educated people's single-minded embrace of rampant consumerism. It ignores social issues; promoting the consumerist ethic drains resources and diverts attention from poverty and deprivation within societies. This perspective is particularly relevant to Thailand.

Underlying this burgeoning ideology of consumerism is the growing global phenomenon of money politics. Not only in Thailand, money politics pervades the whole global system. Transnational corporations have become increasingly influential in defining political and economic realities. The business and financial economists attached to international investment funds and trading banks—with their narrow focus on market risk and returns, and business opportunities—dominate the airwaves and newspaper columns, and draw attention away from the real economic needs and aspirations of people in developing societies. In turn, corporate power, based on mass consumerism and its huge money flows, translates into self-serving political power. In countries as diverse as the United States and Thailand, elected politicians increasingly have become the tools of powerful economic lobbies.

Thus, taking the two standpoints outlined above, we can assert that the international community, especially the economic community, has somehow lost the perspective of development. The crisis in Asia has been seen not so much as a development problem but rather as a financial or institutional problem: that policies were not somehow "right". It is an example of one of the great economic dilemmas of our time, the rush towards growth without development.

The subordination of global ideals such as the development of healthy individuals who are culturally and educationally well-rounded—which were evident in past decades—to short- or medium-term business objectives bodes ill for sustainable global development. Adding to this subordination of humane ideals by business objectives is official bribery, often through so-called aid grants or loans or investment. Many governments of the developed world offer such inducements in order to secure advantageous terms for the donor governments' favoured transnational corporations. This kind of "bribery" again can thwart genuine development.

Then there is government-sponsored actual bribery. Global money politics has reached the point where governments will actually encourage or condone bribery and corruption on the part of their country's corporations to buy favourable commercial considerations from corrupt third-world ministers. Some so-called developed countries allow their corporations to claim tax deductions for money spent as bribes to foreign governments.

Additionally, as economic sovereignty migrates from governments to transnational corporations and investment funds, facilitated by instant telecommunications, we witness another blow to genuine democracy, to peoples' empowerment, and to genuine development.

Thailand's Prelude to Crisis

As I indicated at the beginning of this chapter, a consensus has now emerged about the technical and structural causes of Thailand's financial collapse, leading subsequently to economic crisis and social distress. I will look at these causes briefly here and then comment on the cultural factors underlying them.

Financial Liberalisation

In the early 1990s, with Thailand hungry for foreign investment flows, the Bank of Thailand decided to liberalise Thailand's financial system, particularly in its relationship to the rest of the world. There were two important milestones in this liberalisation of the foreign exchange system, as noted by the Thailand Development Research Institute (TDRI):

The first was Thailand's acceptance of the obligations under Article 8 of the International Monetary Fund in 1990. This required the lifting of all controls on all foreign-exchange transactions on the current account, most of which had in fact been already removed.

The second was the opening of the Bangkok International Banking Facility (BIBF) in 1993, designed to make Bangkok a centre for financial services by encouraging foreign financial institutions to set up operations in Thailand. These financial institutions were to make loans both to borrowers in other countries in the region and to domestic borrowers.[2]

These actions, in conjunction with a fixed exchange rate, set the stage for the flood of yield-hungry foreign capital into Thailand. Indeed, Asia as a whole was experiencing an inward flood of "surplus" capital from the "developed" world. The World Bank estimated that net inflows of long-term debt, foreign direct investment, and equity purchases into Asia and the Pacific were only about $25 billion in 1990, but exploded to more than $110 billion by 1996.[3]

But dangers lurked, dangers that the Thai system was ill-equipped to handle. The Nukul Commission, in its report, *Analysis and Evaluation on Facts Behind Thailand's Economic Crisis*,[4] published in March 1998, noted that

> . . . because a large portion of the foreign capital inflows were debts, prudent and efficient management was required . . . debt levels increased substantially since 1990. In 1996, it shot up to 50.14 per cent of GDP. Anything more than 40 per cent of GDP is considered quite dangerous.[5]

Fixed Exchange Rate

Thailand's policy of pegging the baht to the US dollar, at a rate of around 25 baht to one dollar, was established in 1984 following a devaluation of the baht. The peg came to be regarded as an anchor for Thailand's spectacular economic growth, especially in the early 1990s. It allowed for the massive influx of foreign money into the country to fuel that growth. But as economic conditions changed, with Thai industries becoming less competitive and exports faltering, Thai officials were unable to see the necessity to change the currency regime.

The baht–dollar peg had led to the baht appreciating against other currencies as the dollar appreciated, thus making Thai exports less competitive. This was particularly true with the yen, which by mid-1996 had depreciated 50 per cent against the dollar. The fixed baht exchange rate maintained by the Bank of Thailand gave an illusion of (devaluation-proof) security for large flows of foreign money both inwards and outwards. Thus, just as a massive amount of money flowed into Thailand since 1993, a massive outward movement of "hot money" took place in the first half of 1997, as economic indicators began to deteriorate, and as currency speculators began to attack the baht, leading to fears of a devaluation. Subsequently, the TDRI noted:

> First of all, the central bank should not have continued with an essentially fixed exchange-rate regime. An open capital account has repeatedly been shown to be incompatible with such a regime (unless there is a very strong currency board that strictly limits the use of monetary policy). The crises of Chile in 1982, Sweden in 1990, and Mexico in 1994 can be cited as examples of the failure to heed this rule.[6]

The tragedy of maintaining the baht at a fixed rate against the US dollar continued until the central bank spent almost all of its foreign reserves defending the rate, at which time it was forced to float the currency on 2 July 1997. The baht then experienced a steep fall.

Key central bank officials apparently believed they could fend off the speculators' massive selling of the baht with their foreign reserves, even as exports were experiencing a decline. Their explanation was that they believed the decline was merely a cyclical downturn and that high export growth rates would soon return. But the IMF's analysis did not see it that way. *The Nation* reported:

> In June 1996, the IMF completed a report on Thailand in which it urged the economic policy makers to tighten their fiscal policy, adopt a more flexible exchange rate regime, devalue the Thai currency by 10 to 15 per cent, and take precautions against the

looming financial sector crisis. Bodi Chunananda, Banharn's second finance minister, told Rerngchai Marakanond, then BOT governor, that he would be willing to go along with the IMF's suggestions should the BOT pass on the recommendations on the adjustment of the foreign exchange policy. It was an unusual political move, yet Rerngchai did not take up the offer. When Banharn stepped down from office in November 1996, by which time the capital market had collapsed, the economy was well on the way to a meltdown. . . .[7]

The Nukul Commission's report devoted much of its research to examining why the Bank of Thailand depleted its reserves defending the baht. It documented the earlier warnings given to Thailand by the IMF and its advice to devalue the baht, and asked why they were not heeded. The report puts the beginning of the crisis around the middle of 1996:

Before Moody's [Investor Services] reduced Thailand's short-term debts credit rating on 3 September 1996, money market analysts had quietly become suspicious of the economy's future. The lower credit rating, however, made the problems much clearer to both foreign investors and Thais . . . [particularly] the current account deficit problem which might lead to the country devaluing the baht eventually.[8]

Thailand's current account deficit in 1995 had escalated to 8.2 per cent of GDP, exacerbated by wealthy Thais who spent heavily on luxury items in the midst of the bubble economy. In addition, financial institutions were facing growing bad debt problems, and there was a fear that some might not be able to survive. Other economic indicators were worsening:

These problems undermined foreign investors' confidence in the Thai economy. Foreign capital inflows began declining in the third quarter of 1996 but net capital outflows didn't begin until the second quarter of 1997.[9]

In 1997, the IMF contacted Thai officials many times. An IMF regular mission to survey the economy in March 1997 concluded:

As we have discussed on previous missions, we continue to believe that the introduction of a more flexible exchange rate arrangement is a policy priority, both to increase monetary policy autonomy and to improve the composition of the capital account by reducing the incentives for short-term inflows. . . . In addition, the present system can hinder adjustment to external shocks; in particular the heavy weight of the US dollar in the basket has clearly been unhelpful in present circumstances.[10]

The IMF encouraged the government to introduce greater exchange rate flexibility "promptly". During the mission's visit, the managing director of the IMF, Michel Camdessus, telephoned governor Rerngchai and pleaded for a baht devaluation to make the system more flexible. But the governor disagreed.[11]

The baht came under pressure in December 1996, mainly resulting from foreign investors' withdrawals, and increasing dollar buying by Thai companies, which were losing confidence in the exchange system—but not from speculators. In the last week of January 1997, there was a devaluation rumour, and – additionally—an economic data report showed the government would incur a budget deficit of 54 billion baht for the first three months of the year. The speculators' attacks began. They continued into the first three weeks of February. The Exchange Equalisation Fund and the Banking Department of the Bank of Thailand spent $7.8 billion in foreign exchange to defend the baht over January and February, with the official reserves falling to $38.1 billion, and the forward swap commitment rising to $12.2 billion.[12]

A more intense attack began on 8 May. After 14 May, Thailand had run out of choices when it came to resolving the foreign exchange issue. On that day, the country's reserves fell to $2.5 billion from an outstanding balance of $24.3 billion at the beginning of the month.[13] Apparently, only a handful of officials in the central bank knew how low the reserves had fallen; the Commission concluded that finance minister, Amnuay Viravan was not fully informed until a memorandum dated 28 May reached him. Meanwhile, the IMF made another attempt to urge policy changes on Thailand:

On 14 May, when the baht was intensely attacked, Michel Camdessus wrote to Deputy Prime Minister Amnuay, pressuring for Thailand to proceed with the proposed IMF package of March 1997. . . . The letter was rather vague. But six days later on 20 May, Camdessus sent another letter to Prime Minister Chavalit and held no reservations. He clearly outlined the package's details this time:

- A devaluation of 10–15 per cent, accompanied by a move to greater exchange rate flexibilities. "While we recognise the difficulties in moving in this direction during periods of exchange market pressure, this shift in exchange market regime is now overdue and can only be postponed further at the cost of substantial erosion to reserves."
- A fiscal tightening of at least 1.5 per cent of GDP.
- A tight monetary policy.
- A comprehensive package of measures to strengthen the financial sector. . . .[14]

During the consultations with Thailand, and up to the time when the baht was floated, the IMF never received information on the net reserves.[15]

Up until the point where the BOT was forced to float the baht, Rerngchai continued to insist it was necessary to intervene to maintain confidence in the currency. The central bank's failure to adjust the exchange rate much earlier raises the question of whose interests it believed it was serving. This question, up to mid-1999, has not satisfactorily been answered. Once it started using swap contracts to defend the baht, the bank stood to lose large amounts of foreign exchange when those contracts became due later, if the baht was devalued in the meantime. Did the BOT officials think they were serving the interests of Thai businessmen who were massively overborrowed in foreign currencies, by trying to defend the baht exchange rate at all costs? Did these businessmen also use their political connections to urge maintenance of the rate? If so, there would be a parallel (discussed below) to the BOT's indiscriminate bailing out of failing finance companies to the tune of hundreds of billions of baht. Ammar Siamwalla, a former president of the TDRI, noted:

When the time came to alter the pegged exchange rate, clearly at the beginning of 1997, it appears that the BOT was reluctant to do so for fear of political repercussions. . . . The combination of the decline of the civil service section of the technocracy and the severe internal tensions in the BOT meant that it was a dispirited and demoralised technocracy that confronted the economic crisis. . . .[16]

The truth about the baht defense, which had been carefully concealed, became apparent in August 1997, after Thailand entered the IMF's bail-out programme and was forced to reveal the BOT's swap contracts. *The Nation* wrote:

When the financial markets learnt that as of 19 August 1997, Thailand's outstanding swap contracts due to mature over the next 12 months had reached $23.4 billion, they responded in one voice: Thailand is bankrupt. Rerngchai, along with his strategists, had little understanding of the implications of the foreign exchange swap contracts they accumulated as a smoke-screen to conceal the BOT's dwindling reserves in the baht defence. . . . Upon learning about the gigantic scale of the central bank's swap activity, Hubert Neiss, the director of the IMF's Asia-Pacific Department, said, "I have never seen any central bank in the world do this kind of thing."[17]

Hot Money, Bad Investments

Tens of billions of dollars of cheap capital poured into Thailand following the 1993 liberalisation of the foreign exchange regime. Most of it flowed into speculative investment such as the stock market and property development, causing severe asset price inflation, and—predictably—a property bubble. *The Nation* summed up the situation aptly in a 1998 New Year special report:

. . . [financial institutions and corporations] went on a borrowing binge that built up foreign debts to US$70 billion, half of which accounted for loans with short-term maturity. The foreign loans came with low interest rates of 6–7 per cent, while the baht interest rate was 13–14 per cent. Thai corporates sensed they could make easy profits . . . borrowing cheaply from overseas and making money from the interest rate differentials. Who cared about profits from actual operations. . . ?

Foreign lenders lent financial institutions and corporates easy money because Thailand was an economic tiger, a model of the newly-emerging industrialised economy. At $90 billion in total external debts, including public debts, Thailand's debt service burden was running at about half of gross domestic product. . . . The financial and economic system was in need of more foreign debts to refinance old debts, which had been mis-allocated into the speculative property and stock markets. With the deteriorating macro-economic conditions, foreign investors began to lose confidence. That was how the trouble started. . . .[18]

The property bubble dealt a fatal blow to the finance sector. Finance companies and banks lent recklessly to grandiose property schemes, and foreign lenders continued to pour money into those institutions despite the warning signs. Fuelling it, among other things, was the Chinese-Thai business community's deeply-ingrained belief that holding land was propitious and that the fastest way to get rich was through investment in real estate. Andrew Hilton surveyed the mass lunacy that seemed to be prevailing in Thailand (and in some other parts of Asia), and remarked:

Take Thailand. . . . Surely, anyone with half a brain could have gone out to, say, the "Golden City" development in the Bangkok suburbs and counted the empty offices, the "see-through" buildings. Americans should have learned the lessons of the 1980s Savings and Loan crisis; Japanese bankers . . . had even less excuse since they are still living the downside of their own property bubble. . . .[19]

The TDRI put the beginning of the property boom in the late 1980s, when Thailand was enjoying double-digit growth:

With that kind of growth rate, there was indeed a shortage of office and residential space, particularly in Bangkok. The resulting construction spree was only to be expected, but by 1994 it was becoming obvious that supply was overshooting the requirements. There was an Indian summer of construction activity, when everyone raced to complete their projects, helped along by the cheap money that was becoming available at that time. . . .

The property sector has a special place in the Thai financial system. The majority of Thai bank loans are based on collateral, with property as the asset of choice. . . . However, while the bubble arose in large part out of private decisions, there were major policy and regulatory failures also.[20]

A Bangkok-based securities analyst, Michael Stead, recalled:

During the boom years, the banks and finance companies were eager to lend. People had a lot of cash in those days. They didn't know where to put their money. The banks were brimming. They lose money if they do not lend it out at a higher rate of interest. . . .

Everybody was getting richer, wages were going up, banks were enjoying very sizable increases in their deposit base, and of course, they had to lend the money somewhere. In the case of property . . . it was mainly the local banks who were to blame. . . . But for petrochemicals and steel, it was perhaps more difficult to foresee they would run into problems. . . .[21]

Stead noted that after 1993, the big capital inflows caused a lot of problems in the economies of the region, particularly in Thailand. They caused inflation to heat up. The BOT tried to stop inflation by raising interest rates, but with a fixed exchange rate, higher interest yields led to the capital inflows growing stronger. The problem only really became noticed in early 1995. Once again, lack of accurate information on the Thai economy worsened the situation. Stead conjectured:

I think there were fault lines in the banking system, in that maybe the banks underreported or distorted their amount of property lending. It can be a confusing issue because the banks can say only 10 per cent of their loans go to the property sector. . . . But that does not tell the true story, because perhaps 20 per cent of loans go to manufacturing, [where] a company may say that it

wants to build a new plant or production line, but then uses a
part or all of that money for new offices, for example.

The easy money that flowed into Thailand had an intoxicating effect.
The international fund management community, with its myopic and
lemming-like behaviour, fuelled the bubble. When the bubble burst and
the value of the baht crashed (40 per cent down against the US dollar a
year later) the banks and finance companies were left with huge non-
performing loans and practically worthless collateral in the form of
property—and a chain-reaction to follow of financial and economic crisis.
Despite the recklessness of foreign lenders, Prime Minister Chavalit
generously placed all the blame on Thais by promising that the Thai
government (that is, the nation's taxpayers) would guarantee all foreign
loans to Thai private financial institutions. The Nukul Commission Report
noted that, after suspending 16 finance companies, the BOT issued a
statement (No. 44/2540) on 29 June 1997 announcing that:

> The prime minister insists:
> 1. Apart from the 16 suspended finance companies, no more
>   finance companies will be suspended.
> 2. The government will guarantee local and foreign deposits
>   and loans of all finance companies still operating.[22]

The intoxicating effect of the "growth-without-end" syndrome had
somehow led the country's financial regulators to suspend their
professional judgement and neglect to carry out their duties. Why? That
is a long story which will be examined in a later section. It has something
to do with money politics, the patronage system, and the cultural
expectations of Thai society. *The Economist* wrote this about it:

> It is not only bankers who are to blame. . . . Consider Thailand. . . .
> For a long time, the government and regulators turned a blind
> eye to growing evidence that lending to a property bubble had
> contributed to a dangerous level of bad debts. In 1996, one of
> the country's 15 commercial banks, Bangkok Bank of Commerce,
> went bust. The government rescued it. The bank had lent large
> sums to corrupt politicians, provoking accusations of a stitch-up
> between the institution and its supervisors.[23]

The Nation's editor-in-chief, Suthichai Yoon, had this to say about lax supervision:

> Cronyism was very much part of business circles and social life during the boom years, and if the central bank's supervisory competence was wobbly then, that didn't mean the prevalent violation of the financial rules at the time was legal. But the central bank's supervisory department didn't suggest it was such a serious breach of the basic rules and regulations at the time. . . .[24]

Thai Farmers Bank president Banthoon Lamsam earlier commented on this "tolerance" by the central bank, in a *Nation* interview:

> Banthoon said financial institutions generating bad loans have never been punished because the authorities and the institutions themselves swept the problems under the carpet. . . . He noted that in the past, the authorities were not transparent in the area of information collection, and would conceal information from the public in order to protect [the institutions'] status. . . . However, as the central bank [becomes] more transparent, the institutions will be unable to conceal the problems again.[25]

There is a deeper tragedy behind Thai businessmen's and politicians' lust for quick riches, behind the speculative bubble, and behind the financial crisis. It is the tragedy of impoverished and low-income Thais who will not benefit from the squandered investment that should have gone into the country's sustainable development—much-needed investment in education, health, rural development, and new technology that will not now be made for years to come. The lives and expectations of a generation of young Thais have been stunted. At the same time, rampant, unregulated property development has added considerably to the destruction of the urban environment (see Section 5, The Urban Challenge).

IMF Bail-Out, Financial Closures

Who could foresee Thailand's Crash and the ensuing Asian and then global conflagration? Institutions such as the IMF and the World Bank were just as surprised as everyone else. Other United Nations agencies had become too used to praising the "miracle" growth rates of East Asian tiger economies; although committed to the concept of sustainability, such agencies were not equipped nor motivated to promoting it conscientiously among Asian governments. Economists working for local and international investment banks and brokerages were too narrow in their focus to perceive systemic risks. And in Thailand, macro-economic management was not a priority at that time, as money politics and expanding political patronage networks were busy feeding off the substantial liquidity. *The Nation* wrote:

> Fiscal tightening was impossible under the Banharn admin-istration, which was good at cutting deals on government projects. However, Bodi Chunnananda, the then finance minister, told Rerngchai Marakanond [the Bank of Thailand governor] that he was ready to support any foreign exchange adjustments. Rerngchai did not take up the offer, saying the BOT was not ready.[26]

When the Crash came, Thailand was forced to turn to the International Monetary Fund to shore up its disintegrating financial system, and signed a US$17.2 billion bail-out agreement in August 1997. The agreement called for the "standard" IMF austerity measures: cutting the government budget; setting limits and progressively lowering the current account deficit to bring the balance of payments crisis under control; and maintaining high interest rates to stabilise the baht (a move which was also criticised for drying up much-needed liquidity in the lending market).

Prior to signing the agreement, the IMF required the closure of an additional 42 virtually bankrupt finance companies, following the earlier closure of 16 others. The central bank replied that the firms would "temporarily" stop most of their operations, including lending, for at least three months. The 58 firms accounted for two-thirds of total deposits in Thailand's finance industry, which was then estimated to be worth a total of about one trillion baht.[27] The closures sparked a run to claim deposits, money which was made up by loans from the central bank.

The closures, on a "temporary" basis while the various firms were given time to raise new capital and seek mergers or buy-outs, sparked a flurry of lobbying by company owners with their political friends in the

Chavalit government. It seemed likely that many of them would get additional infusions of (politically-motivated) loans, up until the collapse of the Chavalit government on 6 November 1997. The Democrat Party, on taking power later in the month, permanently closed 56 of the 58 firms.

Adding Up the Cost

At the beginning of 1997, the Bank of Thailand held net foreign reserves of $33.8 billion.[28] From November 1996, foreign speculators mounted continual attacks on the baht, trying to make big profits by massively short-selling the currency. The most fierce attacks came in May 1997. The BOT spent $30 billion of its reserves in the baht's defence, $23.4 billion of which was in forward contracts. . . .[29] Finally, when the reserves were depleted, there was no choice but to let the baht float, leading to its steep devaluation. UBS Global Research estimated that Thailand lost $12 billion as the final cost of the failed attempt to defend the baht's fixed exchange rate.[30] Add to that lost money the amount spent by the central bank in keeping afloat the floundering finance companies. *The Nation* wrote in August 1997:

> IMF officials must have been amazed by the blatant misman-agement of the Thai banking regulators who seemingly granted unlimited financial support to the ailing finance companies. The total 450 billion baht bail-out, excluding the 70 billion baht bail-out of the Bangkok Bank of Commerce, is so far the largest in the history of world banking. . . . Instead of separating the financially sound firms from the troubled firms by using non-performing loans or net worth as a standard, the central bank just threw money at any finance firm with liquidity problems. . . .[31]

The bail-outs were dispensed by the Financial Institution Development Fund (FIDF), an arm of the central bank. The TDRI wrote in May 1998:

> The amount lent out by the FIDF, including the finance companies' notes taken up by the [state-owned] Krung Thai Bank at the request of the central bank, totalled more than a trillion baht. The current interest cost on this sum alone is in excess of 100 billion baht. . . . Eventually, some of this money will be

recovered, but most estimates put the figure at around fifty per cent of the total.

Together, the cleaning up of the FIDF problem and the recapitalisation of the remaining banks will cost the taxpayers annually some 100–200 billion baht, a non-marginal addition to the Thai budget, the total size of which is currently 800 billion baht. Such a discrete jump may require a restructuring of the tax system.[32]

Thus, tax increases were on the cards for future years, as the cost of damages incurred by wealthy Thais would be passed on to the middle and less-wealthy classes. The TDRI reported in May 1998 that Thailand's foreign debt stood close to $80 billion, compared to a GNP level of $110 billion at the prevailing exchange rate of almost 40 baht to the dollar.

Deficiencies in the Thai System

Following the plunge of the baht, many stories surfaced about former financial executives continuing to lead a lavish lifestyle despite the collapse of their companies and sacking of staff. Following the suspension of the 58 afflicted finance companies (most of them were suspended in August 1997), a number of their failed chief executives were still enjoying monthly salaries of 700,000-plus baht, while at the same time seeking financial and liquidity support from the Bank of Thailand.[33] Finally, under its new leadership, the BOT began prosecution of some finance executives in August 1998. Out of the 56 closed finance companies, 46 were believed to be victims of wrongdoing by their executives, and reports circulating at that time indicated that more than 200 executives of finance firms and banks were expected to face charges brought by the central bank.[34] Central bank Governor MR Chatu Mongkol Sonakul, who was appointed on 6 May 1998 to begin a clean-up and restructuring of the bank, began by pressing charges against two high-profile, former finance executives.

Narongchai Akrasanee, a former commerce minister in the Chavalit Government, was charged with making an illegal, under-collateralised loan worth 338 million baht when he was previously the head of the (subsequently closed) General Finance Corporation.[35] In September 1997, the parliamentary opposition had alleged that Narongchai was behind the injection of 14 billion baht into General Finance and Securities during the Chavalit government, to ease its liquidity problems despite the fact that the company had been exposed to overwhelming property loans.[36] Narongchai, a free-trade advocate, was an architect of the ASEAN Free Trade Area, and once served as the dean of the Economics Faculty of Thammasat University.

The chief executive of Finance One, the former high-flying "takeover king" Pin Chakkaphak, was the other. Chatu Mongol reportedly refused Pin's offer of a compromise deal, saying the central bank had brought charges to establish righteousness and social norms, and not merely to recoup financial damages. The collapse of Finance One, formerly Thailand's largest finance company, created a shock wave in the financial system in 1997, since the company had acquired almost 40 billion baht in bail-out money from the Financial Institutions Development Fund.[37]

The BOT charged that between November 1996 and February 1997, Pin and two of his senior executives made loans worth 1.5 billion baht to Ekkaphak Holding Co. and 623 million baht to Business Consolidate Co. without collateral. The loans were made despite the fact that the Finance One executives knew that the two companies would not have the ability to repay them, according to the charges. At the time, Ekkaphak Holding Co. was suffering a loss of 1.6 billion baht, while Business Consolidate was reportedly losing 92 million baht. The two companies were closely tied to Pin and his business associates.[38] The editor-in-chief of *The Nation*, Sutichai Yoon, commented:

> After all is said and done, standards must be set, culprits punished, and wrongs righted. Friends of Narongchai argue that lax lending by financial institutions during the boom years was a common phenomenon and if that's the criterion for prosecution, many of the country's "best and brightest" will end up in the courthouse charged with similar damaging accusations. Everybody, it seems, was doing the same thing. The high-risk, high-return mentality was the order of the day. . . . But don't forget that part of the high risk was to end up in jail if laws were broken to achieve the high returns. . . .[39]

Why did so many financial executives employ dubious or illegal practices in running their finance companies? Why did they make huge, questionable loans without sufficient collateral? Why did the central bank officials at the time not take action? Why were no elected members of the government interested in scrutinising and rectifying the abuses and the attendant deterioration of the financial system?

The answers to some of these questions lie in Thai attitudes to the rule of law, and in the pervasive nature of political patronage with its system of protection for client members. (I describe these in some detail in Chapters 7 and 8.)

Since feudal times, and continuing through the decades leading up to Thailand's financial crisis, loyalty to and favours for friends and relatives within the patronage system were the "normal", preferred and effective ways of doing business—preferred over an abstract system calling for strict observation of laws and regulations, which at the close of the 20th Century was still seen as somewhat alien to Thai society. Add to this the common Thai perception that the legal system does not really apply to "high-status" Thais. A feeling has permeated Thai society ever since feudal times that the country's high-status elite are a special class deserving of respect from "ordinary people" and deserving of special treatment, often including exemptions from regulations. In modern times, this elite includes the old aristocratic families and the newly-rich, Chinese-Thai business families who have prospered from the country's free-wheeling entrepreneurial environment.

I got a glimpse into this syndrome of deference and privilege during my early years in Thailand as a freelance journalist. By coincidence, it arose from a request I made to the Bank of Thailand. In 1979, I was writing an article for a business magazine in Bangkok and needed some information about foreign exchange controls which existed at that time and were administered by the Bank of Thailand. I telephoned a BOT official. He told me that there was a regulation which limited the amount of dollars (foreign exchange) that a Thai person could take out of the country—it was something in the region of US$100 per day (I forget the exact amount). But, the official explained, this regulation did not apply to high-status people, because "they need more money" when they travel overseas. This is just one example of how the lifestyles of "higher" people are not encumbered by regulations designed to regulate "ordinary" people. As I have learned from my Thai friends, government agencies (and quasi-government agencies such as Thai Airways International) are constantly bombarded with requests from highly-placed people for special favours and treatment.

It is hard to say "no" to such requests because of the notion of *kaurop*, the attitude of deference (submission, compliance, or reverence) or paying respect to one's superiors. It is an unquestioning respect, a respect which is due because it conforms to the "natural order of things"—not necessarily because a person has achievements or talent, but because a person has position, power, or wealth. Thai society's unquestioning adulation of the wealthy—whether their wealth is gained by legal or illegal means, or whether it is inherited—has been criticised by many knowledgeable Thais as a major deficiency of Thai society. It is deeply ingrained.

I once asked a well-regarded Thai academic, during a conversation about the Thai elite's frantic overinvestment in the property market, and it's scorn for regulation and planning, what can be done to educate the Thai elite? "You cannot educate the Thai elite," was his reply.

In a similar vein, a foreign friend with connections to Thai high society once offered me the convivial observation, "You can't tell high-status Thais what to do." Enforcing regulations and penalties on members of Thailand's elite is difficult. No matter if they are bad managers and ignore rules of financial prudence. Regulators are shy about inflicting loss of face on supposedly "high" members of society. The moment of truth gets postponed to avoid embarrassment.

Now, perhaps, it is becoming clearer why Thai tycoons could act so recklessly *en masse*, and why officials of the BOT found it difficult to regulate and act against the so many delinquent finance companies and banks. In 1992, 1993, and 1994, the BOT told the banks many times to stop lending to property developments, but the instruction was ignored.[40] A whole culture of moral laxity had grown up based on a person's status, connections, and a notion of individual freedom without responsibility. Who could presume to order the tycoons what to do? What should have been regulations and laws that were universally applied to everyone, ended up becoming guidelines that could be followed or ignored at will. Politics, which should have been instrumental in devising solutions to such problems, has in fact made them worse.

Of course, it is clear after the Crash of 97 that Thailand's corporate culture has many weaknesses that are in need of remedy. The answer lies in professionalising management and creating corporate professional standards through better education, through peer review (as suggested in Chapter 6, through stronger professional associations), and through more effective, official supervision. The culture of the family-owned and family-managed business, now reeling from economic meltdown, is destined to disappear or to undergo transformation. As Suchart Thadathamrongvej of Bangkok's Ramkamhaeng University has noted, the crisis has trimmed the ranks of Thai billionaires. He observed that the big banking-family names like the Sophonpanichs, the Lamsams, and the Tejapaibuls, which have dominated the economy since the 1950s, will fade away and be replaced by transnational corporations and institutions moving in as new strategic partners.[41]

In conjunction with the notion of *kaurop*, the Thai attitude of *krieng jai* is seen as another major impediment to informed decision making. *Krieng jai* is a form of etiquette governing one's personal behaviour which requires that one should avoid intervening in another's affairs, avoid contradicting or upsetting someone. Thus, one should not challenge or question the actions of others (particularly those who are of equal or higher status). It seeks to avoid personal confrontation, especially in face-to-face situations. Hence, disagreement is sometimes conveyed through intermediaries.

The reluctance to speak frankly arising from *krieng jai* has been identified as a contributing factor to the decline of professional competence within the Bank of Thailand, which contributed to Thailand's broader financial crisis. Communication among staff, and open, frank discussion of policy alternatives was sorely missing in the months or years leading up to the Crash of 97. Central bank governor, Chatu Mongol singled out the attitude of *krieng jai* as one of the Bank's weaknesses. He said that to solve the finance sector's problems

> . . . we need to make the country's survival a priority and not practice *krieng jai* which could result in the country collapsing.[42]

The attitude of *krieng jai* is also a companion of dishonesty and corruption. Thus, staff members at a company or government office may be aware that other staff are cheating and causing damage to the organisation or to the Thai people, but adopt the attitude that "it's none of my business. . . ." In fact, dishonesty amongst tycoons and would-be tycoons of the business world seems to be quite common. In so many cases, the principle seems to be: if you can cheat to win, you had better cheat. Many executives have tended to treat their company as a personal fiefdom whose resources are available for their personal enrichment. As Harvard economics professor Jeffrey Sachs noted:

> [As is the norm in most emerging markets] owners [and managers] of banks look to them not as equity investments, but as personal pocket-books from which they can draw for whatever hare-brained real estate scheme takes their fancy.[43]

Additionally, there seems to be a widespread acquiescence that a government official or employee of a large private company may use his position to pursue personal gains.

In a culture where businessmen often resort to the payment of tea-money or large-scale bribes to purchase exemptions from regulations and to secure contracts, who would want to strictly comply with financial regulations covering capital adequacy or sufficient collateral for loans? Who would want to strictly comply with a directive to cease lending to the property sector? The question of underdeveloped public morals must figure largely in seeking the underlying cultural causes of Thailand's crisis. Here are the reflections of two Thai academics. Dr. Gothom Arya, a leading Thai pro-democracy advocate, in June 1997:

> The Thai culture is considered a "soft" culture as opposed to the "hard" ones of some Asian countries like Singapore, which has more rigid values regarding good and bad. The same system would not work in Thailand because we tend to compromise. We as a people are too soft to enforce the law. We don't want people to get hurt. Enforcers of the law in Thailand always face a dilemma of whether to uphold the principle or to be nice to family and friends. They invariably choose family and friends.[44]

Prof. Kriengsak Chareonwongsak of the Institute of Future Studies for Development, in August 1996:

> [If Thais condone dishonesty] then Thai society is corrupt and headed toward self destruction. . . . The prevailing utilitarian values and principles of Thai society have resulted in society attaching greater importance to wealth than to honesty. . . . Many people will do anything possible, including dishonest or illegal acts, for material gain, as society overemphasises the value of material wealth—which always brings much prestige and power. . . .

> Throughout history, the people of Thailand have never known the true meaning of an egalitarian society. Consequently, Thais do not attach importance to the concepts of freedom, individual rights, and equality. Instead, they submit to people with power and material wealth—and many grow up to believe that cheating without getting caught is an achievement of which they can be proud. . . .[45]

Securities analyst Michael Stead reflected the concern of the foreign business community working in Thailand:

> In fact, this question of ethics is a very real issue. I am disturbed by the lack of honesty in Thailand, in the corporate field, in the political field, basically at all levels. It's because of the unfairness of Thai society. . . . The poorer people don't get a good deal. There is a snowball effect. People believe "I am getting ripped off here, so I am not going to be so honest myself." They can see that among the most dishonest people are the politicians, people who are getting huge amounts and mismanaging the country in a dreadful way. . . . Again, the civil servants see this, so there is less incentive for them to be honest; the police see this. . . . [Thus] I think there is this cascading effect of corruption. Thailand is a very unfair and inequitable society. . . .

How can Thailand reverse this perception of cheating as an achievement? Start with the law enforcement system and the schools. Cheating during school examinations is widespread in Thai schools and most often goes unpunished by teachers, while the principle of enforcing academic standards is neglected. (See Chapter 9, the section Education for Quality of Life.)

Cronyism, Transparency, and Disclosure

The issues of cronyism, lack of transparency, and lack of disclosure have been pounced on by international analysts in searching for explanations of why Thailand's (and Asia's) financial crash could take place apparently without warning. The term "cronyism" has often been used in the Asian context to denote a distortion of free-market, competitive principles by the creation of "sweetheart" contracts and monopolies, generally between political power-holders and their business friends and supporters. The most famous crony economies in Asia belonged to the presidencies of Ferdinand Marcos in the Philippines (1965–1986) and Suharto in Indonesia (1966–1998), both of whom were deposed by popular uprisings.

The concept of cronyism is less easily defined in Thailand since the political culture is more fluid and multi-polar than in other Asian countries. Thai cronyism has been centred more on the relationships of extended families and their close business associates, especially where such families also owned banks or finance companies. In a political context, however, the seeking of a crony relationship becomes a gamble on which political party to support financially; some business interests, ambitious to guarantee that all-important political connection, will give money to more than one political party during election time. (See Chapter 7.)

The line between political cronyism and just plain payment for favours is somewhat blurred; the only certain thing is that payments for influence have been so common that they were a major component of governance both during the era of military dictatorships and during the tenure of elected governments in Thailand's recent history. We may even venture an opinion that for some political parties the spoils of power—the generation of revenue from influence-dispensing activities—are the major reason for their existence. This conjecture may account for the perception that politicians within the two governments immediately prior to, and during, the onset of the financial crisis had little interest in supervising, or in guarding, the integrity and standards of financial institutions such as the Bank of Thailand.

Let's examine one sequence of events in the months following Thailand's entry into the IMF "rescue" programme (6 August 1997), and the collapse of the Chavalit government (6 November 1997). A condition of Thailand's entry into the IMF programme was the suspension of an additional 42 delinquent finance companies. The government and the IMF agreed that a failed finance company with a large proportion of non-performing loans had to achieve and maintain a strict capital adequacy ratio of 15 per cent in order to qualify for reopening. A new body, the Financial Sector Restructuring Authority (FRA), was created to implement this and other provisions for financial restructuring agreed with the IMF, in order to win back the confidence of international investors. But the capital-adequacy prescription, a beginning towards restructuring the finance industry, immediately became the object of lobbying from finance companies with political connections to the two largest parties in the governing coalition: Prime Minister Chavalit's New Aspiration Party (which held the finance portfolio) and Chatichai Choonhavan's Chat Pattana Party. *The Nation's* business writer, K. I. Woo, wrote of the situation:

> In their fervour to protect the moneyed interests of poorly-run finance company operators and shareholders, Thai political leaders have refused to coldly prescribe the bitter medicine necessary for righting the country's troubled financial system—letting bad financial institutions fail. Instead of forcing insolvent financial institutions to immediately cease operations during the past year, government officials have poured billions of baht into a vain effort to protect their political friends who have been shoddy and sometimes dishonest caretakers of deposits from millions of this country's small savers.[46]

In this kind of politically-charged environment, finance ministers came and went in rapid succession. Earlier, in June, the first casualty of the manoeuvring between the Chat Pattana and New Aspiration parties had been Finance Minister Dr. Amnuay Viravan—a non-MP technocrat brought in by Chavalit on New Aspiration's cabinet quota. Chat Pattana's Korn Dabaransi, then a deputy prime minister, reversed Amnuay's proposal to raise excise tax on two-stroke motorcycles, granite, and batteries, which was an attempt by Amnuay at fiscal tightening during the growing crisis. Amnuay resigned on 19 June, sending a sharp reverberation throughout the financial markets. *The Nation's* analysts Vatchara Charoonsantikul and Thanong Khanthong gave this report:

> The Chat Pattana Party, the second largest coalition partner, had been pressing for his resignation so that it could take full control of the finance portfolio. . . . Amnuay's lack of political leverage also jeopardised a plan to solve the financial mess through the cabinet or the legislative body. As a matter of principle, Amnuay could not stay on after Korn shot down his tax increase proposal. Amnuay had been recognised by the financial markets as a staunch defender of the baht. Thereafter, confidence evaporated.

In less than 10 days, the BOT lost more than $4.3 billion as a consequence of Amnuay's departure.[47]

Chavalit then brought in Thanong Bidaya, a former president of the medium-sized Thai Military Bank to be finance minister. Thanong resigned the following October after Chavalit flip-flopped on a decision to impose a tax increase on oil products, reversing the imposition of the tax only a few days later in the face of public protests against it. *The Nation* wrote of this farce:

> The political environment has made it impossible for a man of Thanong's integrity to institute any radical reforms in order to save the country from utter ruin. The political end-game tactically espoused by core members of the Chat Pattana Party to force a sweeping cabinet reshuffle and to support their leader, Chatichai Choonhavan, as the next prime minister, has dealt a big blow to the economic and financial reform package. . . . Under Chat Pattana's guidance, the contents of the financial sector reform will also be significantly watered down to appease vested interests, particularly the shareholders of the 58 suspended finance companies, who would like to salvage some of their assets from the wreckage.[48]

Another casualty in October was the respected technocrat Amaret Sila-on, the chairman of the Stock Exchange of Thailand, who had been named chairman of the newly-created FRA only the previous month. Amaret complained that the process of rehabilitation of the financial system had become a "political football".[49] The FRA had the power to review the required rehabilitation plans submitted by shareholders and creditors of the 58 suspended finance companies, and either to accept the plans or to close the companies. Amaret was upset that representatives of the 58 finance companies succeeded, without his knowledge, in seeking a meeting with Prime Minister Chavalit at Government House. The group also twice visited Chatichai, who was the chief adviser to the government for foreign and economic affairs, to ask for help and sympathy.[50]

Following the resignation of Amaret,[51] the outcome of the group's lobbying became apparent with Chavalit's appointment of new deputy finance minister, Surasak Nananukul, who declared on 27 October that he would revise the capital adequacy ratio for the failed finance companies back to its original 7.5 per cent which would make it more "realistic" for the troubled finance companies to recover.[52]

Despite bringing in a succession of neutral technocrats into key executive positions to solve the burgeoning financial crisis, Chavalit and his rivals within the coalition government could not avoid scheming against each other and interfering in the work of their "neutral" appointees to benefit themselves and their favoured clients.

It was thanks to this climate of political interference and infighting, coupled with the fact that none of the coalition parties had the expertise or commitment within their own political ranks to tackle the crisis, that public confidence in the government began to plummet. Chavalit was forced to resign on 6 November 1997, paving the way for the Democrat Party to form a new coalition government. With a new government in place, the FRA decided on 8 December to close 56 of the 58 suspended finance companies. Right up until the date of announcement, politicians continued to lobby for special treatment on behalf of the companies. *The Nation* reported:

> A source close to the event said that on Saturday, just two days
> before the announcement was made, telephone calls were made
> to FRA executives from politicians wanting to lobby the agency
> to approve the rehabilitation plans of finance companies believed
> to have connections with them. However, the FRA executives
> declined to take the calls. . . .[53]

Let us not underestimate the impact of the Thai way of doing business which is revealed by this single example of Thai-style cronyism founded on the linkages between the wealthy elite, bureaucrats, and politicians (including the notions of *kaurop* and *krieng jai*). After all, close to 500 billion baht was poured into saving the face of elitist owners and managers of mismanaged finance companies without so much as a glance into the companies' loan portfolios or management practices.

Can cronyism, and indeed the broader political patronage system, be dismantled or at least greatly diminished? In some respects, a watershed was reached with the closure of the 56 firms, despite their political connections. But much will depend on the on-going financial and political reforms, and the actualisation of provisions for transparency of the new 1997 Constitution.

The closures struck at the heart of an obsolete and (with hindsight) dangerous system. Members of Thailand's business elite had routinely maintained finance companies as offshoots of their businesses, and their associated cronyism had led to a huge misallocation of loans to family and friends, especially for risky, severely under-collateralised projects. This system had come to dominate and neutralise legalistic attempts at regulation; it had, indeed, given rise to a mindset of tolerance of bad practices. Lack of transparency and lack of disclosure are the companions of cronyism. *The Economist* gave a glimpse into the problem of disclosure in December 1997 as the financial crisis continued to spread in East Asia:

> Many of Asia's listed companies are tightly controlled by powerful families. Typically, Asia's moguls list only part of their empires, while maintaining a string of affiliated private companies. "You get to see one room, not the whole house," says John Donald of Jardine Fleming, a Hong Kong investment bank. Even when times were good, some families routinely manipulated the prices their various companies charged each other to skim profits from their listed vehicles and tuck them away in their privately owned ones.[54]

Up until 1997, the Bank of Thailand had "blessed" the moguls of the banking and financial system with some of the world's most lenient disclosure rules. These allowed banks and finance companies to regard a secured loan as "performing" even if no interest had been paid for a year.[55] The Bank of Thailand itself was woefully inadequate in its own disclosure, to the extent that it misled the whole economy. It had never punished financial institutions for generating bad loans; rather, it had bent to their managements' pleas to conceal information about such loans, apparently to protect the institutions' public image.[56] Analysts inside the country said they were unable to detect a coming crisis, as vital information was concealed by the Bank of Thailand.

This pervasive lack of honesty amongst the business community and its regulators apparently also extended to the nation's auditors who, a year after the Crash, were coming under increasing criticism for failing to uncover the dubious accounting that allowed many companies to gloss over financial irregularities during the boom years. The Securities and Exchange Commission (SEC), in August 1998, suspended two chartered accountants for 1996 audits of subsequently-shuttered finance companies. The AP Dow Jones financial news agency reported that auditors came under enormous pressure during Thailand's boom not to nose too closely into company accounts. The lack of clear accounting principles and the lack of a single body to enforce standards made it easy for companies not to fully disclose information to investors. AP Dow Jones wrote:

> Despite the lack of clear regulations, however, some responsibility for the failure of auditors to forewarn Thailand's economic collapse must lie at the door of the international "Big Six" chartered accountancy firms, according to analysts. "There was definitely a willingness to please people so they could get more accounts," said Vikas Kawatra, an analyst at Paribas Asia Equity. . . . Jeff Earhart of Seamico Securities also noted that international auditors have been lax in not applying the same standards to Thailand as to Europe or the US.[57]

Considering these problems of transparency and disclosure, we may ask, is there a tradition of secrecy in Thailand? Foreign securities analysts complain that Thai company executives have often been reluctant to give information. Many executives give very little information and some refuse to speak to analysts at all. However, calling this secrecy often causes Thais to bristle with indignation. It is not secrecy, not that Thais are trying to hide things, some say. Rather it is just that in Thai culture people try to avoid conflict with each other, or causing pain. But there is another dimension to this phenomenon of secrecy: that of keeping up appearances. In this context, we may coin a maxim that gives an insight into Thai psychology: *the image is more important than the reality.*

Thais are very sensitive (perhaps even more sensitive than other Asian cultures) about "image", whether it is one's company or one's personal image or face. (This also applies to the country's image; Thais will often condemn negative but factually correct news reports about Thailand as "damaging to the country's image".) Of course, causing damage to someone's "face" (reputation, image) even if it is through disclosure of accurate information, is thus also seen as a painful event that should be avoided. In Thailand, image is an often obsessive concern; an integral part of establishing one's status or hoped-for status. People will go to all lengths to keep up appearances of success and wealth, especially among the *nouveaux riches* or upwardly mobile professionals. They will go deeply into debt in order to maintain the two luxury cars, the golf club membership, the condominium, and in order to indulge in "luxury" consumption to maintain the image. This syndrome undoubtedly played a large part in Thailand's collective denial of reality that led to the bubble economy.

The lessons arising from lack of transparency and disclosure have now been learned. New standards are being introduced and, hopefully, economic shocks such as the Crash of 97 can be avoided in the future as accurate and comprehensive financial information is released to the public in a timely way by both government institutions and private companies.

Political and Bureaucratic Ineptitude

The vexing question arising from the Crash of 97 is, why couldn't Thailand's political and administrative institutions take action to avoid it? Of course, I have attempted to show that the answer to that question lies in the broader theme of this book, in the notion that patronage and money politics are failing Thailand's quest for rational development. Much of what has conventionally been seen as "development" in Thailand is, in fact, unsustainable and damaging growth without development.

Concerted government action to address macro-economic imbalances 12 months before the Crash, or even six months before, could certainly have lessened the pain that followed. But perhaps this whole episode should be taken as a warning that the rot within Thailand's political and governing structures had gone so far that only disaster could follow the oblivious intoxication of the boom years. In fact, when one talks about the *security* of the Thai nation—not only about its development— one need not look outside the kingdom's borders for military or economic threats. It is now apparent that the threat to the nation's viability and to its people lies within the country, among the moral decay that has accompanied the misuse of power and privilege that cares little about the wellbeing of the whole society. Following this observation, the really worrying question is whether Thai society, or society's leaders, will learn the lessons of the Crash of 97, or whether this unfortunate event will soon be shrugged off and the reckless power of money, privilege, and patronage reassert itself. Just weeks after the plunge in value of the baht, *The Nation* interviewed a former cabinet minister, and reported:

> Sadly, Thailand is broke. Even more tragic is the fact that most local politicians, bureaucrats, and farmers hardly realise the depth of the trouble the Thai economy is in. "The politicians are acting as if nothing is happening to the economy. This is because they never have had to make a living. While the country is on fire, they're still fighting for toys," said a retired cabinet minister. The bureaucrats, too, are complacent, with a narrow self-interest born of the confidence they will always receive government pay cheques at the end of the month. . . .[58]

The Thailand Development Research Institute (Thailand's major development NGO, albeit somewhat conservative and establishment-oriented) politely interpreted the failure of the Chavalit government to cope with the crisis in the following words:

> The prime minister ruling Thailand for most of 1997 [Chavalit] resigned in November as the economic crisis deepened, and as the feeling became widespread that his cabinet could not cope with the myriad problems. A new prime minister who had within his party what was felt to be a more competent team of potential economic ministers was voted into office by Parliament [the second Chuan government].[59]

The TDRI sidestepped any analysis of the deeper causes of the political failure, but had some praise for Parliament (despite the low public perception of it) for bringing about a peaceful transition to a new government during a time of severe stress, saying it indicated a certain maturing of Thailand's democratic traditions. Rather, the TDRI put more blame on Thailand's declining "economic technocracy":

> It was another important political institution that failed the test badly, namely the economic technocracy. This was surprising, inasmuch as this institution had in the past been considered a tower of strength, particularly in times of crisis. The biggest

disappointment was of course the Bank of Thailand, which now badly needed extensive reforms. But the central bank is not the only institution that failed the test; the other economic agencies, the Ministry of Finance, the Budget Bureau, and the National Economic and Social Development Board were all found wanting. . . . Just as important, their lacklustre performance was part and parcel of the general decline in the quality of Thai bureaucracy, as the abler civil servants were siphoned off to the private sector.

Without the technocrats or able economic technicians in the ministries, and with the central bank demoralised, the elected politicians had to fashion a strategy on their own. They were eminently unfit for this task, nor did they have any infrastructure, within their own political parties or elsewhere in the civil society, to help them in their task.

In fact, the decline in the economic technocracy and lack of political ability to counteract the trend is not attributable to any one government, although a series of inept decisions by the Chavalit government finally brought about the collapse. Rather, a series of elected governments, coming to power under the system of money politics and cabinet quotas, presided over the decline.

The governments of Prem Tinsulanonda (March 1980–August 1988) were seen as making intelligent use of the economic technocracy, at a time when its organisations were strong and focused. The planting of the seeds of collapse, the beginning of the financial/property bubble, may be traced to the Chatichai Choonhavan government (August 1988–February 1991), in which corruption is widely regarded as having reached new heights. The next elected government (omitting the short-lived, military-backed Suchinda government), was the first government of Chuan Leekpai (September 1992–May 1995). It had more economic and financial expertise, backed up by academic advisory teams. Notable was the team of deputy prime minister, Suphachai Panichpakdi, run by Chulalongorn University academic Teerana Bhongmakapat, whose research ranged from Thailand's export competitiveness to what the country's international and regional roles should be.[60] Yet, the first Chuan government proved incapable of counteracting endemic corruption and

117

patronage, and finally disintegrated through the contradictions that this inability generated within the coalition.

The successor government of Banharn Silpa-archa (1995–96) was criticised as masterful in the art of dispensing patronage, especially through manipulation of the state budget and the cutting of deals with the private sector. It was during Banharn's term that the macro-economic imbalances began to worsen. Banharn had no academic back-up team, nor indeed *any* back-up team, but chose to rely on the bureaucracy, whose decline was far advanced by 1995. Pana Janviroj, editor of *The Nation*, commented:

> Banharn, despite his *lung jiu* (Chinese one-man management style), found himself unable to understand the issues and problems that were facing the country and, in short, things were running out of control.[61]

Many knowledgeable Thais, and expatriates stationed in Thailand at that time, judged the Banharn administration as the worst elected government the country had ever had. That was before Chavalit—who was a deputy prime minister and defence minister in the Banharn government—manoeuvred to oust Banharn and form his own administration (1996–97). The Chavalit government was perceived as being at least as bad as Banharn's. Pana Janviroj noted:

> The Chavalit government has too many advisory teams—none of which work because Chavalit had no idea what role they should play. . . . His economic "Dream Team" consists of second-rate bankers and economists who lack academic skill, vision, and a hands-on management style. It isn't a complete surprise that Chavalit remains ignorant of many issues. . . . Chavalit's aloofness and confused mind, and his lack of an active approach to key issues, has resulted in the mismanagement of the economic crisis. . . .[62]

(See Chapter 8 for further examples of patronage under Banharn and Chavalit.)

By contrast, the best government Thailand has had is generally taken to be the interim government of Anand Panyarachun, appointed by the military junta that overthrew the Chatichai government in 1991. That government, coming to power in a quite unique fashion, was composed mostly of highly respected technocrats. During its tenure of 13 months, it passed more legislation, including the 1992 Environment Act, than any other Thai government.

Returning to the Crash of 97. . . . It was thus not just an "accident". It had many complex causes, most of them resulting from internal systemic weaknesses and unsustainable practices—plus some unsustainable international ones. Fred Hiatt of the *Washington Post* produced a valid observation on some of these internal weaknesses, in writing about the Southeast Asian scene in general:

> In some ways, the Southeast Asian nations are victims of their own success. Their schools, governments, bank regulators, and other institutions were good enough for nations just beginning to industrialise and grow. But as they attracted more investment and became more integrated into a global, fast-moving economy, those institutions didn't keep up.[63]

Moreover, in Thailand's situation, key officials were not only not upgrading fast enough, their quality was actually in decline, as indicated by the TDRI. Michel Camdessus, the IMF's managing director, came up with a similar "systemic" explanation as to why Thailand did not heed the IMF's warnings until it was too late:

> One [reason] is quasi-cultural. When a country perseveres and follows a policy which yielded great successes for at least 10 years, between 1983 and 1993, it is very hard to convince it that things have changed and that it is time to adjust.[64]

Camdessus also noted that the crisis broke while the country seemed ungovernable because of political division and government priorities that weren't in the right order. The Nukul Commission report into the Bank of Thailand's failings in the crisis echoes the remarks of the TDRI and the IMF chief, noting that the unsuccessful political leaders of 1995–97 had little knowledge of the importance of macro-economic policies, and were more assertive in their acts only within the bounds of their own vested interests.[65] Academic Thitinan Pongsudhirak further specified these vested interests by noting that some cabinet members of the Chavalit government were directors with seats on the boards of haemorrhaging finance, securities, and property companies—companies that would benefit from government attempts to keep them alive with massive and expensive infusions through the creation of the Finance Ministry's 100-billion-baht Property Loan Management Organisation.[66]

Documenting the weaknesses and the decline of the Thai bureaucracy would constitute a large-scale endeavour in its own right. (Further insights will be offered in Section 2 of this book, particularly regarding corruption and patronage.) However, some brief, additional perspectives on bureaucratic weaknesses can be offered here:

- promotions within government departments on the basis of seniority rather than on merit, leading to a growth of mediocrity at executive levels in the bureaucracy as talented staff leave government service;
- failure to adopt a progressive salary policy for professionally qualified staff, to pay them a close equivalent to private sector salaries;
- lack of clear responsibility in various agencies—for example, in the Bank of Thailand and the Finance and Commerce ministries, for the issues of the current account deficit, unemployment, and inflation;[67]
- a lack of coordination among government agencies, especially regarding the country's economic management;
- a prevailing culture of competition, rivalry, and non-communication within agencies, rather than a conscientious atmosphere to foster a culture of cooperation and sharing of information and ideas; and
- more recently, a politicisation of certain agencies, where key officials form alliances with certain politicians in the hope of gaining security or promotions, or other benefits.

Singh Tangtatsawat, the president of the Stock Exchange of Thailand, noted four main reasons for listed companies getting into an unhealthy position. Some had used company funds to support other businesses owned by the management team. Some listed companies had been able to raise money easily via the SET, and invested it in businesses in which they had limited experience. Additionally, managers of many listed companies had not made the most efficient use of personnel. Finally,

Singh noted the low credibility of the management teams and their balance sheets.

The Thai corporate culture has also suffered from a decline in the quality of its managers, a phenomenon which no doubt goes part of the way to explain the abuses outlined earlier in this chapter. Indeed, the present generation of young, gung-ho managers who came to the helm during the 1990s boom years, has been blamed for the excesses that led to the Crash; the older generation of more prudent managers would not have been so reckless, that thinking goes.

The Economist touched on this decline in quality of corporate executives in an interview in October 1997 with Thai Farmers Bank president Banthoon Lamsam, who had gained respect for his far-sighted reform of the bank:

> In both the crowded banking halls and in back offices, there was considerable resistance to reform. It threatened the snug feeling of belonging to a family, which had brought enviable corporate loyalty but a rather weak work ethic. Promotion and pay had tended to be assessed in length of service rather than performance. Everyone received an eye-popping "13th month" bonus equivalent to $5^1/2$ months' salary. Mr. Banthoon found that executives were not judged by results, and that "quality" was not rewarded. In consequence, there was an "averaging down" of talent. To change this, he introduced flexible bonuses, and individual staff evaluations. This was particularly contentious. "Thai people don't want to be tested. They like to feel we are all moving along together."[68]

Bangkok business columnist Larry Chao gave another insight into Thailand's "expansion mentality" fuelled by the massive inflows of cheap capital and high consumer demand:

> Over time, the name of the game became "increase sales volume". This attitude led to continued expansion—more and more production lines, more labour, more assets. Without the benefits of IT early on, operating and overhead costs soared. Booming sales masked the need to control this excess. . . . There was no sense of urgency to operate cost-effectively. . . . For every

> business reason to reduce costs there were two or three reasons
> to continue adding to them to fuel this grow, grow era. In this
> feeding frenzy, people forgot about the importance of operating
> cost-effectively and productively. . . .[69]

Add to the political, bureaucratic, and corporate woes, the whole misorientation of the economy, based on the promotion of an unsustainable lifestyle. Thais were being encouraged from all sides to borrow their future earnings to become part of a high-spending consumer class while a significant sector of the country remained in deprivation or poverty. Finance companies granted loans for extravagant consumer behaviour, further adding to the bad debts caused by property speculation when the economic crash finally came. Hire-purchase schemes for the low-income group abounded. Thais, in effect, were being led by the media and status-driven peer pressure to live beyond their means, mesmerised by their compulsion to own cars, motorcycles, imported clothing, and other luxury items. Then came the Crash, and a bitter dose of stringent realism.

With cronyism, patronage, and corruption rife in the government sector, and wild optimism rife in the private sector, many Thais welcomed the dose of stringent realism brought in by the IMF, despite an apparent loss of sovereignty, and despite the subsequently discredited austerity component of the IMF package. Former prime minister, Anand Panyarachun expressed the Thai attitude to the Foreign Correspondents Club of Thailand in August 1997:

> Thai people are happy that the IMF came in and took over our
> economic sovereignty because we do not trust our government.
> At least we hope the IMF would be as incorruptible as we think,
> and see to it that the people in power here would manage the
> IMF fund with integrity and honesty. . . .[70]

The Bank of Thailand's Decline

Inadequacies within the Bank of Thailand are largely to blame for the failure of Thailand's economic and financial institutions to properly manage Thailand's macro-economy, and to foresee and avoid the financial crash. This, at least, is the conclusion of the The Nukul Commission report. The Commission, named after its chairman, Nukul Prachuabmoh, a former Bank of Thailand governor, was tasked with making recommendations to improve the efficiency and management of Thailand's financial system.

The Commission, comprised of eminent economists, succeeded in exposing a degenerate and apathetic management culture within the BOT. It assigns responsibility for the failed defense of the baht, and for the indiscriminate (and admittedly inexplicable) pouring of huge amounts of bail-out money first into the ravaged Bangkok Bank of Commerce and then into the collapsing finance companies. For the collapse of the baht, the Commission places overall responsibility for the BOT's failings with political figures outside the bank: the then prime minister, Chavalit and the then finance minister, Amnuay Viravan. But it stops short of making specific accusations of wrongdoing, or of providing details into the alleged political interference which undercut the independence and the competency of the bank.

Perhaps a failing of the report—or perhaps the commissioners regarded it as outside of their mandate—was a lack of analysis of the social context within which the leadership and personnel of the BOT were operating, and particularly of the set of expectations inherent in the patronage culture of Thai high society and of Thai politics.

The Commission, in Chapter 6, outlines the weaknesses in the structure and the management of the BOT which contributed to its mismanagement of the crisis. Standards and work ethos of the bank had been declining, to a large extent mirroring the decline in the government bureaucracy as a whole. But the decline within the BOT was all the more serious, since it was regarded as the elite government institution entrusted with protection of the country's finances. The report notes:

> Over the past four to five years, the BOT has experienced an unprecedented situation in its history. Former governor Dr. Puey Ungphakorn was a man of vision who wanted to develop quality manpower for the benefit of the central bank's future. He sent first-rate students to be educated in the most famous academic institutions in Europe, the USA, Australia, Japan, and New Zealand, hoping that they would return and become an important force, and produce positive results for the Bank and win the credibility and confidence of both Thai people and foreigners. They were junior and middle-ranking officials of the bank, who

loved and worked with one another well, but when they had climbed close to the top of the Bank's hierarchy, regrettably, both love and unity dissolved, and jealousy and hate set in, as often featured in the press. . . .

The rift among the top officials made it difficult for their subordinates to carry out their duties and responsibilities, but the greatest damage resulted from a lack of coordination between different divisions, because of individuals who mutually disliked each other. The damage affected both the bank and its work. This situation came about because of a lack of good leadership.[71]

Competition among the careerist staff led to severe factionalism within the bank, and thus the pool of available talent was not put to effective use. Worse still, the dedication to the public interest that suffused the bank's ethos in the period before 1990 had all but disappeared, according to the TDRI's former president, Ammar Siamwalla.[72] A former BOT official said the management system of the central bank rested on the enormous power and leadership of the governor. But over a period of time, it had developed into a moral hazard as the governor sought to rely on the assistance of the number three or number four official, intentionally avoiding any dealings with the number two through fear that his governorship would be undermined.[73]

Other problems within the BOT, common to the general bureaucracy, included salary-level appraisals and promotions being based on seniority rather than on capability and merit. Staff appraisals were not systematic nor carried out seriously.

The Report also criticised the "one-man-show" system of the bank, with decisions largely resting on the governor. Open debate on policy and exchange of views were not encouraged, as the report indicated:

Key issues such as policy, even if discussed among top officials, were often not seriously considered, because the culture of the bank, as explained by assistant governor Siri Ganjarerndee, was not to "oppose" one another. . . . In meetings, people who disagreed with policies usually stayed silent rather than speak out. Consequently, without good leadership, problems occurred. . . . Some divisions were often quite clueless about the

activities of other divisions. The coordination was poor because
there was no system to exchange information.[74]

Regarding the BOT's leadership, the Report is scathing about the
capabilities of Governor Rerngchai Marakanond (governor from 13 July
1996 to 28 July 1998) who presided over the plunge in value of the baht:

> It may be said Rerngchai was unfortunate to have risen to the
> BOT governorship during an unprecedented Thai economic crisis.
> It can also be said for Thailand and the Thai people that they
> were unfortunate when the then prime minister, Banharn Silpa-
> archa appointed Rerngchai to succeed Vijit Supinit as the central
> bank governor, at a time when competence, ability, and
> decisiveness were badly needed qualifications to help restore
> Thailand back to economic health. The Commission had
> reservations about Rerngchai's qualifications in all the above
> areas. According to Rerngchai's own testimony, he had no foreign
> exchange or international fiscal policy expertise.[75]

How could such an unsuitable person be elevated to such an important
position? What precisely was the relationship between Prime Minister
Banharn and Rerngchai, and what understanding had they reached prior
to Rerngchai's appointment? How should we understand such an action?
It is already known that Rerngchai was appointed at a time of intense
politicisation of the central bank. There is a political parallel that may
offer some clues: the manner in which ministers gain seats in the cabinet.
Thailand's political patronage system, lubricated by money politics during
elections, has regularly placed unqualified people in charge of important
ministries on the basis of political loyalty and service to the party's
patronage network. The impact of politics on the central bank is
mentioned by the Nukul Commission, but not discussed in detail. It had
this to say:

> Recently, political interference has become a greater hindrance
> to the bank's operations than in the past. This may have come
> about because top officials wanted to please politicians in order
> to keep their positions secure. The activities affected by political
> interference caused the bank to lose its independence in terms of

decision making and policy setting. Lacking good leadership, the bank had to be cautious about its opinions for fear of political repercussions. The decision-making process was therefore not sharp or decisive.[76]

But what the report does not state explicitly is how political figures influenced bank decisions, and how they profited from the suspension of sound banking practices. The TDRI, likewise, in its analysis skirted this problem of how apparently criminal behaviour among politicians contributed to the Crash. Three major disasters were precipitated during the 1990s by the Bank of Thailand, with politicians taking a major role in at least two of them:

1. The Bangkok Bank of Commerce fiasco (outlined in the next section).
2. The flawed defense of the baht, resulting in billions of dollars of foreign exchange lost (already discussed).
3. The pouring of billions of baht of public money into the bottomless hole created by mismanaged finance companies.

The latter action was carried out by the Financial Institutions Development Fund (FIDF), a branch of the central bank whose board of directors was chaired by the bank's governor. The tragedy of the FIDF's operations is that it fell into the same trap as the insolvent finance companies it was trying to help: imprudent, excessive, and unmonitored lending.

The FIDF was set up in 1985 to "rehabilitate and improve financial institutions and to improve their stability," and was given wide authority. It could deposit money at a problem institution to ease liquidity, and consequently to prevent runs on other institutions. It could extend low-interest loans. It could buy capital increase shares before an institution's troubles became known to the public. It could take over institutions and liquidate bad assets before rehabilitating the institutions. It could transfer good assets and liabilities from troubled companies to healthy companies. It could institute policies for improving an institution's management team.[77]

But, as the finance companies did, the FIDF threw money indiscriminately into companies without a clear idea of what it was trying to achieve, or without an overall vision of development for the finance sector. The Commission noted that the measures the BOT adopted were confusing, usually changed, were indecisive, and unsuccessful. The BOT was not prepared for a crisis, and therefore saw no urgency in solving a serious and growing problem; this lack of preparedness put at risk the whole financial system.

These severe shortcomings reflected the decline of commitment and efficiency within the bank's administration. Regarding one of the bank's crucial duties, its examination of financial institutions, the bank lost touch with the overall objectives of examination. The Commission wrote:

> Considering the financial institutions' problems, there is always a question: If BOT's examinations were efficient, why was there a systemic risk. . . ? Sometimes, a report was issued a year after the examination. The lengthy procedure resulted in:
> 1. The person receiving the report could not use the information to deal with the problems because the information was out of date.
> 2. In troubled times, the BOT took a long time to find out the root causes of the problems and adopt measures. Moreover, the examination department's orders—though apparently stringent—were relaxed for, or ignored by, some companies. [Some] troubled companies ignored the orders for years before the BOT investigated, relaxed, or re-examined the problem.[78]

The Commission's report documents how the bottomless hole of the financial institutions' "rescue" expanded:

> As of August 1996, the Fund had extended liquidity assistance of only about 9 billion baht to two financial institutions, the Bangkok Bank of Commerce and Thai Fuji Finance and Securities. By the end of 1996, the number of recipients had risen to seven, and the amount totalled 27.5 billion baht. By February 1997, the number of recipients had risen to 15, and they had borrowed 53.8 billion baht. Of the total, 14 were finance and finance/securities companies, clearly showing that the sector was in trouble. . . .

On 31 March 1997, when the BOT ordered 10 finance companies to raise capital, the public began sensing that finance
and finance/securities companies were in trouble. . . . The
finance and finance/securities companies had borrowed 132.3
billion baht. By June 1997, they had borrowed 288.9 billion
baht from the Fund. The number of borrowers rose from 30 to
57 between March and June, showing that there were many
financial problems. . . . On 27 June, the authorities suspended
16 finance and securities companies. On 2 July, after the BOT
floated the baht, the Fund's loans to 68 institutions increased
to 384.3 billion baht. Now, even many commercial banks
sought the Fund's help; the total loans to banks skyrocketed
to 12.7 billion baht in April 1997, and rose to 128.1 billion
baht in August. In that month, the BOT suspended an
additional 42 finance companies. At the end of 1997, the Fund
had loaned out 700 billion baht to financial institutions.[79]

According to *The Nation*, Rerngchai had ordered the Fund to provide
universal protection to the finance sector. Part of the money spent was
borrowed directly from the BOT, hence a flouting of monetary discipline
at a time when the central bank had been calling for the government to
tighten its belt. IMF officials expressed their deep concern about this
double standard.[80]

By the end of 1997, the Fund was not receiving interest from many
of its loans, and large amounts of principal were turning sour. After giving
money to the financial institutions, the Fund had no role in tracking the
companies' operations despite being the largest creditor who would have
to bear the burden of any damages caused by the institutions. The
Commission criticised the BOT for its failure to resolve the financial
sector problems despite spending a huge amount of taxpayers' money. It
notes:

The Fund advanced unlimited funds to companies whose assets
were so poor they probably could never repay the loans even if
liquidated. The Fund did not act as the leader in negotiating with
other creditors of the companies for rehabilitation purposes, and
sometimes it caused problems by refusing to join negotiations.[81]

The Nation reported that Finance One took more than 30 billion baht from the fund, compared to 20 billion baht by General Finance & Securities, and more than 10 billion baht by CMIC Finance & Securities. It quoted the finance minister in the second Chuan government, Tarrin Nimmanahaeminda, as previously indicating that the Fund had lent its money to these troubled finance companies even though it realised it would never recover it.[82] Tarrin had also blamed the monetary authorities for failing to distinguish between those companies that had fundamental problems with bad debts, and those that faced liquidity problems.[83]

The Commission notes that the Fund borrowed money at a high interest rate of 20 per cent from the short-term money market, finally resulting in annual interest expenses of around 100 billion baht, which will eventually be borne by taxpayers. The government should not have guaranteed the deposits and liabilities of the additional finance companies suspended after the original 16 companies were closed on 27 June 1997, the Commission concludes.[84] In addition, the 700 billion baht bail-out was conducted without public knowledge:

> The public has a right to ask what decision-making processes and operating procedures are used by a government institution which has the power to spend hundreds of billions of baht of taxpayer's money.[85]

The Bangkok Bank of Commerce Scandal

A time-bomb was quietly ticking away throughout 1999, waiting to explode and to create shock waves throughout Thai politics and society. The time-bomb was the on-going legal action being taken against former executives of the Bangkok Bank of Commerce (BBC) arising from the massive fraud and theft cases surrounding the gutting and collapse of the bank from 1991–1996. And linked to those cases were possibly a dozen or more politicians who had benefited from under-collateralised loans issued in dubious circumstances; at least one of them in 1999 was a minister in the second Chuan government.

Rakesh Saxena, a former advisor to the bank who stood accused of being the mastermind of the US$2 billion looting of the bank, was under arrest in Vancouver in 1999, awaiting the outcome of the Thai government's attempt to extradite him to Thailand to face charges. During his detention, he had remarked to the Thai press that "scores" of politicians had received money from the BBC. He had told the Canadian court that he expected he would be killed "extra-judicially" if he was returned to face trial in Thailand.

The collapse of the BBC has been called the largest in world banking history, eclipsing the highly-publicised collapse of Barings Bank in 1994, caused by the massive trading losses incurred in Singapore by rogue trader Nick Leeson. The shaky condition of the BBC was publicly revealed in May 1996 during a no-confidence debate in the Thai Parliament, when Suthep Thaugsaban, a Democrat MP, revealed information from a confidential Bank of Thailand report on the BBC. The report placed the value of non-performing loans at 77 billion baht (at that time US$3 billion) and the BBC's links to politicians were revealed. (A longer account of the alleged political involvement in the BBC scandal appears in Chapter 7.)

The significance of the BBC scandal became much more than just a common case of political corruption, with which the cynical Thai public had become all too familiar. This scandal revealed a complex web reaching into the highest echelons of Thai society, into the political culture, and encompassing senior central bank officials who were entrusted with protecting the country's financial system. Many financial analysts in Thailand saw the BBC's collapse as the beginning of Thailand's financial crisis. It exposed the inadequate supervisory regime and the woeful decline in standards of the Bank of Thailand, and even raised questions of whether or not there was collusion among senior officials of the BOT in covering up criminal actions. The then central bank governor, Vijit Supinit, resigned in disgrace following revelations of the BBC's plight. The BBC scandal was the first major event that caused foreign investors to begin to lose confidence in Thailand's financial system, a loss which culminated in 1997 in a massive withdrawal of foreign investment funds from the country.

The Nukul Commission condemned the Bank of Thailand's lack of action against the BBC when it should have realised the severity of BBC's problems from very early on. Particularly, it condemned governor Vijit for not replacing the management of the bank and for not reducing the capital of the bank before embarking on recapitalisation. These failures benefited existing management and did not solve BBC's problems. In addition, when serious problems were detected at BBC, the BOT merely continued with its routine audits and did not intensify its scrutiny. Such failure to take firm action led to a steady worsening of the BBC's position, and seriously affected the BOT's image and credibility.[86] Regarding the BBC bail-out and impacts on the financial system, the Commission stated (in Chapter 4 of its report) that:

> The BBC problem was evident after a bank examination on 30 April 1991 discovered non-performing loans of 18.2 billion baht, which represented 26.73 per cent of total assets, which was considered a heavy problem. At that time, the average non-performing loan ratio for the banking industry was only 7.41 per cent. . . . The BOT immediately ordered BBC to increase capital by 800 million baht in 1992, and draw up a strict plan to increase its capital for 1992–1994. A 31 March 1993 examination showed that non-performing loans had risen to 38.5 billion baht or 39.57 per cent of total assets.[87]

A March 1994 examination showed that the NPL problem had risen further, with many of the loans used for mergers and acquisitions of companies listed on the stock market. The bank had approved takeover loans involving Rakesh Saxena and other senior BBC executives, had approved overdraft loans with no contracts or collaterals, and had approved loans valued higher than the authorised level. The BOT ordered BBC to ban Saxena from the bank's activities. It also ordered BBC to increase capital by 3 billion baht by June 1995, and another 3.7 billion baht by the end of 1996. . . .[88]

From 8–10 May 1996, BBC's problems were exposed in Parliament by Suthep Thaugsaban. The revelation led to public panic and a run on deposits. The BOT took control of BBC and set up a control committee on 17 May 1996. Saxena flew to Vancouver on 23 May 1996, entering on a visitor's visa issued four days before the central bank assumed control of the BBC.[89]

On 6 June, the BOT dismissed BBC president, Krirk-kiat Jalichandra. In the same month, 20 lawsuits were filed against Krirk-kiat for damaging the BBC. It had become apparent that massive fraud had taken place. *Asiaweek* magazine reported that in the same month:

The Kingdom of Thailand accused Saxena, Krirk-kiat Jalichandra, then president of the Bangkok Bank of Commerce, a clutch of their associates, a handful of Thai politicians, and Saudi arms merchant Adnan Khashoggi with embezzling as much as $2.2 billion from the BBC. . . .[90]

The *Far Eastern Economic Review* of 8 November 1996 gave this perspective:

When an American trader phoned the Bangkok Bank of Commerce about $126 million in Russian bearer bonds it was selling on the secondary market, he was astonished to learn that the bonds had gone missing. What kind of bank, he fumed, could allow that kind of paper to walk out of its doors and then fail to notify the international trading community? The answer: a renegade bank with allegedly criminal management and $3 billion in mostly outstanding loans—and one so unencumbered by regulation or oversight that it is now in dire need of rescue. . . .

Privately, bankers say they believe that senior regulators at the Bank of Thailand knew exactly what was going on, but were simply afraid to act. Social and political connections may have overwhelmed their integrity, as the BBC served well-connected clients, stretching up to the highest echelons of Thai society. The late MR Kukrit Pramoj, a former prime minister closely related to the royal family, was chairman of the bank.

Was BOT governor Vijit being pressured by politicians or influential people, or had he been drawn into the dubious activities of the BBC? Vijit later told the Nukul Commission that he did not order a capital writedown of BBC shares because the BBC was the only bank facing problems at that time, and because the economy was still in good shape. Because the bank was under close public scrutiny, capital writedown, he said, would confirm market fears and fuel public panic which might be followed by a chain reaction against other financial institutions. . . .[91]

However, press reports subsequently alleged that Vijit also benefited from the BBC's dubious practices and the BOT's lack of corrective action:

that he also had a large, unsecured BBC overdraft.[92] Vijit was apparently a friend and golfing partner of Krirk-kiat, who, prior to taking up the BBC presidency, was himself an official of the BOT. In addition, *The Nation* columnist "Bangkokian" reported that Vijit was a member of the council of advisors of the Chat Pattana Party of former prime minister, Chatichai Choonhavan, so that he could be protected when the party was part of the Chavalit coalition government. . . .[93] How far did the complicity between the central bank and the BBC go? A few months after the revelations in Parliament, *The Nation* wrote:

> The BOT knew the bank's shaky financial position all along. As of the end of 1995, it told Krirk-kiat to terminate all lending related to corporate takeovers or leveraged buy-outs. But Krirk-kiat kept on defying the central bank's orders. In return he received a pat on the back from Vijit Supinit, the central bank governor. Vijit did not give Krirk-kiat any final notice. He did not act at all, and eventually this was instrumental in costing him his job.[94]

Just weeks after the takeover of the BBC by the central bank, *The Nation* commented that the central bank was experiencing one of the most turbulent periods in its history, particularly through a wave of politicisation hitting the bank:

> Because the prime minister [Banharn] has friends in the property and business sectors, like many of his cabinet members who own businesses, they feel they have the legitimate right to order the central bank to tell financial institutions that they have to reduce their interest rates. They have thought little of the credibility of the central bank but rather tried to politicise the already weak governor. . . .
>
> A closer look at the BBC's loan extension reveals that its lending for takeovers and other related doubtful loans virtually doubled in 1995—when it was certainly known that some members of the Group of 16 MPs in the Chat Thai government [of Banharn], who are clients of the bank, were set to be appointed to the cabinet.[95]

133

Asiaweek commented:

> It was a heady era. Those with the right information could
> make millions on the soaring stock market. It was common
> practice to buy companies, pump up the books, and flip the
> firms for huge profits. The same attitude applied to the boom-
> ing property market: land was routinely overvalued so deve-
> lopers could use it as collateral for loans to build condos. . . .
> Yet, at the same time, the central bank and Ministry of Finance
> were increasingly undisciplined and ever more responsive to
> the needs of politicians. It was in this environment that the
> BBC saga unfolded. . . .
>
> Saxena's strategy was fairly simple. He would identify publicly
> traded but stagnant Thai companies, find buyers for them, pump
> up their balance sheets by shedding unneeded assets and staff,
> then resell the firms for a profit. Throughout 1993 and 1994,
> Krirk-kiat, Saxena, and their backers launched takeover bids. . . .
> In all, some 15 public companies were attacked. They also took
> the plan global. . . .[96]

The Nation added that this strategy, in which 35.8 billion baht was
poured into takeovers, was also a smoke screen to cover up other money-
making activities of loan recipients:

> All the deals could be traced to the management, which
> according to investigators set up as many as 97 paper companies
> to loot the bank. The BBC's takeover bids quickly turned sour
> because, in the words of the BOT, "The loan approvals were
> grossly negligent, without any fundamental analysis of the
> business or the ability of the borrowers to service the debts. The
> collateral offered on the loans was not enough to cover the
> debts. . . ."[97]
>
> "There's nothing complicated in the gutting of the bank. Money
> was simply taken from the bank outright," said [one] financial
> executive. . . .[98]

Following Vijit's departure, Rerngchai Marakanond became governor of the Bank of Thailand, but the folly did not end there. In order to "save" the BBC, the BOT had to undertake another round of capital increase in August 1996, but still the best solution of a capital writedown was not forthcoming. The Financial Institution Development Fund (FIDF) bought BBC capital shares totalling 22.5 billion baht.[99]

The Nukul Commission concluded that the BOT ought to have ordered the BBC to write down capital before ordering the FIDF to inject new funds:

> The capital writedown is applied to preserve the principle that old shareholders must be responsible for all damages caused by their mismanagement. When the BOT ordered the Fund, the Government Savings Bank, and others to buy new shares before requiring a capital writedown, it precluded the old shareholders from having to pay for their previous mismanagement mistakes.[100]

In early 1997, the FIDF acknowledged that BBC had problem debts of 60 billion baht, and hired the Industrial Finance Corporation of Thailand to manage BBC and gave them an option to buy BBC shares from the FIDF in stages. . . . In a masterpiece of understatement, the Nukul Commission noted at the end of its chapter on the bail-out of the Bangkok Bank of Commerce:

> The Commission views that the BBC bail-out policy was not transparent and there were questions which have no answers.

How many years would it take to resolve the criminal cases arising from the BBC fiasco? As of September 1998, some 23 cases involving former management and debtors of the BBC had been forwarded to the public prosecutors. Three cases had made it to court. Several of the debtors facing possible prosecution were politicians. The new BBC president installed by the Bank of Thailand, Aswin Kongsiri, said that 70.5 billion baht had been loaned to politicians during the lending spree. But the government was not about to name the political borrowers. Deputy finance minister in the second Chuan government, Pisit Lee-atham, said the names of borrowers involved in the mammoth BBC loan scam could be disclosed within three months of the BBC losing its banking status and becoming a company merely to manage bad assets. By mid-1999, no names had been disclosed. Perhaps influencing that decision was the fact that the Chat Thai Party of former prime minister, Banharn—to which several of the suspected politicians had belonged—had been brought into the second Chuan government in mid-1998 to give it added "stability".[101]

What Next? Learning the Lessons

As 1998 came to a close, Thailand was still mired in a tangle of debt problems: non-performing loans in the banking system were thought to be around 40–45 per cent of total loans; the government was still struggling to pass the bankruptcy and foreclosure bills that were seen as crucial to restoring international investors' confidence in the Thai economy; and corporate debt restructuring was not moving forward. The Chavalit government's generosity in June 1997 (under pressure from the World Bank and the IMF) in guaranteeing all the external debts of the yet-to-be-closed finance companies, was undoubtedly a factor in foreign creditors delaying restructuring of Thailand's massive debts.

Many heavily-indebted tycoons, who personified the carefree behaviour that had caused the country's economic collapse, continued to use their influence in an attempt to resist legal reforms such as the bankruptcy and foreclosure bills that would force them to liquidate their assets to pay debts. Such legislation was seen as crucial to unlocking the outstanding non-performing loans of 2.7 trillion baht in the banking system.[102]

In August 1998, Dresdner Kleinwort Benson Research said that the bail-out cost for the Thai banking system was expected to amount to 1.5 trillion baht. At the end of 1998, preliminary calculations valued the 1998 GDP at around 4.295 trillion baht.[103] Thus, if the bail-out estimate was accurate, it would cost 35 per cent of GDP. *The Nation* commented:

> Considering that the major crises of the past decade in the United
> States, Japan, and Mexico all cost less than 5 per cent of their
> respective GDPs, the gravity of the disaster in Thailand remains
> apparent.[104]

A debate was continuing into early 1999 on how far the government could go to relieve the many heavily-indebted tycoons who relied on personal guarantees to obtain loans for their businesses. How much would they be allowed to keep of their personal assets, and how much would be confiscated? One tycoon pointed out that the credit system in Thailand put trust in individuals rather than in companies, so business-men had no choice but to become personal guarantors of their own companies. . . . Businessmen-Senators with large debts were trying to delay implementation of the legislation "until Thailand recovered". The debate was striking at the heart of the (formerly-wealthy) Thai elite, who had enjoyed so much privilege under the system of money politics and who had come to expect special treatment from politicians when things went wrong.

The finance minister, Tarrin Nimmanahaeminda, was stressing that the overall principle of repaying loans to creditors must be kept, otherwise the entire financial system would break down. The government, however, was in a dilemma. Social hardship was increasing, and political opponents were able to attack the government on the charge that it was more interested in bailing out the wealthy and well-connected while the poor got little. In fact, the pouring of 700 billion baht into failing financial institutions began under Banharn and continued under Chavalit, before the second Chuan government put a stop to it.

The shocks of the Crash of 97 were still reverberating throughout the Thai governmental and corporate culture. But, ironically, one benefit from the Crash was beginning to be seen. Finally, a movement towards good governance, based on principles of accountability and transparency in government, was beginning to emerge as a reaction to the poor governance that had led Thailand to disaster. And in the private sector, the perceived need to embrace the principle of corporate responsibility was leading to attempts to modernise management and to introduce international standards in corporate financial practices and auditing. These developments held out promise that Thailand's economy and society could be redeveloped on a sounder institutional basis in the future. In many ways the Crash was a hurdle that the country had to overcome in its striving to become a mature and sustainable society.

But, there was a major doubt remaining about whether these progressive moves could lead to a genuine turning point for Thailand. How far could such moves transform the society as long as the legal system was failing to prosecute, convict, and punish political figures who were co-conspirators and prime movers behind the host of dubious and illegal practices that brought down the financial system and caused so much suffering?

Bank of Thailand Reforms

A major restructuring of the Bank of Thailand was taking place, based on recommendations of the Nukul Commission and other agencies such as the IMF, and on initiatives taken by the government to bring in respected central bankers from the developed world to advise on the process. A major objective was to increase the central bank's independence and to insulate it from political interference, especially the kind of interference that led to massive infusions of money into insolvent banks and finance companies.

The Nukul Commission made recommendations about how to choose the Bank of Thailand's governor, to help ensure that a capable and far-sighted leader would head this important institution in the future. It recommended that the governor should have a five-year term, which should not be extended more than once. Respected persons from different sectors should be recruited to nominate and appoint the central bank's governor. The finance minister would make the proposal to the cabinet, with the Senate's endorsement. The desired qualifications of the central bank governor should also be determined.

The world congregation of central bankers is an important source of guidance on restructuring. For example, more than 130 governors or former governors of central banks met in London in 1994, where Stanley Fischer, a professor at the Massachusetts Institute of Technology and the first deputy managing director of the IMF, had some lessons on the case for central bank independence:

- The central bank should have a clearly defined mandate, which includes price stability.
- The bank should publicly announce its intermediate-term policy goals.
- The bank should be accountable in two senses: it should be held responsible for meeting announced goals, and it should be required to explain and justify its policies to the legislature and the public.
- The government should have the authority to override the bank's decisions, but an overridden decision should carry a cost for the government.

- The central bank should be given the authority to set interest rates and other monetary policy variables in order to achieve its policy goals.
- The bank should not be required to finance the government deficit, and should not manage the public debt.
- There cannot be a separate responsibility for setting interest rates and the exchange rate so long as the exchange rate floats.[105]

Auditing to International Standards

The Thai people have suffered immeasurably from poor standards of auditing, both within government and in the private sector; poor standards which have allowed massive fraud to take place. The Crash of 97 provoked a close examination of malpractices within mismanaged and overborrowed Thai companies, with concrete measures for positive change emerging.

Singh Tangtatsawat, the president of the Stock Exchange of Thailand, called for more transparency in auditing listed companies, to restore the confidence of foreign investors. In August 1997, he spoke about measures introduced by the SET to force listed companies to improve their internal controls:

> The SET has brought in a long-term measure to support the establishment of auditing committees in the firms. Independent directors will sit on the committees and supervise the company's management. Meanwhile, the listed companies will set up another committee to monitor management expenses to ensure they are as transparent as possible.[106]

At a subsequent forum for chief financial officers, organised by the Thailand Management Association, Singh said that CFOs will be expected to be involved in all of the decisions a company makes regarding finance, employees, resource allocation, auditing, and reporting the company's financial status to the public. The CFO would have to endorse all announcements to ensure that the listed company told only the truth to the public. Speakers at the forum agreed that most Thai companies were still managed in a family style, and there had been no separation of the roles of CFO and CEO, which resulted in a lack of foresight into future risk. In the past, CEOs thought only about company expansion.[107]

In November 1998, the cabinet approved in principle a Finance Ministry proposal to form independent budget-audit committees that would work full time in all ministries to check corruption in state agencies. Finance Minister Tarrin said the audit committees may comprise representatives from the Counter Corruption Commission, the Office of the Auditor-General, the Comptroller-General's Department, the Budget Bureau, the National Economic and Social Development Board, and independent experts from the public sector. . . . The committees would also work on the highly controversial project-bidding systems of each ministry, where corruption through collusion between officials, politicians, and private firms is thought to be widespread.[108]

Other recommendations were coming forward to combat fraud within financial institutions. Paul Carter, a fraud investigation expert at Price Waterhouse Cooper and the Institute of Internal Auditors of Thailand, proposed the setting up of fraud-control committees within companies.[109]

Ultimately, a key factor in achieving financial stability is building up a culture of responsibility—to include businessmen, officials, and politicians. This means focusing on concepts such as fairness, and commitment to a regulatory framework which is objective, automatic, and favours no one. The biggest obstacle to this in Thailand is the patronage system: fairness and even-handedness have hardly been conspicuous in Thai society. Where there have been senior officials dedicated to honesty, they have often been educated overseas; their influence is soon negated by power exercised through the patronage system.

The Political Factor

With our knowledge of elitist behaviour in Thailand and of the links of patronage between the elite and politicians, it is not too far-fetched to conclude that the disastrous "flexibility" in the central banks' monitoring and regulating of the finance companies, outlined earlier in this chapter, was coloured by a desire not to upset powerful people. The Nukul report does not touch on this question of underlying motives of the BOT's officials; it merely reports the damage. The report states— very sparingly—that politicians deserve a share of the responsibility, but offers no details. The report does state that (serious) unanswered questions remain about the financial crash. One question this writer would ask:

How much of the money handed out by the finance companies and the Bangkok Bank of Commerce, and how much of the 700 billion baht handed out by the Bank of Thailand to cover those companies losses, ended up in the bank accounts of politicians and their friends?

Who will expose and prosecute the political criminals?

Apparently, the fear of repercussions is too great for agencies such as the Nukul Commission and the Thailand Development Research Institute to directly accuse politicians of wrongdoing. We can see that issues of criminality were skirted in the analyses these bodies undertook into Thailand's Crash.

One commentator explained the dilemma involved in such an action, when looking at the mission of the newly-appointed central bank governor, Chatu Mongol Sonakul, to crack down on reckless or unscrupulous executives of finance firms who had evaded legal action. The commentator said:

> It's not about having evidence or not, it's about having the guts to cross those people.[110]

Up to the end of 1999, we have seen that no elected government in Thailand has wanted to prosecute MPs or current or former cabinet ministers for criminal activity, even when that activity has done great harm to the country. There seems to be a pervasive assumption cutting across all major political parties that "we are all in it together". After all, today's accused opponent in politics may be tomorrow's potential coalition partner. Thus, those within Thai politics who are guilty of abuses remain protected.

If my above question cannot be answered, and culprits not punished— no matter how high a position they held or still hold—no amount of political reform appearing on paper can lead to a healthy and sustainable Thai society in the future.

There has been no countervailing agency in Thai society that has so far been able to say, "Stop. Enough is enough!" The political system should have been able to guide and safeguard the financial system. It failed. The legal system, including the courts, should have been able to expose and prosecute criminals within the political system. It has failed, and continues to fail.

What is needed in Thailand is a political purge, carried out according to the rule of law and due process, to put offending politicians in jail and set a precedent for future political development in the country. It remains to be seen whether Thailand's new, and yet-to-be-tested Constitution, with the powers it embodies to root out corruption, could provide the momentum for this.

There is another major, unanswered question underlying the whole of Thailand's Crash: Can it happen again? If the root, political causes are not addressed, no amount of talk about good governance and corporate responsibility will solve the problem. Disaster awaits when the required high standards of administration and public responsibility cannot be attained and maintained. If there is no mechanism in the society or government that can insist upon and enforce standards within public life and politics, then the country cannot succeed in an international competitive environment that now demands higher standards of governance and accountability.

There is another requirement for the survival of a healthy Thai society over the long term, apart from good governance and corporate responsibility: it is an appreciation of what is genuine sustainable development. Sustainability means living within ecological boundaries, both nationally and globally, and therefore redirecting personal pursuits away from vanity consumption towards a non-materialistic quality of life.

Thailand's recent pursuit of money-by-all-means through eco-destructive growth has failed in terms of sustainability, as have the prevailing financial and political practices of the 1990s. The financial and political practices have come under close scrutiny following Thailand's Crash, but commitment towards a genuinely sustainable society has yet to be placed on the nation's agenda. (More about this in later chapters.)

Chapter 5

Transparency and Accountability: The New Zealand Experience

Thailand badly needs greater transparency and financial accountability in government, even more so following the economic bubble of the 1990s, culminating in the Crash which virtually bankrupted the country.

This chapter looks at the experience of New Zealand, which faced a similar problem in the 1980s. New Zealand became mired in economic problems over two decades of virtually no growth and mounting foreign debts, largely caused by the government's inability to adjust to changes in the international economic environment. The government became technically bankrupt, relying on foreign loans to cover chronic deficits. Finally, the country's massive problems gave rise to a political movement which demanded wholesale changes to the way government worked— including increased transparency, fiscal accountability, deregulation, and a reorganisation of the bureaucratic structure along corporate lines. These are precisely the areas in which progressive Thais are now seeking to promote change.

New Zealand overcame its crisis through a decade-long legislative programme of radical reform, begun by a determined group of young cabinet ministers—and the country now arguably has the most transparent system of government in the world, with an unprecedented degree of financial accountability required from its politicians and government officials. In the years after the reforms, New Zealand recorded healthy economic growth and budget surpluses, and was able to pay off substantial amounts of its foreign debt. As of 1999, the rate of growth had slipped back somewhat, partly a result of the Asian crisis. The reforms drew a stream of international visitors to Wellington to examine the new set-up.

I visited the capital in 1995 and gathered information on the philosophy, the measures, and the implementation of New Zealand's "quiet revolution". Following is my report:

Systems of government and public administration in most countries are not responding very well to the demands for change brought about by the rapid globalisation of economies and the need for sustainable development. State sectors—characterised by bloated bureaucracy, secrecy, inefficiency, ill-defined goals, and often preoccupied with their own self-interest—have largely come to be seen as burdens on their societies. Amongst the developed countries, New Zealand suffered more than most—almost 20 years of economic stagnation from poor macro-economic management and an unresponsive state system. In the early 1980s, the country of 3.4 million people found itself virtually bankrupt with a large debt burden, high inflation, low or no economic growth, and a tradition of extensive involvement by the government in running commercial enterprises and infrastructural services.

All that changed in the space of a decade, following the accession to power in the 1984 general election of a well-informed group of dynamic, young reformers under the Labour government of Prime Minister David Lange. They began a programme of radical reform which turned the old bureaucratic order upside down, eventually resulting in robust economic growth. In 1994, the government achieved a current account surplus, reduced inflation to less than 2 per cent, and began making inroads into repaying its public debt, which amounted to 48 per cent of gross domestic product (GDP) in 1993.

New Zealand began its reforms with a sweeping "downsizing" and deregulation of government, in line with the macro-economic prescriptions of the early 1980s being advocated by such agencies as the World Bank and the IMF: the removal of state subsidies and the privatisation of government-run commercial activities or their conversion into state-owned enterprises. It gave the central bank (the Reserve Bank) independence to set interest rates and control inflation, freed up currency controls, and liberalised markets. The key piece of legislation here was the Reserve Bank Act of 1984. The reforms became known as "Rogernomics", following the direction of the then finance minister, Roger Douglas.

But that was just the beginning. A new regime of presenting government accounts, under Generally Agreed Accounting Principles

(GAAP), the set of accountancy rules followed throughout the private sector in New Zealand, added an increased transparency to government accounting.

The reformers created worldwide interest by redefining the relationship between the public service and government ministers, and by transforming the state sector through the introduction of corporate-style management. Permanent heads of ministries and departments were placed on contracts of three to five years, and renamed "chief executives". The State Services Commission (SSC) became the employer of the chief executives, and not the ministers, to retain the neutrality and apolitical nature of the public service. The chief executives are now selected through an elaborate search process run by the State Services commissioner.

The SSC chooses a candidate for a chief executive's post by advertising for a high-profile selection panel, either nationally or internationally, to remove political influence and add transparency to the process. The commissioner then recommends the candidate to ministers. The ministers have the power to reject the candidate, but that has seldom happened.

A chief executive is now required to enter into an annual performance agreement (a written contract) with the minister, which specifies what the chief executive is required to deliver on behalf of the ministry, and the amount of money the minister will provide through the government's budget. In effect, the minister formally purchases the outputs of the ministry at specified standards of quantity, quality, timeliness, and cost under the new, transparent accountancy methods. The chief executive has almost complete freedom to hire the staff of his choice, organise his department, and contract functions out to the private sector—following the basic rationale that the state should not be involved in any activities that would be more efficiently and effectively performed by the private sector. His performance, as measured against his contractual obligations, is subject to an annual review by a special panel convened by the SSC, which used to be the agency in charge of employing all civil servants and regulating the government bureaucracy.

Refocusing Political Responsibility

The rationale for this contract system between the minister and chief executive was to introduce as many of the disciplines of the commercial operating environment as practicable to the state sector. Administrative and policy-advice functions were also separated. The system also removed the minister from day-to-day intervention into the workings of departments; his function was thus refocused on responsibility for broader policy. This amounts to a radical departure from the doctrine of ministerial responsibility which New Zealand inherited from the British Westminster model of government. The chief executives are responsible for the contracted "outputs", while the ministers are responsible for their policy "outcomes"—their actual impact on the society or economy.

Contracts and agreements between the ministers and chief executives are written down and are accessible to the public under New Zealand's Official Information Act, an important piece of legislation reinforcing the financial and bureaucratic reforms, which was introduced in 1982 to replace the Official Secrets Act (a legacy of British colonialism, which the British still maintain). The Official Information Act requires that official information should be released to the public unless there is a reason in law why it should not be released. Once information is received by a government agency it becomes official information. The Ombudsman is the appeal agency in cases of disagreement on the release of information. John Martin, a senior lecturer in public policy at Victoria University of Wellington, commented on the financial and bureaucratic reforms:

> This really is a revolution, a quiet revolution, in the sense that the status quo has been overturned. It is well imbedded, there is no going back. It has changed the ethos; an entrepreneurial spirit is now there, and ministers would say they have a much more responsive bureaucracy.

Key pieces of legislation in this drive were:
- the State-Owned Enterprises Act 1986, which provided the basis for converting the old trading departments and corporations into businesses along private-sector lines;
- the State Sector Act 1988, which made departmental chief executives fully accountable for managing their organisations efficiently and effectively, and changed the role of the State Services Commission from employer and manager of the Public

Service to employer of chief executives and advisor to the government about management of the state sector;

• the Public Finance Act 1989, which changed the basis of state sector financial management from a focus on inputs to a focus on outputs and outcomes; and

• the Fiscal Responsibility Act 1994, which forces the government to display the state of the nation's finances twice a year and before an election, and commits it to running financial surpluses rather than deficits.

The last piece of legislation came under the National (conservative) government of Prime Minister Jim Bolger, first elected in 1990. While in opposition, during Labour's restructuring of the public service, Bolger was sceptical about the contract system. On gaining power, he appointed a committee which examined and subsequently vindicated the reforms, and then pressed ahead with fiscal and economic reforms of his own. Thus, the durability of New Zealand's decade of reforms achieved the consensus of both major political parties.

The outcome of the reforms has had tremendous importance for economic policy, according to Alex Matheson, the branch manager for state sector development of the SSC:[1]

> The move to contracts between the public service and the politicians means that [everything] gets written down and is accessible under the Official Information Act. In economic policy, this has been tremendously important. There is very little incentive for politicians to spend up in the final year before an election or to manipulate the economy [to make things look a bit better than they are] because they will be seen to do it and they will take a political hit. . . . None of this represents necessarily bad intent, but because ministers could manipulate the exchange rate and the interest rate, and all of this could occur really with little outside scrutiny, there was a quite high level of moral hazard in that whole system.

Public servants tended to connive with politicians in pre-election spend-ups, especially in marginal electorates, added Matheson, because often it was a chance for the public servants to increase their kingdoms. . . .

> This situation was tremendously damaging to New Zealand because we had a post-war history of governments spending up in their final year. . . . Every country is finding that public administration and government systems are not coping as well with modern conditions. The trends of globalisation and democratisation have changed the conditions in which governments operate.

New Zealand's "quiet revolution" prompted Steve Hanke, professor of applied economics at Johns Hopkins University in Baltimore, USA, to recommend New Zealand as a first-class investment opportunity:

> The 1994 Fiscal Responsibility Act made New Zealand the only country in the world with proper public sector accounts. With everything out in the open, corruption becomes riskier. . . . It is not surprising that Transparency International (a Berlin-based anti-corruption organisation) ranks New Zealand as the least corrupt government in the world.[2]

A publication of the SSC, entitled *New Zealand's Reformed Sate Sector*, says:

> Other countries have undertaken very significant reforms of structures and/or systems over the last 10 years but none have attempted anything of quite the comprehensiveness or on the scale that New Zealand has, and sustained it for as long. . . . These were changes on an enormous scale—dynamic solutions for major problems. The government saw the state sector, with its traditional focus on resource distribution, regulation, and control, and with relatively little transparency in its processes and activities, not so much as a tool for reform, but as a significant part of the problem. It felt the state cost too much, contributed too little to wealth-generating production, and was a dead weight on our society.

The SSC noted that in the 1993 *World Competitiveness Report*, New Zealand's overall ranking moved from 15th to 8th within the OECD (the Organisation for Economic Cooperation and Development, grouping the developed economies). The report ranked New Zealand first in quality of government, while ratings in domestic and economic strength moved from 21st to 7th, in management from 18th to 8th, and in infrastructure from 13th to 6th.

In May 1994, then finance minister, Bill Birch, in introducing the Fiscal Responsibility Bill for its second reading, summarised the negative trends of the past that had been overcome:

> For almost 20 years New Zealand governments have spent more than they have earned to try to shelter the country from the effects of major changes in our international environment. Many New Zealanders have been locked into long-term unemployment, ill-equipped with the skills needed for success in a modern economy. High debt has constrained our ability for success in a modern economy. . . . Fortunately, we are now on the way to recovering [from] this sorry position. This government has moved over the past four years to put its finances on a much more secure footing. This year [the fiscal year ended 30 June 1994], for the first time in 15 years, the government will deliver a budget showing the financial balance in surplus. . . .

With proceeds from the government's privatisation programme and from the 1994 budget surplus, New Zealand was able to reduce its foreign public debt from 48 per cent to 42 per cent of gross domestic product (GDP). It was the first decline of public debt for nearly 20 years. In the 12 months up to March 1994, the economy grew by 5 per cent, and 57,000 new jobs were created amongst New Zealand's population of 3.4 million people.

What were the major changes in New Zealand's international environment that Birch referred to? They included the two oil shocks (steep rises in oil prices) of the late 1970s and early 1980s, and declining revenue from New Zealand's agricultural exports. New Zealand was seen to be living beyond its means as successive governments borrowed heavily from international sources to cushion the shocks. By 1984, when the then National Party prime minister, Robert Muldoon, called a snap election, there was a sense of mounting crisis—both economic and constitutional—as the post-war political consensus about the role of government was breaking down, according to John Martin.

Following the victory of the Labour Party in the 1984 general election, the Treasury (Finance Ministry) struck the first blow for change with a briefing paper, *Economic Management*, which it tendered to the Lange government as it came into office. The Treasury document was, in effect, a mainstream economic prescription of the OECD, and it carried a warning that if the problems of the state sector were not tackled, the economic crisis would continue, according to Martin. This "manifesto for revolution", coupled with a new generation of radically-minded ministers who had no association with the old order, set the stage for major change.

What does the government structure look like under this new set-up?

According to the SSC, when the reform process began, nearly 88,000 people worked in the departments of the public service; in 1993 the figure was just over 36,000. Today, the public service (or "core public service" as it is often informally termed) is characterised by relatively small departments with quite sharply-defined purposes covering policy advice, service delivery, regulatory functions, and sectoral funding. The streamlining has resulted in many semi-independent and independent agencies. As of May 1995, there were 80 Crown entities, ranging from the Auckland International Airport Ltd, to the Electoral Commission, and the New Zealand Artificial Limb Board. There were 16 state-owned enterprises (SOEs), including big ones such as Electricity Corp., Forestry Corp., New Zealand Railways Corp., and New Zealand Post. Earlier SOEs, such as the Petroleum Corp. and the Shipping Corp. had already been privatised. The enterprises are run by a board, devoid of politicians or public servants, and pay an agreed dividend to the government.

The SSC summarised the organising principles for the reform process:[3]

- The state should not be involved in any activities that would be more efficiently and effectively performed by the community or by private businesses.
- Trading enterprises would operate most efficiently and effectively if structured along the lines of private sector businesses.
- Departments would operate most efficiently and effectively with clearly specified and non-conflicting functions, and particularly

with policy and operations functions separated, and with commercial and non-commercial functions separated.

- Departmental managers would perform most effectively if made fully accountable for the efficient running of their organisations, with the minimum practicable central control of inputs.
- The costs of state activities should as far as practicable be fixed through real market factors—in other words, the quality, quantity, and cost of products should be determined by the purchaser's requirements, rather than the producer's preferences.

A lot of work for the government is now short term, employing the private sector, and tendering for contracts. This has led to the growth of a culture of quite highly-paid, independent consultants and specialist firms seeking government work. There is general agreement that great gains in efficiency have been achieved.

Among the core public service are three key agencies: the Department of the Prime Minister and Cabinet, the Treasury, and the SSC—which operate, individually and collectively, as key advisers to the government, and coordinators of its business. Another important development, according to a senior official at the Parliament buildings, is that government has moved towards "strategic management". From the top down, government has indicated nine strategic results areas to achieve social cohesion and sustainable economic development. Everything the government does is to be attuned to those nine areas.

Impact on Ministers and Officials

Said Alex Matheson:

> Initially, the ministers felt a little uncomfortable with the apparent transparency of contracts, the fact that what they are doing is very open. But most of them have taken to the principle of being able to define their objectives with their chief executives very well.

As for the civil servants, the reforms have led to a deregulation of pay and conditions (which are negotiable), and to greater managerial freedom. According to Matheson, those factors mean that the public service can probably attract better people than previously because they can have a more interesting career and can go in and out of the public sector more easily. The reforms have created a lot more energy and made the public service a far more interesting environment to work in. Senior public servants no longer have tenure, but are being paid salaries comparable with the private sector. For example, the secretary of the Treasury receives NZ$180,000 (US$117,000), as do the other top two or three secretaries, according to John Martin.

ASEAN Countries Welcome

Could New Zealand's reforms effectively be transplanted to other countries? There are several aspects of New Zealand culture that facilitated acceptance of the reforms: the country's small, relatively homogeneous population, and a good basic level of education. The senior parliamentary official cautioned that New Zealand's experience may not completely suit other countries because of differences in the societies and levels of development, but added:

> Most countries aspire to having transparent public finances, so people can see where their taxes are spent. They aspire to having efficient public sectors that can provide utilities as efficiently as the private sector. Most desire governments whose bureaucrats are not corruptible—a requirement for genuine service to the public in a parliamentary democracy.

> New Zealand does encourage the ASEAN countries (the ten-member Association of Southeast Asian Nations) in particular to visit and talk about these areas of public sector reform and economic reform.

The New Zealand experience suggests there are seven key elements to a successful reform process, as enumerated by the SSC:
1. Unflinching political determination.
2. Very clear objectives, agreed at the highest levels, and based on an intelligent appreciation of the community's tolerances.
3. A set of comprehensive and well integrated basic principles agreed at the highest levels.

4. Sound legal architecture that redefines the rules outright.
5. A demanding but realistic timetable.
6. A core of unified, highly motivated, experienced, and imaginative senior public servants, provided with sufficient resources and discretion to manage implementation.
7. Very effective information and public relations systems.

The Negative Side

The state sector reforms appear to be generally accepted by the people; perhaps the greatest resentment may be on the part of formerly protected public servants who lost their jobs as staff numbers were cut back and their functions contracted to private service providers on merit. The reforms seemed to have caused more disruption than originally envisaged. The SSC notes:

> Together, the major corporatisations, structural reforms in education and health, and departmental restructurings since 1984 have affected the lives and careers of thousands of employees. . . . In many cases surplus staff from shrinking or abolished organisations were quickly hired by the newly-created agencies and enterprises that sprang up, while others were able to establish their own businesses as contractors to the new organisations. . . . However, the reforms did bring an end to state sector careers for a very significant number of people, and dramatically changed a number of rural communities that had previously depended upon a single state industry. There is no doubt that the scale and significance of these impacts were underestimated.

In fact, there was a general feeling that reforms in education and health were proving difficult after several attempts. The social security system was another difficult area, and a subject of political debate in New Zealand. What level of support should the state provide for the disadvantaged? All of these sectors are part of a readjustment problem being felt by many countries in a rapidly changing world posing new demands. Societies everywhere are experiencing a growing gap between rich and poor, partly a function of deregulation and cutting of subsidies in favour of the "user pays" principle, and partly a function of greater premiums placed on expertise and skill in a globalising economy.

While there is a general agreement on the benefit of New Zealand's radical reforms and the efficiencies they have brought, there is also some nostalgia for the old regime. Analysts such as John Martin question whether something has been lost in the transition:

> I have some reservations about what has been done to the core public service, about the ethos of the public service. . . . There is a lot of questioning about whether we have taken this contracting too far, decoupled activities too much from government. With the emphasis on outputs rather than inputs, we are interested in results rather than how you get them. . . . The new architecture of the state, with its emphasis on "decoupling" ministers from the day-to-day management of public functions, has left a dangerous vacuum in respect of responsibility. . . . The nature of widespread short-term contract employment is having an effect on the capacity of the public service to offer "free and frank" quality advice.

Contracts and performance-based criteria have led to competition rather than cooperation becoming the dominant style. Martin added:

> Public servants need, in my view, a sense of vocation which carries with it a distinctive ethos.

Additionally, Martin points out in his writings, the bureaucracy in Western democracies has traditionally been the repository of knowledge peculiar to the service of the state: knowledge of the functioning of the system of government itself, and—secondly—an accumulation of the precedent and experience of the state's dealings with its citizens.

Perceptions about the changing ethos of the public service arising from the reforms are acknowledged by SSC senior staff such as Alex Matheson. Officials have had a lot more professional scope not having to work to tight bureaucratic rules, but this also changes the way they had to address issues like ethics. In a regulated system, ethics are imparted through central regulations, and through replicating the same kind of people through the culture of the organisation. Matheson added:

> Now, I think we have got a harder job with ethics and fundamental principles. . . . There was a concern that with the changes, a lot of knowledge, if you like, would be lost.

In response, the SSC has developed a set of books to fill the gaps between law and legal principles, and administrative devices like codes of conduct. They discuss principles upon which professionalism and ethics are based. However:

> This does not solve the problem of ethics, but we are now about to inaugurate a series of rolling seminars. . . . The only way to keep people conscious of their professional and ethical responsibility is to keep churning: stories, case studies reinforcing good behaviour.

The Fiscal Responsibility Act

To round out the concept of transparency and fiscal accountability, here is a closer look at the Fiscal Responsibility Act.[4] The Act works by obligating governments:

- to follow a legislated set of principles of responsible fiscal management, and publicly assess their fiscal policies against these principles;
- to require the Treasury to prepare forecasts based on its best professional judgement about the impact of policy, rather than relying on the judgment of the government (it also requires the minister to communicate all of the government's policy decisions to the Treasury so that the forecasts are comprehensive); and
- to refer all reports required under the Act to a parliamentary select committee (the Finance Committee).

In addition to bringing in economic and fiscal updates twice a year and before a general election, the Act requires the government to make a Budget Policy Statement and a Fiscal Strategy Report. The government must publish the Budget Policy Statement well before the annual budget. It must reveal the broad strategic priorities for the upcoming budget, the government's fiscal intentions for the next three years, and its long-term fiscal policy objectives. The Fiscal Strategy Report is published at the time of the budget. It encourages consistency between fiscal intentions published in the Budget Policy Statement and actual budget decisions. Inconsistencies must be explained. There is also a requirement to include "progress outlooks" to project fiscal trends over a ten-year period at least.

In addition to the above Statement and Report, the Act requires the publication of a substantial array of fiscal information throughout the year, including:

i) an economic and fiscal update for the next three years to be tabled on budget night;

ii) a half-year economic and fiscal update for the next three years to be tabled between 1–31 December; and

iii) a pre-election economic and fiscal update for the next three years to be published, depending on circumstances, between 42 and 14 days before the date of any general election. . . .

Every economic and fiscal update is to contain statements by:

1) the minister of finance, that all government decisions and circumstances with material, fiscal, or economic implications have been communicated to the secretary of the Treasury; and that the minister is responsible for the integrity of the disclosures contained in the economic and fiscal update. . . .

2) the secretary to the Treasury, that on the basis of the economic and fiscal information available, the Treasury has used its best professional judgement in supplying the minister with the economic and fiscal update. . . .

The Fiscal Responsibility Act requires the Treasury to prepare forecasts based on its best professional judgement about the impact of policy, rather than relying on the judgment of the government. The Act also obliges the government to reduce Crown debt (public debt) so as to provide a buffer against future adverse events, by achieving operating surpluses every year until prudent levels of debt have been achieved—a provision that prevents governments from achieving prudent debt levels simply by selling assets. These requirements mean that the government of the day has to be transparent about both its intentions and the short- and long-term impact of its spending and taxation decisions. Such transparency is likely to lead governments to give more weight to the longer-term consequences of their decisions and, therefore, is likely to lead to more sustainable fiscal policy. . . .

Transparent Accounting Principles

New Zealand governments previously established their own rules of accounting. Now, following the financial reforms, an obligation to follow the Generally Agreed Accounting Principles requirements adds to the integrity and credibility of a government's statements. GAAP rules are made by a body independent of the government, the New Zealand Accounting Standards Review Board, established by the Financial Reporting Act 1994. Its standards apply to both public and private sectors. Therefore government statements are easier to understand, adding to their transparency.

Part of the new, stringent accounting procedures for government is accrual accounting. It recognises expenses when an obligation arises and not simply when cash is paid. Similarly, revenue relates to the Crown's entitlement to future benefits and not the point at which cash is received. (The Crown, as a denotation of government in New Zealand, includes all ministers and all departments of government, but not offices of Parliament, Crown entities, or State enterprises.) Assets and liabilities are separated from current revenues and expenses in a balance sheet or statement of financial position. The SSC's Matheson gave this assessment:

> I think we are the only country in the world that presents Crown accounts [according to] the GAAP. It basically means we give a total picture of government expenditure, including its capital expenditure. [Now] it is possible to look at the New Zealand government as though it were a firm; one can see its net worth. That is most unusual. . . . Most governments probably expose only the annual appropriation and so the past capital sort of just disappears, and they may have huge liabilities of various kinds reaching into the future that would not ever appear on the balance sheet. . . . So the accounting changes and the macro-economic changes are of world standing. . . .

The State Services Commission cited three key aspects of the reforms that had been extremely successful:

Transparency in the activities and processes of the State, the liberation of managers from central input controls (on accommodation, equipment, vehicles, consumables, and the like) and the new financial management and accounting systems are revolutionising the ways in which departments and officials work. Unnecessary and redundant activities and wasteful processes are being exposed and eliminated, and the efficiency with which the service does its business is improving as departments progressively become more skilled in specifying and pricing outputs. The new accrual accounting and financial management systems give much better appreciations of the financial positions of departments, and are part of the overall regime that leads to a rational set of government accounts.

Managers have relished the opportunities presented by devolution; and some, at least, of that flourishing of ideas and energies sought by the government when it began this process of reform has occurred in the state sector. The public service has shed the stodgy, unadventurous, and in some respects secretive character it had for many years.[5]

Finally, in summary, the New Zealand reforms show that information is the key to better, cleaner, and more responsive government. All interactions requiring expenditure, between ministers and their chief executives, get written down in contracts, and are public information. Economic ministers and chief executives are required to provide information on the state of the government's accounts, and on their short-, medium-, and long-term financial plans—and they are required to take responsibility for the veracity of that information.

The system of accrual accounting, in addition, mandates that financial obligations cannot be hidden and must appear on financial balance sheets. Cabinet ministers and MPs alike benefit from free and complete information; it allows the cabinet to act more strategically than it used to. Civil society—the public, academics, and journalists—can participate more fully in the affairs of government. Said Matheson:

There is no doubt in my mind that once you start to create better quality information, you at least have the potential to sort out certain problems. If you have got obscured, blurred purposes and poor quality information that can be manipulated for the purposes of the people within [a certain institution], then the chances of getting any traction on some of these big problems are very limited indeed. . . .

The level of sophistication of the economic debate in this country over the last 10 years has just been transformed, partly through integration into the global economy, partly through the added transparency and accountability brought about by reform.

SECTION 2

REFORMING THAILAND'S DESTRUCTIVE POLITICS

Chapter 6

The 1997 People's Power Constitution

In 1997, Thailand created the best chance in many decades to reform its political culture to remove widespread abuses of the political process and of political power, and to set the country on the path to attaining a responsive, participatory, and sustainable democratic culture. Rising political consciousness among educated Thais throughout the 1990s, in conjunction with the financial crisis of 1997 and the decline of the economy, led to the adoption of a new Constitution on 27 September 1997.

The innovative and exhaustive process of consultation with the public, through which the Constitution was drafted, was at least as important as the resulting document. This process of sampling public opinion through questionnaires and regional seminars was a big step forward in Thailand's democratic development. The chairman of the drafting committee of the Constitution Drafting Assembly, former prime minister, Anand Panyarachun, noted:

> This is the first time in the 65-year history of Thailand's democracy that the draft is being drawn up, not by the elite, not by the people in power, but it's being drawn up by laymen . . . such a diverse group . . . such different conceptions and backgrounds. . . .[1]

The resulting document has drawn praise as the "people's power" Constitution and the "anti-corruption" Constitution. Thailand's 16th charter, it is undoubtedly the best the country has produced. The

Constitution is strong on human rights, on people's participation in decision making, on redress of complaints against officialdom, and on monitoring the activities of politicians and officials. It offers the prospect, through its various anti-corruption measures, of breaking through the barriers of influence and patronage that up to now have prevented any politicians or senior officials from being charged with—let alone being convicted of—corruption.

One month before the Constitution was (surprisingly) adopted by a vote of Parliament, Anand spoke of the growing disillusionment that had finally crystallised into a movement to rewrite the Constitution:

> Nobody can actually tell when this process started. But one sure thing is that in 65 years, the Thai people have become sick and tired of our political system, with [its] different variations, with interruptions of coups d'etat, strong-man rule, authoritarian concepts, and what not. . . . Last year [1996], I think we came to the end of our rope. We completely lost faith in our political system. We simply did not trust politicians (many of whom are very good people and are very good representatives). . . .[2]

What the Constitution Does

The 1997 Constitution creates, for the first time, a comprehensive system of checks and balances that greatly increase transparency and accountability in government, and offer the means to reform politics and usher Thailand towards a more enlightened process of development—and, hopefully, a sustainable quality of life.

Following a period of dictatorship, which lasted until the mid-1970s, Thailand has employed a bicameral system of government, with a Parliament consisting of an elected House of Representatives and a Senate appointed by the prime minister. The Senate has had little power except to scrutinise legislation. Real power, throughout the country, has been concentrated to an overwhelming degree in the hands of cabinet ministers.

The checks and balances of the new Constitution are especially achieved through a decentralisation of some key functions of power from the central government to independent institutions of state—a drastic change from previous constitutions. This new system comprises an array of independent bodies and specialised law courts to monitor and curb abuses at all levels of government. It strengthens some existing institutions.[3] It creates significant opportunities for people's participation in legislative initiatives and planning, and in monitoring officials. Said Anand:

> This constitution addresses the question of the allocation of power between the state and people. . . . The entire rationale is that you deliver state power to the people and you make sure that the people are ready to exercise that power. . . . It's a restructuring of relations between state and people. It's never been done before in our history. . . . Once it starts, it is an irreversible process [people's power]. . . . People are getting wiser.

Among the new institutions:

- A powerful Election Commission will control, arrange, or organise the election of MPs, senators, members of local administrations and local assemblies, and ensure a fair and clean public referendum. It can enlist the help of NGOs to supervise elections. The commission is empowered to order re-counts of votes, annul election results, and call new elections, as well as to investigate and take action in cases of electoral fraud. It is authorised to retrieve relevant documents or evidence from any person, or to summon any person for questioning. It can order government officials and employees of government agencies to carry out any necessary task regarding elections. The commission is obligated to immediately investigate complaints of electoral malpractice.

- The National Counter Corruption Commission, a revamped version of the former "toothless" Counter Corruption Commission, will be called upon by the Senate speaker to investigate petitions of complaint against MPs, senators, cabinet members, and high government officials, including those of the independent government bodies and law courts. It submits reports of its findings to the Senate, which may vote to remove the office-holder in question. The NCCC will consist of a chairman and eight experts, nominated by a 15-member selection panel. It will have a free hand in its staffing, budgeting, and other aspects of its management permitted by law. Removing it from the supervision of the prime minister (or a minister of the prime minister's office) and making its involvement automatic when the Senate speaker receives a corruption complaint, should make it much more effective in pursuing corrupt cabinet ministers.

- Parliamentary Ombudsmen will consider and investigate people's complaints against government officials, and employees of government organisations, state enterprises, or local administrations.

- The National Human Rights Commission, including members from NGOs, will investigate and report acts or omissions which have led to violations of human rights, or which have not complied with international treaties to which Thailand is a signatory. It will also support activities that promote human rights, and compile an annual report.

- The Administrative Court will try cases arising from disputes among government agencies, local administrations or officials, involving the performance of a duty or failure to perform a duty. Ordinary citizens have the right to sue government agencies through the regular courts.

- The Constitutional Court will rule on complaints that actions or laws contradict provisions of the Constitution, and on disputes regarding the power or duties of state organisations under the Constitution.

- The Public Finance Audit Commission and its public finance commissioner.

An elaborate system has been created to place these bodies beyond the control or influence of politicians or political parties. The nomination of members of the bodies will be made by neutral and well-qualified selection committees and forwarded to the Senate for confirmation—a new and important role for the Senate. In the case of the Election Commission, the Supreme Court also reviews the nominees before submitting the list to the Senate speaker. Members of all of the bodies are subject to scrutiny and removal. Anand commented:

> In the past, politicians could sin, commit wrongdoings, and they
> would go scot-free. We introduced a system of monitoring, a
> system of impeachment. We strengthened all the existing

institutions and we created new ones, to make them more independent—not subservient to the government, but responsible to the Parliament. . . . We have converted the Senate from a rather ineffective law-making body, into a monitoring institution. Senators will not have the power to initiate legislation . . . but they will have much more power to monitor the performance of the government and the performance of the elected members of the House of Representatives.

Civil rights and civil liberties are expanded under the Constitution in such a way that they could also be enforced through the introduction of people's participation. Measures here include:

- Right of access to information that is in the pubic domain and which is possessed by a government agency. This right was defined in detail by the Information Act, passed by Parliament in December 1997. Some examples of information that government agencies must provide to the public on request are: plans, projects, and their budgets during the year they are implemented; manuals, orders, or instructions on official works that affect the private sector; contracts, concessions, or joint ventures between the government and the private sector that provide services to the public; cabinet resolutions, or resolutions from committees set up by law or by the cabinet. The Prime Minister's Office minister, Supatra Masdit told *The Nation* in April 1998 that:

This [law] is a revolution, because we have grown up in a society where government bureaucrats consider it to be their duty to protect state information. We will have to change this long-entrenched attitude to make them think that it's honourable, not degrading, to serve up the information to the public.

- At least 50,000 eligible voters may submit a draft law for consideration by Parliament, in cases where the government fails to submit a draft law, or issues a law that is inconsistent with public demands.
- At least 50,000 eligible voters may submit a petition to the Senate speaker calling for the impeachment of the prime minister, a

cabinet member, an MP, a senator, a chief justice, or a ranking bureaucrat for corrupt conduct in office, or for an unjustifiable increase in wealth.

- The government may not impose a ban on printing, newspaper publishing, radio or television broadcasting, except when it is imposed by a court judge corresponding to law. Employees of media organisations, including those of state owned organisations, must not be ideologically controlled by the organisations' owners.
- The government is to provide free a minimum 12 years of basic education.
- The cabinet will be able to call for public referendums.

People's empowerment through local administration gains a significant boost through measures in the Constitution, including:

- election of members of local councils;
- a requirement for mechanisms to be enacted to ensure true independence for local administrations in terms of power, function, finance, and taxing ability;
- the power of local residents to remove chief executives and members of local councils; and
- the power of local residents to propose a local ordinance, signed by 50 per cent of a local administrative region's residents, to be deliberated in the local legislative body.

Local participation in environmental protection is guaranteed in the Constitution:

- Indigenous communities have the right to conserve and revive their traditions, mores, folklore, art, and culture, and to participate in the maintaiance and management of natural resources and the environment.
- Local communities have the right to demand information, clarification, and justification from a government agency before it actually approves, licences, or carries out a project that has an impact on the environment, the health, or hygiene of the people or the community.
- Any activity or project that can seriously affect the quality of the environment is prohibited unless an environmental study and evaluation is undertaken. The study must receive endorsement

from independent agencies, which include representatives from environmental NGOs and university academics, as provided by law.

- Individuals are guaranteed the right to cooperate with state agencies and local communities to conserve and benefit from natural resources and biodiversity, and to protect, promote, and maintain the quality of the environment.

People's organisations have other participatory roles to play in the political system, as well as protecting the environment:

- NGOs may assist in regulating elections.
- NGOs may participate in activities of the National Human Rights Commission.

Many new anti-corruption measures are introduced in the Constitution. Scrutiny of politicians and officials by the NCCC can be initiated through one of four channels to obtain legal proof of corrupt behaviour and unaccounted-for wealth:

1. A motion by the opposition for a no-confidence debate against the prime minister and cabinet members for corrupt behaviour or unaccounted-for wealth which automatically requires an NCCC investigation.
2. A demand made by one quarter of the total MPs.
3. A demand made by 50,000 eligible voters.
4. Demands made by persons sustaining damage as a consequence of corruption. . . .

The last three methods to initiate an investigation also apply to MPs, senators, chief justices, judges, tribunals, members of monitoring bodies, the attorney-general, and ranking bureaucrats. If the NCCC finds the accused party guilty, it must refer the case to the Senate, where the removal from office of the accused must receive a five-eighths majority vote. Other anti-corruption measures require that:

- codes of ethics for political office holders and bureaucrats; and codes of ethics for MPs, senators, and members of House committees be compiled;
- MPs, senators, and cabinet members forego access to concessions or contracts monopolistic in nature awarded by the government—

the private interests of office holders and the interests of the state must not conflict during or beyond their terms in office; and

• public office holders and ranking bureaucrats declare their assets and liabilities, as well as those belonging to their children, prior to assuming office, and after leaving office, by means of official audits.

Anand noted that prior to the 1997 Constitution, scrutiny of government was possible through only one political channel: that of a no-confidence debate in Parliament.

> Proof of corruption is difficult to produce during debates in Parliament. . . . The draft charter attempts to address these problems by creating separate measures for monitoring the political and legal aspects of the application of power. . . .

> On the whole, I don't think that the corruption level or money politics are much greater than what is in existence in many other countries. The only difference is that in our society, under whatever rule—authoritarian or strongman rule—there has been a relative degree of freedom of the press and freedom of expression. In a way, all through this turmoil we have experienced, Thai society has been a very open one. . . . In many countries the corruption level is even greater, but it is very much hidden because of the lack of freedom of information.

Other political restructuring touching the electoral system has the aim of reducing money politics, particularly vote-buying and the seeking of cabinet positions through money. Said Borwornsak Uwanno, secretary to the Constitution Drafting Assembly's drafting committee, and a professor of law at Chulalongkorn University:

> We have to know why politicians invest in elections. . . . Thai law is not like American law, which has details that constrain the discretion of officials. But under Thai laws, full discretion has been given to cabinet ministers. So, that is the main cause of corruption. Politicians foresee that if they invest, for example,

only 30 million baht in an election, they can get back more, even
one billion baht [through corruption]. So they invest.

The constitution attempts to combat vote buying through stronger
monitoring and through the newly-instituted powers of the Election
Commission to pronounce immediately on election fraud. Additionally,
the Constitution stipulates that the counting of votes will be conducted
at a single, specified locality in each electorate. Under the old system
votes were counted at each polling station where vote buyers could control
bribed voters by inspecting electoral returns. Additionally, it is thought
that the newly-introduced system of proportional representation through
party lists (described below) would also serve to diminish vote buying.
The reasoning is that senior party figures who may have bought votes in
the past would stand in the party lists where vote buying is impractical
because the entire country is the constituency for the party lists.

An "entirely new political structure", as Anand described it, offers to
make inroads into abolishing the old-style politics which precipitated
the country towards crisis. The keys to this are the independent Election
Commission (already described), proportional representation through
party lists, the separation of executive and legislature, single-member
constituencies for the House of Representatives (abolishing the multi-
member constituency system), the redefinition of powers of the Senate,
and a requirement to introduce new legislation for the increased regulation
of the affairs of political parties.

The introduction of a party list system of proportional representation
follows other countries such as Germany, Japan, and New Zealand. One
hundred seats in Thailand's House of Representatives are to be filled by
election from party lists, and 400 by single-member constituency
elections. Thus, voters have to fill in two separate ballots. Each political
party presents a list of one hundred candidates who are available for
election from the party list, and the number of MPs it gains from the list
corresponds to the percentage of votes it receives among parties gaining
at least 5 per cent of the votes for party lists. Parties receiving less than
5 per cent of the national vote for political parties are not entitled to
seats from the party list quota; this provision is expected to consolidate
the multi-party system of coalition government by screening out small
parties.

It is thought that the perceived low quality of MPs gaining election under the old system can be remedied under the party list system, which will open the door for qualified persons to make their way into Parliament without becoming immersed in cynical or corrupt election practices. The list system would allow parties to display their "selling points" by putting prominent, respectable names at the top of the lists, who could then be portrayed as a "shadow cabinet".

The separation of executive and legislature is another measure, particularly promoted by Anand, which was thought to offer the prospect of reducing corruption among cabinet ministers. It calls for all cabinet members, including the prime minister, to resign their seats in the House upon being appointed to cabinet. Anand explained:

> When candidates enter the electoral process, many of them, or most of them, have the ambition to become cabinet ministers. They are not just happy and contented to be legislative members. . . . Their aim is to get a seat in the cabinet. So, with money politics, anyone with a group of five or six cronies subservient to him or beholden to him can demand a seat in cabinet if his faction should be included. So that gave rise to the quota system. So when you have such a cabinet of 50 [as in the old system] the major parties may control 40 seats, but another 10 are controlled by chieftains from this province or that province. . . .
>
> So we thought that if we could devise a method which would keep them away from cabinet posts, it would, to a certain degree, reduce the temptation to invest money in an election. So the separation of duties is designed that if you should be appointed a cabinet member, you have to resign from your legislative duties. . . . The moment you leave the cabinet, you cannot go back to your seat; you are no longer a member of Parliament; you cannot engage in the extortion game or in blackmail; you become an ordinary citizen and you have to stand in the queue for by-election or whatnot. . . . But, the moment [an MP] becomes a cabinet member, and if he is still a member of Parliament, he can wield very large influence. So the idea is to put a break in [such MPs'] thinking.

Before they join the cabinet, they are not sure how long they can remain in cabinet. They have to think very hard as to which cabinet they are joining, which prime minister they are joining. In the past, they could become an MP, they could rise up to become a cabinet minister, they could engage in blackmail, extortion, in any kind of very devious manipulative politics to serve their own ends, because they knew that even if they were chucked out of the cabinet, they could always go back to the Parliament and create trouble for the prime minister and the cabinet. This [new separation of executive and legislature] is only one example [of measures] to reduce corruption and money politics. . . .

The redefinition of powers of the Senate, in the words of Anand, converts it from "a rather ineffective law-making body, into a monitoring institution". The Constitution sets the number of senators at 200, to be directly elected from Thailand's 76 provinces, with each province being one constituency and electing at least one senator. It is intended that the Senate should be a neutral body. Therefore, senators cannot be members of political parties, or hold positions in political parties; additionally, they must not have been an MP within one year before elections for the Senate. The Senate is entitled to participate in general debates, and to scrutinise laws, but not to introduce legislation. It meets for specific purposes in joint session with the House. It may delay, and offer amendments to, legislation submitted to it by the House, but it cannot vote down such legislation. Its main functions are monitoring politics and administration of the country; scrutinising appointments to the various independent state commissions, bodies, and law courts; and initiating corruption investigations and conducting impeachment processes. However, the function and membership of the Senate remains a contentious issue. (This is examined in the section below.)

The question remains, when will Thailand's political mess come to an end? This was asked of Anand during his visit to the Foreign Correspondents Club of Thailand, following his explanation of the various points about the new Constitution. He answered:

> The Thais are pragmatic people. If you look at our history, there
> are times when things changed very quickly in Thailand, without

any planning, any organisation. Pragmatism is a tremendous asset. Things can get worse and worse, but when you reach a certain point, somehow there is a correcting procedure. . . .

The learning process has begun. A new social force has emerged, not from street demonstrations, not from fighting in the street . . . but [from] a learning process by a larger body of citizens in this country. . . . And [once they secure the Constitution] they will maintain it, they will cherish it. It will make them into stakeholders. And that is the ultimate objective of the whole exercise.

How the Drafting Progressed

The movement to reform the Constitution gained increasing support from political activists and academics following the 1991 military coup and the imposition of a new constitution by the coup makers, and following the May 1992 bloodshed when troops opened fire on demonstrators opposing the military's apparent manipulation of the 1992 election.

The major questions of contention were, who would write it and how would it be done? At issue was Article 211 of the 1991 Constitution, which stipulated that the Constitution could be amended only by a simple majority of parliamentarians, then comprising 391 members of the House of Representatives and 270 senators. There was a prevailing feeling among political observers that entrusting the writing of a new constitution to politicians and their appointees in the Senate would serve only to perpetuate perceived abuses of power and of public administration, which were seen as threatening the future development of Thai society and economy. *The Nation* noted that:

The bid to amend Article 211 stemmed from a 1991 article called *Constitutionalism: A Way Out for Thailand* written by public law expert, Prof. Amorn Chantatasomboon. He proposed that a new constitution should be drafted to become a tool to control the power of representatives of the public. Changes in Article 211 were proposed to set up an apolitical, constitution-drafting committee that [would] include no parliamentarians. The proposals were later adopted by the Democracy Development

Committee, which was appointed by then Parliament president Marut Bunnag in June 1994, following pressure by pro-democracy groups. The panel, led by academic Prawase Wasi, proposed changes to the charter's Article 211, to allow non-parliamentarians to draft a new constitution.[4]

A breakthrough came on 22 November 1995, when coalition partners of the Banharn government agreed in principle to amend Article 211.[5] An influential player in this decision was the prime minister's brother and member of Parliament, former academic Chumpol Silpa-archa, who headed the government-appointed Political Reform Committee. Subsequently, the government announced on 2 January 1996 that it would submit a draft to Parliament the following March to amend Article 211, to allow non-parliamentarians to participate in a constitution-drafting committee.[6]

Political debate and manoeuvring continued throughout 1996 on how to select the Constitutional Drafting Assembly (CDA). Some politicians proposed that the assembly should be elected, drawing a rebuke from committee chairman Chumpol that such an arrangement would allow politicians and capitalists to buy their way into the charter-drafting process. An alternative proposal was made by an alliance of opposition MPs, academics, and senators that a 99-member assembly be set up. It would consist of one representative from each of the 76 provinces who would then select another 23 members—experts with an academic background—to the assembly. The proposal was endorsed on 13 June by the joint House-Senate *ad hoc* committee vetting a charter amendment bill.[7] However, many old-style politicians continued to fight the growing movement to curtail their influence through a drastically revamped constitution.

The showdown came on 22 August, when Parliament agreed to set up a constitution-drafting assembly that would exclude MPs and senators. But Parliament voted to empower itself to elect members of the drafting assembly and to retain the power of veto over the assembly's draft. Parliament would vote whether or not to accept the draft in its entirety; it could not single out portions of the draft for rejection. In the event of a veto, a public referendum would be held to either accept or reject the draft.

Amid continuing controversy over political influence on the drafting process, Parliament adopted the following formula to elect the 99 members of the CDA:

- All candidates in each province would select 10 nominees from among themselves, and forward the nominations to Parliament.
- Parliament would meet to elect one member from among the 10 nominees forwarded from each province.
- Parliament would likewise select 23 members of the CDA from nominees in the academic "expert" categories.

It was stipulated that the candidates could not be affiliated to a political party. But, as the process began and the provincial candidates were announced, fears were expressed that political parties were covertly pushing forward their own supporters. The *Bangkok Post* of 15 December 1996 noted that:

> Over 19,000 candidates vying for seats in the CDA will today choose among themselves 760 nominees of whom only 76 will be picked by Parliament. . . . [The selection process] has already been marred by widespread allegations that some of the candidates have resorted to "bloc vote" tactics by arranging their supporters or stooges to register as candidates in order that they can vote for them.

The first phase of the process resulted in lawyers making up the largest single group among the 760 provincial nominees for seats in the CDA— following earlier urgings from the Law Society of Thailand for its provincial members to stand as candidates. A total of 270 lawyers were nominated, followed by 174 businessmen, 148 retired government officials, and 50 former MPs.[8] The final election of the provincial members of the CDA took place in Parliament on 26 December. *The Nation* noted that:

> The government came under a storm of criticism . . . after [a parliamentary vote for the CDA] produced a membership remarkably similar to a shortlist allegedly circulated by the coalition before the crucial vote. The uproar was particularly directed at the ruling New Aspiration Party. . . . The shortlist shown to reporters by NAP MPs matched the final result in all but 11 provinces.[9]

Among the 23 expert members, Thailand's leading reformer, the former prime minister, Anand Panyarachun, was very narrowly elected in the university nominations category. His near-defeat was attributed to influential politicians of the coalition government lobbying Parliament against his election. On 20 January 1997, Anand was elected chairman of the CDA's key charter-drafting committee. Uthai Pimchaichon had earlier been elected president of the CDA as a whole.

The Constitution Drafting Assembly was given 240 days to write a draft constitution. To carry out its various tasks it initially set up five committees: for charter drafting, public relations, research, gathering public opinion and organising public hearings, and for secretarial functions.

Apart from the many important new provisions to guarantee human rights, popular participation, and checks and balances in politics, four major issues created considerable debate prior to, and during, the constitutional drafting. Some of them are still not resolved entirely satisfactorily:

1. Whether or not to have direct election of the prime minister?
2. Whether or not to institute a separation of the executive and the legislative functions of Parliament, and if so, how to do it effectively?
3. How to choose the Senate?
4. Whether or not the mixed election system, with both proportional list representation and directly-elected constituency MPs, would be effective or divisive?

(Some of these issues are examined at greater length later in this chapter.) Other issues generated a lot of heat, especially from those sectors of society with vested interests to protect. These included:

• The status of the various new, specialised courts created by the draft constitution and whether or not they would be under the control of, or independent of, the existing legal establishment. This issue provoked protests and demonstrations from existing judges, and split the legal profession.
• The further empowerment of *tambon* (local) councils to decentralise power to local communities at the expense of the powerful Interior Ministry.

177

- The stipulation that tens of thousands of village headmen around the country, who had lifetime tenure and most often strong links with political parties, would have to submit themselves for election. Village headmen, defensively jealous of their guaranteed tenure and the political influence they could wield in alliances with political parties, threatened to march *en masse* to Bangkok in protest. A compromise was reached that vacancies for the position of headman would be filled by election, while current headmen would not have to submit to elections for 10 years.
- Whether or not the supposed political party allegiances among provincial members of the CDA would, in the end, lead to sabotage of reform proposals put forward by the academic, "expert" members?

The final outcome was much more favourable to political reform than the great majority of analysts had anticipated even a few months earlier. The expected rejection of the charter by Parliament, under the feared influence of old-style political leaders, did not happen. The charter was passed on 27 September 1997 by a vote of 578 to 16, with 17 representatives and senators abstaining, and 40 absent.[10]

The country's deepening financial and economic crisis and the ineptitude of successive governments in preventing it, undoubtedly played a part in discrediting the draft charter's influential opponents among the old-style political elite (the "dinosaurs"). The crisis certainly underscored the need for political reform, and helped to crystallise public opinion in favour of the new charter.

Also very important in generating national, pro-charter sentiment was the comprehensive process of consultation with the public through seminars and committees at regional and provincial level, and through questionnaires and the press. Provincial consultations were enthusiastically attended across a broad spectrum of society, representing a unique upsurge of civic consciousness which undoubtedly led people to feel for the first time that the Constitution was really "their" charter.

The draft charter's various monitoring systems and mechanisms to fight corruption and abuse of power came through virtually unscathed. Perhaps the most controversial issue, the requirement that cabinet ministers give up their seats in Parliament, also survived the often bitter opposition of prominent politicians.

The Struggle for the Senate

If the influence of the old-style politicians was felt in the CDA, their biggest victory came perhaps with the last-minute changes to the chapter governing the election of the Senate. Many reformers had envisaged a revamped Senate as a body where independent expertise could be assembled, an expertise that had been sorely lacking in the House of Representatives and in the cabinet.

Giving new powers to the Senate under the draft Constitution—as part of the drive to clean up politics—made it more important than ever to get "good" senators elected. For example, the Senate now has the key role of giving final approval to nominees to the various new and reorganised commissions and courts before they are appointed by His Majesty the King. These independent bodies—designed to monitor politicians and to carry out certain high-level political functions—include the Election Commission, the Ombudsman, the National Human Rights Commission, the Constitutional Court, the Administrative Court's judicial commission, the National Counter Corruption Commission, and the Public Finance Audit Commission and its Public Finance Commissioner. (In addition, the Senate selects two members of the 14-member commission of the Court of Justice.) But there was no ready consensus on how to choose senators prior to, or during, the deliberations of the CDA. Proposals on how to select senators underwent a number of changes and reversals as the debate went on, with the academic members of the CDA in conflict with the provincially-elected members.

The first concrete proposal on how to elect the Senate came from a sub-committee of Anand's charter-drafting committee on 24 February. It proposed that the number of senators be reduced to 200 and that they come from indirect elections. Official bodies such as provincial councils and *tambon* administrative councils would elect 10 people from each province to a so-called assembly of experts, making up a total of 760 candidates. Former prime ministers, House speakers, Senate speakers and opposition leaders would jointly name organisations which would be empowered to nominate 10 people each to the assembly. The prime minister and opposition leader would each nominate 100 people to the assembly.[11] This proposal underwent significant changes in the main committee.

Anand presented his committee's first complete draft of the charter to the full CDA on 7 May. Chapter 6, defining the Parliament, set the maximum membership of the Senate at 200 senators divided into two chambers. Chamber one was to have senators directly elected from each province at a ratio of one senator per one million people. Chamber two was to have specially-selected senators numbering three-fourths of the total membership of chamber one. These latter senators would have been picked by a special selection committee comprising a former House speaker, a former Senate speaker, a former deputy Parliament speaker, and a former deputy Senate speaker, none of whom could hold any politically-appointed positions, but who were allowed to be members of political parties.[12] The special selection committee would divide chamber two candidates into two groups:

1. Those with political experience, legal expertise, or academic credentials. They were required to have served as chief of a judge's quorum on the Supreme Court, as deputy attorney-general, as director-general of a government agency at the departmental level, as a university rector, or as head of the Law Society of Thailand.
2. Those in other professions. They were required to have worked in an organisation selected by the committee that is lawfully certified and widely recognised.

Opinion polls had shown that the people favoured a directly-elected Senate. However, the idea was not favoured by members of the prevailing Senate. They took a stand in May criticising the idea of an elected Senate, saying that such a move would likely destroy the Senate's political neutrality in supervising legislation, as elected senators would have to be accountable to their constituencies.[13] (The Senate of that time had been appointed by the since-discredited Banharn administration, which governed from July 1995 to October 1996. However, it was probably the best assemblage of senators yet seen, as many respected people had been appointed, going somewhat against the historical trend of appointing party supporters and military officers to the Senate.)

Thus the debate about the merits of an elected or appointed Senate, or a combination of the two, continued. Public hearings of the CDA also found a substantial body of public opinion that wanted no Senate at all.

Meanwhile, a vetting committee was set up in the middle of May to scrutinise and amend the completed draft. Anand, despite some opposition, was chosen once again to chair that committee. The question of how to choose the Senate became increasingly contentious in June. *The Nation* reported:

> In one of the first major amendments to the charter draft, the CDA's vetting committee [on 2 June] decided to scrap a provision on the direct election of the Senate, citing concerns over political influence in the upper chamber. . . . The vetting committee agreed to keep the maximum number of senators at 200, but abolished the clause on direct election. Debate was inconclusive on how senators should be selected. . . .[14]

Tongchat Rattanawicha, spokesman for the vetting committee, said the clause on direct election was scrapped because panel members agreed that it would be difficult to bar political parties from asserting their influence:

> Senatorial candidates could be secretly supported by political parties and we would never know. . . . The most important qualification of the Senate is that it has to be politically neutral. We decided against direct election to protect this principle.[15]

Two weeks later, the vetting committee set the stage for indirect election of the Senate by proposing senators be chosen from certain groups. A proposal elaborated by committee secretary Borwornsak Uwanno and executive member Kaewsan Atipo called for three main groups: 70 specialists, 60 representatives of various occupations, and 70 representatives of local administrative organisations. The first group would comprise 20 academics, 20 specialists, 20 former government officials, and 10 representatives of non-governmental organisations. The second group would comprise 20 farmers, 20 labourers, 10 merchants, and 10 industrialists. For the third group, Bangkok's district councillors and city councillors would elect five representatives, while other provincial administrative organisations would elect a total of 15. Municipalities nationwide would elect 25 senators, and *tambon* administrative organisations would elect 25, bringing the total in the third group to 70. However, the committee could not make a final decision and suggested that the method used for the selection of senators be finalised in a supplemental law to be enacted by Parliament later.[16]

Meanwhile, the decision of the vetting committee, led by university academics, to rule out direct elections caused a reaction among a large bloc of provincial representatives. They denounced the vetting committee for refusing to heed public sentiment, revealed in surveys, for the direct election of senators. They set up two committees to "shadow" the vetting committee.[17]

The vetting committee finished its scrutiny of the articles concerning senators on 17 June, after 14 hours of deliberations over three days. The proposed formula for the Senate changed once again, as *The Nation* reported:

> The committee resolved to have Parliament issue a supplemental law to determine the selection method of 200 senators. The panel stipulated that senators would comprise 60 specialist senators, 60 representatives from different professions, and 80 representatives of local administrative organisations. The panel stipulated only that the specialists should include academics, former government administrators, and representatives of NGOs. The rest would be decided by Parliament when passing the supplemental law.

When the vetting committee completed its work and the CDA's second reading of the newly-amended draft began on 7 July, the antagonism of the provincial representatives against the committee's academic membership became apparent. The CDA embarked on a rewriting, "article by article" as *The Nation* put it, of the committee's draft. Eight days after the second reading began, the newspaper wrote that the chief spokesman of the academic bloc, Borwornsak, had borne the brunt of the provincial members' ire:

> CDA members who have not taken part in drafting and vetting the draft have turned the second reading into a personal fight between themselves and Borwornsak. The non-panel members have stood up against Borwornsak's proposals or voted for the amendment of some articles, only because it was Borwornsak who was defending them.[18]

On 16 July, the CDA voted to scrap the vetting committee's preference for the selection of senators and reverted to the previous proposal for direct elections of senators, this time for the entire Senate. *The Nation* reported the vote as 42–30 for direct election.[19] The decision created another storm of contention. The *Bangkok Post* highlighted the issues at the centre of the storm:

> Critics say the resolution will replicate the system by which members of the Lower House come to office. They say candidates for the Upper House will buy votes and engage in the worst of practices the political reform drive was designed to eradicate. . . . Borwornsak said elected senators would repeat the mistakes of MPs. For example, they would try to divert resources from the central fund to develop their constituencies in order to secure their political bases. Borwornsak was worried senators would be unable to perform their duty in monitoring state power since they would lose neutrality.[20]

Yet another committee was set up by the CDA, following the victory of the direct-election advocates, to review the roles and duties of senators coming from a direct election. On 1 August, the CDA accepted the wording of the draft, pending a final vote on 15 August. Senate Speaker Meechai Ruchuphan, meanwhile, warned that direct election of senators may destabilise the parliamentary system:

> I think elections of senators will be affected by vote buying. The CDA empowers the Senate to appoint key monitoring agencies, but if we don't get neutral senators, the whole system may collapse.[21]

Lingering Doubts

Given the manoeuvring, politicking and influence-mongering that underlay the drafting of the Constitution, what are the chances that the new charter can deliver the good government that the country so badly needs following a steady decline in the competence and sincerity of governments coming to power in the 1990s (up to November 1997).

The legacy of those governments was an economic crisis arising from the Crash of 97. An environmental crisis from decades of neglect and corruption continues throughout the country. Thailand is experiencing an urban crisis in Bangkok and other major cities and towns. These growing crises have, more poignantly than ever, exposed the country's major political weakness: that cabinet ministers, recruited through political parties and the cabinet quota system of coalition government, cannot measure up to the task of rational development of the country.

Thailand has many highly-qualified, talented people with administrative capability who, if they were to take up all the key positions in the cabinet, could raise the development of Thai society to a much higher level—a sustainable level—than we see at present. However, up to now, these people have largely been excluded from power by the cynical, get-rich-quick mentality that pervades Thai politics. Following this observation, there are two points of concern regarding the new charter:

1. It does not do enough to ensure that capable, honest, and dedicated ministers will be appointed to cabinet. The draft does not actually provide a mechanism specifically designed to recruit high-quality cabinet ministers. The controversial proposal to require ministers to relinquish their MP status once they are appointed to the cabinet has been commended as a separation of legislative functions from executive functions that will improve the quality of cabinet. But is this guaranteed? It seems that this "separation" is somewhat superficial. It has diverted attention from the real obstacle to good government: cabinet ministers will continue to be recruited through the self-serving political party system, which has most often produced businessmen-politicians who are unresponsive to the needs of the country's development.

2. It still basically perpetuates the cabinet quota system of coalition government, whereby parties place in the cabinet a proportionate number of ministers corresponding to their number of seats in the House. Members of Parliament who are ambitious to become cabinet ministers may be more cautious if they stand to lose their House seats; but such a provision seems unlikely to negate their need for money to obtain cabinet positions in the first place, and unlikely to negate political parties' inclination to demand cabinet quotas according to their relative strength in the House. While the quota system persists, there will still be no transparent screening process to impede the entrance into the cabinet of politicians who merely represent money-making, vested interests. Under the new Constitution, the rectitude of ministers may be

challenged, but the competence and hidden agendas of ministers cannot easily be challenged.

Additionally, the cabinet quota system in Thailand is a factor contributing to political instability and to a damaging lack of continuity in policy making, as MPs vie for positions of influence. It will likely still remain a major incentive for vote buying. Cabinet posts dealing with the economy need to be filled by persons with high-level competence and understanding of how the twists and turns of the global economy affect Thailand. They must be able to resist the pleas for "special treatment" by vested interests, while keeping their focus on the macro-economy.

There has been some hope expressed that the proposed mixed electoral system for the House of Representatives, comprising MPs elected from constituencies and from party lists, will improve the quality of cabinet ministers and help reduce vote buying. This, too, is subject to doubt. When we consider the huge sums of money seeking to buy influence in Thai politics, how can we expect that, merely by creating a proportional representation system, "good" men (with no money to spend) will somehow replace representatives of vested interests in cabinet positions? This may, however, happen in the long term as other anti-corruption measures in the Constitution start to bite, and as the electorate becomes more knowledgeable.

But in the short term, the party list system could, in fact, become a more convenient avenue for patronage-dispensing politicians to buy their way into cabinet portfolios. Positions at the top of the party list will simply go to wealthy politicians making the biggest contributions. This would suit ministerial aspirants who previously relied on money-dumping in their constituencies to win election. That practice is illegal and everybody knows about it. And, under the new, independent Election Commission, there are increased chances that enforcement of laws against vote buying may actually result in disqualifications and prosecution of dishonest candidates. Under proportional representation and the list system, large sums of money need only change hands among senior party members—a much safer, in-house method of buying cabinet positions under the cabinet quota system.

All of this offers compelling logic that cabinet appointees should emerge from a screening process. Such a provision does not exist in the new Constitution, and most observers would be inclined to give the new system a chance before calling for a renewed attempt at constitutional reform. But, if the need arises, how could it be done?

Screening Candidates for Cabinet

Democratic principles can be upheld and even enhanced by a process to screen candidates for cabinet. For example, in the United States, cabinet and high judicial appointments must be approved by the Senate, which has often voted against dubious nominees. Although Thailand does not follow a presidential system, this fact does not overrule the value of a screening system for cabinet appointments. But how to do it?

This writer favours a politically-neutral Senate, comprising highly-respected and independent senators from a wide range of occupations, to conduct a screening process and propose a short list of nominees to head each government ministry. The prime minister could then choose his cabinet from those lists with a view towards enhancing harmony and competence in government. This would be a genuine separation of executive and legislature. MPs and cabinet ministers would come from different sources and the latter would have no obligations to party patronage systems. The checks and balances already devised in the 1997 Constitution could then also be implemented more effectively.

Such a screening system to choose (mainly) non-political cabinet ministers would make it somewhat easier to prosecute ministers indulging in corruption. At present, corrupt ministers are never prosecuted because their political influence within the party and the government is too great. Ministers suspected of corruption may often control a faction of MPs that is necessary to maintaining the government's majority in Parliament. Governments can simply arrange for any attempts at prosecution of such ministers to be abandoned. A minister may be discredited and thus dropped from the cabinet without any admission of guilt forthcoming. Such a discredited minister may come back again, thanks to the cabinet-quota system, to join a subsequent government.

Where ministers do not originate from the political party system, they do not influence the balance of power in Parliament; they are simply executives chosen by the Senate and the prime minister to carry out a job. The prime minister or the government, therefore, will find it much easier to disown a corrupt minister under this system. Such ministers, with no factional support in the House of Representatives, can be prosecuted and jailed. Therefore, the proposal (which will be elaborated upon shortly) to have the Senate involved in selecting cabinet ministers could have an enormous effect on cleaning up politics.

The method of choosing senators which was finally adopted by the Constitution Drafting Assembly and endorsed by Parliament, emerged from controversy. Many political critics regard the direct election of senators by the same voters who choose members of the House of Representatives, as a blunder. Such direct election mistakenly assumes a need for senatorial representation on a geographic basis (a need that is already fulfilled by direct election for members of the House); but it leaves unfulfilled the need for high-level and well-recognised expertise from a broad cross-section of occupations, to contribute directly to the political process from within the Senate. This is perhaps the most serious flaw in the 1997 Constitution's bid to achieve good governance. It is a situation faced by many countries, where the parliamentary system (especially in coalition politics) often places partisan and incompetent ministers in the cabinet. Thus, future reform in Thailand may well centre once again on the Senate.

A Senate of Respected Experts

Senators should be elected (rather than appointed as in earlier constitutions), but this does not mean they should be chosen from the same pool that the professional politicians come from, or chosen by the same electors who elect members of Parliament. The Senate can be used to recruit highly-qualified and politically-neutral people into the governing process.

I recommend a system of functional constituencies (which can also be described as professional or sectoral constituencies). Groups such as educators, lawyers, engineers, workers' organisations, farmers' groups—to name some—would directly elect senators. The certified members of each group would have their own electoral register, maintained and updated by the Election Commission. It follows that the members of a certain profession who are most respected by their colleagues would gain election. One would suppose that this arrangement would serve to undermine the destructive system of government by political patronage, which still may surface in a popularly-elected Senate, as mandated in the 1997 Constitution. Powers of the Senate could include:

- the power to approve, amend, or reject the budget, which would first be approved by the House; and
- the power of senators to introduce legislation into the Senate, which, if adopted, would be forwarded to the cabinet and House for consideration.

Thus, the Senate could enhance its role as a think-tank on legislation, and keep alive beneficial legislation which might be threatened as coalition governments come and go. It would be much more difficult to reverse a well-thought-out policy merely for personal or party interest. Continuity of important legislation would be maintained if it stayed alive in the Senate and could be reintroduced into the House by cabinet ministers. It would be worth considering whether or not a reformed Senate should vote on all legislation passed by the House.

Under this proposed system, senators would be eligible to serve in the cabinet, and—for the sake of improving the quality of decision making—could well take up the great majority of cabinet positions. A constitutional revision might also stipulate that ministerial positions would require suitable qualifications. For example, the minister of finance would need a degree in finance from a recognised university and should have some years of experience in the Finance Ministry, central bank, a large private bank, or as financial director of a large corporation. It might be seen as a great benefit to the country for the minister of finance to come from the Senate, having been first elected by his peers in the financial sector.

There are many examples in other countries of senates that have varied powers and memberships. Many incorporate the principle of the separation of powers as a safeguard towards good government. Thailand's Senate should be tailored for the country's particular stage of development, to address its particular problems.

Some foreign examples: Australia's Senate is chosen during general elections using a proportional system. It votes on the budget, and its members can be government ministers—the most prominent example over recent years has been Senator Gareth Evans, who became a long-serving Australian foreign minister. Japan's Upper House of the Diet is elected in separate elections from the Lower House and has power to pass or reject the government's budget. The American Senate is perhaps the best known; the US Constitution—famous for its principles of checks and balances and separation of powers—gives certain unique powers to the Senate, such as approval of treaties.

Hong Kong incorporated functional constituencies into elections for some seats in its Legislative Council in 1992, beginning an attempt to introduce a measure of democracy into the then British colony. Colonial Hong Kong's system of functional constituencies deserves study to see which elements may be applicable to Thailand.

A proposal for functional constituencies was raised in Thailand during debate on the 1974 Constitution. Difficulties were encountered at that time in defining the requirements of functional constituencies. Such a system was seen as suitable for urban societies, but more difficult in rural societies. Problems surrounding geographical factors were also encountered.[22] Additionally, at that time, professional groups were not well organised into societies. However, the situation by 1997 had changed considerably. Functional constituencies—this time for the Senate—should be seriously reconsidered. In effect, this is a proposal for power sharing between the House and Senate—at the same time enhancing the quality of input into the whole governmental system.

It is not the job of MPs or members of the cabinet to promote business interests while in office; and, by mid-1999, it was still not clear whether cabinet ministers rising up through political parties could escape from the domination of money politics and decision making through the patronage system. Political parties should be debating national policy and not merely devising strategies to make money out of legislative and administrative decisions. A lot of Thailand's accumulated ills arise from the fact that Thai governments have been unable to generate and implement development-oriented policy inputs under the political patronage system, which strives to place politically-loyal party hacks into the cabinet. The best talents available in the country should be the prime choices for the cabinet. There is no need for a large number of professional politicians to be in the cabinet to guide the formulation of policies; this can be done through party caucus meetings and parliamentary committees.

I originally wrote about reform of the Senate in Thailand in 1992, and since then I have become even more convinced that the number of cabinet seats being filled by members of political parties in the House of Representatives should be drastically reduced. The early 1980s saw proponents of democracy calling for a reduction in the number of cabinet members who are non-elected "outsiders". But it is patently obvious that as the percentage of professional politicians in the cabinet has increased, the quality of administration of the country has stagnated or declined.

Thailand should consider giving no more than a minimum number of cabinet positions to politicians coming from the House. Large political parties in a coalition government should be entitled to no more than two cabinet members. They could name a deputy prime minister and another minister of state, while smaller coalition partners could name one minister of state (i.e. ministers without portfolio) if they do not meet the qualifications for a portfolio. India, for example, in the past has made use of ministers of state. The prime minister would continue to be an elected member of the House and a political party leader.

Having senior party MPs in the cabinet as ministers of state would reinforce the proposition that MPs and ministers are there to formulate policy, not to use the ministries and departments of government to further business interests or personal gain. How to actually choose cabinet members to head ministries? Consider this sequence:

1. Senators would nominate candidates from the Senate itself (or perhaps also some from outside the Senate) to head a particular cabinet portfolio.
2. All senators would cast one ballot for one candidate to fill the portfolio.
3. The prime minister would, after due consideration, choose the portfolio head from among the three nominees gaining the highest number of senators' votes.

Having senators thus screen prospective cabinet members should ensure a high calibre of choices to head government ministries, while having the prime minister make the final selection should enhance the prime minister's authority over cabinet and enhance the chances for harmonious conduct of cabinet affairs.

Having cabinet members thus chosen for their expertise and character could be expected to deal a most effective blow to money politics and vote buying. Government policy would primarily emerge from the House of Representatives, but a new process of give-and-take arising from greater power-sharing with the Senate would hopefully generate more progressive and timely legislation. The cabinet, comprising members from both the Senate and the House, could act as a point of mediation in the governing process.

Bringing functional constituencies and sectoral representation to the Senate would also ensure that voices of neglected sectors of society and marginal groups could be directly heard. For example, Thailand's oft-supressed labour movement could have a direct voice.

This move would benefit the country at large. If a mass organisation representing the industrial labour force (or any other sectoral organisation) was given the right to elect senators, then that organisation could be subject to supervision by the Election Commission to ensure that its leadership elections, its election of senators, and its organisational set-up and finances, all conform to democratic rules. We could expect that such a system would lead to greater responsibility within such organisations, and to their greater responsibility in contributing to national development through a broadened political system and promotion of a civil society.

This writer likes the provision of the American system where a senator is elected for a six-year term and one-third of the Senate is elected every two years. This arrangement provides much-needed continuity, which is not found in Thailand's 1997 Constitution, which calls for the whole Senate to be elected every six years, and makes out-going senators ineligible for re-election.

If Thailand, in future, comes to appreciate the merits of a Senate elected through functional constituencies, the major contentious point may be what number of seats to allocate to various sectors. Here are some principles, and a tentative composition of Senate constituencies which may act as a prototype for further discussion. Since the Senate may best be chosen following the principle of electing one-third of its members every two years, the number of senators to be elected from each occupational and sectoral group could conveniently be allocated in multiples of three. The following tentative list is not comprehensive; finalising a list would require broad discussion:

Educators	9
Businessmen	9
Farmers	9

Financial	9
Lawyers	9
ex-Military	9
ex-Officials	9
Workers	9
Economists	6
Medical	6
Architects	3
Engineers	3
ex-Diplomats	3
Media	3
NGOs	3

Some rationale is needed for my allocation of various numbers of seats to each profession/sector. For example, general workers and farmers constitute the largest (and most under-represented) sectoral groups in the country, and therefore merit the maximum allocation.

Educators cover the whole range of teachers, up to the rank of university professors. There is a great deal of high-level expertise in many fields here to be tapped. This is also the case with former government officials.

Businessmen are central movers of a free-enterprise economy, and the most respected businessmen have much knowledge to contribute to economic policy making.

Financial experts will be needed in monitoring the finance system, and in devising improved accounting methods and financial legislation to eliminate graft and misuse of funds.

Respected lawyers are needed in substantial numbers to facilitate the drafting of legislation, to monitor the functioning of the legal system, and to push for reforms to the legal system.

Although the military has sometimes been regarded as acting against democracy, it has a large capacity to contribute towards democratic development, with a wealth of experience amongst its retired officer corps. Hence, the maximum allocation. Active military officers, as with active government officials, should not be eligible for Senate election because they cannot be both masters and employees of the state at the same time.

The best among retired diplomats should be welcome in the Senate to add their contribution to foreign policy debate. This is a small professional group, but with a highly-relevant expertise in international statecraft. Thus they are recommended for the minimum number of seats (three). Likewise, other small professional groups with particularly relevant expertise may be considered for representation.

The object in adopting functional constituencies is not to achieve proportional representation of the various sectors, but to create positions in the Senate for men of ability coming from a broad range of professions. The 3-6-9 formula (this could be modified if it were decided that the number of senators should be greater) recognises that mass-based organisations with potential membership of hundreds of thousands, such as small farmers, could expect nine representatives of ability to emerge, while professions demanding high qualification and specialisation, while small in membership, could be expected to put at least three outstanding people in the Senate.

My proposal for Senate reform may not look like anything in operation in other countries, but Thailand is a unique society at a transitional stage of its development. The proposal, I believe, is suitable for Thailand's present stage of development.

Choosing the Prime Minister

A dilemma has arisen on this question. During the debate on constitutional reform, opinion polls consistently showed that a majority of respondents wanted to elect the prime minister directly. Leading CDA members, including Anand (chairman of the CDA's drafting committee) and Borwornsak (secretary to the Constitution Drafting Assembly's drafting committee) said this was too problematical for Thailand at present.

Anand said on 18 March 1997 that direct election was not yet suitable for Thailand as many changes needed to be made to the overall system first. One problem was that a prime minister coming from a direct election could be corrupted by the power of the people's mandate:

> It could be a good system, but practically it still has a lot of weak points. . . . It's human nature to be corrupted by power, especially when one thinks he has so much because it came from the people. This is not an easy issue to give clear-cut answers to. We have to know what good and weak points it will lead to. . . .[23]

193

Borwornsak objected about possible government instability if the prime minister came from a party other than the one with the most MPs. Another objection regarded the perceived problem that Parliament would not be able to revoke the premier's status, and another problem that the prime minister would not be able to dissolve the House.

Ammar Siamwalla of the Thailand Development Research Institute noted that direct election of the prime minister would result in a dramatic change to the political system and would require major legislative amendments. He suggested the country play safe by changing the system gradually.[24] In April, the then prime minister, Chavalit, said his party would support direct elections of the prime minister if it would lead to better government stability, but His Majesty the King would have to retain the power to appoint the prime minister. Candidates in such a leadership election should also be leaders of political parties.[25]

In May, another suggestion surfaced that the prime minister should come from the party list; an arrangement that would be closer to direct election, while avoiding many of its problems. However, opponents of this arrangement argued that vested interests would still be behind the party list system.[26]

Nonetheless, this writer believes that there are advantages in having more participation of voters in choosing their prime minister, especially given the current factionalised and mercenary nature of Thai politics. It is not necessary for a prime minister to come from the largest party in Parliament. There have been instances globally (and in Thailand) where prime ministers were not the leaders of the largest party. Consider this: the largest party after an election may be the one that spent the most money on vote buying. However, the nation as a whole may favour a prime ministerial candidate whom they perceive as honest and dedicated to the people's welfare, and so may choose the leader of a smaller party.

To achieve a greater public role in choosing the prime minister, it is not necessary to invest new powers in the position of prime minister, nor to directly elect him or her. Voters could merely indicate on their ballot which party leader will be given the first choice to form a government. This would not change the powers of the prime minister, but give the first choice to the popular candidate rather than to the leader of the biggest party. (Alternatively, the party that won the most votes in the party list ballot could be the first to nominate a prime minister.) The principles of coalition building would still apply. If the voters' first choice failed to form a coalition and win a vote in Parliament, their second choice would be given the chance. This provision should satisfy voters and also help to counteract vote buying.

Although fears about abuse of power of a directly elected prime minister may have some justification, there are advantages to strengthening the position of prime minister provided that certain constraints and checks and balances are put in place. Prime ministers emerging from the party system—especially where money politics, vested interests, and the cabinet quota system prevail—have often had little room to manoeuvre and to take decisive action for the public good. The quota system very much restricts the authority of the prime minister, especially in punishing corruption among ministers, and breeds government instability as already mentioned. My earlier proposal to have non-partisan cabinet ministers nominated by the (further-reformed) Senate and chosen by the prime minister, would also serve to reduce vested interests and the influence of money in government decision making.

Given a strengthened prime minister and a strengthened Senate, political parties in the House would have to redefine their roles: towards policy making and increased sensitivity to the needs of their electorates— which is what representative democracy is all about.

Political Party Development

Since the transition to elected governments began in Thailand in 1973, Thai political parties have remained somewhat underdeveloped, mostly representing business interests or coalescing around one or more influential or charismatic characters. Internal party affairs are typically carried out in an autocratic manner. Democratising the internal structure of political parties would go a long way towards strengthening representative democracy.

In the so-called developed world, political parties have broad memberships consisting of people who subscribe to the ideology of the party and are prepared to work for the party (for free!) at election time and take part in policy formulation. The leaders of political parties and their senior officers are elected by this rank-and-file of the party, usually at party conferences. Policies, in turn, should be adopted by a vote of all party members before becoming part of the official party platform. Transparency is called for in this process of electing officers and determining policy. Political parties in the mature democracies generally hold annual conferences of members.

Thailand's 1997 Constitution called for the writing of a Political Parties Bill, as one of the three key pieces of enabling legislation to carry out the aims of the Constitution. (The other two were the National Election Commission Bill, to define the structure and duties of the Election Commission, and the Parliamentary Elections Bill for House and Senate elections.) The main thrust of the Political Parties Bill is to regulate political party finances and to introduce transparency to election campaign contributions. The account books of political parties are to be audited by certified accountants appointed by the Election Commission, and to be made public. The legislation also empowers the registrar of political parties (the chairman of the Election Commission) to regulate the operations of a political party, and to seek a ruling by the Constitutional Court to remove an official or the entire staff of a political party.

It was widely hoped that the 1997 Constitution and its attendant supplementary legislation would lead to a consolidation of Thai politics into fewer, more democratic, political parties, and consequently to greater stability in coalition politics. It was hoped that cleaner politics would result from closer regulation of political parties, thereby attracting more people of talent and conscience.

Bureaucratic Reform

Another major need to improve Thailand's governing structure is bureaucratic reform. The country has been committed to this since 1997, but substantive progress remained to be seen by mid-1999. Major aims of bureaucratic reform should be to make the bureaucracy more efficient, to make it more responsive to the people, and to greatly reduce corruption.

As of December 1997, there were 2,074,805 officials and employees on the government payroll, with their salaries and benefits accounting for 42.5 per cent of the total budget for the fiscal year 1998.[27] It is conceivable to reduce the number of civil servants to one-half or one-third that number and use the savings to greatly increase the salaries of remaining staff, especially for talented middle-level professionals and high-level management. Thus, highly qualified staff, better managers, and modernised office procedures could produce higher efficiency than large numbers of poorly-paid and unmotivated officials, as seen at present.

A lot of duplication and fragmentation of work among government departments could be avoided through judicious restructuring of the whole system, while building up neglected areas such as environmental management (see a proposal for a full Ministry of the Environment in Chapter 13). There are also many ideas floating around about redefining the purpose of bureaucracy and the relationship between government and the governed. Government is trying to do too much, with too many layers of authority getting in the way, say many analysts. In the decade and a half preceding the Crash of 97, brain drain from the bureaucracy was rampant, aggravated by the poor image of the bureaucracy and poor rewards compared to booming salaries for skilled professionals in the private sector. The number of bachelor's degree holders joining the civil service after graduation was more than 60 per cent in 1981, but fell to just 24 per cent in 1994.[28]

The Nation, in an editorial of 6 September 1996, noted that a strategic framework for the urgent task of bureaucratic reform was beginning to take shape:

> The Civil Service Commission (CSC) has initiated an action plan in preparation for bureaucratic reform. Sukhothai Thammatirat University has been assigned to look at the present system, while the Thailand Development Research Institute (TDRI) has been tasked with charting the future direction of the bureaucracy. Comparative examples from Japan, New Zealand, and Canada are being evaluated. . . .
>
> TDRI president Chalongphob Sussangkarn said the bureaucracy must have a new philosophy, utilise new legal and working systems, have an outward-looking attitude, and realise the values of dignity, transparency, proper working ethics, and account-ability. . . . As pointed out by a recent roundtable discussion in Chiang Mai, the country's education system must be revamped in order to create a new breed of people who want to enter the civil service. . . .
>
> Time, though, is certainly not on the side of the reformers. Politicians have furthered their objectives by shamelessly interfering in the machinations of the bureaucracy to suit their

> own needs. Both sides have ended up colluding for the sake of
> their own vested interests. The best and the brightest today are
> leaving the bureaucracy, which has also failed to attract new and
> capable recruits. . . .

Earlier, at a seminar hosted by the above three institutions and the
Thai Research Fund, the country's top thinkers and former senior
bureaucrats and technocrats issued a unanimous warning: Thai
bureaucracy urgently needs to be overhauled or it will die. The participants
called for an immediate campaign to inform the public of the magnitude
of the problem so that a push for drastic changes could gain quick and
effective momentum. They called for thorough research and the drafting
of a bill on overall bureaucratic reform to replace vague government
strategies which seem to be going nowhere. The participants also
advocated the establishment of a neutral, independent body to adopt the
reform mechanism and ensure a continuous implementation of the
necessary measures.

In May 1997, the Chavalit government unveiled a master plan for
bureaucratic reform which would reduce the number of civil servants by
one third by the end of 2001.[29] But could the government act, in view of
the number of master plans for various purposes that had been shelved
by governments in the past? Following the advent of the second Chuan
government in November 1997, *The Nation* editorialised:

> It is . . . crucial that Chuan acts boldly in the management of the
> government amid the decline in the capability, and even
> responsibility and morality, of the Thai bureaucracy. . . .[30]

On 8 December 1997, in response to the economic recession, the
Civil Service Commission approved reform measures to radically change
the roles and responsibilities of government agencies to comply with the
new Constitution and citizens' rights to fast, efficient and cost-effective
public services. It advised the Chuan administration to implement
sweeping crisis management measures that would also accelerate
government bureaucratic reform. Thailand had already agreed with the
IMF, as part of its rescue plan, to reduce the public-sector workforce and
improve efficiency of government agencies.[31]

According to the CSC's 8 December resolution, government agencies must in future confine their role to policy making, planning, supervising, and upholding the standard of public services, which would be contracted out to private companies. The CSC recommended reform measures to allow systematic dismissal of government officials deemed inefficient, and of those who persistently failed to meet professional standards. Its measures required each government agency to draw up a plan within six months to downsize by:

- merging units, dissolving redundant or non-essential decision-making powers;
- shortening the line of command and delegating decision-making powers;
- decentralising powers to provincial and local government organisations;
- contracting out a wider range of work to the private sector;
- investing in high-tech equipment as part of efforts to cut back on staff; and
- setting key performance indicators to evaluate performance.[32]

A former advisor to the CSC, Vuthiphong Priebjrivat, urged that during the economic crisis was the best time for the government to take decisive action on restructuring:

> The economic crisis will provide the necessary pressure and impetus for decisive action to reduce inefficient government bureaucracy which is excess baggage that will weigh down Thailand's economic recovery.

The plan should aim to deconstruct or break down huge government ministries and departments—which he described as gigantic pyramids—into smaller, flexible, and efficient workgroups doing policy making, supervising, regulating, and other essential works.[33]

Bureaucratic reform must also ensure that the morale and self-respect of the civil service is improved in order to reverse brain drain. It should remove political influence from the appointments process and institute promotion on merit rather than on seniority. (The previous chapter examined the radical legislation of New Zealand, adopted during the

1980s and early 1990s, which apparently has been the most successful exercise in bureaucratic reform up to now.)

Towards a Civil Society

Without a doubt, through the coalescence of a range of political initiatives in the mid-1990s, Thailand has embarked on a journey towards achieving a civil society. This is evident through several provisions of the 1997 Constitution: for example, those guaranteeing participation of communities and people in the decision making of governmental bodies on issues which affect them; and through other mandated measures such as provisions which allow voters to recall their representatives, or to place legislative proposals on the parliamentary agenda. This journey towards a civil society is also apparent in the exhaustive process of consultation with the public that accompanied, for the first time, the drafting of a Thai constitution and of the country's Eighth National Development Plan.

The growth and acceptance of non-governmental organisations in Thailand is another fundamental aspect of movement towards a civil society. NGOs have gained an enhanced status to the point where they are now invited to participate in official committees dealing with various issues. Another aspect is the decentralisation of government administration to the local level, through the upgrading of *tambon* councils to become legal entities capable of entering into contracts, and to be progressively elected by local villagers. The new Information Act also enhances the movement towards a civil society.

This movement, both in Thailand and globally, aims to empower people and communities while recognising the limitations of government: that large government bureaucracies cannot generate good decisions in isolation from the people, nor can they hope to carry out efficiently and cost-effectively all of a nation's developmental and service activities. Thus, the concept of civil society advocates the transfer of certain state functions to enhanced local government and citizens groups, and to guarantee the latter groups' participation in governance through consultation and power sharing. It advocates increasing opportunities for voters to make decisions directly on certain matters affecting them. It embraces transparency in government. This movement to a civil society is a dramatic change for Thailand, where top-down decision making under a highly-centralised system of government has traditionally treated people as subjects of government rather than participants with certain rights.

Another opportunity which has been slow to galvanise so far, but which offers great prospects for the advancement of Thai society, is greater involvement of the professional community in national and community affairs. This is a call for professional bodies and organisations to become socially-oriented organisations—not merely social clubs as most of them now are. Thailand lacks a strong tradition of independent charitable organisations, or of philanthropy. It has been pointed out that there is a lack of socially-oriented groups in Thailand's individualistic society working for the common good.

Professional organisations could fill this void by developing outreach programmes to help communities in various ways. Such organisations could, in effect, become NGOs. Thus, NGOs set up by branches of lawyers' associations could inform disadvantaged groups of their legal rights and assist with legal problems. They could, for example, encourage people to report corruption in ways that action could be taken against the corrupt. Medical NGOs could mount community health awareness programmes—an area in which the formal health establishment has largely failed in Thailand.

Every professional group has the potential to form an association to set standards and monitor professional conduct, to work in the community, to propose and comment on government policy, and—in the case of larger groups—also to elect representatives to the Senate as outlined in my recommendation for further reform of that body. The Senate could be an avenue for introducing legislation into the system through such direct links to professional associations.

Thus, the need is now apparent for civil society to become more active on two fronts: outreach to communities disadvantaged by lack of resources and lack of access to information, and input into the political system. The proposal earlier in this chapter to empower professional associations to elect senators would at once be a powerful galvanising factor in turning professional organisations into effective instruments to contribute to both of these needs. It would create a new dynamic for the rational development of Thai society. As mentioned previously, a professional or sectoral organisation which elects senators would be subject to supervision by the Election Commission to ensure that its leadership elections, its election of senators, and its organisational set-up and finances, all conform to rules of democracy and accountability.

Thailand's financial and economic crisis—which is best seen as a systemic breakdown arising from an accumulation of unsustainable practices—contains a wake-up call for Thailand's professional classes. The intelligent minds amongst Thailand's various professions knew how professional standards and best practices were being violated by the corrupt and the influential, yet they did little or nothing to create public awareness or to rectify the abuses. It was not until the crisis became full-blown that some professional associations, such as the Thai Banker's Association, made their voices heard.

Professional people have much to lose in a disintegrating economy and society. They also have a unique responsibility, because of the specialised knowledge they possess, to ensure that government policy reflects the actual needs of society. The failures which led to Thailand's collapse are also failures of Thailand's professional community. The activation of professional associations could certainly be a major step in promoting a higher standard of governance and the enhancement of civil society. Professional associations may begin by reflecting on what the broader aims of their profession should be; on how to raise the standards of practice, on how the profession as a whole can raise standards of behaviour in the society, and on what projects the profession could undertake in cooperation with communities.

Politics and Sustainability

As 1997 came to a close—with the new Constitution adopted but with the process of writing enabling laws to implement key provisions of the Constitution continuing—Senate Speaker Meechai Ruchuphan issued a warning. He said that the next election, the first to be held under the new Constitution, would be a make-or-break election for the country. If vote-buying continued as in past elections, political reform would be doomed:

> Before, [the politicians] could be corrupt and get rich with little consequence [to the people]. Now the nation has been damaged and everyone is affected. . . . The world has become technical and the government will need to have people with technical expertise to work for it. . . .[34]

The first general election following adoption of the 1997 Constitution will be an indicator of how the newly-devised system of safeguards and accountability can work. Much will hinge on how the newly-instituted, independent Election Commission organises and supervises the election.

The Commission must send a clear signal that a new era of politics is beginning; that the old era of money politics, which has damaged the country so much, is ending. It must be tough, and demonstrate a will to exercise its full power regardless of the consequences.

Undoubtedly, there will be cheating and influence-mongering during the election. The Commission must be determined to punish the worst offenders, and it should annul polls in the ten or twenty worst electorates. Where clear evidence of malpractice is available, candidates and their agents should be prosecuted and the worst offenders jailed, no matter what party they come from and no matter which influential patrons criticise the Commission's actions. If the Commission does not immediately and determinedly exercise its powers, those powers will erode. The old-style politicians will come to believe that, despite all the fine words in the Constitution, politics is just "business as usual".

Certainly there would be bitter complaints from affected political parties against such a pro-active Election Commission. The Commission must prove who is the boss: the influential, old-style politicians with their networks of allegiances, or the newly-appointed officials of the various organs set up by the Constitution to guide the country towards good governance? The Commission must have the courage to nullify the whole election and undertake large-scale prosecutions if necessary.

With such high expectations of the Election Commission, it was therefore disappointing to read that most of the 21 candidates nominated by a provincial screening committee in July 1998 to staff the seven-member election committee of the Northeastern province of Buriram, were close to deputy agriculture minister, Newin Chidchob and his father, Chai Chidchob, who are the province's House representatives.[35]

Another disappointment, regarding the application of laws covering election fraud, occurred following the election for the Samut Prakan Municipality, south of Bangkok, on 2 May 1999. That election was regarded as one of the most fraud-ridden in Thai history, as men stormed into polling booths and stuffed fake ballots into ballot boxes. One blatant example was captured on video tape. The use of fake identity cards and tampering with boxes was also widespread. During a subsequent examination, large numbers of fake and illegally marked ballots were found in ballot boxes at a majority of polling stations. The Progressive Pak Nam 2000 party, led by Chonsawat Asavahame, son of Deputy Interior Minister Vatana Asavahame, won that election, taking 22 of the 24 seats on the municipality council.

Following exposure of the massive fraud, the election was annulled and another held on 9 October. More than 700 police officers, 300 election volunteers, and two fast-moving police units were assigned to the municipality to prevent a recurrence of fraud. However, it appears that corrupt candidates stepped up vote buying in the face of intensive monitoring. Samut Prakan Election Commission chief Paitoon Sunthornwipak, admitting that the election was not free from vote buying, said he had been informed by election volunteers that voters would receive as much as 1,000 baht per vote.[36] Chonsawat still emerged overall winner capturing 15 of the 24 council seats.

The tragedy of the election was that despite clear evidence of massive fraud in the original poll, the perpetrators were not disqualified from contesting the re-run. Neither members of the Chuan cabinet, the provincial courts, nor the provincial administration were willing to apply the full force of the law, and pursue criminal charges. Despite attempts to clean up politics, through reform and through an invigorated legal system, big money and big influence prevailed.

A major theme of this book has been that money politics has corrupted the legal and administrative systems to such an extent that financial, economic, environmental, and social crises have wrecked Thailand's development efforts. The more enlightened among the Constitution's drafters recognised this and set about restructuring the political landscape, adding many new institutions and processes designed to fight corruption and abuse of political influence, so that genuine political reform can take place.

Thus, a whole "first generation" of officials and judges to take charge of these new bodies will face a test. It will also be a test for the Thai nation. Prospects for successful political reform depend a great deal on these officials and judges carrying out the duties for which they were selected in an uncompromising way. They will face threats from established political interests that have benefited for too long from various malpractices. In the context of elections, these have already been enumerated and described: vote buying; the misuse of funds;

intimidation; the enlistment of government officials (including teachers and police) whose duty is to be neutral, to act as political canvassers; and so on.

Can this "first generation" pass the test? A brief story from my experience shows how the weight of *krieng jai* (the reluctance to intervene for fear that it would upset some people), patronage, and tradition has weighed heavily upon such officials in the past.

After the 1992 election—the first one monitored comprehensively by the political NGO, PollWatch—thousands of complaints of electoral abuses and violations of the law were recorded. At a subsequent luncheon with a senior official of PollWatch, I asked if at least one offending election candidate would be prosecuted and punished. Full of indignation, the official replied that the organisation would take action to initiate the prosecution of five or six electoral offenders. In the end, no-one was prosecuted. The web of influence and collusion of political parties with government officials and police was so pervasive, and the weak electoral laws so predisposed against proper enforcement, that all of PollWatch's good intentions could not prevent electoral criminals from taking seats in the House and ultimately in the cabinet. The bad governance which the country has experienced since 1992 has certainly resulted, in part, from the inability of the state to conduct honest elections. Electoral abuses have, in fact, escalated throughout the 1990s.

Therefore, it is important to emphasise my earlier point: the Election Commission must have the courage to nullify the whole election if electoral fraud continues to be pervasive.

Another important objective of political reform arising from the Constitution redrafting process is to introduce the concept of sustainable development into politics. Good governance as a single concept is not enough; there must be continuity and sustainability arising from it. Good governance will not arrive overnight, but will arise from an accumulation and institutionalisation of good political and democratic practices. Enlightened political leaders, who hopefully will emerge following the full implementation of the Constitution, must make a point of introducing and nurturing political best practices (just as the financial crisis has revealed the absolute necessity for adherence to internationally-recognised financial best practices). Citizens who recognise the need for higher standards in government following Thailand's economic collapse, must also support such efforts to institute political best practices.

In the mid-1990s, as the movement to redraft the Constitution gained momentum, a debate emerged between people who maintained that in order to cure Thailand's political ills, political structures must be changed; and others who maintained that people's attitudes must change. Officials and politicians who are determined to be corrupt will always find a way, whatever the political structure, say the latter group. The need is to produce good people, to change people's attitudes through education, they say.

This writer is sympathetic to the latter point of view. But how does one begin to produce good people? In fact, this is an age-old question, going back at least to the ancient Greek philosophers in the Western tradition, and to Confucius and the Taoists in the Eastern tradition. In Thailand, it is widely known that education curriculums, policies, and teaching methods are very much out of date and largely inadequate in preparing students to respond to the new realities of the age of globalisation, both economically and socially. How can the education system be revamped and new approaches devised without strong political support? Recent attempts to begin revamping the education system have foundered through the lack of political will, and through the proliferation of "just visiting" education ministers who come and go as frequently as discredited governments.

Obviously, political guidance is needed to begin to change major institutions such as the education system. A stable, progressive government would certainly help. In July 1999, with the passage of the National Education Act, Thailand was poised to begin its long-overdue, major reform of the education system. The Act mandates the setting up of an Education Reform Office, with a term of three years, to begin implementing the many-faceted and far-reaching reforms. Will the political climate continue to support this major effort?

Education is just one area in which the inertia of the past must be overcome to enable Thailand to progress in the changed and difficult circumstances following the East Asian financial and economic collapse. Positive political changes must lead, or at least accompany, Thailand's quest for a sustainable and just society. The predominant task for Thailand is to place its best people in executive and legislative positions. The advancement of democracy and sustainability now demand that people of integrity and ability set an enlightened agenda for the country. This is the crucial second stage of political reform to follow Thailand's history-making, Constitution redrafting process.

In that process, the structuralists proved successful in introducing far-reaching structural and institutional reform. But major battles still lie ahead to make the Constitution work by generating a will to clean up the system among the first generation who will staff the new monitoring and legalistic bodies. Many democratic and legalistic values, and not least a coherent vision for Thailand's future, need to be developed or strengthened through the country's political institutions. The prevailing cynicism about politics, that prevents "good" people from contesting elections, must be dispelled by the incoming first generation of officials and judges who administer the newly-created institutions. The emergence of a new political era calls for the creation of a critical mass of judicial will to imprison those people—whether they inhabit the financial, political, or law-enforcement sectors—whose illegal or negligent actions can be proved to have contributed to the country's crisis.

Thailand in the 1990s has seen too many short-term governments, too many "just visiting" cabinet ministers who showed little concern about pursuing long-term policies to benefit the society, too many instances of projects and policies being revised or reversed merely because they were initiated by "rivals".

There is a need to encourage more grassroots democracy where the politically-dispossessed and the politically-manipulated—especially among the rural masses—can exercise real power through a vigorous civil society. Professional classes, as indicated in the previous section on civil society, may also take a lead. A fashionable viewpoint, especially among university academics in pre-collapse times, held that a responsive democracy would develop "naturally" in Thailand as a result of economic development, prosperity, and a growing middle class. Such a view was expressed, for example, by Dr. Waraporn Samkoset, former dean of Thammasat's Faculty of Economics, in a compendium of views on the future of Thai politics published by *The Nation* in February 1996:[37]

> Better financial status over the next two decades will influence
> the public to better protect their rights. After seeing the positive
> changes in other countries, those reaching a good financial status
> will take a look at themselves and start to demand their basic
> rights and push for changes that have benefited foreign countries.

207

But, such a supposedly emerging ethos among the growing middle class did not prevent the collapse of the economy and the worsening strains apparent in Thai society. On the contrary, this book argues that the materialistic, egocentric assumptions that often accompany affluence and consumerism actually contributed in a great measure to the collapse. The size of the middle class also shrank somewhat along with Thailand's evaporating wealth. In the future, could a resurgent middle class, once the victim of a consumerist and speculative bubble, lead the way toward an economically and democratically sustainable society? One imagines that this can no longer be expected to happen "naturally". Leadership is needed at many levels.

The middle class has received a painful burn. Its suffering should logically lead to a realisation that personal responsibility for society on the part of educated individuals must replace the "go-along-with-it" complacency which has previously allowed the rise of political and economic abuses. Such a transformation, in turn, depends on enhanced public education and public involvement in the society; in short, a transition to a robust and responsible civil society. Middle-class anxiety and broader aspirations of the middle class for long-term stability can be channelled into meaningful political participation. My proposal in previous sections was designed to promote this: the proposal to encourage professional groups to develop active community programmes, and to give the professional groups political power to elect senators and ultimately to influence the choice of cabinet ministers.

Chapter 7

The Failure of Money Politics

The previous chapter documented Thailand's big step forward of September 1997 with the adoption of the "people's power" Constitution. That event raised hopes that stronger measures to combat corruption and ensure clean elections would spur much needed political reform, and set the country's development on a sustainable course. But would the measures be successful against the many layers of ingrained corruption in Thai society? Could they lead to political and social stability?

The first eight years of the 1990s had seen numerous political woes: a military coup, bloodshed in the streets of Bangkok, allegations of massive corruption in government, politicians' meddling in the country's once-venerated financial system, and finally a financial collapse and economic downturn caused in part by gross political indifference.

A decade of high economic growth had brought rapid changes to Thai society—but how many Thais could say that they were genuinely better off after the bursting of the bubble economy? Thailand as a whole had experienced an increase in material affluence while at the same time undergoing a decline in major aspects of the quality of life: increasing stress in the society, a dangerously widening gap between rich and poor, continuing environmental decline, and a debasement of culture through rapid commercialisation that changed the values and expectations of Thais. Riding on top of this political instability and decline in the quality of life was the scourge of money politics.

Increasingly, Thais have come to understand that money politics has failed to meet the country's larger challenges of sustainable development and economic competitiveness. It is now becoming apparent that money politics—through its many destructive aspects—has become the major threat to the security and cohesion of Thai society. Accusations of impropriety, and even of criminal activity, have dogged ministers of every elected government during this decade up to mid-1999. Public perception has been that political parties, more often than not, mainly exist to enrich their members and supporters. The low quality of party politicians obtaining cabinet positions has led to a feeling of despondency among concerned and educated Thais. At the root of this problem is money politics: vote buying during general elections, the payment of money to enter the cabinet, and the political patronage system of favours and rewards which dominates Thai politics and society.

The stakes in Thailand's black game of money politics have been getting higher: the money spent on vote buying was seen to be increasing. Analysts believe that under-the-table "commissions"—paid during the initiation of mega-projects and mega-purchases, and whose existence was routinely denied by politicians—were growing ever larger as Thailand's economy boomed. And add to that, political meddling in the day-to-day affairs of ministries—and particularly the country's financial institutions.

Thailand's general election of 17 November 1996, won by Gen. Chavalit Yongchaiyudh's New Aspiration Party, verified these destructive trends. General elections, as well as providing democratic means for changing governments according to the people's will, also provide a window on the current state of a nation's politics. The election was labelled as the dirtiest and most violent ever, with more money spent on gaining illegal influence, corrupting government officials, and on vote buying than ever before. There were numerous complaints of intimidation of party canvassers and of independent election monitors working for the election-monitoring body, PollWatch. Its chairman, Gen. Saiyud Kerdphol, said each candidate spent between 15–30 million baht during the campaign. Canvassers for political parties resorted to intimidation while government officials failed to remain neutral.[1]

All of this raised the prospect that Thailand's politics would continue to suffer instability, and that corrupt politicians who participated in abuses of the country's financial system (for example, in the Bangkok Bank of Commerce scandal) would become ever bolder in future—increasingly threatening Thailand's economic security.

Dr. Arthit Ourairat, a former speaker of the House of Representatives and a former minister of health, had succinctly expressed Thailand's dilemma at a panel discussion of the Foreign Correspondents Club of Thailand in August 1992. He said:

> Politics in Thailand is so backward that it cannot follow economic development, and it even tries to pull down the economic achievements.

This comment came 18 months after the military *coup d'état* of February 1991, and just three months after the shocking events of May 1992, when troops shot dead 44 Thais[2] who were among a large group demonstrating in Bangkok against military intervention in government, and for a cleaner, more democratic political system.

Four years later, the economy began to falter as export growth suddenly stagnated, the current account deficit ballooned, and external debt soared—accompanied by a decline of confidence in Thailand's financial system. The system collapsed the following year, precipitated by apparent policy misjudgments by the Bank of Thailand and the consequent plunge in value of the baht.

Dr. Arthit's words of 1992 did indeed seem prophetic. Was Thailand's success story finished? Could ordinary citizens, the nascent middle class, the members of the newly-impoverished elite, and especially those with political ambition, learn the lessons of the economic collapse? Some analysts called it a blessing in disguise. The collapse focused attention with a new urgency on the abuses and irresponsibility of patronage and money politics, generating a popular upsurge of support for the Constitution Drafting Assembly's efforts to write an anti-corruption constitution.

Let's take a brief overview of events following the military coup of 1991. The coup leaders attempted to justify their action in overthrowing an elected government by citing the unprecedentedly high level of corruption which had gained hold in the overthrown cabinet of Prime Minister Chatichai Choonhavan.

After 19 months encompassing military intervention in politics, two interim governments, a military attempt to manipulate an election, and the violent May Incident—a relatively free general election was held on 13 September 1992. It generated high hopes, as a coalition government of so-called "angelic" parties which had opposed military intervention in politics took power.

But the high hopes proved to be tempered by disappointments. The government of Prime Minister Chuan Leekpai, with his Democrat Party as the core of a five-party coalition, proved to be weak in leadership, and promises of meaningful political reform failed to materialise. The Democrats placed some highly-competent ministers in the cabinet, and were, along with a majority of the parties in the coalition, perceived as relatively clean by previous standards. But the political patronage system remained as a negative force in the coalition, putting self-interest and monetary interest ahead of the public interest. Finally, a land reform scandal, in which land that should have gone to poor farmers ended up in the hands of wealthy supporters of the major governing party, led to the pull-out of the Palang Dharma Party from the Chuan coalition, and the government's collapse.

Following the general election of 2 July 1995, and the victory of Banharn Silpa-archa's Chat Thai Party, concerns were again voiced that the political patronage system had led to the placement of unqualified people in key cabinet positions, and that vote buying in the rural constituencies had reached an unprecedented level. Almost a year later, discontent was mounting over the economic performance of the Banharn government. It was reflected in an editorial of *The Nation* on 19 June 1996, which charged that fewer than 10 of Banharn's 40-plus cabinet members were qualified to hold ministerial positions.

It was becoming clear that the problem of money politics and its participants' lack of vision and foresight in economics and in overall national development, was fundamentally a problem of Thailand's underdeveloped political culture. The problem was not so much attributable to this or that government or party (although vote buyers and manipulators tended to gravitate towards certain political parties), but was rather pervasive to the system. A number of undesirable and undemocratic practices (such as vote buying during elections), based on social psychology which dates back to the old feudal era, had crystallised around the representative form of parliamentary democracy, and were able to grow because of a certain passivity or indifference among the population at large.

I am tempted to say that Thailand has not yet experienced genuine democracy. To be sure, Thailand has elements of democracy: a constitution, a parliament, elections, a free press. Yet, the spirit of democracy has somehow been missing. There is an impression that Thai people in general lack the expectation that they can use the political system to improve their condition, and that the political system should, as its first priority, respond to their needs.

However, while the political events early in this decade threatened to negate democratic progress, they invigorated a movement and longing for a responsive democracy. This was apparent in the growing activism of Thailand's educated and professional class through such organisations as the Confederation for Democracy, an independent activists' group, and PollWatch, an independent body (financed by government grant) which mobilised thousands of monitors to watch for election violations and to educate voters since 1992. There had also been constant pressure for a complete and meaningful rewriting of the Constitution since the overthrow of the Chatichai government in 1991.

Other political progress has taken place over the decade of the 1990s. The role of the parliamentary opposition has taken on new vigour. Adversarial politics in Parliament has developed to the point where the opposition has established the right to scrutinise government performance and directly criticise the government through parliamentary no-confidence debates. The public outcry when Prime Minister Banharn tried to escape a censure motion by forcing the closure of a no-confidence debate, further strengthened this process. And, it was a no-confidence motion against the prime minister himself that led to the chain of events which caused Banharn to dissolve Parliament on 28 September 1996. The role of the Thai press as political watchdog in exposing abuses has also evolved along with the invigoration of the parliamentary opposition's role, the two processes supporting each other. In addition, the media have become more sophisticated in monitoring policy and in generating debate, and in proposing alternatives for national policy—given that articulation of forward-looking policy has been a weak point among political parties.

Unprecedented measures for political accountability were introduced into politics during the first government of interim prime minister, Anand Panyarachun in 1991, although subsequent governments have proceeded to dilute them, or have ignored them completely.

Thailand is rapidly changing and the society is becoming more complex. Feudal attitudes may now predominate but are destined to fade as education and development reach the most disadvantaged communities. The development of democracy also depends on this trend. Much depends also on whether or not law enforcement agencies can discover a new sense of purpose beyond the benefits of patronage, and the courage to actually imprison violators of the new and strengthened laws against corruption and electoral malpractices.

The Rule of Law

In connection with this, we need to reflect upon the purpose of the law. One key requirement of democracy is that the rule of law should prevail— that is to say, the legal system should be impartial and favour no one (especially the powerful), and the application of the law should be swift and unrelenting.

Under a feudal system, for example, the law is not applied equally to everyone. It is used by the higher orders of society to compel lower orders to stay in line, but it can rarely be used by the lower orders to exact the same penalties for harmful or criminal activities of the influential or powerful. Developing the rule of law to serve democracy—that is, equal treatment for everyone under the law—seems to be one of the most neglected aspects of Thailand's yearning for democracy.

The fact that no politicians, senior officials, or generals can be convicted and jailed for massive corruption or other crimes in Thailand causes amazement among foreign observers. However, this fact is not so amazing when one considers the size and the beneficiaries of the illegal economy in Thailand. Chulalongkorn University lecturers Pasuk Phongpaichit and Sungsidh Piriyarangsan researched corruption and the illegal economy in Thailand and came up with these findings:

Thailand's economic decline of 1997 had the effect of spurring the illegal economy, including gambling, drug smuggling, prostitution, smuggling of illegal foreign labour, oil smuggling, and sales of illegal weapons, Pasuk reported in August 1997. Such illegal businesses accounted for as much as 20 per cent of GDP, said Pasuk, and would be difficult to eradicate since almost all of them were owned by politicians.[3] A few months earlier, Sungsidh had told *The Nation* that each year over the three previous years, more than 400 billion baht had been taken from such activities:

> Gambling dens and illegal lotteries led the pack and profited by
> 260 billion baht. Prostitution raked in an estimated 60 billion

baht, and the drug trade 30 billion baht. . . . Sales of bootleg petrol and smuggled arms together accounted for nearly 100 billion baht. The police were net beneficiaries of the underworld, benefitting to the tune of more than 5 billion baht. . . . They had the tacit backing of senior bureaucrats and politicians, including members of the cabinet, who ultimately benefitted from their illegal activities, Sungsidh said.[4]

Thailand has yet to use the legal system effectively as a tool to develop, to cleanse, and to guide politics. The legal system has usually shied away from prosecuting, convicting, or imposing prison sentences upon, well-connected or high-status people accused of serious crimes. The principles often cited in these cases are: not causing divisions or disruptions to society, or that the person involved should not be punished because of his/her "contributions" to society. Decoded, these "principles" often mean that those responsible for administering the law fear retaliation from those accused of violating it, or are part of the accused's patronage network.

Mont Redmond, in his column *Thai Whys*, published in *The Nation* on 31 October 1993, gave an indication of how the Western concept of the rule of law is somewhat alien to Thai traditional society:

> The law, for most Thais, is a strange and arcane instrument of privilege, and not a weapon of self defence distributed equally to every man. It must be paid for, if not in money, then with time or favours or fear.

Here is another perspective on the rule of law that arises within the development process, as related to me by a Western political analyst in Bangkok in 1992:

> In a rapidly changing society like Thailand, the tension between what the law says and what people actually do is going to be higher. How can you adapt and modify Asian legal conditions to a rapidly-emerging state joining the global economy. . . ? Law has to be rooted in the traditions. To Americans, law is a statement of governance: "You can't do this". But in Thailand, laws are more as guides or aspirations, something like paradigms.

Pasuk and Sungsidh examined the dominance of corruption and patronage over the rule of law in the context of Thai traditions in their landmark 1994 book, *Corruption and Democracy in Thailand*:

> In sum, several studies on corruption in Thailand have indicated that there is corruption in all levels of the bureaucracy and the political system, and that for many of those involved the practices are legitimate under the patronage system although illegal in the context of modern laws. This conflict between what is legitimate in the traditional culture and what is wrong under the modern legal code has existed in Thai politics for a long time. Thai politicians and Thai elites resolve the conflict by adhering to tradition rather than to the modern standards of official practice. . . .[5]

Pasuk and Chris Baker elaborated on this in their 1995 book, *Thailand's Boom!*:

> The judicial system is heavily biased in favour of the rich and powerful. Straightforward corruption—money paid to policemen, prosecutors, judges—plays a large part in this. But there are also forces that run deeper. The rich and the powerful are reluctant to punish one another. This tendency has its roots in the traditional society of lord and slave. Lords protected the social division by protecting one another. The tendency has been modified and sustained through half a century of military-bureaucratic domination.
>
> When "big people" are found doing wrong, they are rarely punished. Elite society may isolate them, push them out of sight, restrain them from doing further wrong. But it usually saves them from public confirmation of guilt, punishment, humiliation. Court proceedings drag on and peter away. Bureaucratic investigations fail for lack of evidence. Accused parties simply disappear. Often this tendency is attributed to Thai "tolerance", a Buddhist distaste for retribution. But it also reaffirms the equation: might = right. The powerful can do anything.[6]

The rule of law, by definition, means that the law is supreme. It is the supreme ruler over all other systems, networks, individuals, or interests. It is worth saying again: once called into action, the law should move relentlessly, allowing no obstacles; it should be impartial, favouring no one regardless of their social or financial status.

However, while the law may seldom be supreme in Thailand when dealing with high-level influence, it should be said that many Thais view their legal system as being generally fair and generally responsive in dealing with everyday complaints among ordinary people. The legal system thus may be seen as being one of the more advanced in Southeast Asia, especially when compared to the practices of some of Thailand's neighbours.

Corruption Can Destroy Societies

When I was a political science student in the early 1970s, one of my lecturers took what was called a "structural-functional" view of corruption, analysing why it existed and even looking at a presumed "virtue" of corruption; namely, that it helps to get things done. Interestingly, I came across a similar view when I visited Cambodia on a writing assignment in 1992, when a United Nations official pointed to the upsurge of economic activity in Phnom Penh, and remarked that such a level of activity would not exist if it were not for corruption money greasing the workings of the normally lethargic bureaucracy. (However, I don't think the official meant to excuse corruption.)

More recently, in September 1996, this view found its way into the *Asian Wall Street Journal*, as one contributed comment to the newspaper asserted:

> The corruption-free process is more fair to society, but the two are arguably equally efficient, given that both processes are effectively sealed, competitive bids in which the highest tender wins. Indeed, economies where corruption is a way of life may arguably be more efficient than slightly corrupt economies where only a few bidders are willing to pay bribes. . . . Moreover, in countries where widespread bribing is a feature but formal public tenders are absent, corruption actually introduces competitive market processes.[7]

The writer also contended that

> . . . corrupt practices in the public decision making of developing economies could spur growth, particularly if they frustrate inappropriate and anti-development government policies. . . .

And, he added, where corruption is expected, if not accepted,

> . . . such generally agreed "rules of the game" enhance predictability. . . .

If that was not enough, he added:

> Smuggling is another type of "corrupt" behaviour that almost always has a positive economic effect, as long as the goods being smuggled are not of an illicit nature. Smuggling goods across international borders circumvents trade barriers such as tariffs and local-content rules. . . .

The writer starts by saying he doesn't mean to excuse corruption, but then tries his best to do so by stating that corruption that leads to "growth", circumvents trade legislation, and negates certain government development policies (those which are presumably unfavourable to big business or transnational business) is "good" corruption.

Are these comments indicative of the thinking of a new breed of international entrepreneur, intoxicated by the new globalisation of the profit-making game, who believe that anything that gets in the way of "growth" or free markets, or transnational investment deserves to be stomped on, including the rule of law and the sovereignty of governments? Taking such accommodating views towards corruption is wrong and dangerous. When we look at the overall effects of corruption, it becomes clear that it can cause complete lack of faith of people in their government; it can destroy the fabric of a society—not to mention a country's financial system, political system, and its environment—and can plunge a nation into decline, poverty, and misery.

Compare the view presented in the *Asian Wall Street Journal* with that of Rangsan Thanapornpan, an economics professor at Thammasat University, at a seminar in August 1996. He predicted that the number of mega-projects proposed for Thailand would increase because transnational corporations find it easy to do business in Thailand by merging with local businesses and paying politicians and state technocrats to endorse their projects.[8]

The often-furtive introduction of mega-projects into Thailand has aroused many suspicions. Many mega-projects are accused of being either environmentally unsound, being technically unsound, not taking into account the interests of local communities, or not being part of a coherent development plan. Sometimes they can even be financially unsound, and ultimately a call is made for taxpayers' money to bail out the investors. *The Nation* reported Rangsan as saying:

> If there was more transparency and public accountability, politicians and technocrats would have had fewer chances to seek personal gain by colourful, large projects. . . . Transnational corporations which wanted to make maximum possible profits held the trump cards in deals with the government. They drafted contracts loosely and then paid senior technocrats in charge of reviewing the contracts to give approval. . . . Investment in mega-projects by transnational corporations in Thailand would continue to grow in sectors such as transport because the corporations will earn continued revenue by collecting service fees from consumers. . . .

I believe that a corruption crisis is a major underlying cause of the crisis in Thailand's political development, and both were a major factor in the Crash of 97. While there is an outcry amongst the media and amongst well-educated Thais, many people take the accommodating view that you can't do much about it. The studies conducted by the Chulalongkorn University staff into Thai attitudes about corruption seem to indicate that large numbers of government officials, police, and businessmen don't think anything is wrong with small-scale corruption, at least provided no one is "hurt". This, again, is wrong and dangerous.

Yet, the pervasiveness of corruption and this apparent indifference to it can be explained in the context of Thai history, in the way that the state and its bureaucratic administration developed during the era of absolute monarchy and feudalism. (This historical perspective is examined more closely in Chapter 8.)

Corruption is seldom static. It is either growing—both in the number of incidences and in value—or it is declining, through official determination to prevent it and punish it. Corruption reaches new heights during times of economic growth. According to one source, twenty or thirty years ago the stakes were small; perhaps in the order of 100,000 up to one million baht. But in the decade from 1985–1995, Thailand has experienced kickbacks of 50 million to 100 million baht or more per project.

Corruption lowers the quality of life of a whole society. On the one hand, corrupt money generally tends to flow towards the well-off and greedy when it should be spent on government projects to develop the country and benefit the poor. On the other hand, government policies and laws designed to uplift the lives of the people cannot be implemented because so many exemptions are given to businessmen offering bribes. Some examples:

- Wealthy and well-connected businessmen, with collusion of officials and police, grab land off poor, unsophisticated peasants who may have customary rights to land going back generations, but insufficient written titles.
- Factory workers are exposed to dangerous conditions and substances, and suffer health problems because factory managers bribe officials who are supposed to enforce safety regulations.
- Deforestation through illegal logging takes place with the collusion of corrupt officials, and leads to the destruction of the environment through floods, soil erosion, and even disastrous drought—which can impoverish millions of farmers.
- Construction projects become unsafe because contractors use sub-standard materials as a result of corruption.
- Building codes and town planning regulations cannot be enforced, leading to serious degradation of the urban environment such as the overcrowding and pollution we find in Bangkok, and leading to physical and mental diseases among the population.
- Young girls are forced into prostitution, through collusion between traffickers, patrons, and corrupt police officers, threatening the girls' health and ruining their lives. . . .

The list goes on.

Social disparities arise where government policies do not address the needs of the country, but are instead seen as revenue-generating measures for politicians and their (business) supporters. For example, in 1995 the top 20 per cent of income-earners in Thailand earned 87 per cent of the total national income, while the lowest 20 per cent earned a mere 1.56 per cent. By comparison, in 1975 the top 20 per cent of income-earners received 49.3 per cent of national income, while the lowest 20 per cent earned 6.1 per cent.[9] Corruption has certainly played its part in this trend towards greater inequality within society.

As corruption increases at high levels, it finally begins to destroy the free market. Companies which gain lucrative contracts through corruption payments become bigger and more powerful. Their corrupt relationships with political leaders become cemented into monopolies, and the system of cronyism may develop where large chunks of the economy slip more and more under the control of a small, corrupt group. According to recent Thai experience, we can see that a country's financial integrity and economic stability may also be sabotaged.

Corruption: The Philippine Example

The rise of the dictatorship of President Ferdinand Marcos in the Philippines illustrates how a country can become humbled, through complacency and lack of vigilance by its people, and suffer economic and social disaster. Patronage, corruption, deception, intimidation, and payoffs characterised Marcos's rise to power. These ingredients are also present in Thai political society, although power is multi-polar rather than uni-polar as it has been in the Philippines.

Marcos gained the Philippine presidency in November 1965 in a popular vote, and was re-elected in 1969. From there he gradually transformed an elected presidency into a dictatorship. He suspended the legal right of *habeas corpus* in 1971, and declared martial law in 1972— both actions taken supposedly to combat the Philippines' communist insurgency. He consolidated his 20-year rule subsequently through electoral fraud and by virtually taking control of the Philippine economy through his corrupt and pervasive crony system.

Estimates of the amount of money stolen by Marcos range between 5–10 billion dollars. Ongoing Philippine legal efforts have so far been able to recover only a small fraction of this. In the final years of the Marcos dictatorship, the Philippine economy nosedived. It shrank for several consecutive years, and increasingly relied on foreign loans to stay afloat. The education system deteriorated and the number of people living in dire poverty increased until 1995, when a modest economic recovery began.

An example of Marcos's alleged corruption using mega-projects is the case of the Bataan nuclear power plant, initiated by him in 1973. After the fall of Marcos, Philippine government charges of corruption against the plant's contractor, Westinghouse Corporation, were heard in an American court, but were dismissed in 1994. Nevertheless, controversy still surrounds the case, as well as subsequent Philippine government dealings with Westinghouse. A number of allegations were made by Raymond Bonner in his book, *Waltzing with a Dictator*,[10] including the following:

The nuclear plant is located in Bataan, Luzon, less than 160 kilometres from five volcanos, four of them active; and near three geological fault lines. It was the largest and most expensive construction project in Philippine history.

Two companies bid for the plant. Originally, General Electric appeared to have won the contract with a well-documented bid of $700 million for two reactors. Westinghouse, in desperation, approached Herminio Disini, a crony of President Marcos. Shortly afterwards, Westinghouse submitted a bid of $500 million for two reactors. The bid had no accompanying details about cost or even specifications. Westinghouse allegedly set up a subsidiary company in Switzerland for the purpose of channeling corruption money into a bank account owned by Disini (denied by Westinghouse).

After it had locked in the contract, Westinghouse set about submitting a serious proposal. When it came in, it was for $1.2 billion for one reactor. According to Bonner's allegation, Marcos's share of the corruption was almost $80 million. He doesn't indicate what the other allegedly corrupt participants may have got.

The nuclear plant project was already the most expensive in the world. The final cost of the one reactor, according to the Nuclear-Free Philippines Coalition, was $2.2 billion. As of mid-1996, the Philippines was still paying interest to the tune of $500,000 a day on loans for the project.

The nuclear plant has never been operated. Independent nuclear experts identified many unsafe features in the plant, presumably the result of corruption and indifference to opposition. Marcos's successor, President Corazon Aquino, refused to sanction its operation. As of 1996, the government of President Fidel Ramos was on the point of reaching an agreement with Westinghouse for a financial settlement of the protracted dispute, and conversion of the plant for gas-fired electricity generation. But fresh allegations of new corruption in the financial settlement have since been made in the Philippines.

Thai Parallels?

Can one find parallels with the Bataan case in Thailand? The three million-line telephone deal, which was exposed by interim prime minister Anand in 1991, may come close. That deal started as a two-page memorandum submitted to cabinet by a communications minister under the elected government of Chatichai Choonhavan (1988–91). Isn't this somewhat reminiscent of the case of the Westinghouse nuclear power plant bid with no cost details and no specifications submitted?

Anand openly accused top officials of being corrupt in awarding contracts for the telephone deal, causing heavy financial losses to the country. He raised questions about the Telephone Organisation of Thailand's handling of the three-million line telephone project, and the Communications Authority of Thailand's procurement projects for submarine optical fibre cables, international telephone exchanges, satellite communications equipment, and the provision of mobile data communication and in-flight communication services.

There have been other possible examples. The Thai press has also raised questions about contracts awarded to private investors for rapid mass transit systems in Bangkok during the Chatichai government. Certainly, the *ad hoc* manner in which projects were formulated and contracted, without a serious attempt to draw up an integrated mass transit plan and system of complementary procurements, has been disastrous for the city.

Phaichitr Uathavikul, as a minister in the first (1991) interim government of Prime Minister Anand, raised the Hopewell mass-transit, road-and-rail project for Bangkok as an obvious example of a government mistake. Phaichitr was quoted as saying:[11]

> This project is worth 80 billion baht but the government never commissioned a detailed study of its feasibility. I believe that this kind of thing is never done anywhere else in the world. What we did have was only a three-page invitation for private

> investment. We don't even know yet where exactly the proposed
> elevated highways will be built.

In 1997, following delays, confusion and controversy, the Hopewell project was scrapped.

Were the telephone deal and the continuing mess over the privately-commissioned mass transit projects—resulting in contracts for incompatible, overlapping systems—the result of efforts to extract kickbacks? If so (as suspected), they would rank as additional textbook cases of how corruption undermines the economic aspirations of a developing country.

Then, in 1996, the emerging details and accusations of impropriety surrounding the near-collapse of the Bangkok Bank of Commerce (BBC) had already made it Thailand's biggest financial scandal ever. Members of Parliament of Prime Minister Banharn's party, Chat Thai, were accused of benefiting from money looted from the bank. Court proceedings had begun against the former deputy interior minister, Chat Thai MP Suchart Tancharoen, in the Northeastern province of Nong Khai regarding the falsification of land title deeds for land used as collateral for BBC bank loans. The bank's senior management had also been charged. In addition, Thailand's chief of police had hinted that highly-placed officials of the Bank of Thailand (the central bank) were implicated. But it was unclear whether or not "higher-ups" in the central bank or in the Chat Thai party would be formally identified in the scandal.

The scandal broke during a parliamentary no-confidence debate from 8–10 May 1996, when Suthep Thaugsaban, an opposition MP, made public a confidential document obtained from the Bank of Thailand exposing the dire financial state of the BBC. The document said the BBC was beset with 77 billion baht in low-quality, high-risk debts (later revised to 50 billion in bad debts which were thought to be unrecoverable), most of which were incurred through gross negligence, imprudence, and violations of banking laws. Some 37.98 billion baht of that amount was in loans for corporate takeovers with inadequate collateral.

Suthep made a series of charges against then deputy interior minister, Suchart, linking him and political colleagues to massive fraud charges regarding the bank.

Suchart, a prominent member of the so-called Group of 16 political faction, was accused of acquiring cheap land through companies controlled by his family, largely through the falsification of land documents. The value of the land was then substantially inflated before being pledged as collateral for loans from the BBC.

The next step, according to the allegations surrounding the scandal,[12] was for Suchart and his Group of 16 allies to take over financially ill companies and to manipulate their shares for big profits on the Stock Exchange of Thailand. The proceeds were then allegedly used to enable Suchart to become an MP through vote buying, and then, through the political patronage system, to become a minister overseeing the Land Department.

The Tancharoen family was found to have secured 2.64 billion baht from the BBC by the end of 1995, of which 1.55 billion baht was collateralised. Altogether, the Group of 16 borrowed 6.15 billion baht from the bank, of which 3.48 billion baht was collateralised. (However, by 1999 criminal charges against Suchart had failed to materialise. Enquiries to police and state prosecutors drew the response that there was no evidence that he was implicated in the BBC scandal. He and his family members were paying off loans and interest incurred with the BBC. The court case in Nong Khai involving falsified land titles did not go ahead and had been removed from the court agenda. But, the allegations aired in Parliament in 1996 cost Suchart his cabinet position and relegated him to political obscurity. By 1999 he still held his seat in Parliament as the member of a one-man political party, but he remained a controversial figure.)

By the end of 1995, the bank (unknown to the public) was technically bankrupt with net liabilities exceeding its net assets by more than 4 billion baht. The bank concealed this loss while announcing annual profits for the years preceding and including 1995. The precarious state of the BBC was known to the Bank of Thailand and to its governor, Vijit Supinit, but the central bank declined to take action as it should have done. Vijit was alleged to have enjoyed a close and friendly relationship with the BBC president, Krirk-kiat Jalichandra, who himself was found to be personally accountable for 36.22 billion baht of the bank's outstanding liabilities by the end of 1995. Almost half of the 77 billion baht in low-quality loans was poured into the takeovers of 22 companies, both inside and outside the country.

Opposition MP Suthep charged that the Group of 16 had blackmailed Krirk-kiat into approving its share of the excessive loans. Suthep charged that the Group of 16 gained access to records of the BBC's shaky financial status and questionable transactions while its members served on the House of Representatives' Fiscal and Financial Institutions Committee. They then used this knowledge to pressure Krirk-kiat, it was alleged.

It is widely assumed by political analysts that under the patronage system of politics, major financial contributors to a political party are rewarded with ministerial positions if that party subsequently becomes part of the government.

Following the revelations of Suthep, journalists questioned Snoh Tientong, then the Chat Thai Party secretary-general, about whether money from the massive loans scandal went to support the election campaign of the Chat Thai Party, and particularly to Prime Minister Banharn Silpa-archa. Snoh ruled out calls for the party to disclose its election spending, saying the present law was unrealistic:

> Only stupid people wouldn't lie about their campaign expenditures. And if anybody tells the truth, he or she should not be an MP.[13]

It is well-known that under the Banharn government, Snoh coveted the post of interior minister, which Banharn withheld in order to balance the ambitions of factions in his party. Snoh subsequently gained the post following the defection of his faction to the New Aspiration Party, which became the core party of the government following the election of 17 November 1996. The post of interior minister is the second most powerful in the cabinet (following the post of prime minister), and at that time controlled the police force, local governments, and preparations for general elections.

Subsequently, Rakesh Saxena, treasury advisor to the BBC and regarded by many as the "brains" behind its dubious operations, charged that scores of politicians were under his pay. Rakesh had fled to Canada during the early revelations of the BBC scandal, and by mid-1999 was still resisting an extradition attempt to bring him back to Thailand.[14]

As of 1999, the legal proceedings regarding the BBC scandal had barely begun to unfold. It was being suggested that the 50 billion baht in bad debts (prior to the crash of the baht in July 1997, worth $2 billion) may be unrecoverable. (See The BBC Scandal, in Chapter 4.)

Where, finally, did the evaporating BBC money go? Will the Thai legal system be able to punish all those who illegally benefited from this massive scandal? Will the patronage system protect high-level beneficiaries? The implications for future fiscal responsibility in Thailand are also massive.

The Principle of Unusual Wealth

It is ironic that the National Peace Keeping Council (NPKC), established by the military junta that seized power in the bloodless military coup of February 1991, was the first body to hold corrupt politicians to account through its tribunal, the Assets Examination Committee. The Committee's governing principle—a correct one, in my view—was that officials and politicians who could not adequately explain their acquisition of unusual amounts of wealth were deemed to be guilty of corruption.

Of course, the NPKC was an illegitimate organisation. Its setting up of the Assets Examination Committee finally proved to be a cynical and manipulative exercise. And it was subsequently ruled by the Supreme Court in March 1993 during the first Chuan government, that the Assets Investigation Committee and its actions—in attempting to bring "unusually rich politicians" to book—were unconstitutional and void. Indeed, there are reasons to believe the Committee was used by some NPKC leaders to exert political leverage for their own benefit. Yet, despite the tribunal's contentious nature, its conclusions were a revealing insight into Thai politics.

Twenty-five cabinet ministers of the toppled government, including former prime minister, Chatchai, were put under investigation for possessing excessive wealth. Eventually, 10 cabinet ministers were confirmed by the committee as being unusually rich.

The junta appointed General Sitthi Chirarochana, a former interior minister, as chairman of the Assets Examination Committee. Sitthi was known for his integrity and honesty; he reportedly became disillusioned and embittered by the junta's apparent manipulation of the investigations once the committee had accumulated evidence. Commentators at the time questioned why the then interior minister and Chat Thai Party secretary-general, Banharn Silpa-archa, escaped examination. Members of the group of former ministers "exposed" as being unusually rich later ended up joining the Sammakitham Party, a political party subsequently created by the junta as a vehicle for the promotion of military influence in the upcoming election, and which later propelled junta member Gen. Suchinda Kraprayoon to his (short-lived) premiership.

The irony of this whole affair is that no elected, "democratic" parliament ever tried to expose and punish corrupt politicians in such a systematic way, before or since. It appears that the politicians who were ruled "unusually rich" were so confident that the patronage/corruption system would not be effectively challenged that they kept large sums of unexplained wealth in their own personal bank accounts.

Who has ever been severely punished for corruption in Thailand? The norm in Thailand has been that, at worst, a politician or official could suffer public embarrassment or loss of his influential position. Patronage and corruption exists in other Asian countries, but some highly-placed politicians still manage to end up in jail.

For example, in late 1995, South Korea put on trial two former presidents, Chun Do Hwan and Roh Tae Woo, for masterminding and assisting, respectively, the 1979 military *coup d'état* and an army massacre of pro-democracy demonstrators in Kwangju the following year. They were convicted in August 1996. Chun was sentenced to death while Roh was sentenced to 22 years in prison. They were granted clemency in late 1997. The two were also convicted of massive corruption during their tenures, spanning 13 years. Also convicted were nine business tycoons, including the chairmen of Samsung and Daewoo, for bribing Roh.

Meanwhile, other countries in this region are conscientiously attempting to punish the corrupt in high places. The former president of Bangladesh, Mohammed Ershad, was sentenced to 13 years in prison for corruption. The corrupt former police chief of Queensland, Australia, was sentenced to 15 years for illegally amassing A$400,000—then worth about eight million baht. And in 1997, the former prime minister of India, P.V. Narasimha Rao was put on trial for forgery. China continues to execute high officials for corruption, and Vietnam had also managed to imprison a former government minister for corruption.

Meanwhile, several of the 10 cabinet ministers "confirmed" as being unusually rich by the Assets Examination Committee, returned to influential cabinet positions in subsequent governments. The "confirmed" unusually rich politicians were:

    Chatichai Choonhavan, prime minister

    Montree Pongpanit, communications minister

Subin Pinkhayan, commerce minister
Pramarn Adireksarn, interior minister
Pramual Sabhavasu, finance minister
Snoh Tientong, deputy interior minister
Pinya Chuayplod, deputy commerce minister
Chalerm Yoobamrung, PM's Office minister
Vatana Asavahame, deputy interior minister
Pitak Intaravirayanant[15]

Montree did not take up a cabinet post in the first Chuan government, but subsequently became communications minister in the Banharn government, then agriculture minister, and then deputy prime minister. He was deputy prime minister and public health minister in the Chavalit government. In the second Chuan government, he did not take up a cabinet post, but his Social Action Party kept control of the Ministry of Public Health up to the breaking of the nationwide 1998 pharmaceuticals-purchasing scandal.

Snoh subsequently became public health minister under Banharn. Coveting the interior ministry post, he led his faction of 50-plus MPs out of Banharn's Chat Thai Party to the New Aspiration Party of Chavalit for the November 1996 election, and subsequently became interior minister in the Chavalit government.

Chalerm became justice minister under Banharn and then deputy interior minister under Chavalit.

Vatana was poised to return to the cabinet of the Banharn government, but was excluded following a public outcry when it was reported that American drug enforcement officials suspected he was involved in drug dealing. Evidence was not produced and Vatana subsequently became a deputy interior minister in the second Chuan government.

Pitak returned to the cabinet in the Chavalit government as deputy foreign minister. He became a PM's Office minister in a cabinet reshuffle under the second Chuan government, when the Chat Pattana Party entered the administration.

Following the accession of the first Chuan Government, the accused politicians appealed against the verdicts handed down by the Assets Investigation Committee, leading to the Supreme Court's voiding of the Committee's actions. However, it should be noted that while the cases against the politicians were dropped, the evidence that the

Committee gathered—particularly through the unprecedented move of examining the politicians' bank accounts—was not refuted. Thousands of "gift" cheques were found to have been deposited in the bank accounts of those politicians. Some of the accounts contained hundreds of millions of baht.

Chuan could hardly have taken action against the unusually rich politicians, since it would have been too destabilising to his coalition. Coalition governments have almost always been precarious in Thai politics, and an understanding has grown that corrupt politicians cannot be prosecuted under this system, even when exposed. They are merely deposed and are not asked to return the money they have looted.

An attempt at prosecutions in 1993 would certainly have caused the Chuan coalition to disintegrate earlier than it did. Another constraining factor, no doubt, was that such an action would have been too much of a shock and embarrassment to the corporate system of influence-buying, if high-flying tycoons who regularly sought favours through political payoffs were also legally implicated.

By 1998, the ultimate result of this system of tacit and collective condonation of the patronage-payoffs system could be seen as a major factor in the meltdown of the country's finance system. The psychology that had developed and gone unpunished, exemplified by the unusually rich politicians, was undoubtedly at work in the months and years leading to the financial meltdown.

If evidence exists, someone must find the courage to punish the guilty. Failure to do so will guarantee that the same problems return again in the future. All Thailand's fine new reforms under the new "anti-corruption" Constitution will come to nothing if enforcement officials in the new courts and the National Counter Corruption Commission succumb to intimidation when the powerful start threatening those responsible for administering the law.

Vote Buying and Dirty Politics

Of course, vote buying is a form of corruption and is part of money politics. As the Thai economy has grown, opportunities for corruption have become more numerous and more lucrative. Therefore, as an investment and quick road to power and influence, vote buying continues to seem attractive. It is seen as one major cause of unqualified people gaining seats in the House of Representatives and the cabinet.

The prevalence of vote buying is a complex issue, tied to rural poverty, the patronage system, and feudal attitudes. Reports arising from the general elections of July 1995 and November 1996 indicate it has grown rather than receded, despite the efforts of independent bodies to monitor electioneering. As previously noted, the 1996 election was described as the dirtiest and most violent in Thai history.

Here are some of the allegations of election malpractice reported in the Bangkok press:

- Democrat Party leader Chuan Leekpai told a gathering of party members that in Pathum Thani and Prachuap Khiri Khan provinces, ballot boxes were changed and officials at polling stations, as well as teachers, were bought. Chuan claimed that election irregularities were most rampant in Prachuap Khiri Khan where party volunteers had been threatened and beaten.[16]

- Vote buying was rampant in the Northeast, with two major rival parties paying up to 1,000 baht for a vote, said PollWatch officials in the region. Provincial chairmen of the body said many parties had adopted the tactics of kidnapping canvassers of rival parties and of making death threats. A certain party had distributed more than 50 million baht among voters in Nakhon Panom (prime minister elect, Chavalit Yongchaiyudh's constituency) said the secretary of the provincial PollWatch office. In Nakhon Ratchasima, the chairman of the PollWatch Region 2 office said he had received death threats and his house had been under surveillance by a group of men. The secretary of the Si Sa Ket office said vote buying in the election was more prevalent than when he first headed the office four years ago.[17]

- The increasing number of campaign complaints and accusations show a worrying trend that rival parties are using partisan bureaucrats to support their candidates and also to harass their rivals. The most worrying and confusing sign given by a caretaker minister in charge of ensuring fair and free elections was his comment that bureaucrats are free to support any parties and individuals they like.[18]

What was the attitude of senior government ministers to allegations made by PollWatch? On 20 November, caretaker prime minister, Banharn, who was also interior minister, failed to keep an appointment at the Interior Ministry to receive evidence on election irregularities from PollWatch. The body instead presented the evidence, covering alleged irregularities in Pathum Thani, Samut Prakan, and Prachuap Khiri Khan provinces, to a deputy interior minister.[19]

No political parties admit to buying votes, but practically everyone in the country knows that it is going on. In a report three months following the 2 July 1995 general election, a news story of *The Nation* made a point that MP's legitimate income can hardly cover their election expenses. Where does the money come from?

> A new-face politician, who failed in the previous election, admitted during an interview with The Nation that his party gave him 3 million baht to buy votes although his hope of winning was slim. "When I walked into the party's headquarters to get my money, I saw senior politicians emerging with boxes of money, literally. When I entered the room I was even more stunned; there was a huge amount of cash in there, huge," said the man, who is now a House committee official. He later found out that hopeful candidates were given 10 million baht each, or more. "The amount a big party spends in an election is unimaginable," he said. "Believe me, most politicians buy votes, more or less."[20]

In an editorial of 7 November 1990, *The Nation* wrote:

> Vote buying is a serious violation of the election laws. But few violators are arrested because the police are afraid of retribution from politicians and their influential patrons. [To combat vote buying] there is certainly no lack of good ideas running around. What is utterly lacking is the political will to clean up the election process as many top politicians rely heavily on existing loopholes to retain power.

Press reporting on recent general elections indicates that many rural voters do not see much wrong with selling their votes. The phenomenon of vote buying is difficult to understand and remedy unless it is seen in the context of traditional culture. There are some differences amongst analysts on how to interpret it, but basically it reflects the relationship between politicians and people, and the expectations of benefits (even if defined in a narrow, parochial way) that people have from the political system. The previously-quoted, Bangkok-based Western analyst noted:

> Vote buying is different in many ways from the abuse of power. . . . What seems to be emerging is a recognition that for people in the rural areas the money paid is a positive sum. They face threats if the votes are not delivered: cut off from credit, seeds, water, whatever. So everyone has a stake in delivering the goods. Villagers look at politicians as providers of tangible benefits; providing baht is just the icing on the cake. Vote buying is a pernicious practice that needs attention, but [it cannot be stopped] unless circumstances of rural life change to gain services and redefine the role of politicians.

Following are some other insights into vote buying which emerged from my interviews and reading. The *Bangkok Post* editorial, 13 December 1989:

> Vote buying is a major symptom of organisational weakness: no party branches outside Bangkok, no long-term grassroots support, no clear platforms, no party discipline, etc.

The Nation, December 1990:

> Vote buying would be less successful without the active connivance of district chiefs and senior provincial administrators, including the governor of each province. . . . An interior minister can, without difficulty, ensure his re-election by appointing the "right" men to his home province and do the same to help his followers get elected in other provinces. He can also block his rivals and their allies by pulling strings in the provincial administration, and unleashing police on his enemies' vote canvassers. . . .

Thammasat University lecturer Chirmsak Pinthong, interviewed in 1992:

> Most Thai politicians depend on influential figures who serve as their canvassers, instead of trying to create a real following among the constituents. . . . The system of patronage is still dominant in this country.

Suwat Liptapanlop, secretary-general of the Chat Pattana Party, interviewed in *The Nation*, 13 April 1996:

> The problem of vote buying is getting increasingly serious. At a recent provincial council election, more than 40 million baht was circulated. It's hard to believe, but it's true. . . .

The Nation, 28 September 1996:

> Pisan Manoleehakul, the president of Thai Farmers Bank Research Centre, predicted "hot money" circulating during the [17 November 1996] election, part of which would be used for vote buying, would be at least 20 billion baht, up from 17 billion baht estimated to be in circulation in the 2 July 1995 campaign.

Nongyao Naowarat, a lecturer in education at Chiang Mai University, offered some insights in the *Bangkok Post*, 14 November 1996:

> Women's groups have often been mentioned in anti-vote-buying campaigns. . . . One hilltribe housewife said to this writer, "Do you expect us to vote without receiving anything in return? If so, many of us will not leave the home to cast ballots because we don't know whom to vote for. We don't know any of the candidates. But if we don't vote, the government would look at our village in a negative way for not cooperating. . . ."

> The form of vote buying and selling has also transformed over time. Past vote-buying attempts involved politicians discreetly giving materials or food of relatively small value to villagers. Both buyers and sellers were usually acquainted with one another. But as political competition became more intense, the "price" for a vote also increased, and vote-buying activities began to occur more openly. . . .

So it pays for village housewives to organise themselves. To them, an election is translated into at least some minor benefits for their collective wellbeing. The notion of turning an election into a means to punish tardy or corrupt politicians is far beyond their imagination for the reason that these villagers cannot afford to be deprived of state funds under their politician's control.

Political commentator "Chang Noi" wrote in *The Nation*, 20 November 1996, also about vote buying from the villagers' perspective:

> The villagers' electoral behaviour is perfectly rational. They get a cash bonus. They get a chance to bargain with the candidates for some investment in local infrastructure—a new well, a paved road, more electricity connections, a bus service. For them, these are the tangible benefits of democracy. The paved road, water supply, and electricity are facilities which city dwellers take for granted. But many villagers still have to bargain for them in this way. The villagers have arrived at this view of politics through experience. For several decades, the farmers' own attempts at forming political organisations were rigorously suppressed. Even this year, another rural leader was assassinated and there is no sign that the police will unearth either culprit or motive. . . .

As well as vote buying, the use of "dark influence", intimidation, and cheating persist. Likhit Dhiravegin, a Thammasat University political scientist, wrote about ballot-box stuffing, a form of election fraud, in the *Bangkok Post*, 13 November 1990:

> Another method of election fraud is to buy off election officers who will be paid to undertake the three "No's"—no reading, no checking, no looking up when people come to cast their votes. [Thus anyone can come to cast a vote.] In a severe case, toward the end of the election hour, the officers will just cast ballots by themselves. If the voters list is checked against the number of ballots in the box, there may be considerable discrepancy. But such a check can only be done when there is an official complaint, and it has to be ordered by the Court of Justice.

Dr. Suchit Bunbongkarn, dean of Chulalongkorn's Faculty of Political Science, in an interview on 17 August 1992, recounted to me a similar example of election fraud:

> In Thailand, there is no compulsory registration of voters. Each voter has to check the household registration against his name on the voting list. But this system is open to abuse. Very few people check their registration. In one case in the past, a huge number of voters were registered from one house: 100–200. . . . [Cheaters] can add a long list of people to the list in collusion with the district officer or polling booth officer. One or two people will vote 10–20 times. Poll Watchers in the booth can spot these multiple voters.

Dr. Suchit added:

> If we really want to have a clean election, it is up to the people. If you want to get rid of fraud, you have to go to the local level. In most of the rural areas, the local patronage is very strong. People are under the control of the village headman and *kamnan*; they can't escape from them. They are not secure if they don't follow their orders.

In the *Bangkok Post* of 14 January 1996, human rights lawyer Thongbai Thongpao wrote about a case in Pak Chong district, Nakhon Ratchasima province, where influential persons forced nine out of 11 candidates to withdraw from a provincial council election:

> It is no secret . . . that politicians at the national level always stick their hands in provincial council member elections, rendering their financial and moral support to certain candidates, as districts are the important constituencies and vote bases of politicians at the national level. . . . In my view, Thai politics is reaching a crisis. Those who have money can buy practically everything they feel like. Government officials, instead of maintaining the law and democracy, readily agreed to be used.

Thus, we get a glimpse of a vicious circle in Thai politics where local officials, local influential people, and national politicians conspire to reinforce their network's power. Because of that, and because of political influence often exercised from above through the Interior Ministry, and because of the weakness of laws and administrative practices that protect rather than expose and punish poll violators, the huge amount of evidence collected by independent election monitors has yet to result in a legal action that has prevented a fraud-committing candidate from assuming a seat in Parliament.

The prosecution of the Buriram vote-buying case arising from the 1995 election stands out as the best attempt yet to punish candidates involved in vote buying. While the outcome, announced on 16 September 1996, was not very satisfactory, it marked a positive new turn in attempts to use the legal system to clean up politics. None of the three accused Chat Thai candidates led by Newin Chidchob was convicted of vote buying. Subsequently, however, an appeals court sentenced some election canvassers to short jail terms, reasoning that there was clearly a conspiracy to buy votes. This had previously been recognised by the provincial court when it ordered the confiscation of 11.4 million baht found with the election canvassers. Newin later returned to the cabinet of the second Chuan government as deputy agriculture minister.

The Buriram case is a tentative achievement and is part of a positive trend against the oligarchic domination of politics—a trend which could be reinforced in the election due by November 2000, if the newly-empowered Election Commission takes strong action. Also part of the positive trend is the work of political NGOs such as PollWatch and the Confederation for Democracy, and the efforts of students, professionals, and others to strengthen democratic awareness through their individual efforts.

PollWatch grew from concerned Thais' yearning for genuine democracy. It made its first appearance as an independent election-monitoring organisation during the March 1992 general elections which brought army commander Gen. Suchinda Kraprayoon to power (only to be toppled following the bloody events of May 1992).

The founding of PollWatch mirrored an Asian yearning for clean elections, as seen in the Philippines in the reinvigorated campaign of NAMFREL (the National Movement for Free elections) to monitor the January 1986 presidential election, which was widely judged to have been won fraudulently by Ferdinand Marcos. His cheating led to the rise of the People's Power movement and the ascent of Corazon Aquino as president the following month.[21]

PollWatch in 1996 monitored its fourth election. It needs to be given much more financial support and additional powers to be more effective. So far, it has been tolerated publicly but scorned locally by corrupt political party interests who find it expedient to cultivate a democratic image. Although PollWatch worked closely with the police to suppress vote buying in the July 1995 election, it had little effect on the practice, since witnesses of vote buying were reluctant to testify. Some volunteers could not enter their designated areas because of death threats made by party canvassers and influential figures.[22]

Complaints of violations of the election laws recorded by PollWatch in the 1995 election campaign showed 66 per cent of them involved candidates' promises to give money, 17 per cent involved officials rallying support for a particular party, and 5 per cent involved voters accepting money. Investigation of complaints showed that some 14,466 had grounds. According to one volunteer, most accusations of electoral fraud involved candidates taking advantage of the authority of government officials.[23]

The ideal number of volunteers to enable two people to monitor every polling station, is more than 100,000. In 1996, the NGO was aiming for 40,000 volunteers.

PollWatch could monitor the campaign, and on voting day observe the counting of votes in the polling booth, but it had no power to prosecute offenders. Under the electoral laws of that time, this could be done only by the police or provincial governor's office, or by the interior minister in exceptional cases. Candidates could also submit cases to the court.

Business and Politics

Ironically, a thesis supposedly written by Prime Minister Banharn Silpa-archa for a masters degree in law from Ramkamhaeng University exposed some fundamental problems of money politics in Thailand (but was later criticised allegedly for employing plagiarism and for being ghost written). The thesis noted that political parties in people's eyes are a tool of interest groups who provide financial support in return for favours, while politicians exploit parties as a key to social, economic, and political privilege.

It noted that much of the funding for political parties came from interest groups who expect business favours. Their mutual-interest relationship with parties went back a long way. When in power, parties used their muscle to smooth the way for their allies' businesses. There were also those who contributed for future investment. Because the stakes are high and it is hard to predict which parties will gain power, business people usually invested in most parties. Such contributions were usually enormous, the thesis said. In conclusion, it observed that political parties were formed to look after the interests of particular groups. Vote buying was excessive and led to corruption.[24]

Consequences arising from the intertwined nature of business and politics have been cited in previous chapters. Following are some additional perspectives on this matter. Likhit Dhiravegin, Thammasat University, in the *Bangkok Post* of 2 January 1990:

> Allegedly, cronyism has been a prominent feature of the present system. Indeed, one is reminded of the Marcos regime. It is estimated that there are around 10–15 business groups rallying around [Thailand's] power centre who have hastily taken the opportunity to exploit the gold mine. . . . Big projects have been approved quietly and swiftly. . . . The permanent civil servants have been unhappy with the present set-up because of the high-handed behaviour of political appointees who interfere in the day-to-day operation of the institutions.

The Nation, on 17 May 1996, gave a glimpse into the way political lines of influence had formed in big business's lobbying for at least four major projects worth more than 121 billion baht:

> Among the most sought-after is the 32 billion baht Metropolitan Rapid Transit Authority underground mass transit system. Industry sources said Ch Karnchang, Italian-Thai Development, and Naowarat Patanakarn are the strongest of the six bidders. . . . Sources said the consortium led by Naowarat Patanakarn/Philip Holzman is a "political" powerhouse, considering their member companies: Si Saeng Engineering, Prayoonvit Co., Vichitphan Co., and Sino-Engineering & Construction. Si Saeng is known to be close to Prime Minister Banharn Silpa-archa, while Vichitphan is related to a key member of Chat Pattana, which is currently in the opposition camp. The other consortium is led by the country's largest contractor, Italian-Thai Development, which

> is building the elevated train system for Bangkok Transit System Co. Sources said the first consortium clearly has an edge in terms of political connections, but Ch Karnchang and Ital-Thai also have cemented good connections within the political establishment. One source said Ital-Thai seems to enjoy good ties with all the major parties, while Ch Karnchang has built a relationship with deputy premier, Somboon Rahong of the Chat Thai Party.

Similar lines of influence to political parties had been established by major telecommunications companies to secure an inside track for telecom projects and licences—a booming business in Thailand in the 1990s.

We may well imagine, following the Crash of 97, that members of Thailand's (formerly) wealthy elite were given a lesson in the destructive role that influence-mongering plays through money politics. During the latter half of 1997 and throughout 1998, impoverished members of the elite were still trying to use their political connections to avoid liquidation of their businesses. But, in future, would the big business tycoons welcome a government where decisions were made on the basis of technical and rational considerations instead of influence-mongering and monetary payments? The up-and-coming next generation of tycoons have been given cause to reflect upon how the unethical and corrupt practices of their predecessors helped to plunge Thailand into misery.

Chapter 8

Thailand's Culture of Patronage and Corruption

As suggested throughout this book, the biggest hurdle impeding Thailand's political development, its sustainable economic development, and its attainment of a genuine quality of life, is the patronage system which permeates Thai society and politics. What exactly is the patronage system?

The essence of patronage was captured very succinctly by one Somchat Santisook in a letter to *The Nation* of 11 November 1990. He wrote:

> Influence and reward characterise Thai society at almost every level—in the cabinet, the civil service, the armed forces, corporate boardrooms, as well as in provincial society. The links run all the way from the village to the cabinet and Supreme Command and back. Policies are far less important.

Patronage is a surviving element of the old Asian feudal system. Among the rural majority of Thailand, passive and feudal-style attitudes still largely hold sway.

In the modern context, patronage is most often linked to money-making through the attainment of political power. When government decisions are made on the basis of patronage, benefits are shared among a small group of people, often accompanied by corruption and disregard for the general welfare of the people. Patronage is anti-democratic. It distorts the development process. Decisions based on patronage often overlook better, more rational courses of action—and often result in more harm than good to the country and people. Patronage is about building networks of influence. It is about paying money for the opportunity to make more money, for gaining (official) political support, and for protection. In its simplest form, patronage seems harmless: a person of status or wealth helping a less privileged person or group. Sometimes a debt, spoken or unspoken, will be incurred; sometimes not. Thus, patronage can be seen to be a natural occurrence among the many possible forms of human relationships. People help each other every day, for friendship's sake, out of benevolence, or in expectation of considerations to be returned in the future.

Patronage fails and becomes destructive to society where it becomes systematised into a network, becomes a law unto itself, and recognises no other goals but its own expansion and the advancement of its members. Political patronage networks strive to infiltrate institutions, business groups, political territory. Anything that can benefit the network or protect it from the law and from rival patronage groups, becomes an object of coercion. Thus, patronage as a system often embraces illegal activities— and often contradicts public policy—because close adherence to the law reduces the benefits available to its members and restricts the growth of the network.

According to Supatra Suparb, an associate professor at Chulalongkorn University's Sociology and Anthropology Department, the patron-client relationship is very much alive in modern Thai society. Why is this?

> Most people still feel comfortable in a hierarchical system and prefer owing allegiance to those more senior or more powerful in return for protection and maintenance of the status quo. . . . Many Thais believe that karma means those people who did good deeds in a past life are rewarded with material wealth and high social status in this life. . . . Most Thais are mainly concerned with their own welfare, and that of their family and close friends. They have little sense of duty to the community. That's why it's difficult—if not virtually impossible—to organise volunteer or charity activities.[1]

As money politics and the political patronage system continue to grow, feeding off an expanding economy, they continually need to find new sources of finance. New, audacious, and more lucrative forms of corruption are sought, as the competitive cost of buying power through money politics increases. The patronage system abhors transparency in government because transparency—the conduct of transactions and decision making openly for everyone to see—assumes the existence of higher goals of honesty, fairness, and benefit to society: elements which again restrict the growth of patronage.

As mentioned in Chapter 6, one of the most acute problems threatening Thailand's future is the political culture's inability to consistently place honest, capable, and talented people into cabinet positions. In addition, it is widely believed among analysts that most, if not all, appointments of senior government officials are based on political, financial, and electoral considerations—a manifestation of the patronage system. The problem exists throughout the government bureaucracy and state agencies. How many times have we seen a political party try to replace the entire board of directors of a state agency, which it momentarily controls, with its own loyal supporters? Thus, we can see another vicious circle in Thai politics where officials, local influential people, and national politicians conspire to reinforce their network's power.

When loyalty to a patronage network replaces criteria of ability and expertise in appointing an agency's top management, we can expect the agency to flounder, and corruption to flourish. The losers are the Thai people and the Thai nation. When merit is ignored, patronage and corruption grow—and the whole government and bureaucratic system becomes less and less capable of solving the country's problems. This was clearly the case leading up to the Crash of 97.

The demise of the unpopular administration of Prime Minister Banharn Silpa-archa in September 1996, after 14 turbulent months in office, serves as a castigation of patronage politics. *The Nation* commented thus on Banharn's political career:

> It was an [unenviable] career, built purely upon the patronage system at which he had been reigning supreme. For twenty-odd years he had been skilfully brokering power, cutting shady deals, and expanding his influence from his Supanburi base into national politics, until he became the most powerful politician of this country. Banharn's mistake was his belief that he could always rely on the patronage system that had nurtured him into national prominence.

At the heart of the patronage system lies money and *baramee*, or reserved power, as translated by former prime minister, Anand Panyarachun. But *baramee* carries a dualistic quality. There is a positive *baramee* that commands loyalty and respect, without any promise of kickbacks, for it is based on a noble cause or principle. Then there is a negative *baramee* that works insofar as the practitioner could afford to throw the money around while instilling fears and greed. Banharn symbolised the dark side of *baramee*. Insofar as he could cut deals or mediate power sharing, he would keep his power. But he could never command respect. Anyway, does respect matter in the patronage system? His flair was to contract out big deals for the benefit of his family and friends. At one point he was Thailand's most successful contractor. It was exactly this business-minded politics which guided Banharn's philosophy of public affairs. . . .[2]

Neither did Banharn's major coalition partner and rival, Gen. Chavalit Yongchaiyudh, (who became prime minister following the 1996 election), escape charges of patronage. In its editorial of 29 August 1996, entitled "New Aspiration Party Policies Promote a System of Patronage", *The Nation* observed:

The telecom master plan, which would give a broader picture of the government's policy to ensure equal footing for all participants, has not been approved. In effect, the NAP has allowed big telecom firms to influence policies and undermine the process of fair play. . . . Instead of contributing to the creation of a society that is democratic, just, transparent, and accountable, it strives to keep the public helpless and in blinkers. . . . Likewise the quiet changes at the board of the Port Authority of Thailand, and reshuffles conducted at the Highways Department and the Maritime Promotion Commission have been heavily criticised. The reshuffles appear to have been based on a "patronage" mindset rather than on personal qualifications or suitability. This scenario resembles what is also happening in the reshuffles of top officers in the three branches of the armed forces.

The political patronage system will even support the direct entry into the cabinet of big players from the corporate world. *The Nation* reported on such a power grab during the final days of the Chavalit administration, through a cabinet reshuffle involving his New Aspiration Party:

> Non-MP Poosana Premanoch, a major shareholder of telecom giant United Communication Industry Plc (Ucom) . . . assumed that he was coming in to replace NAP party MP Piyanat Watcharaporn, who was in charge of tourism. . . . [Poosana] is being closely watched as he is one of the two top executives of the Ucom group installed in non-key positions in the cabinet. His partner Somchai Bencharongkul was made deputy public health minister. . . .
>
> The entry of the Ucom group's executives into the cabinet reflects its long-time attempt to boost the group's profile. Poosana was quoted as saying that Ucom group should have its own representatives in the government so that it could access information efficiently and at the same time prevent competitors from blocking Ucom's projects in cabinet meetings. He made the statement when he was working for Ucom full-time. Ucom always looks at Shinawatra, its main telecom rival, as having better access to the government, as its owner, Thaksin Shinawatra, is a deputy prime minister.[3]

Considering the numerous negative effects arising from the patronage system, it is no surprise that Thai politics is racked by division, opportunism, and inherent instability. On average, looking at the elected governments of this decade, a cabinet minister will keep his seat for around 12 months or a little more—hardly long enough to maintain continuity in government policy or to establish much-needed, long-term programmes to overcome obstacles that are impeding Thailand's development.

The Cultural Roots of Patronage

There has been a fair amount of academic research documenting the cultural patterns, values, and practices of the old Thailand from which modern-day patronage and corruption have evolved.

The 1994 study of Pasuk Phongpaichit and Sungsidh Piriyarangsan[4] shows that there is much complacency in Thai society about corruption. The two lecturers review earlier scholarship which has traced the origins of this complacency, from writers Lucien Hanks, Fred W. Riggs, Edward Van Roy, Thinapan Nakata, Clark Neher.

The common observation is that old norms of behaviour remain deeply rooted in present-day Thai political and bureaucratic culture, even though Thai institutions have taken on a modern outward appearance. Attitudes necessary for a healthy, modern society—such as the rule of law and commitment to the service and wellbeing of the people—have in a large measure failed to replace them.

What are the cultural roots of the patronage system, with its tendency towards corruption? In the days of absolute monarchy in Thailand, and especially throughout the Ayutthaya period (encompassing the *sakdina* period of aristocrat-officials which existed under the monarchy from roughly the 16th to 19th Centuries), everything was the king's prerogative. The king designated officials of his family to administer various regions of the kingdom. These governors were not paid, and in collecting taxes for the monarch naturally kept something for themselves. This was acceptable as long as there was no complaint from the people. Included in the *sakdina* system was the tradition of presenting gifts to high officials. Once appointed to a senior position, a Thai bureaucrat would tend to treat his office as a private domain and as a legitimate tool for generating revenue. This traditional-style patronage system was then, no doubt, seen as part of the natural order.

It is in the modern era—which is much more complex and requires properly-functioning, rational systems of economics and government—where such practices have come to be labelled "corrupt" and detrimental to the development and maintenance of a healthy society. The modern era (roughly the past 100 years in Western terms) has spawned the concept of equal rights among the people, and the notion that governments, especially in developing countries, have a duty towards national development—that governments should work to end exploitation and inequalities in society, rather than use the mechanisms of office for personal gain or patronage.

In the old agrarian feudal systems, patronage was formalised, where the feudal lord or master (the patron) took care of the needs of his underlings (the peasants) in return for their loyalty. Feudalism defined a person's place in the universe. It contained the attitude that the individual is subservient to higher powers, has little or no power to influence events himself, reacts passively when called upon, and does not challenge or question the existing order. The rights and obligations of both parties under some feudal societies may even have been written down in some kind of charter. At the summit of this system was the ruler—the absolute monarch or emperor—who was the origin of all favour, and to whom everyone held obligations.

In analysing the logic of feudal society, Hanks argued that within the Thai value system, merit could be derived from power, and that this equation was the basis for patron-client relationships which formed the structure of Thai political society. . . .[5]

Riggs showed how the Chinese business community was able to flourish in Thailand, by using and reinforcing the patronage system. Each businessman received protection from an influential Thai official to carry out his business, and in return the Chinese businessman paid his protector or patron for the service.[6]

Van Roy explained the existence and continuity of pervasive corruption in Thailand as a carry-over of patron-client type relationships from the pre-modern *sakdina* period, and especially from the Thai tradition of presenting gifts to high officials.[7]

Neher noted that the patron-client structure existed, and continues to exist, because everyone concerned sees it as a good structure which brings benefits in terms of stability, order, and the resolution of potentially destabilising conflicts. . . . "Little" people must find a patron and offer respect, gifts, and services in order to ensure favour and security. "Big" people try to build up their clientele in order to maximise the flow of gifts and favours. People in high office must generate enough money to provide resources and protection for their followers in order to maintain their loyalty in the context of keen competition among different factions. . . .[8]

Pasuk and Sungsidh note that the coherence of the *sakdina* system

> . . . started to be undermined by the administrative reforms begun under King Chulalongkorn from the 1880s onwards. These reforms introduced the idea of a centralised bureaucracy with professional skills, a system of recruitment and promotion, standards of behaviour, disciplinary rules, and remuneration by salary. . . . However, there were substantial compromises between

247

> the new system and the old which meant that this "age of reform" was very far from a complete replacement of one "feudal" administrative system by another "bureaucratic" one. . . . The bureaucracy remained dominated by members of the royal and noble families, especially at the upper levels . . . linked to monarchy. . . . The revolution of 1932 marked another step away from the traditional system.[9]

Now, there are laws and commissions to deal with corruption, and a code of conduct for officials which explicitly outlaws gifts taken in return for services or activities which the official has the duty to perform, and outlaws the use of official position to grant favours to friends and relatives. But there is still large-scale adherence to these practices by officials. Pasuk and Sungsidh further conclude:

> The concept of public service as a counterweight to corruption has limited meaning when the public opposition to corruption is weak or non-existent. The people themselves are confused about what is corrupt and not corrupt. . . . There has been little pressure from corporate bodies such as business groups or political parties to limit corruption. This ambivalence can contribute to the persistence of corruption.[10]

Within the bureaucracy, officials' expectations of commissions, tips, or "tribute" is well entrenched. It may be defined as corruption by legal experts or advocates of sustainable development—but many others see it as "normal" practice. These others may or may not be aware that it is a destructive practice which lowers the standards of achievement. Corruption in some departments has become institutionalised in the form of syndicates, where officials from the lowest to the highest cooperate to share corruption revenues. This was clearly exemplified in 1998 by the syndicated corruption uncovered in the Ministry of Public Health, when rural doctors exposed a large-scale, drug-purchasing scam. In such syndicates, officials protect each other—especially superiors protect inferiors. This is somewhat similar to a patronage network.

Over recent decades, the major question regarding corruption among the groups surrounding the power centre has been not how to eliminate this plague, but rather who gets to share the benefits. Traditionally, the bureaucratic elite monopolised the benefits arising from corruption, but as new power groups have emerged, new tensions have emerged also. But, having said that, it is worth noting that a new ambivalence seems to have crept in. Political parties in the parliamentary opposition now regularly raise corruption issues to discredit members of the government, in the hope that they may soon replace the discredited ministers. However, while corruption charges have become more common and politicised, MPs practically never introduce specific administrative or legislative measures to get rid of it.

Businessmen seeking special advantages have always cultivated the power holders. Following the rise of military power after the 1932 coup against the absolute monarchy, companies customarily invited high-ranking and influential military and police officers to sit on their boards of directors or advisory boards. There were new upsurges in this practice following the coups of 1947 and 1991.[11] In the 1970s, businessmen increasingly sought access through political parties. In the 1990s, more are looking for individual links into the technocracy.[12]

High-ranking military officers overthrew the Chatichai government in 1991 citing its massive corruption. But later it seemed that the officers' indignation was not aimed at the evil of corruption itself, but rather at the fact that upstart provincial politicians were indulging in such a large buffet. Pasuk Phongpaichit and Chris Baker assessed it this way:[13]

> Corruption [in the form of gift cheques to ministers in the Chatichai government] was not new. But the boom economy made the sums larger. And the shift of power from bureaucracy to business changed the beneficiaries. For many Bangkokians, both businessman and bureaucrat, the provincial politicians seemed greedy upstarts. They had been pulled into politics as an extension of their business interests. They were now promoting those interests from their seats in the cabinet with the business ethics of the provincial frontier. They were grabbing the corruption revenue which once had disappeared into more established pockets.

Perhaps the biggest hurdle to solving the corruption problem is the attitude of the public and of officials (including police) that accepting bribes was not corrupt as long as it did not cause trouble to anyone.

Sungsidh found there was a perception among these career groups that corruption involves only money that you force out of people, and money that you cheat from the government budget. . . . Commissions from purchasing programmes and construction projects were not thought of as corrupt by businessmen as long as officials did not demand more than 20 per cent. But some contractors objected to it as corruption, because it forced them to reduce the quality of their work.[14] Sungsidh found that so many people were indulging in dishonest practices without thinking that they were corrupt.

By and large, Thais still see bribes given to officials as being *sin nam jai*, or gifts of goodwill, which are acceptable or tolerable. At the same time, officials rationalise that since they do not request the bribes overtly, there is no moral or social wrong incurred in receiving gifts which are "willingly" presented to them.[15]

In completing their assessment, Pasuk and Sungsidh conclude that the rise of corruption as an issue was more a function of increasing competition for political power and corruption revenues between the old power holders in the military and civilian bureaucracy, and the new challengers in civilian politics, particularly those with a business background. . . .[16]

The Alternative to Patronage

What is the alternative to patronage and payoffs in conducting the business of government? To achieve good government and create the conditions for a healthy and competitive Thailand of the future, patronage and its relentless use and pursuit of money must be curbed, and a great effort made to base government decision making on selfless principles, such as:

- the insistence on principles of transparency and financial accountability in awarding government concessions and contracts;
- the principle of merit in making appointments to government posts; and
- the principle of rationality in policy making.

The need to embrace these principles became more important than ever following Thailand's financial collapse. Many recommendations, such as instituting better auditing practices both in government and in the private sector, were receiving attention and were addressed by the new Constitution.

Needless to say, contracts for projects and purchases should proceed according to strict bidding procedures, emphasising fairness and impartiality. The enactment of a code of "best practices" to ensure transparency and fairness is recommended. Such procedures should also cover the formulation of the terms of reference for contracts, also covering technical specifications, which should be assessed by a competent and independent panel.

Rationality in policy making would be greatly enhanced by insisting that politicians' self-interest be removed from the process of decision making and policy formulation. A politician should be obliged to disqualify himself from any debate, decision-making process, or negotiation in which he or his associates or relatives have an economic or financial interest. Formulation of a code of conduct for this may be advisable.

Rational policy making, to explain it in simple and practical terms, requires that the process of analysing the problem to be solved, and making a decision on what action to take, be clarified in three areas, namely: objectives, strategies, and policies. Policies are formulated by first defining objectives and strategies, and then determining specific measures designed to achieve them. In a politically ideal world, it is not enough to announce merely that "we have a policy. . . ." without also revealing the strategies and time-frame for implementation.

Additionally, the overriding goal of rationality in a democratic context requires that policies and strategies must include broadly-accepted assessments of the environmental and social impacts. After all, economic growth and infrastructure development are means to the most sublime of rational ends: a better quality of life for the people, which is sustainable far into the future. This requirement is part of the *ecological imperative* (see Chapter 2).

A number of large infrastructure projects promoted by governments in the 1990s, including some dams and transportation projects, would fail the rationality test because they were apparently designed to benefit business interests, rather than objectives such as sustainable development. Such inappropriate projects can distort a country's overall development, gobbling up funds that could be better spent elsewhere.

Politicians and their supporters love massive infrastructure projects, including expensive high-tech projects, given that the rate for under-the-table commissions, by the mid-1990s, seemed to have grown to 20 per cent (some kickbacks are much higher) compared with 10 per cent a decade earlier. High-tech projects give the country merely an appearance of being "modern" and progressive, while fundamental social problems remain underfunded and corruption becomes even more entrenched. This fixation on money-spinning infrastructure is part of the anti-progressive syndrome of *growth without development*.

Members of Parliament love road-building and bridge-building schemes for their constituencies. Billions of baht per year are spent on unneeded multi-lane highways, concrete pedestrian bridges, and trans-railway vehicle bridges which are sprouting up all over the country, not because they are wanted by the community, but because kickbacks from construction projects have become so pervasive and "accepted" as politicians' means of personal revenue generation. Politicians have previously scorned investment in improving educational standards and in implementing primary health care based on preventive medicine, because these investments offer very few opportunities for skimming the budget. Infrastructure projects and equipment purchases offer many more opportunities. That is why so many local government bodies all want to buy their own (expensive) earth-moving equipment, for instance. Money would be much better spent, and development much better served, if private, regionally-based companies invested in such machinery and worked on contract for various local governments needing such services. This kind of psychology of growth without development pervades the political and administrative systems.

The 1997 Constitution can help to dismantle this wasteful and destructive system. Its provisions that local communities must be consulted and must be involved in the planning of so-called development projects in their communities, must be rigorously applied. Villagers know what their priorities are: they mostly want good health services and good education for their families. NGOs and the legal profession can play a big role in insisting upon, and fostering, people's participation.

The Increasing Stakes of Corruption

Creative forms of corruption are arising all the time. A subtle method identified by a researcher[17] in the early 1990s involved MPs keeping quiet and abstaining on votes in Parliament. The tactic was first for an MP to make a noise in the House against a particular proposal so that the company involved would come to see him. After a hidden transaction had taken place, there would be no more noise.

Pasuk and Sungsidh noted how the beginning of Thailand's economic boom of the late 1980s changed the opportunities for political corruption:

> The cabinet had the power to decide on large infrastructure projects without recourse to debate in the Parliament. Individual ministers also had the power to decide on large projects in each ministry without reference to cabinet or Parliament—granting licences for new factories and financial firms, approving immigration quotas, granting concessions for logging or reforestation.[18]

Pasuk and Sungsidh found that misuse of funds and corruption occur in all ministries and government offices. They quote the 1990 report of the Office of the Auditor General (OAG), which classified the magnitude of corruption by ministry. The ministries which garnered the largest amounts were: Defence (especially 1987), Industry (especially 1989, 1990), state enterprises (especially 1990) Agriculture (1989–90), and provincial offices. The office of the Counter Corruption Commission (CCC) ranked ministries with the highest instances of corruption which it investigated in 1990 as: Interior, Agriculture, Education, Public Health, Communications, and Defence.[19]

Pasuk and Sungsidh found that the police department was rated as the most corrupt department of government, with revenue from corruption syndicates within the police being widely distributed not only among police, but also among officials in the military, in the Ministry of Interior, and in the juridical system. They observed:

> Corruption in the police also has a special significance. It encourages crime. It ensures that those who run illegal businesses and criminal activities can buy protection and make super-profits. This in turn leads to criminalisation of both society and politics, since many of those who achieve wealth and power have risen from the super-profits of criminal activity. . . .

Meanwhile, in 1996, an additional rampant form of corruption became evident as the Thai government's budget allocation process came under scrutiny, and some shocking observations were made public.

In February 1996, MP Pichet Phanvichartkul (Democrat Party) claimed he received complaints from Budget Bureau officials that a "second budget bureau" had been set up at the bureau headquarters to deal in under-the-table business. Prime Minister Banharn had often been accused of infiltrating the bureau with his cronies in earlier times as a cabinet minister. He now dismissed additional charges that he was exerting political control over the Budget Bureau in a bid to ensure that politically significant projects of his Chat Thai Party got top priority. He denied knowledge of high-level transfers of staff at the bureau which the opposition claimed were meant to ensure that the prime minister's party would maintain a firm grip on national budget management, and to facilitate "deals" with contractors.[20]

In May 1996, House speaker, Boon-ua Prasertsuan charged that as much as 50 per cent of the budget earmarked for specific government projects was being siphoned off by dishonest politicians in collusion with corrupt officials. He was speaking at a seminar entitled "Budget Reform in the Age of Globalisation."[21] He said budget funding is regularly skimmed as it proceeds from ministries to their various departments, divisions, and provincial offices before arriving at the project sites. Boon-ua said:

> Most of the time corrupt politicians and officials escape punishment. In fact, most of them continue to prosper and command respect in society. . . . The budget is like a popsicle that is passed around. Everyone gets a lick at it when it comes their way, so that by the time the one at the end of the line gets it, there's only a little left.

In August 1996, at a meeting organised by the Civil Service Commission, the Thailand Development Research Institute, the Thai Research Fund, and the Sukhothai Thammathirat Open University, the Budget Bureau was identified as one of the "worst cases" among institutions plagued by blatant political intervention and corruption. It was said that more than half of the projects going through the bureau were not government agency initiatives.[22]

Could new provisions for budget scrutiny in the 1997 Constitution and its subsequent new enabling legislation remedy these appalling abuses?

Other possibilities for large-scale corruption—within the Bangkok Metropolitan Administration—were pointed out by former foreign minister, Prasong Soonsiri during a press interview in May 1996. He identified two activities of the BMA that were susceptible to corruption:

1. Unclear methods of estimation of the annual household tax, which allowed corrupt tax collectors to ask for tea money from building owners in return for not collecting the full amount of tax.

2. The approval of construction projects or licences, which were very hard to get unless tea money was paid to concerned officials. Officials control every procedure, said Prasong, ranging from granting construction projects and all related licences, to the construction methods used. . . .[23]

Here are some other published allegations of corruption:

- MPs told the House Budget Committee in late June 1996 that the Royal Irrigation Department was rigging bids for contracts in order to obtain kickbacks from contractors. A figure of 20 per cent of the value of the contract was mentioned.[24]

- A curious incident took place in Bangkok in August 1996 when the justice minister, Chalerm Yoobamrung, charged that some applicants for new banking licences being issued by the Ministry of Finance were making under-the-table payments of 750 million baht each. Such a charge, coming from the justice minister, could be expected to cause severe ripples within the government, or perhaps even to topple it. However, the following day, photographs in the daily newspapers showed Chalerm and Prime Minister Banharn shaking hands and smiling after emerging from a meeting. The charges of illegal payments were not heard again.

- Education Minister Sukhavich Rangsitphol said on 22 June 1996 that corrupt officials had siphoned off hundreds of millions of baht from budgetary allocations for the purchase of educational equipment, and for projects. Many ministry officials had been involved in corruption for years, particularly in procurement projects in which specifications of the goods to be purchased tended to be loosely written when they should be clear-cut. He

255

cited the Education Ministry's programme to provide primary school children from poor families with school uniforms, saying he had been informed that ministry officials customarily sought a 20 per cent "commission".[25] However, Sukhavich himself came under suspicion over the ministry's procurement of thousands of vastly overpriced computers for schools, many of which lacked an electricity supply or teachers capable of using them.

- The American giant transnational IBM asked to withdraw from its 1.8 billion baht computer system contract with the Thai Revenue Department in July 1997. It was rumoured that officials refused to cooperate with IBM software developers because a modern computer system would cut off their illegal sources of money. An IBM executive said the software phase had been fraught with problems because the department had not pinpointed even its most basic requirements to help developers design the proper software. The failure of the Revenue Department to install an adequate computer system meant the country's tax collection system would become even more obsolete as the department called for a new round of bidding.[26]

- Even Thailand's joining the international Information Technology Agreement, formalised at the World Trade Organisation meeting in Singapore in 1996, became subject to official delays through "red tape". The proposed zero-tax measure for imports of technology included in the trade agreement was apparently perceived by Thai officials as a threat to the substantial income that import duty collectors regularly skim off imports. Even though the official rate of tax on electrical products was 5 per cent, companies had to pay an under-the-table charge of at least 30 per cent to get the imports released.[27]

- Another spectacular example of a lack of transparency was the supercomputer project at the Meteorological Department. The project was initiated in 1993, had been through the hands of two governments, various changes of directors, and in 1997 was facing a third government without nearing completion.[28]

- The Office of the Auditor-General in July 1998 reported many irregularities had occurred involving budget spending at the Education Ministry. Several education offices did not have receipts for spending programmes, some issued cheques to unidentified creditors, and those who signed procurement projects were not authorised persons. Some agencies failed to submit copies of contracts worth more than one million baht to the state auditor, and others also failed to collect delay fines. The Counter Corruption Commission, in its annual report, said 172 complaints were lodged against education officials for corruption and irregularities in 1997. The Education Ministry was second to the Interior Ministry, which had 361 complaints against it. The Agriculture Ministry ranked third with 145 complaints.[29]

- In November 1998, it came to light that the Food and Drug Administration was running a scam, in approving advertisements, that netted officials more than 36 million baht per year in recent years. *The Nation* found that a change in the structure of the public relations and advertisement control division around 1994–95 provided greater authority to the Food and Drug Administration's deputy chief, and did away with the participation of outsiders in approving advertisements. The division handled about 30 print, television, and billboard applications a week. Advertising agencies used to pay a minimum 10,000 baht bribe per advertisement approved prior to 1994–95, rising to a minimum of 25,000 baht during the peak of the bubble era.[30]

- Perhaps the most significant case to reach the light of day in 1998 was the systematic corruption in the pricing of pharmaceutical supplies to public hospitals throughout the country. The Rural Doctors Society, under its president Yongyos Thammawut, in August accused senior officials of the Ministry of Public Health of requiring many hospitals to buy drugs and medical equipment from specific companies according to a price list which set prices two or three times higher than regular prices. The first reaction of health administrators, including Rakkiat Sukthana, the health minister, of the Social Action Party, was to deny that there were any irregularities concerning the use of the 1.4 billion baht budget for such purchases. But the doctors would not abandon their campaign. The Society urged hospitals to send it irregular purchase documents for submission to the National Counter Corruption Commission. Rural pharmacists came out to back them. The minister was forced to resign, sending ripples through the coalition government of Chuan Leekpai. But, like so many similar cases, well into 1999, no legal action had been taken against individual officials. It was obvious that a corruption syndicate existed within the ministry encompassing many senior and lower officials. The syndicate's tentacles stretched far and wide into hundreds of provincial hospitals. The tragedy of this case was that Thailand's economic crisis was already hitting the rural poor, who could not afford expensive medicines. But this was of no concern to the greedy and corrupt officials. The former secretary-general of the Medical Council, Dr. Chuchai Suphawong said:

> Just think how many children could be immunised against deadly diseases with the budget. If the money was stolen, what will happen to a lot of people who get sick and whose lives could have been saved with that money?[31]

And so, the numerous accusations of massive rake-offs continue. There is no agency within the Thai governmental set-up that can be relied upon to relentlessly pursue and prosecute corruption cases, especially at a high level. The Counter Corruption Commission should be one such agency. With its reorganisation and empowerment under the 1997 Constitution, it remains to be seen whether it can now begin to net big fish. Up to 1997, the Counter Corruption Commission was perceived as having been largely ineffectual, perhaps because it had been under the supervision of the prime minister, and therefore subordinated to the demands of patronage politics.

Such is the pervasiveness and destructiveness of corruption in the Thai system. But, if we really want to characterise the attitude of the Thai elite, and their numerous strings and connections that run through the government, the police, and the bureaucracy, one major scam stands out: the Saudi gems scandal.

In 1989, Kriangkrai Techamong, a Thai servant in the Riyadh palace of Saudi Arabia's Prince Faisal, stole $20 million worth of gold, diamonds, other gems, jewellery, and cash. Kriangkrai returned to Thailand with the loot, was caught, was convicted in 1990, and served two-and-a-half years of a five-year sentence before receiving a royal pardon.[32] But the jewels, which had been recovered and placed in police custody, just disappeared!

A frantic hunt for the gems followed, resulting in some being recovered—but many of those subsequently went missing a second time from police custody. A saga of deception, forgery, kidnapping, and murder accompanied the attempts of various players to grab the jewels. The Saudis were understandably very upset, and the whole episode has effectively nullified Thai relations with Saudi Arabia.

The police department set up a centre in October 1994 and appealed for the anonymous return of the jewellery. It received more than 500 pieces. Even while they were awaiting return to Prince Faisal, some of the jewels again went missing from police custody. Many others that were subsequently returned to Saudi Arabia proved to be fakes.

Police vowed they would not give up the search for the missing "blue diamond", the most valuable piece of the stolen jewellery. National police chief Pratin Santiprapop appointed Police Lt.-Gen. Chalor and Police Lt.-Gen. Sophon Sawikamin to lead a team which would hunt for it. Chalor kidnapped the wife and son of Santi Srithanakhan, a gems dealer believed to know the location of the diamond, to force him to come forward with the information. Santi was forced to pay a 2 million baht ransom for the return of his wife and son, who were nevertheless murdered.

In December 1995, Kriengkrai testified as a prosecution witness in the charges of malfeasance and conspiracy in an embezzlement suit filed against Pol Lt-Gen Chalor Kerdthet, then deputy commissioner of the Central Investigation Bureau, and eight other officers.

In the ensuing years, rumours circulated that the wives of prominent politicians and police generals were seen wearing missing jewellery items, including the blue diamond.[33] Ten years after the theft, the prize pieces of the collection were still missing.

The overwhelming desire of members of the Thai elite to steal the Saudi royal family's jewels has led to Thai workers being excluded from working in Saudi Arabia, where they previously formed a contingent of tens of thousands. Saudi Arabia declined in 1998 to attend the Asian Games hosted by Thailand. Every time a new government is formed in Thailand, the current Saudi Arabian *charge d'affaires* raises the issue once again with Thai government officials.

SECTION 3

QUALITY OF LIFE OR GROWTH WITHOUT DEVELOPMENT?

Chapter 9

Defining a New Quality of Life

The bursting of the bubble economy in Thailand has given all Thais cause to reflect upon what is the true essence of a satisfying and attainable quality of life that will endure far into the future. What alternative course, political and economic, should the country follow in the future? Will Thailand's eventual recovery merely follow the same assumptions and attempt to pursue the same goals that contributed to the bubble economy in the first place? (These are questions I attempt to answer in this section and the following one.)

It is worth emphasising that even before the Crash, Thailand's quality of life was in decline despite the country's apparently growing affluence and increasing purchasing power. The economic bubble was fuelled, among other causes, by the society's single-minded pursuit of money by all means, which was overriding quality-of-life concerns such as health, environment, and social equity. At the same time, the notions of fairness and compassion in society were failing to develop, or were eroding. The rural masses were seen as people to be manipulated for power or profit by the ambitious and powerful.

What does it mean when a country's material wealth is seen to increase but the quality of life declines? Some years earlier, the United Nations Children's Fund (UNICEF)[1] succinctly explained this emerging global dilemma:

> The industrialised world is entering an age of doubt about material progress. Many of its citizens are experiencing what the economist Robert Heilbroner has called "the startled realisation that the quality of life is worsening . . . that people who are three or five or ten times richer than their grandparents do not seem to

be three or five or ten times happier or more content or more richly developed as human beings." Coinciding with such doubts is the gradual realisation that such progress is also no longer limitless; that what was once the clear and infinitely extending horizon of material advance is now becoming closer and darker as ecological limits loom.

But while questioning the superfluous nature of rampant materialism, UNICEF warned that

> . . . for at least a billion people in the world, material progress has very different connotations. It holds out the hope of adequate food, clean water, safe sanitation, decent housing, reliable health care, and at least a basic education. This is a definition of progress which remains entirely valid. And it is one with which the rest of the world must keep faith.

As noted in Chapter 3, a philosophy abounds in money-oriented, market-based economics (the ideology of *economism*) that economic growth will solve all of the developing world's problems: if poverty, anxiety, ill health and environmental destruction are prevalent today, we just need to get more money and everything will soon be all right. Thais succeeded in getting more money, as their economy recorded the world's highest continuous growth rates through most of the 1990s.[2] Some of this money filtered through to the poor, but most of it fuelled status-generating consumption among the rising middle class and get-even-richer investment schemes—such as ill-thought-out property development and the proliferation of shopping malls and luxury department stores—among the Thai elite and *nouveaux riches*. Showing off was the order of the day during the bubble economy. Observed *The Nation*:

> In this age of intercontinental shopping sprees, wealthy Thais have taken conspicuous consumption to new levels. "We go to Switzerland to buy Rolex and Victorinox, to London to shop in Oxford St, and to Paris to buy Louis Vuitton bags and to visit the Galleries Lafayette," said Wimol, a 25-year-old Thai office staffer who recently joined a popular shopping tour to Europe, courtesy of her parents. . . .[3]

Dr. Chalongphob Sussangkarn, president of the Thailand Development Research Institute (TDRI) commented that in South Korea, for example, such people would be despised for being conspicuous consumers and flaunting their Mercedes Benz, Rolex, and so on. Some would say such a thing is not what real Koreans would do. And to pay for all this, Thais accumulated debts as never before. Said Dr. Chalongphob, in 1996:

> Thais are now living on credit. The country has overspent as well as the people. . . .[4]

Dr. Chalongphob noted that household savings declined from 21.1 per cent of GNP in 1986, to 9.8 per cent in 1992, and to 7 per cent in 1995. Consumption expenditure in 1995 rose 15 per cent from the year earlier.

An aura of progress and "modernity" was generated as the speculative economic bubble grew, fuelled by a fawning media, high consumption, and a quick-profits mentality among foreign investors. Rural and urban development, and the environment, suffered. When this illusion of progress vanished, it became apparent that the problems generated by such growth without development were bigger than ever.

For example, the National Economic and Social Development Board (NESDB) in its Seventh Plan (1992–96) noted that the rapid transformation from a basically rural society to urban economy, and the ageing of Thailand's population, had increased illness and death from relatively new diseases such as AIDS, respiratory tract diseases, cancer, mental illness, and nervous breakdowns. The NESDB pointed to the decline in social cohesion and noted that Thailand's traditional family structure was breaking down, as one or both parents frequently became economic migrants to the cities, leaving behind children and the elderly. The demands of so-called "modern economic development" thus undermined the sense of security, reassurance, caring, and warmth generally associated with the family institution. They hindered mental, spiritual, and moral development. The NESDB warned:

> These imbalances are destabilising and will have impacts on the peace and calm of society in the future.

What followed was the 1997 meltdown of the economy—and a deteriorating social situation that affected millions of Thais.

Even as Thailand was recording its world-beating economic growth, the NESDB was lamenting that environmental development to enhance the quality of life was almost non-existent. In its 1994–95 economic outlook report, the agency noted the many ways in which Thailand was neglecting its environment, particularly:

- Administration and management systems for environmental protection and enhancement were inefficient and fragmented.
- There was no mechanism for supervision and coordination among the public agencies under different ministries at the national and local levels.
- There was no specific legislation which dealt directly with prevention (and solution) of pollution problems, and development of the needed manpower and technology was lagging behind and had not kept pace with the extent and seriousness of the problems.
- The polluter pays principle, regarded as an important legalistic and fiscal approach towards maintaining a clean environment, was being ignored, and the burden of cleaning up pollution shifted to the taxpayer, letting polluters off the hook
- People's participation in environmental causes, particularly in monitoring environmental quality, was lacking.

Can Thailand, in its post-Crash doldrums, create a new wave of sustainability and enhanced quality of life, rather than aspire once again to ride the receding wave of growth without development, characterised by the pursuit of ever-increasing consumption which disregards social and environmental concerns? Quality of life is not just some abstract dream worldof academics and disaffected writers. When economics, politics, and so-called "development" become detached from the quality of life and sustainability, the result will surely be social upheaval and/or ecological disaster. Thailand thus needs a new awakening, a new focus for national priorities.

Money Politics Harms the Quality of Life

In compiling material during the mid-1990s about the quality of life in Thailand, this writer sought information from three prominent people in the medical profession. All of them indicated that the low quality of politicians coming to power under the money-oriented, political patronage system was a major impediment to advances in the quality of life. Dr. Hatai Chitanondh, director of the Thailand Health Research Institute, expressed it this way:

> Democracy in Thailand has existed only for a short time. The representatives who are elected into the Parliament are not of a high quality. There are a few, but the majority are not. Many of them have to buy their way in. Political decisions are not made on a scientific basis; they are made on [an uninformed basis], out of consideration for profits or personal benefits or group benefits. That is why our urban health is poor, because of political power plays.[5]

Dr. Hatai is a proponent of political decentralisation and administrative reform as a major starting point for improvements:

> Take for example, the Bangkok Metropolitan Administration (BMA). We can elect good people in Bangkok, but the BMA has to be under the Ministry of Interior. The BMA does not control all the infrastructure of Bangkok; for example, water supply is under a government unit controlled by the Ministry of Interior. It is the same with electricity and other agencies. This is a very bad system. Everything should be under a mayor, who should be responsible. This haphazard organisation is the main reason why you cannot do anything to make Bangkok a healthy city. . . . This is why there have been attempts to decentralise. . . . This change is coming. The change must be painful, otherwise you cannot cure the illness. You must at times take drastic action. . . . This system must be changed; it can be changed by law.

Another example of Thailand's counter-productive administrative tangle came in March 1995 from Prof. Debhanom Muangman, dean of Mahidol University's Faculty of Environment and Resource Studies, who was quoted as saying that the single most important factor preventing the Public Health Ministry from adjusting to change is that management and decision making in the field of urban public health is still in the hands of the Interior Ministry's Local Administration Department (LAD). He said:

> The LAD and the municipalities have a vested interest in barring
> the Public Health Ministry from taking an active role in urban
> public health management and policy making.[6]

He alleged that many officials in the LAD were known to have abused their authority by soliciting bribes for turning a blind eye to violations of ordinances. The result was a lack of coordination between the Interior and Public Health ministries over the management of public health programmes for urban residents. Additionally, the NESDB noted that the bureaucratic system is unable to adjust to changes and cannot adequately respond to national economic and social transformation:

> The bureaucracy has been unable to restructure and adjust itself
> to respond to this dynamic because of constraints in manpower,
> legal framework, rules and regulations, administrative system,
> and organisational structure of the government. All of these need
> major modifications.[7]

Education for Quality of Life Is Essential

Thailand is attempting to initiate reform of its education system—something which has taken on a sense of urgency since the onset of economic crisis. To be overcome are the country's culture of political

Table 9.1

Secondary School Enrollment in Selected Countries in Asia 1993 (Per cent of age group)

Country	Female	Male
Sri Lanka	78	71
Malaysia	61	56
China	51	60
Indonesia	39	48
THAILAND	37	38
Bangladesh	12	26

Source: World Bank, *World Development Report 1997*.

mediocrity and the corrupt educational bureaucracy, which have hindered development of the creative thinking needed for far-reaching reform.

Thailand began, in 1996, to extend the basic education of children from six years to nine years, coinciding with the formulation of the Eighth National Economic and Social Development Plan (1997–2001). For the first time, the plan attempts to shift the emphasis of state planning from traditional, growth-oriented, economic prescriptions for the country's development, to long-term people-centred development. But merely extending the reach and duration of education to achieve this is not enough, say many critics.

Thailand is experiencing many difficulties in its approach to education, not the least of them the low priority it has traditionally received. *The Economist* magazine commented in August 1997:

> In terms of GNP per head, Thailand is more than twice as well off as the Philippines. Yet the proportion of Thai children who go to secondary school is much lower. . . . Yongyuth Yuthavong, director of Thailand's National Science and Technology Agency, estimates that Thailand needs 35,000 more technicians each year. It also produces too few university graduates: 12,000 engineers and 6,000 scientists each year, when 17,000 and 10,000 respectively, are needed. . . . Public and private expenditure on education, at less than 4 per cent of GDP, is the lowest in the region. . . .[8]

Thailand's Crash has further emphasised the need to concentrate an increasing proportion of Thailand's dwindling budget on human development—the upgrading of professional and intellectual skills among the general population—in other words, starting with young children and teaching them how to think.

This necessity, now widely recognised amongst East Asian countries, means minimising rote learning and memorisation in the classroom. It means relying less on multiple-choice questions in examinations and instead switching to essay-type examinations which force students to learn how to express themselves and to think sequentially and laterally. It means introducing a whole range of new teaching techniques that will compel students to employ logic, analysis, and creative thinking in the classroom. It means developing a spirit of inquisitiveness by encouraging students to ask meaningful questions.

But however necessary this new prescription may be to Thailand's future stability, it still has opponents. For example, following the initial financial crash, some legislators called for the National Economic and Social Development Board, the authors of the Eighth Plan, to put these new objectives on hold and to go back to the traditional theme of short-term economic stimulation. The wisdom of such a shift from the Eighth Plan's long-term objectives is very questionable, especially since much of what Thais previously regarded as "growth" or "progress" was in fact an illusion leading to the bubble economy and to the subsequent Crash. In a globalising, increasingly competitive world, substantial and well-thought-out investment in human development will be the key to longer-term prosperity, regardless of short-term economic difficulties; and the means to all this is major educational reform.

Thailand embarked on this major reform in July 1999 with the passage of the National Education Act, with trans-party support in the Parliament. It was the fruition of mounting concern that Thailand would be left behind in the era of globalisation unless it could drastically change its educational system. An Education Reform Office, with a three-year mandate was to be set up later in 1999 to decentralise and reorganise the education system, and to modernise and raise teaching standards.

Senator Wibul Kemchalerm highlighted Thai governments' past deficiencies in bringing about genuine development, at a national roundtable on the future of agriculture in October 1997, when he spoke about the plight of rural communities. *The Nation* summarised his viewpoint:

> Despite the success of many communities, the majority of people in the rural sector still lack skills and the ability to deal with the drastic changes in their community. Rural farmers, mostly small-scale, still do not know the objectives of their plantation, let alone have the knowledge to manage it properly. Many are still subject to exploitation by middlemen and other traders, and have no bargaining power over their products.

> To blame are the national social and economic development plans that focus on economic growth and promotion of production for

export only, together with an education system that discourages rather than encourages people's ability to think and learn. Instead of developing the rural community physically and intellectually, the development plans and the education system have led to the destruction of natural resources as well as local wisdom, to the extent that villagers, unable to think by themselves, have become heavily dependent on outside support.[9]

Improving the quality of education will now have to start from a smaller economic base; the chance has been missed to channel the apparent wealth of the mid-1990s into real investment in people. Following the Crash of 97, fears arose that children of poor families would be forced to drop out of school—marking a setback in the already-stated goal of extending the reach and duration of education among the population as a whole. In addition, in October 1997, the permanent secretary for education, Surat Silpa-anan, said about 3.6 million students nationwide were too poor to afford lunch, and about one million were suffering from malnutrition.[10]

Thailand needs a new model for development, and it must focus in the first place on the education system. Economic competitiveness is important, but in the final analysis economic progress must be recognised as a means to achieve (not to contradict) the higher goal of a genuine quality of life for Thai society as a whole. However, as various chapters in this section show, few people among the general public have a vision of what a healthy and sustainable society should look like. A massive educational effort is needed to raise awareness of people about their own responsibilities towards the quality of life, to counteract the negative aspects of the runaway commercial culture that strives more and more to dominate practically every aspect of our lives.

Thais, particularly during the bubble years, have increasingly taken their lifestyle values from the commercial system, especially advertising. The unhealthy messages of consumerism—buy junk food, buy polluting vehicles, buy things you don't really need—are overwhelmingly much more numerous and persuasive than messages that promote sustainable and healthy lifestyles. Commercial enterprises, the media, and the advertising industry—largely responsible for spreading these harmful fantasies—have been dynamic and flush with cash. On the other hand, the education and health systems—which should be spreading alternative, healthy visions of the quality of life—are underfunded and stagnant. The priorities of politicians lie with commercial, money-making activities, not in promoting a major and sustained campaign to educate people for healthy lifestyles and critical thought about the consumer culture that the commercial system attempts to impose on them.

Dr. Suvit Yodmani, then the regional director of the United Nations Environment Programme (UNEP), based in Bangkok, was asked in 1994 about progress in Thailand towards sustainable development and sustainable lifestyles:

> It is an intellectual exercise at the moment; people are talking about it, but it is not happening in practice. This new way of thinking will take a long time and it can be done only through education and information. . . . The consumerism that is invading us is posing so many problems, especially in terms of waste—normal waste and hazardous waste. It affects our lives, our health. We must stop to think. We must try to change our way of life, really.[11]

Dr. Suvit pointed to the implications of the United Nations Conference on Environment and Development (the 1992 Earth Summit) and its blueprint for ecological survival, *Agenda 21*:

> We have to change the consumption pattern, we have to change the production pattern, we have to change the value system, what you call the quality of life concept has to be changed. Producing a lot [of products] cheaply is simply not enough at this time. Traditionally, when we think about the quality of a product, we think about its utility and durability. Now, the new way of thinking should definitely incorporate how it is produced. Has there been clean production nor not? Does it entail using so much energy? We have to think about waste during the production process, and waste after the use of the particular product (its disposal). . . .

Dr. Suvit is an advocate of green schools, where some progress is beginning to be made guiding society towards environmentally sustainable, healthy lifestyles:

> I am encouraged by the way that the education system in Thailand and in other countries is undergoing this scrutiny now, a very critical examination of what we should be doing. They are incorporating, bit by bit, environmental aspects of life into the curriculum, starting from the primary and now to the secondary, and later to universities. . . . But the practical [application] must come, rather than [having it remain] just an intellectual exercise.

Summarizing the above observations, we can assert that Thailand is faced with an urgent, dual task:

1. Producing a comprehensive and forward-looking national educational curriculum that will equip students with intellectual and analytical skills, and with a greater awareness of a globalising world, that will enable Thailand to achieve sustainable economic prosperity far into the future.
2. Using this redesigned curriculum to introduce a new set of values aimed at achieving social stability and harmony, and at achieving a sustainable quality of life that downgrades high-energy, high-waste consumption, while promoting an enhanced reverence for the natural environment.

Now, taking advantage of the opportunities created by the 1997 "people's power" Constitution, we can add a third major task for the revision of the national educational curriculum:

3. Introducing to students nationwide the concept of participatory democracy and the meaning of a civil society based on the rule of law and on the rights and responsibilities of the people.

Emphasis on human responsibilities is long overdue, to counter the abuses of freedom without responsibility which has characterised much of so-called global development in the closing decades of the second millennium. A group of international statesmen, calling themselves the InterAction Council, has taken up this challenge in drawing up a Universal Declaration of Human Responsibilities. It lists duties that individuals, governments, and the media have towards others in society in order to enable people to enjoy their existing freedoms better. In a statement, the council argued that by bringing freedoms and responsibilities into balance, societies would be able to move

273

> . . . from the freedom of indifference to the freedom of
> involvement. . . . If human beings maximise their freedom by
> plundering the resources of the Earth, then future generations
> will suffer. . . .[12]

While upholding the rights guaranteed in the 1948 Universal
Declaration of Human Rights, it noted that these rights carried with them
obligations and responsibilities.

A new curriculum to bring Thailand into the third millennium is
certainly needed, but what about the teachers? Senate speaker, Meechai
Ruchuphan addressed this question on the last day of 1997, when he
told the press that Thailand needed to begin working for its future
generations now, and the place to start was with teachers:

> Let me ask you, who goes into teaching? There are some
> competent people, but they are in the minority. The rest consists
> of those who could not do anything else and applied to become
> teachers because they have no other choice. . . . Nobody talks of
> merit but of the patronage system. Everyone asks for favours
> from MPs and other people to get their children into school.[13]

The Senate speaker said the current system neither demands nor
provides quality and discipline. People, for example, absorb democracy
superficially and think other people must follow its demands rather than
offer opinions.

How to undertake design of a new curriculum and produce capable,
committed teachers in the current climate of indifference? Certainly, the
government will have to accept that recruiting high-quality graduates
into the teaching profession will require greatly increased expenditure.
It will also take years before a newly-designed curriculum can make a
significant impact throughout the education system. This writer
recommends several key steps:

- The country's top educationalists and thinkers meet together in a
  working group to design the new curriculum, based on the best
  assessment available of the country's present and future needs.
- An initial, outstanding group of trainers is selected to become
  well versed in the philosophy and requirements of the new
  curriculum and new teaching methods. Their financial reward

should be in line with the high expectations and importance of their task.
• These initial trainers will have the task of training large numbers of second-level trainers, who in turn will train active and prospective teachers.

This, in effect, is a top-down, pyramid-style scenario. The process can replicate itself over some years until extension is achieved throughout the country. It is difficult to see how a far-reaching educational reform can take place without such a dynamic process. However, in accordance with recent moves towards decentralisation of authority and devolution of governmental decision-making powers from the central to the local and community levels, a mechanism should be created to link this process with community organisations to give it more local relevance. By mid-1999, it seemed that these necessities were on the way to fruition through the new National Education Act. But, beyond abolishing an out-of-date curriculum and raising the competence and status of teachers, there are other obstacles to creating an enlightened education system that must be overcome.

One such obstacle is the culture of patronage and favouritism in schools (remarked upon above by Senate Speaker Meechai), which in turn condones cheating and fails to nurture values of perseverance and objectivity among students. These practices undermine educational standards and the important principle that rewards (i.e. the students' grades) should be commensurate with merit.

Thailand's (feudalistic) culture of patronage and favouritism is perpetuated within Thai society right from childhood. It starts early in the schools: teachers will often give high marks or an undeserved passing grade to certain children following school examinations, merely because the teachers are acquainted with the parents of the child in question or because the child comes from a prominent family in the community. Such teachers do not understand that this practice of attempting to bestow "a pleasing face" on these students damages the society by devaluing educational standards—which should be recognising and rewarding talent among all children. This practice of favouritism also damages the recipient students because they will come to believe that they automatically deserve rewards, not because of talent or hard work, but because of their families' wealth, position, or connections.

This writer knows of an incident at a Thai secondary school where many of the teachers gathered in a group following semester examinations and conspired to inflate the grades of their children who were attending the school, so that their children would score among the top five in their classes. Teachers in this particular school also were reluctant to punish cheating during examinations. Students in the examination room would overtly copy from other students' exam papers, or pass around answers on pieces of paper, and would receive, at most, only a mild rebuke from the teachers supervising the examination. One teacher estimated that as many as half of all the students in the school indulged in cheating.

Hopeless students get promoted from one year to another. Students who fail the entrance exams to private schools can get in on the basis of acquaintance with teachers, or through the payment of money.

One suspects that these examples of lack of discipline and lack of commitment to high educational standards are widespread amongst teachers in the Thai education system. These examples also shed light on the reluctance of many Thais working within corporate or government organisations to report corruption and crime. Such an attitude is first learned in the schools. It also undermines the rule of law, a principle which is so necessary to Thailand's quest for a well-functioning and progressive society.

I would like to mention another major obstacle to creating an enlightened education system: the patronising attitude of many of Thailand's elite towards education of the masses. From time to time, we hear the notion expressed that workers need only education that will allow them to function as economic entities—i.e. skills for factory work such as high-tech assembly. The ideal of producing a well-rounded, thinking individual through education is foreign to their outlook. This is a paternal—indeed, a feudal—attitude. It is still quite common amongst the Thai elite and *nouveaux riches*, although educators who focus on the future viability of Thai society are gradually overcoming this old-fashioned and somewhat right-wing attitude.

No doubt there is also an undercurrent of apprehension that a thinking population might be dangerous in future to the status quo which favours Thailand's privileged classes. Of course, education for economic advancement and for democratic participation (as mandated in the new Constitution) will foster analytical skills which will also enable people to reflect upon and analyse their society and their situation in it. Certainly, the nature of politics and of power will change when the feudalistic paternalism inherent in the present-day, vote-buying mentality gives way to voter choices based on reason and assessment of the higher interests of the community—not merely on deference to "higher" people.

Lastly, Thailand's culture of patronage, money politics, and corrupt administration is a major impediment to even beginning a comprehensive reform of the education system. A major problem spanning recent Thai governments has been the inability to appoint a minister of education who thoroughly understands the need for reform, and of the role that education must play in transforming Thai society to make it viable and prosperous in the future.

In 1998, *The Nation* convened a forum of prominent foreigners working in Thailand to ask for their opinions about Thai education. Forum attendees noted that:

> The fact that successive governments have complained that Thailand cannot afford to extend compulsory education past the ninth grade . . . critically hindered Thai industry's ability to move into higher value-added production. . . . With regard to government spending on the country's education level, many attendees said most Thai governments had grossly miscalculated and underestimated the importance of education. Even though they have cried poverty, local politicians have not been loath to spend billions of baht on new road construction while scrimping on increased funds for education.[14]

It has been well documented (see Chapter 8) that Thai politicians and bureaucrats favour spending money on large-scale equipment purchases and public works projects rather than expenditure on "abstract" things such as upgrading education and on preventative health programmes. After all, kickbacks cannot be extracted so easily from programmes to upgrade the skills and knowledge of teachers. And the first priority of political parties is to recoup the huge amounts of money spent on buying power.

The Education Ministry has been rife with allegations of corruption scandals in recent years, including a billion baht fiasco over the purchase of vastly overpriced and obsolete computers for schools under the tenure of the Banharn and Chavalit governments. The Education Ministry in

1998 was named as the second-most corrupt within the administrative system, following the perennially first-placed Interior Ministry.

Unhealthy Media

What to do about the media? It must be said that news and documentary productions in the electronic media have done much to bring environmental problems into public view. But, are media, in the final analysis, part of the problem or part of the solution? Are they tuned into promoting sustainable consumption and sustainable development? I am afraid I must say that they are not. Media are part of the problem. Commercial media promote consumption of all kinds as the most desirable form of personal gratification, regardless of the negative health and social consequences. Opulent lifestyles and the flaunting of status symbols are depicted in films and television programmes as positive; ironically, medical experts see this kind of behaviour as contributing to many of Thailand's mental health problems. Commercialism and consumerism reinforce personal vanity, self-centred values, and *status sickness* (see Chapter 11).

The negative impacts of the flood of consumerist images became evident throughout Thailand in the 1980s. These impacts were described in a memorable article by the award-winning environmental writer of the *Bangkok Post*, Sanitsuda Ekachai. She wrote on 2 November 1988 about the arrival of television in Thailand's impoverished Northeast. Some excerpts:

> In the barren Northeast, TV sets and refrigerators are the biggest enemies of hungry and malnourished children. "Because that is where the money has gone," says Prof. Dr. Sakorn Dhanamitta, director of the Institute of Nutrition. "When the parents have money, they don't necessarily buy more or better food for children. Instead, they tend to invest it in status symbols like television sets, stereos, and refrigerators."
>
> The decision makers, meanwhile, tend to think that if we can generate more income among the villagers, the children and pregnant women will automatically eat better. "But that's a myth,"

stresses the expert, who has done extensive research on child malnutrition in Thailand. . . .

In Trakan Phutphol district of Ubon Ratchatani province, where wickerware making has been a great success, a survey has shown that child malnutrition is at its worst in the villages where business is best. "Mothers just no longer have time to take care of the children," explains Prof. Sakorn. . . . A survey on the spending patterns of Northeastern villagers [in 1988] shows that they spend 20 per cent of their income on electronic appliances. Only 16 per cent goes to food. Their average income is less than 5,000 baht a year [then US$200 a year].

While decision makers view electricity as a sign of progress, nutritionists are less unequivocally positive about what they view as a two-edged sword. "Electricity brings TV, and TV changes the villagers' values and consumption patterns," says Prof. Sakorn. "All of a sudden, the electronic appliances they see on TV advertisements become a necessity in life as they want to imitate the lifestyles of city people. . . ."

The big transnational corporations—take for example the automobile companies and the soft drink companies—can afford multi-million dollar advertising budgets in one year. The beauty of their position is that it is their customers—we may say, their victims—who pay for the companies' huge advertising budgets with each item they buy.

We can see that most cities of Asia are clogged up with petrol-burning vehicles, and horrendous pollution problems have resulted. In Bangkok, people have fainted in the streets, overcome by pollution, and have had to be carried to hospital.[15] Yet the media continue to bombard us with images of the consuming individual, happily driving his car or motorcycle, amongst the blue skies and leafy trees, oblivious to any social or environmental responsibility. The economic crisis in Thailand caused an immediate decline in the number of vehicles on the road, but by mid-1999 numbers were climbing again.

Mass media, with their superstars and advertising models, seldom teach us to be happy the way we are. They create feelings of insecurity and deficiency, and false needs which—the media tell us—can be satisfied by buying the right consumer products. Commercialism cares nothing about whether you will die young from a heart attack caused by eating junk food and leading an unhealthy life. It cares about how much you will spend on its products while you are still alive.

Can societies, hooked on this consumerist addiction, willingly change their behaviour *en masse*?

Dr. Hatai Chitanondh, director of the Thailand Health Research Institute, is an advocate of providing information about nutrition to the Thai through the mass media:

> Give them information that fast foods are not healthy. We can compare, for example, a hamburger with Thai foods such as *kanom jin*, *nam yaa*, or what not. . . . We propose to promote healthy Thai foods in the future, instead of condemning Western fast foods. We just give the public information, that's all. We don't want to protest, or condemn, or make a negative campaign about that.

Dr. Hatai does not go as far as recommending the banning of advertising of unhealthy foods, but he has suggested placing a tax on such messages in Thailand and using the money to fund health promotion foundations, as he has seen in the Australian states of Western Australia and Victoria.

It may come as no surprise that media are guilty of promoting unhealthy lifestyles, just as they are guilty of promoting unsustainable lifestyles. In Asia and the Pacific, epidemics of the so-called "lifestyle diseases"—obesity, cardiovascular diseases, cancer, diabetes mellitus—arising from overnutrition, poor diet, and lack of exercise, are rapidly on the rise, spurred on by self-indulgent lifestyles depicted through electronic media. The World Health Organisation (WHO) has recognised this growing problem of lifestyle diseases; it is now up to societies and governments to recognise the media's role in promoting it.

A similar pattern emerges in Thailand and across Asia. Does anyone doubt that media have a pervasive influence on people's behaviour and on lifestyles? Here is a news item dealing with this subject which originated in San Diego, USA, in June 1995:[16]

Television food advertisements aimed at children promote unhealthy eating habits by pushing products loaded with fat, sugar, and salt, researchers have said. In analysing seven television stations broadcasting children's programming in San Diego, researchers found 91 per cent of foods advertised during the shows promoted nutritionally unsound products. In addition, the scientists from the University of California, San Diego, noted an average of 21 commercials were shown per hour, 47 per cent of them related to food.

"Perhaps obesity, which has been associated with television viewing, may also be associated with how television is influencing food selection," said Dr. Howard Taras, associate professor of pediatrics and co-author of the study published in the journal, *Archives of Pediatrics and Adolescent Medicine*.

The commercials have become shorter but more numerous since new limits on commercial programming were imposed by the Children's Television Act in 1990, the study indicated. While fewer ads sing the praises of cereals and sweet snacks, more aim at getting youngsters to eat processed, canned, and prepared foods and dairy products. The proportion of foods high in fat, salt, and sugar has not changed since before deregulation of the television industry by the Federal Communications Commission in 1984, said Sheila Broyles of the Division of Community Paediatrics at USCD.

"The Children's Television Act was supposed to reduce the number of commercials per hour and create more time for meaningful and healthful public service messages," said Dr. Miriam Gage, study co-author and now in family practice in the San Francisco area.

The British Broadcasting Corporation (BBC) broadcast on its Asian satellite television service this item on 22 Jan 1996:

In Britain, 50 per cent of the advertising aimed t children is for confectioneries and sweets, and soft drinks containing sugar. . . .

> RTE, the Republic of Ireland's national channel, has banned
> advertisements during children's hours, and replaced them with
> "infomercials".

Congratulations are due to the Republic of Ireland's broadcasting regulators. Sweden and Norway have also adopted bans on commercials aimed at children; for example, those for toys, breakfast cereals, and sweets. Several other countries also restrict commercial advertising targeting children. But, in other countries, particularly the United States, marketers are increasingly targeting the young. Says Alan Durning in his book, *How Much is Enough?*:

> One specialist in marketing to children told the *Wall Street
> Journal*, "Even two-year-olds are concerned about their brand
> of clothes, and by the age of six are full-out consumers."[17]

The United Nations Development Programme, replies:

> Societies need to consider the powerful impact of advertising on
> young children, for whom all information has an educational and
> formative impact. Children constitute an important market for
> consumer products, but society has a responsibility to educate
> them, not to exploit them.[18]

If we seek to protect children from such pollution of the mind, how should we consider the many adults who are lacking in education and failed to develop critical and analytical faculties? We may question whether we need intrusive and persuasive advertising at all; whether or not we would be better served, in the current progression towards interactive media, merely to have databases of product information which are accessible by choice.

In the light of the newly-emerging priority of healthy and sustainable consumption, unhealthy media practices need to be reassessed with a view to eliminating them. Freedom of the media to report truthfully on events and to comment responsibly on them is a desirable thing. But a supposed "freedom" to promote unhealthy and unsustainable lifestyles for commercial purposes certainly cannot be equated to journalistic freedom.

Unsustainable consumption assessed as a threat to ecology at the global level arises from unsustainable lifestyles at the individual level. Thus, it has now become a matter of global urgency to define and propagate sustainable lifestyles throughout the global population. Global warming arises from unsustainable consumption; following the commitment of industrialised nations to reducing greenhouse gas emissions, the media will also have to play their part. Even though Thailand, as a developing country, has not yet been called upon to reduce emissions, is there any justification to continue using the media to promote the sale of polluting vehicles?

Public sentiment is turning against cars in the West, especially in congested and polluted European cities. Not so in developing Asia, where, despite the economic crisis, the desirability of such status symbols does not seem to be diminishing. The media pander to this aura of vanity and self-indulgence surrounding automobiles purely for commercial reasons. Do they have to? There are clear reasons for governments and the media themselves to act now, to help break this consumer addiction.

What we are up against is the so-called "American dream" of limitless consumption, which is becoming repackaged for export as a "global fantasy land", sponsored by the country that already is the world's largest consumer of natural resources and the world's biggest polluter.

Advertising, reinforced by the depiction of consumptive lifestyles in the entertainment it sponsors, is a major driving force for unsustainable consumption. It is a huge business. It does not create anything of value in itself, but is indispensable in propagating the spread of the material economy. The *1998 Human Development Report* notes:

> Advertising is now a $435 billion business. But that's a conservative estimate of annual global expenditures. If all forms of marketing are included, the figure rises to nearer $1 trillion. Global advertising spending—up seven-fold since 1950, [grew] a third faster than the world economy. . . . In 1997, American companies spent more than $100 billion on TV advertising, paying up to $8,000 per second of air time.[19]

Over the 10 years leading up to the East Asian financial crisis, Asian countries showed spectacular advertising growth: for China more than 1,000 per cent, Indonesia 600 per cent, Malaysia and Thailand more than

300 per cent, and the Republic of Korea and the Philippines more than 200 per cent, according to the report.

The considerable creativity that has up to now been harnessed by the commercial machine to create a dream world of vanity consumption must now be considerably redirected through the transfer of financial resources to entertainment and educational pursuits that de-emphasise materialism, and—by exclusion—depict other forms of fulfillment. I propose regulating the mass-media market using the same principles and strategy now being advocated by proponents of environmental taxation. The commercial mass media machine that promotes unsustainable consumption can be taxed, just as the actual consumption itself needs to be taxed.

Let's not be too modest in our approach to taxing advertising-driven entertainment media, particularly television programmes. The huge revenues from advertising allow TV networks to mass produce costly television series, many of which depict lifestyles that the planet cannot afford to see replicated globally. Using the principle of environmental taxation, let's target that sum of superfluous spending, which ultimately is paid for by the consumer anyway, for programmes which are based on the premise of sustainable lifestyles.

Let us place a tax of 30 to 50 per cent on expenditures towards television advertising. This would, predictably, channel a large share of networks' programming budget to not-for-profit agencies, where they could be used to generate a new wave of ecologically-friendly television programming. It would also serve to reduce the amount of advertising on television. Commercial television stations, under this scenario, would surrender at least 30 percent of their advertising revenues to a taxation authority. That authority, in turn, would use the money to commission high-quality programming for public television, or for "infomercials", or for the placement of "acceptable" programming on commercial channels. There is a very wide scope—through additional funding redirected from commercially-financed programming—to promote eduction through the media.

Imagine a TV series where the actors and actresses ride bicycles and there are few or no cars to be seen; or where intelligent and appealing subjects depict a lifestyle of simplicity rather than ostentatious materialism. Thus, the staple fare of national television, the inexpensively-produced but advertisement-laden soap opera may be devised against a backdrop of sustainable lifestyles. It means having a clear idea about what a sustainable lifestyle is, and how it can be subtly and convincingly presented as part of entertainment.

Try another suggestion on for size: Thailand, along with other governments, ban all advertising of cars, motorcycles—all fossil-fuel burning vehicles. Instead they place an environmental tax on these products equalling or exceeding the amount their manufacturers previously spent on advertising. Such revenue, again, can be used for funding eco-friendly programming.

There are other issues involving the media which could be taken up in relation to the mental health of individuals and society. Commercialism has served to popularise base instincts in the media, especially through mass-market, Hollywood-style TV and film productions. I have in mind here the repetitive display of such attitudes as:

- violence as a legitimate element of society;
- crime as a normal means of achieving wealth;
- aggression pays;
- confrontation as "entertainment"; and
- personal vanity as being more important than compassion for fellow human beings.

The sudden explosion of youthful violence and killings of children by other children in the United States since 1998 should give us cause to reflect upon how violence and aggression depicted in the media influence people's—especially children's—behaviour.

Buddhism and Sustainability

Thailand is fortunate: it can look towards the ancient wisdom of the Buddha to evaluate the negative aspects of commercialism and materialism that have frayed Thailand's social fabric and contributed to its economic bubble. Buddhist philosophy already contains fundamental principles of sustainability which are increasingly more relevant today for protection of the global ecology: the denial of material gratification as a way of life (the wanton despoliation of natural resources and natural systems); and reverence for all living things (the preservation of biodiversity).

But the tragedy for Thailand is that these enlightened principles are seldom observed as a way of life, compounding the country's environmental crisis. Rather, Thais have become preoccupied with the ceremonial aspects of offerings and Buddha worship, and have injected a superstitious element into the religion by seeking blessings from monks and even supernatural interventions into their lives. These practices, as some learned monks point out, have turned the meaning of Buddhism upside down. As a leading Thai thinker and social activist, Prof. Prawase Wasi points out:

> Materialism and consumption are very high in Thailand—
> opposite to Buddhism.

In surveying all the ills that are pulling down the quality of life in Thailand, Dr. Prawase calls for a revolutionary approach to development, promoting compassion, working together, and balance. He sees the key for sustainable, healthy development as community building and community education:

> If communities are strengthened, they can protect the environment
> and can solve social problems such as crime, drugs, and
> prostitution. The community is the place where cultural
> development—the real life of the people—takes place, and where
> they can also practice democracy.

Another leading contemporary Thai thinker and noted proponent of Buddhist values, Sulak Sivaraksa, is more acerbic in his lament that Thais have abandoned ancient wisdom for fashionable illusions:

> Consumerism is the new religion. . . . Shopping malls function
> like a temple. They are stealing people from temples and
> churches. I don't think many people believe in God these days
> as their new religion preaches to them to consume. Be it Dream
> World, Mah Boonkrong, Seacon Square [shopping malls]—they
> are all there to deceive you.

Could a revitalised, activist Buddhism become a social force to correct the recent excesses in Thai society? Social activism has not been a part of Thai Buddhism up to now. The religion (if one can call it that) has rather advocated introspection and the achievement of personal enlightenment through reflection and detachment. In addition, Buddhism, as an institution in Thailand, has suffered a series of scandals in the monkhood during the 1990s. But, could a Buddhist-based response to Thailand's crisis now emerge? Would ordinary Thais respond?

Now, the pervasive, new religion of consumerism is seen to be threatening global ecology by putting the Earth's natural systems out of balance. Buddhism, with its emphasis on the sanctity of life and the achievement of equilibrium and balance as preached by the Buddha, contains the potential to help counteract negative, global trends. Can Buddhism become an activist force without denying its own non-aggressive nature, in protecting the global ecology?

In recent years, apparently as a response to the stress and feelings of spiritual emptiness that accompany the demands of the consumer society, there has been an upsurge of interest in Buddhist teachings from young people in Thailand and in some Western countries.

A new balance is needed between self-centred materialism, consumption, and competition on the one hand, and the personal contentment and serenity that comes from being part of a higher purpose on the other hand. This seeking of a higher purpose beyond oneself is often characterised by theologians as transcendence, as a dimension of spirituality.

After all, isn't this what the major religions have taught over the millennia? To place faith in something higher than one's self, higher than one's desires for self gratification?

It may be argued that this act of going beyond oneself, to put faith in a higher ideal, has been necessary for the rise of civilisation. Civilisation cannot survive if its every member simply follows impulses of immediate self-gratification. But, in our modern, "progressive" society, that is what the alliance between consumerism and the mass media teach us to follow. That is why a society may have the appearance of progress, an appearance that dazzles us through its great variety of consumer experiences and material possibilities; but at the same time, it contains a debasement of the human spirit and causes social decay through greed, jealousy, and conflict in the society. (Perhaps this is the greatest lesson in trying to understand Thailand's economic bubble).

If a new spirituality can arise from the materialist frenzy of our present age, its need is to treat Nature as an object of veneration, a cause for celebration that all living entities are linked through a spirituality that diffuses life and Nature. . . . A reaffirmation that man is part of Nature, and that as Nature suffers, man will also suffer.

Chapter 10

How We Measure Progress Affects the Quality of Life

We are seeing increasing concerns in Thailand (and elsewhere) that the quality of life in its many aspects is declining, even as wealth measured in monetary terms such as gross national product (GNP) and gross domestic product (GDP) has registered significant numerical gains. The basic fault of these indicators is that they assume that all growth that makes money is positive. However, it is all too apparent that much of what we call "growth" is destroying natural resources, polluting the environment, and negatively affecting people's mental and physical health.

Somehow, the objective of economic growth has got out of perspective. Growth has become an end in itself, losing sight of its responsibility to improve, not worsen, the quality of life of the masses of people. Globally, a new generation of green economists points out that part of the problem lies in what we regard as progress, and how we measure it.

GNP/GDP, until recently, has been held up as the paramount indicator of progress, as though it were some kind of divinity overseeing modernisation, increased production, and consumerism. But, if we look through the green spectacles of sustainability, it is absurd to think that increased sales of cars and motorcycles, for example, are taken as a measure of economic health and become a plus factor for GNP/GDP, while they are jamming up the centres of Thailand's cities and towns and creating pollution that damages people's health. Billions of baht are wasted in Bangkok's streets every year as vehicles burn massive amounts of polluting petrol while stuck in Bangkok traffic jams. Yet, money made from refining and providing this wasted petrol in Thailand is calculated as a plus factor towards GNP/GDP because it is regarded as a value-added activity within the commercially-defined economy.

Similarly, under this value-added principle, Thailand's rush in the 1990s to construct hundreds of high-rise concrete towers in Bangkok and at beach resorts such as Pattaya and Cha-Am, added several "points" to GDP growth, as land prices skyrocketed and construction companies worked overtime. But after the crash of the property market, dragging down the financial system and then the economy, who would want to glorify the high growth rates of that bubble era?

Let's accept it: greed and egotism were behind the property boom and bust. Rules and regulations, sustainability, and social and environmental impacts, were ignored. The unimpeded rush to cram huge buildings into every conceivable piece of overpriced "prime" space further destroyed Bangkok's overbuilt environment, subjected city workers to ever-increasing overcrowding, and thus lowered every city dweller's quality of life. But this lunacy was recorded as "progress" in monetary and GDP terms.

Who would want to feel euphoric, or even just proud, in worshipping GDP growth? What do numbers—such as 11.6 per cent, 8.9 per cent, 8.8 per cent—mean when we witness the suffering and bewilderment that followed the Crash?

New thinking, along with many new initiatives, are needed to salvage a decent quality of life out of this destruction. Devising scientific approaches to measure the cost of the destruction, the pollution, and the hospital bills—and to offset these costs against GNP/GDP growth, will help. One approach towards this is to revise the system of national accounts—what has been called the "greening" of national accounts—to also include the negative costs of economic exploitation. Additional indicators to measure progress in the quality of life are recommended.

Hazel Henderson, a leading guru of the green economics movement, describes GNP as a malfunctioning strand of our "cultural DNA code", carrying erroneous information and signalling to the body-politic a form of growth analogous to that of cancer cells which consume the host's body. Henderson writes in the January 1995 issue of *Our Planet*, the magazine of the United Nations Environment Programme (UNEP):

> The new national accounting methods being redesigned to correct
> or even replace GNP/GDP will function like healthy "cultural

DNA strands", newly spliced in to govern healthier growth and more normal development patterns for human societies. . . . Quantitative growth is dominant as children grow to adulthood, but once their mature size and weight are reached, this gives way to qualitative growth: education, social skills, broader awareness, and even greater ethical understanding and wisdom. . . . The statistical shift from GNP/GDP to sustainable development indicators mirrors such maturing of societies, recognizing new goals and the traits human beings must now rapidly develop if we are to restructure our societies for sustainability.

Henderson notes that the concept of GNP/GDP was adapted into national accounting systems by the United States and its allies during World War II to measure and maximise war production. With little re-examination, it continues to value bombs and bullets highly while setting the values of education and public infrastructure—not to mention clean air and water and other environmental assets—at zero, writes Henderson.

Official sources put Thailand's GDP growth rate[1] during the 1990s at:

1990	11.6	per cent
1991	8.1	
1992	7.6	
1993	8.5	
1994	8.9	
1995	8.8	
1996	6.6	
1997	-0.5	
1998	-9.4	

But, if the destructive impacts of the country's economic activity on the quality of life were included, those figures would be much lower.

The concerns of economists at the National Economic and Social Development Board (NESDB) during the bubble era were in contradiction. On the one hand, sought-after foreign investors put faith in GNP/GDP figures. Said one senior economist during a pre-Crash interview:[2]

> When people visit me, they don't ask what are environment problems, they ask what is the GDP growth rate, for investment.

291

> They are interested in Thailand because the economy is dynamic and has purchasing power. Businessmen are looking at where they can produce and sell their product.

On the other hand, she added:

> It is difficult for policy makers and planners like us. We care for the environment and quality of life. How can we make the balance?

However, new thinking was emerging in those pre-Crash days within the NESDB and the Thai intellectual community, to change the goal of national development from economic growth to human wellbeing in its Eighth Plan (1997–2001). It resulted in more concern over human resources development and the social and environmental impacts of development projects (see a brief summary of the plan in Chapter 1). But would the politicians go along?

At a seminar, in March 1995, to discuss priorities of the new plan, participants agreed that development of the Thai political system is lagging behind economic development and growing social and environmental awareness. The senior NESDB official added:

> I never worry about quantitative growth. . . . Now I concentrate on quality of growth, quality of life, and better distribution, rather than the quantity of growth itself.

She said that no one has yet succeeded in incorporating damage to the environment into the national account. The NESDB was working on a method to incorporate it, perhaps by deducting the cost of repairing damage. But there are many problems with such an exercise. The new accounting method may result in a new index to stand beside GNP/GDP.

Putting a Cost on Economic Destruction

The realisation that sole focus on the GNP or GDP index is failing the quality-of-life test has led to a number of new approaches to redefine wealth and progress, and thus to change the direction of development on a global basis. The United Nations Statistical Office, in its *Handbook of*

National Accounts, offers such innovations as: environmentally adjusted net domestic product (EDP), environmentally adjusted national income (ENI), sustainable national income (SNI), framework for indicators of sustainable development (FISD), and the human development index (HDI) of the United Nations Development Programme (UNDP).

The value of national indices is that they allow the public to monitor governments' performance and to hold politicians accountable (in responsive democratic systems). They also help policy makers focus on national deficiencies. The newly-proposed indices should increase pressure on governments to curtail money-making activities that harm people's quality of life or go against sustainability. But their national adaption seems to be progressing slowly, if at all.

UNDP devised the HDI, published for the first time in 1990, as an alternative to GNP for measuring the relative socio-economic progress of nations. The HDI began as a composite of three basic components of human development: longevity, knowledge, and standard of living. Longevity is measured by life expectancy. Knowledge is measured by a combination of adult literacy (two thirds weight) and mean years of schooling (one third weight). Standard of living is measured by purchasing power, based on real GDP per capita adjusted for the local cost of living (purchasing power parity, or PPP). In its *Human Development Report, 1994*, UNDP raised the possibility of adjusting the HDI to reflect a country's environmental performance—a crucial aspect of the quality of life. But, at that time, it was proving to be difficult to gain sufficient agreement on which indicators would be appropriate, or how it might be done.

Chapter 11

From Socrates to *Status Sickness*

The ancient Greek philosopher Socrates, who was born around 25 centuries ago, formulated what he called the most serious question a man must ask:

In what way should one live one's life?

This question is still very much relevant, perhaps even more so in our commercialised, self-indulgent, overblown civilisation of the late 20th Century. If Socrates could visit our world today, he would probably be shocked to discover the existence of lifestyle diseases—caused by things that people do (or don't do), or what they eat—which lead to an early death. Socrates and his philosopher colleagues, who strove to live by the tenets of logic, reason, and empirical observation, might well ask today, "If your lifestyles are flawed, and you know the reasons why, why don't you change?"

Indeed, can Thais change their lifestyles for the better? Illnesses of so-called "modern" life, such as heart disease, cancer, hypertension, and diabetes are all on the increase—and the first three, along with accidents, are now the leading causes of death in Thailand. According to a profile of Thailand's behaviour-related illnesses,[1] such health problems are increasing in every part of Thailand, and among all age groups: children, adults, and the elderly.

Mental illness is also increasing. This was true before the Crash of 97 and especially following it. A study by the World Health Organisation (WHO) said the (pre-Crash) problem of mental health, from minor to major illness, was affecting 15 per cent of Thais (nine million people).

The morbidity rate of schizophrenic diseases in Thailand increased from 41.88 per 100,000 in 1989, to 245.45 in 1993.

Children most at risk of mental health problems are those of poor families, those with physical disabilities, orphaned children, those with one parent only, those with mothers who are not prepared for childbirth, gypsy families, children in isolated areas or not having early educational opportunity, or children forced to go to work. As for the elderly, surveys found 42 per cent of them had mental health problems, especially those who have no relatives or friends, or cannot survive by themselves.

Social indicators compiled by the government show negative trends which reflect the growth of health-related social problems among adults:

- The estimated annual consumption of alcohol per person aged 15 years and over increased from 3.7 litres in 1987 to 4.7 litres in 1990, and 6.1 litres in 1992. The first National Health Examination survey in 1991 showed that 31.4 per cent of Thais aged 14 or older had an alcohol drinking habit.
- The number of people seeking cures at government drug detoxification clinics increased from 57,874 in 1987, to 63,978 in 1992, and 82,620 in 1993;
- Convictions for crime around the country increased from 62,219 in 1978, to 94,768 in 1987, and 96,184 in 1992;
- The divorce rate in Thailand increased by 30 per cent between 1994 and 1996, according to Dr. Akom Sornsuchart, a psychologist at the Police General Hospital. In 1994, divorce registrations were 46,903—representing 10.8 per cent of the 435,425 marriages recorded that year;[2]
- The suicide rate (per 100,000 people) increased from 4.7 in 1976, to 5.8 in 1987, and 6.7 in 1993. In 1993 there were 3,925 suicides. The suicide rate for males was 9.1, and for females 4.3. The Central and Northeast regions had the highest rates, 11.7 and 10.9 respectively.[3]

Stress and *Status Sickness*

Stress is a major disorder which is rapidly increasing in Thailand, and which makes people vulnerable to mental and physical illness. There is some difference among experts as to the prevalence of stress in the society, but all agree it is increasingly a problem.

According to Dr. Chutitaya Panpreecha, director-general of the Mental Health Department of the Ministry of Public Health, about 12 million Thais, approximately 20 per cent of the country's population, are suffering from chronic stress. He predicted the 21st Century would become "the century of stress", partly due to the increase in the information people will need to absorb to successfully do their work, arising from today's burgeoning information explosion.[4]

In a 1995 survey,[5] Health Ministry staff put the stress rate around 5–6 per cent in the general population aged 15–59 years. It was higher in the younger group (15–34 years) than the older group (35–59 years). The stress rate increased correspondingly with the intensity of urban development, it said. Sporadic surveys have been conducted in various groups, e.g. school children, youths, and teenagers, showing that about 10–30 per cent had certain mental illnesses including stress.

What is causing the stress? Society is rapidly changing, and people must also change just to maintain their economic position. People's expectations are changing. Competition is increasing and people must increasingly strive for advancement. Cravings for the "good life"—a nebulous concept often depicted by unrealistic images of self-indulgence borrowed from the industrialised North and featured in the mass media—are also stress-inducing. Stress is increasing in society despite the growth of material comforts and the proliferation of technological toys (both the juvenile and adult variety).

Even during the high-consumption psychology of the bubble economy, people were not so satisfied compared with the old days, said the Centre for Non-Communicable Diseases Control. It also blames the rapidly growing income gap between the rich and the poor—along with increasing prices of goods—as a source of stress. Many problems are a result of *status sickness*, as people tried to look better than others, according to the Centre. People pursued luxury consumption and became selfish. Their main aim was to seek benefits for themselves, and more people tried to take advantage of society through dishonesty.

Dr. Prawase Wasi, a leading quality-of-life advocate and chairman of the National Health Foundation, had this to say about *status sickness*:

> Thais are too materialistic; they like to show off. They want more cars, thinking that it is a sign of success, of development. But, when a society is developed, people want to use less. . . . They

297

want to use bicycles and public transportation. . . . You can see [this *status sickness*] when children go to school. If the children do not go in cars, they feel ashamed. Then, the car must have air conditioning. They will put the windows up in the car, even when they don't have air conditioning [to create the appearance of air conditioning].[6]

Dr. Prawase noted that, even in the pre-Crash days, stress was increasing in Thailand among the poor, the middle class, and the well-to-do. A measure of this was the three best selling medicines in the country: tranquilisers, and medicines for heart disease and peptic ulcers. The problem of stress represents conflict between biology and the environment: humans cannot cope with the new situation, said Dr. Prawase. Social breakdown was another factor, fuelled by the rapidly developing (bubble) economy:

> There is social disruption of the family and community. New economic development has divided the family community—because of the economic strain, it can't stay together. Houses in the country are empty of parents. We call this "house divided", home broken down. The community used to be everything. People would help each other. Now it is broken down by the economic drive. . . . These two breakdowns lead to other social problems [such as] poverty, [where] 25 per cent of people live in slums. There are 1,000 slum communities in Bangkok. They are growing everywhere in Chiang Mai, Khon Kaen . . . because of the failure of rural society.

Dr. Hatai Chitanondh pointed out similar changes in society as causes of Bangkok's high level of stress: Thai society has been changing from one based on the extended family, to smaller families, or even nuclear families. The warmth is not there, he said. Industrialisation, urbanisation, and all the consequences of rapid economic growth, cause people to struggle and make life harder, Dr. Hatai said:

> Sometimes [people] have more money in the pocket, but they are not very happy. . . . The mental health service must concentrate upon the family and upon the community and create

a special programme for them. So far there is only individual counselling or treatment. . . . The level of stress [in Bangkok] is quite high. . . . The government sector has not been helpful in reducing stress of the population, I should say. The mental health facilities have not been active and successful.[7]

Food Safety

Then there is the persistent problem of food safety. In 1994, Her Royal Highness Princess Maha Chakri Sirindhorn told the opening of the Second Asian Conference on Food Safety:[8]

It is imperative that regulatory agencies put in place a plan of action to ensure the implementation of health regulations.

She said there was sufficient food in rural areas but it had been found that certain groups still do not have access to proper, or quality, food:

In rural Thailand the majority of people lack a proper understanding of food quality and its nutritional value. . . . By consuming street food, city people put their health at risk.

The Princess said there was a need to support efforts to produce food which meets quality and safety standards:

Farming must be done right so the produce is free from toxic chemicals. Care to prevent contamination must be taken from the beginning of the production process to the finish. Care must be taken to prevent the harmful residues of insecticides or pesticides from contaminating food.

The Princess also had a warning about uncritical acceptance of technology. Science and technology had enhanced economic development, but they have also had a detrimental effect on the environment, she said. Never before had we witnessed such a high level of air pollution or soil and water contamination, as at present. Frequently it is found that food is contaminated by heavy metals and toxic substances which are harmful and can cause serious diseases like cancer, she said.

A glance at *The Nation's* library files on food safety found many recorded instances of food contamination from heavy metals and toxic substances, including insecticides and pesticides. In 1996, officials of the Bangkok Metropolitan Administration, inspecting roadside food quality throughout Bangkok, found animal saliva and urine were among the many hazardous substances detected in cooked and fresh food. The findings were included in a BMA study jointly conducted with the World Health Organisation to inspect food sold in several fresh markets. Meat was laced with excessive amounts of saltpeter, and vegetables were rinsed with formalin—a chemical used to preserve corpses. The study also found that vegetables contained hazardous levels of insecticide residue. Cooked foods were also found to have been repeatedly reheated.

An earlier survey conducted in 1994 by the Medical Science Department of the Ministry of Public Health in Bangkok found that food and drinks for sale on the street were often below standard in terms of hygiene and toxic chemical contamination. The use of preservatives and artificial colouring was excessive; many beansprout samples in the markets were bleached with sodium hydrosulphide; most vegetable oil and fat used for deep frying bananas and other snacks contained acid and peroxide, which produce a rancid smell.[9]

The situation is thought to be much worse in Thailand's poorest region, the Northeast. Consumer groups in Khon Kaen complained about cancer-causing dioxins in tap water, chemical contamination in foods, and pesticides on farms. In Ubon Ratchatani, cloth dye and hazardous preservatives were found in street food. Bacteria and arsenic were found in certain locally-packaged foods.

Are government and non-governmental agencies able to protect consumers? The short answer is "no". The Office of the Consumer Protection Board (OCPB) had a staff of only 43 people to cover a wide area of responsibility, and it lacked sufficient power to deal with the private sector. This conclusion emerged from a seminar in 1995 on how to effectively protect consumer rights. One participant, Associate Professor Susom Supanit of Chulalongkorn University, said she did not see the OCBP helping consumers very much, and called on NGOs to take a major role.[10] Other observers have noted that Thailand has several small NGOs and government agencies focusing on consumer issues, but there is little cooperation among them.

Meanwhile, uneducated consumers unthinkingly buy what the market offers. In addition, there is little awareness about proper nutrition (as well as the need for exercise) throughout Thailand, experts say. People eat high-calorie foods and have low vegetable intakes. The number of patients suffering from diabetes and obesity has already increased dramatically over the past decade, and if consumption of junk food continues to increase at the current rate, more and more Thais can expect to be afflicted with those problems, as well as heart disease, bone marrow deficiency, excess fat in the bloodstream, and constricted blood vessels, according Dr. Songsit Srianuchat, deputy director of Mahidol University's Nourishment Research Institute.[11] Urban Thais scarcely have time to cook or eat hygienically prepared food, he said. They are compelled by their hectic schedules to eat fast food at almost every meal.

Since the mid-1990s in Bangkok and in the towns, we have seen a rapid proliferation of mini-marts or 24-hour convenience stores. They are typically stocked almost completely with junk foods: processed, packaged foods; soft drinks; high-calorie snacks—and lack any fresh fruits or vegetables.

Diabetes

Diabetes is especially surging throughout Asia and the Pacific, as traditional healthy diets give way to junk foods, many of which are heavily promoted in the mass media. In August 1996, deputy public health minister, Tawatwong na Chiang Mai said that about 900,000 people nationwide were suffering from diabetes, with most living in the Central region. About 10 people died each day from the debilitating affects of the disease, he said. The Ministry of Public Health's 1995 report on non-communicable diseases[12] adds that the mortality rate of diabetes mellitus increased steadily from 1983 to 1992, with the deaths in 1992 of 3,583 Thais. The case admission rate in all public health facilities, except in Bangkok, doubled between 1988 and 1993. Females had twice the prevalence rate of males; a low level of education was associated with an increasing prevalence rate. Of those who were found to be diabetic, only 42.6 per cent were aware of their condition.

Diabetes is now a global health problem, with the number of sufferers expected to exceed 100 million worldwide by 2000, according to the WHO. In 1991, the number of diabetics worldwide was estimated at 60 million. As well as being life-threatening, severe complications of diabetes can lead to blindness and kidney failure, and a higher risk for development of coronary heart disease.

Cancer

Stress, environmental pollution, and food contamination from chemicals are all factors that can contribute to development of cancer. Cancer is a major public health problem worldwide with a higher rate in developed countries than in developing countries. However, the WHO predicted that the incidence of cancer will double between 1995 and 2015 in the developing countries.

In Thailand, the incidence rate of cancer in 1990 was estimated at 153.6 per 100,000 people. By comparison, in the United States, the cancer incidence rate in 1993 among whites was about 432 per 100,000, and was 317.4 among blacks. The rates in Canada and Japan were 311.6 and 205 respectively. The mortality rates from cancer in Thailand have been increasing steadily since 1967. Recent rates are: in 1987, 31.5 cases per 100,000; in 1990, 39.3 cases; in 1993, 45 cases.[13]

Hypertension

According to the WHO, by the early 1990s, hypertension (high blood pressure) affected about 20 per cent of the world's adult population. In Thailand, the rate was around 15 per cent. Hypertension is a major risk factor in heart disease. If left untreated, the WHO pointed out, hypertension can lead to heart attack, stroke, kidney failure, and other potentially fatal diseases.

The WHO projects a rise in major cardiovascular disease epidemics in developing countries unless the prevention of hypertension though lifestyle-linked strategies is carried out.[14] In the United States alone, some 50 million people (one in every four adult Americans) suffer from hypertension. Likely sufferers are those who are overweight, have a low level of physical activity, consume excessive amounts of salt or alcohol, smoke cigarettes, and those who have high blood cholesterol levels.

Thus, despite so-called progress measured by the quantity of consumption, we can say that the quality of life for a large percentage of people, linked to habits of consumption, is in fact declining.

Thailand has had a good record over previous decades in developing medical services throughout the country to deal with infectious diseases, maternal and child health, sanitation, and other concerns related to rural development. These represent major advances in the quality of life (see Table 11.1).

Table 11.1

Trends in Health Development in Thailand

Life expectancy
1960: 52.3 years
1993: 69.2

Infant mortality rate
1960: 103 per 1,000 live births
1993: 36

Population with access to safe water
1975–80: 25 per cent
1990–95: 86*

Underweight children below age five
1975: 36 per cent
1985–95: 26

SOURCE: United Nations Development Programme, *Human Development Report, 1996*. Table 6, Page 148.

(*Data refer to a year or period other than that specified in the column heading, differ from the standard definition, or refer to only part of the country.)

However, these results have come from traditional programmes which have been in place for many years—initiated before the present era of rampant money-politics. In recent decades, it seems that Thai governments' priorities have changed. Now, political leaders seem little interested in dealing with the causes of declining health in the cities and with the lifestyle diseases. In some cases, authorities are promoting or condoning commercial activities which are a threat to people's health. To overcome this, making environmental health a priority is an absolute necessity. The promotion of a healthy lifestyle is another necessity.

Ominously, the priorities of the Thai medical system are misdirected, emphasising cure rather than prevention. In 1994, the then health minister, Dr. Arthit Ourairat, had this to say:

> Our system of prevention is not there at all. . . . The state tends to focus only on using the health budget to buy medical equipment. It is a wrong concept. . . . We must promote among the people to have a better quality of life. We must give importance to the environment we live in. Prevention is something we have to stress.[15]

Dr. Arthit has stressed decentralisation of decision making and reliance on health volunteers in *tambons* and villages nationwide to help educate the people on how they can prevent illness and stay in good health. Prof. Debhanom Muangman, dean of Mahidol University's Faculty of Environment and Resource Studies, said (also in 1994) that a major restructuring at the Public Health Ministry is urgently needed:

> The Public Health Ministry now spends between 80 and 90 per cent of its budget every year on medical treatment and administrative costs. It should try to cut costs and spend more on preventive measures and on promoting healthier lifestyles.[16]

The Ministry of Public Health's 1995 report on non-communicable diseases noted that:

> The number of disabled and elderly people is increasing together with the number of people suffering from chronic illnesses, most of which are non-communicable diseases (NCDs). These have resulted in a number of people who are economically and socially dependent on other people or on the social welfare system. In addition, those who are afflicted with NCDs may experience a decrease in their work efficiency. It is therefore necessary for the society to critically look at itself to promote awareness, understanding, and concern in these regards.

It is clearly seen that NCDs are spreading rapidly in Thailand. Based on experiences from other countries, the ministry identified three patterns of disease evolution:

1. Transition from an agrarian society to an early industrialised period—most of the diseases were infectious and in maternal and child health.
2. Attainment of an industrialised and service-oriented society—cardiovascular diseases, cancer, accidents, drug addiction, substance abuse. The change was a result of changing lifestyles, and increasing and indiscriminate use of technology.
3. Entering the era of globalisation—most health problems are drug addiction and substance abuse, genetic disorders, family problems, and violence.

The ministry said that the WHO has predicted that the newly-industrialised countries and developing countries will face the dual problems of the first and the second cycles. Most of the NCDs, in the next ten years will concentrate in these countries, which include Thailand.

In summary, NCDs are caused by genetic disorders, inappropriate behaviour and lifestyles, poor environmental conditions, and—partly—inappropriate medical treatment. Most NCDs are chronic and have some distinct characteristics. They are:

- multi-factoral and complex;
- behaviour-related (eating, working, transporting, leisure);
- lifestyle related;
- having some risk factors that can be altered or chosen; and
- requiring a long time before appearance.

Some NCDs have unknown or unclear causal factors, or factors that cannot be modified, or are hard to modify:

- imitating behaviour—for example, eating fast foods;
- social, cultural, and economic values;
- media influence—for example, advertising; and
- environmental contamination.

Certain conditions in Thailand fuel NCDs:

- demographic changes;
- urbanisation;

- industrialisation and service orientation;
- technological changes and flooding; and
- environmental contamination and degradation

Needed: Healthy Lifestyles

Again, making environmental health a priority is an absolute necessity, and the promotion of a healthy lifestyle is another necessity. The attainment of a healthy lifestyle is not dependent on an individual's wealth (except, perhaps, for the absolutely poor). It is dependent on public awareness brought about through the media and the education system, and on enlightened political leadership that will create the right environment to enable people to pursue healthy lifestyles. But, the lack of such requirements coupled with a widespread fixation on materialism, personal vanity, and self-indulgence seemed to be thwarting this desirable goal as Thailand entered the 21st Century.

Can Thailand break out of its obsession with money, consumption, and status? The *Human Development Report, 1994*, of the United Nations Development Programme (UNDP), had this to say this about opulence and human development:

> First, accumulating wealth is not necessary for the fulfillment of some human choices. . . . Second, human choices extend far beyond economic wellbeing. Human beings may want to be wealthy. But they may also want to enjoy long and healthy lives, drink deep at the fountain of knowledge, participate freely in the life of their community, breathe fresh air and enjoy the simple pleasures of life in a clean physical environment, and value the peace of mind that comes from security in their homes, in their jobs, and in their society. . . .

> The concept of sustainable development raises the issue of whether present lifestyles are acceptable and whether there is any reason to pass them on to the next generation. . . . Sustainable human development . . . puts people at the centre of development and points out forcefully that the inequities of today are so great that to sustain the present form of development is to perpetuate similar inequities for future generations.

That is the challenge for Thailand in defining a new, sustainable vision of the quality of life. There has been much talk in Thailand about redistributing wealth, to ensure that poor Thais get a larger share of the country's increasing wealth. But, enhancing the quality of life calls for other approaches as well: for example, creating public facilities—such as parks, open spaces, sports grounds, community centres—especially in the towns and cities, aimed at providing the means for a healthier lifestyle and enhanced community life. A major programme is needed to create such facilities.

Bangkok is notorious for its lack of open space and public parks. Governing authorities failed to carry out their responsibilities to ensure sustainable development during the bubble era, as property developers continued to cram ever-larger structures into every space they could acquire. Dr. Prawase deplored the unhealthy impact that this uncontrolled, so-called "development" had on urban populations, especially children:

> [In these high-rise] buildings, kids have no place to play. It is very bad for their development. Playing is very important. They need exercise. We don't think about this, only about making money. . . . Now, school children spend their time in supermarkets—they don't understand Nature and society.

Perhaps more than anyone, children in Bangkok suffer from having unhealthy lifestyles forced upon them. Apart from the pressures to excel in school (and even pre-school education), in preparation for pursuing future economic advantage, they also have to spend hours per day stuck in polluting traffic and suffer malnutrition from junk foods and overconsumption.

The suicide of a tenth grader at the Kasetsart University Demonstration School in February 1996 momentarily highlighted to the nation the question, who is to blame for the untimely death of Chakrit?[17] Fifteen-year-old Chakrit jumped from the fourth floor of a dormitory near his school and died after lying in a coma in hospital for two days. Chakrit had complained to his sister about the selfishness of society. A debate ensued which asked whether the depression he sustained may have been caused by pressure to achieve the high academic excellence demanded by the school and expected by his parents and teachers.

Chapter 12

Go Fast, Make a Big Noise

This account arises from observations made in Hua Hin (the writer's town of residence) although it applies in a similar measure to virtually all medium- and large-sized towns throughout Thailand.

In 1989, a tourism brochure of the Hua Hin municipality office described Hua Hin as the "Queen of Tranquility." It had for decades been a sleepy, charming, seaside fishing town and beach resort where hardly anyone stirred on the streets during the middle of the day. In that year, the whole of Hua Hin district had fewer than 1,000 motorcycles. By 1994, according to residents' estimates, the number of motorcycles had grown to around 20,000. By 1999 it seemed to have reached 35,000—representing about one machine for every two children or adults in the district capable of riding one.

Thailand's booming "love affair" with the motorcycle has left clouds of blue smoke and noise where the Queen of Tranquility used to live. Hua Hin town's streets and lanes are now subjected almost constantly, from morning to late at night, to the abrasive sound of motorcycle engines. Children as young as seven years old can be seen riding motorcycles, often with two or three friends on board. Young men often drive at high speed, generating much noise, through lanes which are used by residents and tourists as walkways.

More than 99 per cent of Thailand's eight million motorcycles have two-stroke engines. Vehicles with these cheap and nasty engines have been banned in many countries—in Europe, for example—simply because they are too noisy and too dirty.

Will Thais, especially those living in the densely-packed towns and cities, tolerate increasing noise levels and higher concentrations of toxic gases? Unfortunately, it seems so, under the prevailing passive political culture and consumerist philosophy, unless there is a concerted move by concerned citizens and officials to give priority to health and environment. There is not much understanding about air pollution in Thailand. Most people think the smoke which comes from the exhaust pipe of motorcycles is just a bad smell. Most don't know about the damage that this pollution can do to their health, and especially their children's health.

Acute noise levels contribute to nervous tension, while small children and old people suffer the most from smoke, toxic gases, and particles coming from motorcycles, especially in the town's narrow, enclosed streets.

Air pollution in Thailand increased during the boom years faster than in any other Asian country, according to data compiled by the United Nations.[1] In Thailand, the average motorcycle produces at least five times as much pollution as the average car. This is because the small, two-stroke engines of motorcycles do not burn fuel efficiently, emitting a lot of smoke and unburned oil particles. The pollution is worse if the motorcycle engine is badly tuned, if the rider travels at high speed, or if the motorcycle is overloaded with people. Badly-tuned and overloaded motorcycles are a common sight in Hua Hin.

Studies published by the United Nations[2] show that pollution from two-stroke motorcycles contains about six times more hydrocarbons than pollution from cars. It contains 40 per cent more carbon monoxide. These are dangerous substances.

Hydrocarbons cause unpleasant effects such as eye irritation, coughing and sneezing, drowsiness, and symptoms akin to drunkenness. They are largely the result of incomplete combustion of fuel. Hydrocarbons include thousands of different chemical compounds, some of which can cause cancer. Some combine with diesel particles and may contribute to lung disease. Carbon monoxide decreases the amount of oxygen carried in the blood, which is bad for the heart and nervous system, and for the foetus of pregnant women. The classic symptoms of carbon monoxide poisoning are headache and dizziness.

Because of their high metabolism, both infants and young children assimilate more air-borne pollutants than adults. Acute respiratory infection (ARI) which sometimes leads to pneumonia, is one of the biggest causes of death for young children in Asia. It is aggravated by exposure to air pollutants. Additionally, two-stroke engines running on a mixture of petrol and lubricating oil produce very high levels of unburned oil particles. There is growing evidence that oil particles, along with smoke, can provoke chronic lung disease.

Motorcycles became popular because they are a fast and effortless means for travelling longer distances—and in many cases the whole family can fit on one. Thus, motorcycles were a welcome advent in isolated rural areas. But the popularity of motorcycles goes beyond mere usefulness. Motorcycles have become the new status symbol, in an age of growing affluence, among low-income Thais. Thus, anyone who can afford the installment payments "must" have a motorcycle to declare himself or herself a part of the "progressive" consumerist, technologised society. The "image" created by riding a motorcycle started out by being more important than the actual travel. Now, it is assumed that owning a motorcycles is just as "necessary" as owning a refrigerator or television set. You are "crazy" if you don't want one.

In Hua Hin, for example, most motorcycles are owned by people who live within the town itself. They are used for trips as short as 100 metres. The boundaries of Hua Hin town stretch for only about four kilometers along the southern highway. Therefore it is arguable that motorcycles are not needed at all within Hua Hin township.

The alternative, of course, is the humble bicycle. Bicycles are non-polluting, quiet, inexpensive, and healthy—because they provide exercise. Why would people want to reject them in favour of dirty, noisy, unhealthy,-and more expensive, petrol-burning motorcycles? Is affluence making people so lazy that they do not even want to walk down the street, or feel incapable of the moderate physical effort required for bicycling? The simple answer is that the clean, humble bicycle is "low class" while the polluting, noisy motorcycle has gained a "sexy" image of speed and prestige.

An incident related to this writer in Hua Hin illustrates the point. A young European woman got a job as a managerial assistant working for a new, medium-sized hotel in Hua Hin town. When she arrived for work riding a bicycle, she was told by the management that it was not acceptable, and that she must get a motorcycle. Only prestigious polluters are wanted there!

Teaching Children to Be Polluters

Now, we have the growing phenomenon of children on motorcycles. Children used to walk or ride bicycles to school. They used to play running games. Exercise has long been regarded as essential for the growth of healthy young bodies. Now, displaying their newly-found "status" to 10-year-old schoolmates in the shape of riding around on a motorcycle seems to be more important, and many parents don't seem to care. In the absence of parental or educational guidance, large-scale advertising in the mass media teaches children to "want" motorcycles and to become polluters. Wouldn't it be just too much if every child of seven and older wanted one of these shiny toys, just to be part of the new status-seeking, "easy-living" crowd?

Studies in European and North American cities, published in 1996 by the *British Medical Journal*, prompted researchers to declare that the health effects of air pollution from vehicles are more serious than previously believed. Researchers from St. George's Hospital in London now claim that even among healthy people, motor pollution in cities like London may eventually lead to serious lung damage. Another report shows that emissions from vehicles increased the likelihood of children developing breathing problems. Findings from other cities confirmed that a rise in air pollution is linked with an increase in death and disease, especially among those with heart and lung problems.[3]

Does any Thai government agency care enough to try to turn back this unhealthy tide of motorcycles? The Hua Hin municipal government does not have the authority (it says) to ban or restrict motorcycles. Under Thailand's highly-centralised system of administration, the real power lies in Bangkok. But up to now, the government has suffered near-paralysis in its attempts to alleviate congestion and pollution in the capital, never mind about the country's towns. Reversing this unnecessary growth of motorcycles requires a combination of strong pro-environment, pro-health policies at the central government level, improved public education, greater effort in the schools, tax disincentives for polluting transportation, and strong local action.

There is little evidence that such political will is materialising, perhaps because of the powerful business lobby promoting the ever-increasing manufacture and distribution of two-stroke motorcycles. In late 1994, it was reported that the Industrial Economic Office wanted to lift a seven-year-old ban preventing existing factories from expanding production of motorcycles with two-stroke engines. Its secretary-general wanted to create a "competitive environment" and strengthen Thailand's position as a manufacturer of such motorcycles. He called for government assistance.

There have been moves to get rid of polluting motorcycles. Kraisak Choonhavan, an environmental advisor to the Bangkok Metropolitan Authority, said that plans were made during the 1988–91 administration of his father, former prime minister, Chatichai Choonhavan, to legislate against them.[4] He lamented:

> We have had several postponements of the cessation of production of two-stroke motorcycles. Change of government: it gets postponed again. The air is almost unbreathable now in [towns and cities of] Thailand, and yet the government has not been able to touch the automotive industries, nor to make legal demands for a more international system [to control] exhaust. This is very crucial now in Thailand, and yet they keep postponing it.

Additionally, the then permanent secretary of the Ministry of Science, Technology, and the Environment, Kasem Snidvongs, in 1996 indicated[5] that new anti-pollution standards would be introduced. However, the years roll by and nothing happens while air pollution gets worse. One can only surmise that under Thailand's system of pay-offs and corruption, motorcycle manufacturers and distributors pay handsome "contributions" to ministers to indefinitely delay the introduction of the relevant legislation into Parliament.

Meanwhile, well over one million people in Bangkok suffer from chronic respiratory disease, due in a large measure to Bangkok's 1.6 million polluting motorcycles. The problem is also fast increasing in virtually all medium- and large-sized towns around the country.

Section 4

Protecting and Enhancing the Environment

Chapter 13

Legislating for the Environment

It is well documented that Thailand's single-minded pursuit of a high-profit, high-growth economy has wrought large-scale destruction on the country's natural environment. In 1999, Thailand continued to experience an annual net loss of its woefully-depleted forests, ten years after commercial logging was banned in the country, and despite attempts to promote tree planting.

By the mid-1990s, Thailand was experiencing the fastest growth in air pollution of any Asian country;[1] the incidence of lung cancer in Bangkok was three times the national average by 1992[2] and by 1999 that ratio was probably significantly higher. There were growing problems with hazardous waste disposal, soil degradation, water quality, chemical safety, coastal and marine degradation, and the loss of biodiversity—problems common to most developing countries.

There were some bright spots in this worsening picture, however.

Environmental NGOs were becoming more active, and some business leaders had taken up the challenge to adopt environmentally-friendly techniques in their production processes, and to promote the adoption of environmental standards in industry and commerce. Environmental consciousness was rising in the country, but not yet to a critical level where community action could reverse pervasive environmental degradation. But new provisions in Thailand's 1997 Constitution held out prospects that community action could be invigorated.

The Constitution incorporates several measures to enhance citizens' rights to environmental protection (see Chapter 6). The people are guaranteed the right to access information from the records of government agencies (except sensitive security or personal information), including information on projects having potential impact on the environment. This provision was already written into the 1992 Environment Act, but would take on broader scope through the Constitution (which also mandated the subsequently promulgated Information Act, further guaranteeing the public's right to official information). People also have the right not only to challenge, but also to demand participatory decision-making roles in, developments in their communities or near their homes. Local communities are guaranteed the right to participate in the management, maintenance, and use of the natural resources and the environment in ways that are balanced and persistent, as provided by the law. The state is also charged with promoting and accepting public participation in planning and implementing environmental and natural resource conservation and management.

These constitutional provisions, and other mechanisms to promote transparency and accountability, held out promise that the 1992 Environment Act could be made more effective in reversing the tide of environmental destruction in Thailand.

The 1992 Environment Act

The 1992 Environment Act (officially known as the Enhancement and Conservation of National Environmental Quality Act B.E. 2535) is one of the more enlightened pieces of legislation promulgated in Thailand in recent decades. It was proclaimed by the authoritarian government of Anand Panyarachun, who was named prime minister in 1992 by the military junta which overthrew the government of Chatichai Choonhavan. Therein lies one of the major ironies of Thai politics and the quest for democracy in Thailand: it is doubtful that an elected government, arising from Thailand's prevailing culture of political patronage, would have wanted to enact such a progressive piece of legislation. In fact, accusations have been made against ministers of the subsequently elected governments of Banharn Silpa-archa and Chavalit Yongchaiyudh of violating, or attempting to violate, provisions of the Act.

Officials of the United Nations and the Asian Development Bank have described the Environment Act's purpose as

> ... improvement of the efficiency of agencies at the policy-making level to make them centres for environmental policy making; encouraging the decentralisation of environmental

quality management to local authorities; introducing guidelines to systematically alleviate problems by devising a policy-oriented implementation plan at central and provincial levels; applying monetary and financial measures to supplement other incentives and controls which will help involve the public in the process of solving environmental issues; and creating legal rights and obligation of each individual and those of NGOs to take part in the protection of the environment and the conservation of natural resources.[3]

The Act set up the National Environment Board (NEB), which replaced the previous Office of the National Environment Board inaugurated in 1975. The previous board was part of a department within the Prime Minister's Office; the new board was placed in the Ministry of Science and Technology, which became the Ministry of Science, Technology, and Environment.

The NEB's number of departments expanded from one to three: the Pollution Control Department, the Office of Environmental Policy and Planning, and the Department of Environmental Promotion. The NEB is now a political-level, decision-making board, chaired by the prime minister. It comprises nine cabinet ministers (instead of permanent secretaries as previously) with eight experts who may be university professors, for example, or retired civil servants or advocates of environmental management, plus four other ex- officio members.

The NEB now has authority both in planning and in budgeting, whereas it previously had authority in planning only. The main thrust of the law is the decentralisation of environmental planning to the provincial (*changwat*) level, and local administration of budgets provided through the approval of the NEB. The Act requires each of Thailand's 76 provinces to draw up its own environmental plan, which provincial governors have to submit annually to the NEB's Office of Environmental Policy and Planning. It places initial emphasis on the installation of waste-water treatment facilities, following a flexible approach.

There are other major innovations:

- The setting up of the Environment Fund, subscribed at 5 to 6 billion baht, to fund urgent environmental activities without going through the normal budgeting process. It has its own committee to make decisions.

- The power to set up protected areas, which consist of two types—pollution-control zones and environmental conservation areas. Once a protected area is declared, the provincial or local government authority must prepare a mitigation plan.
- The recognition of NGOs. This provision attempts to promote non-governmental organisations' participation in environmental management. NGOs may request financial support from the Environment Fund, but they are required to register first with the NEB and meet certain criteria—for example, employing a grassroots approach.
- The setting of minimum standards. Other government agencies that are mandated by law may also set standards, but they must be more stringent than the NEB's.
- Environmental impact assessments (EIAs) can no longer remain "confidential" and withheld from the public by government agencies, as had been a practice previously with big projects such as dams that were opposed by environmentalists. Agencies now must give such information to anyone who asks for it.

Kasem Snidvongs Interviewed

On 11 July 1996, the author interviewed Kasem Snidvongs, then the permanent secretary of the Ministry of Science, Technology, and Environment—Thailand's senior official dealing with the Environment—on the 1992 Act and other environmental topics. Following are edited excerpts from the interview.

Author: How is the 1992 Environmental Act shaping up? Is it achieving its purposes?

Kasem: It's getting better. But the problem is really with human resource development, the manpower development. The local authorities have very little idea about environmental management. They don't have engineers or enough engineers. To run a [waste-water] treatment plant or a garbage dumping site, you need good engineers. So, more or less, we are starting from scratch when we try to implement the idea of provincial environment plans. . . . A training programme is going on now, working together with the Interior Ministry to upgrade environmental skills of the staff of the local governments, but that is difficult. We are talking about many thousands [of staff] over the country's 75 provinces, excluding Bangkok.

Author: The local bodies at the *changwat* level are not able to do a lot at this stage?

Kasem: No [not a lot]. But we have a provision that they can ask for help from the Pollution Control Department (PCD) or from any government agency. The PCD and the Public Works Department can help them review the design, or [can provide] the design of the treatment system.

Another point: a mistake in the past was that we did not try to privatise this management part of the environment. So the law provides that if a local government doesn't have the capability for feasibility study or design, or in construction supervision, apart from asking some government agency to help it, it can go to a consultant to do the whole project on a turnkey basis. Or, it can ask the consultant to do the design work, and then open bidding to select a construction firm. Or, it can ask the consultant to run the whole plant.

We saw all the problems over the last 17 years, why the treatment plants in the various provinces never sprang up: the [authorities] couldn't prepare the projects. They didn't have the budget and they didn't have the technical capability. So these are the three difficulties that the law tries to provide the answer to. . . .

The PCD is now moving in such a way that many of the projects can be privatised. Garbage and refuse disposal, and waste-water treatment, are the two major problems now. We set up the Waste-water Management Agency, a state enterprise, to manage and invest in water treatment for Greater Bangkok. It's starting to function now. You have to tackle the waste-water problem in Bangkok as a regional approach rather than a provincial approach, because Bangkok's five neighbouring provinces discharge everything into the Chao Praya River.

The idea was to set up the agency as a mother company, [like the Petroleum Authority of Thailand]. . . . Subsidiaries of this Waste-water Management Agency can become private companies where the agency can hold up to 25 per cent equity. The idea is for them to become investing and implementing [entities]. . . . The agency's priority is Greater Bangkok, but it has authority to service other provinces as well. If the local governments feel they don't have the capability, they can look to this agency to handle the whole investment, running and operating a plant.

Author: You have previously called for the establishment of an environment ministry. How far has this gone? Would it need a constitutional amendment? Is the government seriously considering such a move?

Kasem: Yes, that is the key thing. We discussed [setting up an environment ministry] during the drafting of the 1992 Act, but at that time the Anand government didn't want to establish a new ministry because the government was only a caretaker [administration]. It was a pity. Anand agreed in principle, but didn't want to do it. So I'm now pushing that. We need a ministry separate from Science and Technology.

Author: What would be the advantage?

Kasem: There are two [major] issues for sustainable development within the Thai economy: you must have a good management system for the environment, and you have to use science and technology to achieve sustainable development. . . . Considering the heavy load that the minister and I are bearing, and the magnitude of the problems, both [these tasks] need 100 per cent attention, not just 50–50, to make things work.

The minister and permanent secretary [should] concentrate 100 per cent on one issue. [Additionally] if we create an environment ministry, we would be able to regroup the natural resource aspect of management, and the pollution control aspect of management. For instance, I believe that the protected areas which now are coming under the Royal Forestry Department—such as the national parks, wildlife sanctuaries, non-hunting areas, watersheds—all these aspects of conservation should be put into the new ministry as a separate department. The problem at the moment is that you have a department which exploits resources; at the same time, it is responsible for conservation. This is a contradiction. Look at other departments: the Ministry of Industry's [purpose] is to promote industries, so its section dealing with pollution management should be separated and put into the new ministry.

I hope these things will happen, otherwise management of the environment will be half-hearted. To be more effective in environmental management and for the long-term objective of sustainable development, you need to integrate all the environmental management aspects of the country into one ministry—like what they have done in Europe, and in the USA with the federal Environment Protection Agency and even the state EPAs. They are becoming implementing agencies rather than planning agencies. The 1992 Environment Act is not fully making the ministry an implementing agency.

Author: This means a ministry of the environment would take on more power in a certain sense?

Kasem: I don't want to talk about power. If you talk about that, people are always holding back—bureaucrats don't want to lose power. You should build it from the point of view of how to manage the problem in a better way. It becomes more centralised environmental management if you put [all functions] into one ministry, rather than if you disperse them among all other ministries. . . . No director-general would put emphasis on the conservation part of his responsibility. They always put weight on the exploitation part or the promotion part, which creates environmental degradation. So you need a ministry that could counterbalance this; this is the reasoning behind setting up a separate ministry.

One other thing: we cannot manage the environment in such a way that I would like to see because of the political aspect. Members of Parliament, the politicians, take environment as a fashion. They are not serious about trying to see what will happen to the country 10 years from now if we don't manage the environment well. [Are they looking at] the economic situation, our depleting resources, our pollution problems? They are only interested if these affect their popularity. Many people say this happens everywhere in the world, but I think . . . MPs in the developed countries are more sincere as a percentage. . . . The percentage may be 80–20 rather than 20–80 [as in Thailand]. I hardly see any [Thai] MP who is an advocate of environmental improvement. They use environmental issues when they are canvassing. When they come into power, they don't really put their efforts into trying to give the country a better environment. I think their own personal gain, personal interests come first. So this is the quality of MPs in Thailand. We are facing an uphill battle.

The other side of the coin is the people themselves: quality of life is linked to the wealth of the people, everywhere in the world. In the USA, 30 years ago, maybe you had the same kinds of problems with industrial pollution. But once you become more and more wealthy, you consume better products. The same thing is true with the environment; people want to [enjoy] a better environment if they are getting wealthy.

So you find that to tackle the environment problems in Thailand, you cannot generalise your policy and try to implement it. You have to take the so-called poor people, rural people approach. The approach is different for the urban poor and the urban rich.

What worries me about Thailand is that the income gap is widening. I'm not proud at all when people say we are in the upper income bracket of the developing countries. They look at the GDP, but people should look at the income distribution. I am not begging for aid, but I am talking about the true picture that people should see before they classify us. They never use income distribution as an indicator of the wealth of the country. They use per capita income, the percentage of exports as GDP, as an indicator of the wealth of the nation. It's inadequate. The income distribution factor is the most serious thing. I don't know why the economists—the World Bank and others—never take this as a very important indicator.

Author: Is there much support for this idea of an environment ministry in Thailand?

Kasem: There is support for an environment ministry among environmentalists, whether they are in a government agency, or among those who care about Nature. Those who really care about the prospect of sustainable development, our economy, would support this. Politicians, I think 50–50. They should support it because there would be more ministers.

Author: How about legal powers over the environment, powers to prosecute?

Kasem: This is also stipulated in the 1992 law, by the concept of the polluter-pays principle, in which the polluter has to pay for what he has done, whether the pollution is on public land, in public waterways, or even [caused by] the individual. But there is a weakness in the law. It isn't clear that [a complainant] could take the matter to the court and that he or she would win the case.

Author: So you can't take people to court just now under this polluter-pays principle?

Kasem: We cannot take people to court. But people affected by an industry polluting their rice fields, for example, can take the industry to the court to get compensation. But I think there is a loophole in the law at the moment so we are now trying to amend it.

Author: Will businessmen in the government support it?

Kasem: They have to: the climate is there. The government has to support it. There is no way the government can think otherwise. It is fairness to society. . . . [Businessmen] have been taking advantage of the poor people for a long, long time. This type of thing—for example, air pollution in Bangkok—is not only affecting the poor, it is affecting the rich also.

[The polluter-pays principle] is one of the very important measures so that we can have better management of the environment. Why should people get away with it if they create environmental problems? I am worried about industrial development. If we go more towards becoming an NIC (newly-industrialised country), to a higher income level, it means our industry will be expanding quite fast. And the type of industry that is coming on-stream is mostly polluting industry. Even the electronics industry creates problems with heavy metal disposal; not just petrochemical industries create problems. So, it would be more difficult to manage the industrial pollution problems. What I would like to see is [an increased] role for the public in helping environmental management. This is something government alone cannot do.

Author: It seems there isn't a lot of consciousness. . . .

Kasem: You will create consciousness through education. It's a long-term process. . . . But for the general public, you must have a different kind of approach: public relations programmes, participation programmes. You need to create the awareness.

Author: Are you happy with the way these concerns. . . ?

Kasem: Education is moving too slowly. The curriculum is not geared enough to [environmental concerns]. We have been working on it for 20 years, but still it's not enough. The problem is with the curriculum design. It's the same problem with science and technology: these are the crucial [issues] that you need to impart to the youngsters even at primary school, not secondary. There are ways and means to make them aware apart from teaching them in the classroom. There are games which they can play that stimulate their thinking, stimulate [correct] behaviour towards the environment or towards thinking about science in their way of life.

Environment Act Under Siege

Under the patronage system of Thai politics, even legal requirements embodied in legislation gaining royal assent can be negated by the manoeuvrings of influential cabinet ministers striving to maximise their financial leverage. At least two major instances have been recorded in recent years where cabinet ministers have attempted to by-pass provisions of the 1992 Environment Act—reminders of how the underdeveloped rule of law in Thailand can be overruled by political expediency.

One such alleged case surfaced in March 1997, when a high-ranking official of the Ministry of Science, Technology, and Environment charged that the Interior Ministry was attempting to transfer the budget for provincial water treatment and garbage disposal from his ministry. The official complained that the attempt was "obviously illegal" under the 1992 Environment Act.[4] *The Nation* reported:

> Advisors to Interior Minister Snoh Thienthong last week submitted a letter to Interior permanent secretary Chuwong Chayabutr asking for a review of [a] 1995 cabinet resolution and the permanent transfer of the water treatment and garbage disposal budget to the Interior Ministry.... According to the advisors, many provincial governors have complained of difficulties in getting reimbursement from the Science Ministry for spending on waste disposal and have claimed that, as a result, garbage and waste-water has not been properly disposed of, leading to environmental problems....

> Article 39 of the Environment Act states that provinces must draw up their own environmental plans, to be approved by the Science Ministry. As of 1995, when the article was first implemented, 12 provinces had drawn up environmental schemes, according to the source, but only three of them—Kanchanaburi, Phitsanulok, and Chiang Rai—were able to follow through with their plans. Plans in the other provinces were suspended because the Interior Ministry's Public Works Department refused to cooperate with provincial authorities and the Science Ministry [according to the ministry official].... Transferring the budget to the Interior Ministry would mark a return to the old bureaucratic system in which the central government has full authority to designate and control funds allocated to local agencies. According to the law, the budget does not actually "belong" to the Science Ministry. The ministry only acts as a consultant to local governments, reviewing provincial environmental plans and submitting budget proposals to the Budget Bureau on behalf of provincial authorities.

Other perceived abuses of the Environment Act include the lack of strict adherence to obligations involved in conducting and approving environmental impact assessments (EIAs), especially regarding the controversial construction of large dams in rural areas.

Environmentalists have criticised the building of large dams in Thailand as being destructive of biodiversity and of forests; and as being socially disruptive, requiring the relocation of thousands of villagers almost invariably to less hospitable locations.

The controversy over the Kaeng Sua Ten dam project in Phrae province was emerging in 1997 as another prime example of how lack of transparency and the avoidance of legal obligations on the part of politicians accompanied the commissioning of a mega-project worth billions of baht.

One of the final cabinet meetings of the collapsing Banharn government approved the project on 19 November 1996, along with more than 2,600 other projects which were approved *en bloc* in defiance of criticism that many of them had not received proper study.

The Nation reported that cabinet ministers Samak Sundaravej and Yingphan Manasikarn (the minister in charge of environment), along with the prime minister, supported the Kaeng Sua Ten dam project and pushed it through cabinet—ignoring the 1992 Environment Act, which requires such a large project to first carry out an acceptable environment impact assessment (EIA) and have it gain the approval of the National Environment Board.[5] A lack of transparency, particularly the government's failure to make public all information about the project and failure to hold genuine dialogue with affected local communities, showed a disregard for democratic practice and the needs of sustainable development.

The Royal Irrigation Department had been promoting the project for 14 years, and several attempts to have an EIA approved by the NEB had failed, according to one source.[6] The dam's proposed location is the Mae Yom National Park in Phrae province. The initial estimated cost was 4.6 billion baht. Environmentalist critics estimated that some 42 square kilometres of teak forest would be submerged if the dam was built. In addition, a geological expert pointed out that there is a geological fault line 31 km from the proposed site, and ventured that the already-dubious cost would have to be increased by at least 30 per cent to ensure the dam is resistant to earthquakes.[7]

327

Attempts to promote the project were full of deceptive practices designed to create an impression of viability and popular support. The Bangkok Thai-language newspaper *Krungthep Turakit* reported:

> At the public hearing on 1 August 1994, a mob in favour of the dam was organised with local politicians dividing up respon-sibility for gathering as many villagers as possible. In comparison, the villagers actually affected did not participate because they had not been invited and spent the day planting trees in the Mae Yom National Park.[8]

In December 1996, an official of the Ministry of Science, Technology, and Environment quoted a study of the Kaeng Sua Ten dam project carried out by the United Nations Food and Agriculture Organisation (FAO) which contradicted justifications for construction of the dam given by its proponents. The study suggested that the Royal Irrigation Department had overstated the dam's capacity to control floods. . . . The environment official, who declined to be named because science minister, Yingphan Manasikarn fully supported the project, said:

> To prevent floods, the dam must be larger and it shouldn't store any water in the reservoir during normal times. But the Kaeng Sua Ten is a medium-sized dam with the initial purpose of producing electricity [which means it will have to store a certain amount of water at all times]. Looking at the RID data, it is still unclear whether the dam is worthwhile, but the FAO study says the dam is not cost-effective.[9]

Two weeks earlier, Dr. Adul Wichienchroen, a member of the National Environment Board's expert committee, revealed that the project proposals for the Kaeng Sua Ten dam presented to the NEB and the cabinet contained many differences:

> The size of the dam in the NEB version is larger than in the information presented by the RID to the cabinet. But while the size of the dam presented to the cabinet is smaller, the amount of farmland expected to benefit from the project is larger. I am sure that the RID and the ministers who made the proposals want to

make it seem that the dam will affect less forest area and provide more benefits.[10]

The Nation reported that in Chiang Mai on 25 November 1996, local academics, environmental activists, and students, led by Chiang Mai University's Social Research Institute, said they would join opposition to the dam as the project's approval violated environment laws which state that an environmental impact assessment must be approved first.

The Interior Ministry's Damrong Rajanupharb Institute observed Phrae officials' attempts to promote the project among local residents. Rakkij Srisurin, an official of the institute, said that it

> . . . found that local officials presented one-sided information to convince residents to agree with the project. The officials were also found to have distorted information to benefit the pro-dam case when speaking to the public.

Academics supported public participation in the project

> . . . but local officials said public participation could delay the government decision-making process for the project.[11]

(As of February 1997, another 12 new, large dam projects had been proposed for construction, at a cost of about 163 billion baht. Seven of those would be built in conservation areas such as natural parks and wildlife sanctuaries, according to Decha Siriphat, a leader of the Alternative Agriculture Network.)[12]

The two examples outlined above display the prevailing essence of Thai politics, and how networks of self-interested people would group together to facilitate tasks such as approval of unpopular projects and transfers of budgets. (This question of patronage politics is discussed more fully in Chapter 8.)

Apart from environmental impact assessments, another key provision of the Environment Act was suffering as of 1997—the polluter-pays principle—through lack of implementation. Permanent Secretary Kasem indicated that the Ministry of Science, Technology, and the Environment did not have the power to take violators of the principle to court—a significant loophole in the law. Environment officials are responsible for issuing regulations and investigating suspected violations, but the responsibility to take legal action lies with other agencies that are not always cooperative.

As of 1997, taxpayers were paying most of the bill for cleaning up pollution, with pollution-control projects financed from the government budget or the environment fund. The polluter-pays principle, when translated into wide-ranging legislation and effective implementation, can be a powerful tool for discouraging all kinds of pollution. Not only commercial and industrial enterprises, but also individuals, should be obliged to pay the full cost of cleaning up and mitigating the effects of pollution they create.

This principle should also apply to motor vehicle owners. In an age when fossil-fuel-burning vehicles are a major contribution to global warming and to health hazards in cities and towns especially, environmental taxes should be charged to the operators of all such vehicles. The revenue generated could then be used to pay for monitoring of pollution and implementation of pollution control measures. Producers and consumers of products whose manufacture, use, or disposal have an adverse impact on the environment, should pay—whether through fines or taxes.

Collecting fees from the public for waste-water treatment and solid waste disposal is part of the polluter-pays principle, but the public has yet to accept its responsibility in this, environment officials say. Such public acceptance is also a key to effective privatisation of environmental management.

Lack of political will seems to be the major obstacle to implementing the polluter-pays principle, considering that under the political patronage system, cabinet ministers may protect favoured industries from financial impositions while expecting rewards in return. Various polluter-pays proposals have advanced through the government bureaucracy, only to "get lost" at the political level (see Chapter 12).

Evidence of other breaches of the Environment Act by government agencies is apparent. In February 1997, Saksith Tridech, the secretary-general of the Office of Environment Policy and Planning (OEPP), said that large-scale transportation projects in Bangkok being run by five government agencies were causing dust, noise, and vibrations that exceeded acceptable standards.[13] The agencies were not complying with the Environment Act, which stipulated that agencies managing large projects must not only conduct environmental impact assessment studies, but also find measures to relieve environmental impacts both during and after construction work. He singled out the Bangkok Metropolitan Authority's Tanayong elevated train project, where, in three months since December 1996, all 49 monitoring checkpoints of the OEPP had found the level of dust particles exceeding the prescribed maximum of 0.33 mg/cu.m., while noise pollution exceeded the prescribed maximum of 70 decibels.

Environmental Issues in Thailand

This section briefly outlines some recent developments in certain key environmental areas. (The issues of deforestation and the need to develop sustainable, chemical-free agriculture are regarded as being of high priority, and are taken up at greater length in the next two chapters.)

Environmental Policy

Stated policy is one thing, implementation is another. If politicians find it difficult to follow the provisions of existing legislation such as the Environment Act, how should we regard their statements about environmental policy? At present, one major thrust of policy focuses on waste-water treatment throughout Thailand's 76 provinces. This much-needed pollution-control measure is mentioned numerous times in the Environment Act, often in conjunction with decentralisation of environmental management to the provinces. Privatisation of waste management is also a major thrust, as indicated by Kasem Snidvongs.

Public participation in environmental matters is another policy direction being promoted by environment officials. The PCD wants to formalise and institutionalise the public hearing process, particularly with regard to selecting project sites, to remove "confusion" from the hearing process. We have already noted, in the case of the Kaeng Sua Ten dam project, how this process has been abused in the past to serve the interests of politicians and their allies in officialdom.

Another policy thrust that reflects on bureaucratic inadequacies was the announcement by Sirithan Pairojboriboon, deputy director-general of the PCD, who said local volunteers will be trained to carry out environmental monitoring because government officials have not been effective at this task.[14]

331

Emissions Control

Thailand has made progress in controlling emissions from factories or power plants—but mainly when emissions have reached dangerous levels and caused visible health problems within nearby communities. Thailand has banned petrol containing lead since January 1996, making it the first country in Southeast Asia to do so. New cars are required to have catalytic converters to minimise pollution. However, air pollution from vehicles was growing every year in Bangkok up to the economic crisis of 1997, when many cash-strapped motorists sold their cars or left them at home more often. But, by mid-1999, it seemed that aspiring middle-class Thais were once again seeking to fill up Bangkok streets with new vehicles. Realistic alternatives to private transportation have been slow to materialise, and government has been slow to implement workable disincentives to private transportation. Two-stroke motorcycles remain a growing source of dangerous pollution in urban areas (see Chapter 12).

Thailand was, however, paying some attention to curbing vehicle emissions, as environmental officials proposed a policy to have all cars undergo yearly inspection and maintenance checks when owners apply for their annual registration, to ensure that engines were properly tuned. Additionally, Thailand was planning to adopt Euro I auto standards for vehicle manufactures, with tax penalties levied on laggards. As European vehicular standards advance, Thai manufacturers will have to follow suit, but will have a two-year grace period.[15] The Bangkok Metropolitan Authority, in 1997, mounted a limited programme to conduct spot checks on vehicles to test for excessive emissions.

Thailand has made no effort to control carbon dioxide emissions; up to mid-1999, proposals to institute car-sharing schemes and other disincentives to the growth of traffic, had not materialised. The government's anaemic reforestation policy had failed to increase carbon sinks in the form of new forests or plantations, now a major requirement in the task of abating global warming. Meanwhile, accompanying the 1998 climate-change negotiations in Buenos Aires was the release of more information which showed that global warming was already a reality.

In late 1996, officials of the PCD were preparing to introduce a scheme to allow firms to trade "rights to pollute" as an incentive towards pollution control. The scheme would allow a firm that can reduce its emissions to lower than the required limit to sell its remaining quota to another firm.[16] This type of scheme is in operation in some other countries, and became a major (if controversial) initiative at the Kyoto session on climate change in December 1997. Other incentive measures were planned in Thailand, such as tax reductions on imports of environmentally-friendly equipment and products.

Industrial and Toxic Waste

How to manage the disposal of rapidly growing amounts of industrial and toxic waste is now a major problem facing Thailand. All industrialised or industrialising countries have faced, or will face, this problem at some point in their development. During Thailand's economic boom and rush to industrialisation, such disposal received little attention. At the end of 1996, waste treatment facilities in Thailand could dispose of only 10 to 15 per cent of the total hazardous waste.[17]

Agenda 21, the global environmental master plan produced by the 1992 Earth Summit in Rio de Janeiro, states:

> Effective control of the generation, storage, treatment, recycling and re-use, transport, recovery, and disposal of hazardous wastes is of paramount importance for proper health, environmental protection and natural resource management, and sustainable development. This will require the active cooperation and participation of the international community, governments, and industry.
>
> Prevention of the generation of hazardous wastes and the rehabilitation of contaminated sites are the key elements, and both require knowledge, experienced people, facilities, financial resources, and technical and scientific capacities.[18]

It is difficult to quantify the exact amount of toxic and hazardous waste being generated in Thailand because of reporting difficulties and differences in definition of what constitutes hazardous waste. One commonly used authority[19] forecast that the amount of hazardous waste to be generated in the year 2001 would be triple the amount generated in 1991, which stood at about two million tonnes. It placed the 1996 amount at around 3.5 million tonnes. Another estimate of the amount of Thailand's hazardous waste, attributed to the Asian Development Bank, currently places it at more than 1.2 million tonnes and predicts its rise to almost 3 million tonnes by 2000.[20] However, these estimates came before the East Asian economic crisis.

Under the current division of environmental responsibilities among government ministries, it is the duty of the Ministry of Industry to provide hazardous waste treatment through industrial estates under the management of the Industrial Estates Authority of Thailand. However, recent industrial policy has been criticised for neglecting the question of safe disposal of hazardous waste. An industrial master plan unveiled by the government late in 1996 failed to spell out how the government would get rid of toxic waste, according to Thien Mekanontachai, director-general of the Industrial Works Department.[21] He said that if the government wanted to promote industry, it had to face the industrial waste problem. Thien said that although the master plan, to run from 1997 to 2001, has a policy to relocate factories from Bangkok and its outlying areas, it lacks provisions to prepare rural areas to deal with pollution and industrial waste from the factories.

Thailand's first major attempt to involve the private sector in industrial waste disposal has had a rocky road. The project of Genco (General Environmental Conservation Co. Ltd), designed as Thailand's first such national facility, faced resistance to the siting of its plant from local inhabitants, and resistance from factory owners to pay for waste treatment. Firstly, local residents of Pluek Daeng district of Rayong province, where the plant was originally to be sited, opposed the project and forced it to be relocated. It moved to the Mab Ta Phud Industrial Estate on Thailand's Eastern Seaboard, with a reduction of the planned landfill area for the project from 1,065 *rai* (170 hectares) at Pluek Daeng, to only 62.5 *rai* (10 ha) at Mab Ta Phud, *The Nation* reported.[22] Secondly, the newspaper interviewed Edward Corcoran, Genco's chief operating officer, who said that the two major groups of customers for Genco's services are circuit board factories and the steel products industry, which produce toxic sludge during the smelting process. Corcoran said:

> The problem is they [factory owners] are not used to paying [for waste treatment]. So, we must educate them a lot to convince them to pay, even though they are supposed to do it by law.

Meanwhile, toxic wastes end up in conventional rubbish dumps and in rivers. A 1994 survey of water quality from 1,584 factories along seven major rivers in Thailand showed that 40 per cent were disobeying laws on water discharge quality. A study by the Thailand Environment Institute of pollution from factories in Samut Prakan province (the largest industrial area bordering Bangkok, at the mouth of the Chao Praya River) found that toxic waste from factories totalled 140,000 tonnes per annum, with those involved with food processing, chemicals, metals, textiles (especially leather tanning factories), and electronics creating the most pollution.[23]

Government agencies have reported that pollution by heavy metals is increasing, particularly in the manufacture and unsafe disposal of dry cell batteries.[24] The Pollution Control Department estimated that dry cell factories produce about 147,000 kg of sludge—including about 44,000 kg of manganese dioxide, 28,150 kg of zinc, 2,000 kg of zinc chloride, 58 kg of mercury, and 22 kg of cadmium per year. In addition, the Ministry of Public Health has reported an increasing level of cadmium, lead, and mercury in river water nationwide. Traces of heavy metals are also being found in humans. A major contribution to the accumulation of heavy metals in river waters is the careless disposal of dry cells. Community participation for separating dry cells from other household wastes is important and needs to be promoted on an urgent basis.

The problem of hazardous waste disposal is immense, and a dynamic, comprehensive approach is needed to ensure safety. Hazardous waste poses considerable potential risks to human health and the environment. Heavy metals and other toxic substances can accumulate in ecosystems and find their way into the food chain, causing serious health problems.

Agenda 21 offers strategies for the prevention and minimisation of hazardous waste by:

- encouraging industry to treat, recycle, re-use and dispose of wastes at the source of generation, or as close as possible thereto, whenever hazardous waste generation is unavoidable and when it is both economically and environmentally efficient for industry to do so;
- encouraging industries to be transparent in their operations and provide relevant information to the communities that might be affected by the generation, management, and disposal of hazardous wastes;
- encouraging industrial training programmes incorporating hazardous waste prevention and minimisation techniques, and

    launching demonstration projects at the local level to develop "success stories" in cleaner production;

- providing awareness, education, and training programmes covering all levels of society; and
- conducting environmental audits of existing industries to improve in-plant regimes for the management of hazardous wastes.

Proper disposal of accumulating industrial and household wastes, and toxic substances discharged from industrial plants and vehicles is essential. This calls for strict industrial standards in the production and waste disposal processes to protect the environment—with rigorous punitive action against violators of environmental laws. Diagnostic procedures at health facilities need to be improved to accurately determine whether an illness is related to exposure to dangerous chemical or toxic substances discharged from industrial plants. All of these call for political commitment and better coordination among government agencies involved in environmental protection and health care.

A related problem to the careless disposal of hazardous waste is the massive and indiscriminate use of pesticides in agriculture (outlined in Chapter 14).

Biodiversity

The term biodiversity has entered into the general vocabulary within the past 20 years to help us focus on an urgent need: halting the growing, and alarming, disappearance of living species globally. Biodiversity refers to the total range of plants, animals, and organisms—in effect, all living things—present in Nature.

The current decline in biodiversity is largely the result of human activity, and represents a serious threat to human development. Urgent and decisive action is needed to conserve and maintain genes, species, and ecosystems, with a view to the sustainable management and use of biological resources. Although about 1.7 million species have been scientifically described in Nature, it is estimated that there are at least 13 million species.[25] Most of these are in the tropics, particularly in tropical forests. Human encroachment is driving many of these species to extinction.[26] As of 1997, one conservationist source put the number of species being lost per day at between 50 to 100. According to *Agenda 21*

> . . . our planet's essential goods and services depend on the variety and variability of genes, species, populations, and ecosystems. Biological resources feed and clothe us and provide housing, medicines, and spiritual nourishment. . . .[27]

It might also be added that the presence of such a rich, global biodiversity has been a major factor in regulating the global climate. A stable climate, in turn, is a major factor in maintaining overall ecological stability.

How can dwindling biodiversity threaten human wellbeing? In Asian agriculture, for example, thousands of varieties of rice have disappeared over the years as scientists and agronomists concentrated on promoting a small range of high-yielding varieties to increase food production. But reliance on a small number of varieties can be risky. In future, plant diseases and pests that can wipe out whole varieties of rice (or other crops) may appear. With the gene pool for rice narrowed down to a small number of varieties, the prospect of breeding new strains to overcome disease and pests is greatly diminished. The United Nations Environment Programme, for example, notes that by 2005, India is expected to produce 75 per cent of its rice from just 10 varieties compared with the 30,000 varieties traditionally cultivated. In Indonesia, 1,500 varieties of rice disappeared between 1975–1990.[28]

This is just one example of how the depletion of Nature (i.e. biodiversity), often in the name of economic progress, can undermine the quality of life—which is inextricably bound up with the quality and diversity of the natural environment that sustains humankind.

I believe that human beings are also impoverished culturally and spiritually when species disappear from the Earth, often caused by humankind's carelessness. To take one example: the noble elephant, long a treasured and beloved part of Thai culture, is facing disappearance as its forest habitat is taken from it by human beings. Elephants come into direct conflict with man, encroaching on agricultural plantations for food. Their numbers have dwindled in Thailand to between 3,000 and 4,000. They may soon disappear from the wild altogether, conservationists warn.

Then, reflect upon this notion: there is a spirituality which traverses the whole web of life, such that when a major part of that totality is destroyed, the other parts of that web, including humankind, are somehow spiritually diminished. This may not be demonstrable in scientific terms, but we know from the empathy that we are capable of feeling for animals and plants, that there is some transcendent force that links the various elements of life. It is not enough to value other organisms merely because of their utility to humankind.

Animals, plants and organisms are interdependent. They need each other for their own survival, and therefore we are justified in talking about a web of life. If humankind persists in its large-scale destruction of species, could this unravelling web ultimately undermine humankind's existence?

The table below indicates threatened biodiversity in Thailand. It gives only a glimpse, since species—particularly in the plant kingdom—are far from being fully catalogued and may disappear even before they are identified. The United Nations has recognised that the fauna and flora of Asia and the Pacific are more threatened than ever before; this is surely true in Thailand as commercial and infrastructural expansion—much of it unnecessary and motivated by greed—has relentlessly destroyed natural systems.

Table 13.1

Biodiversity: Threatened Plants and Vertebrates in Thailand

	Threatened species[*]	Total known species[**]
Plants	68	—
Mammals	26	265
Birds	34	915
Reptiles	1	298
Amphibians	0	107
Fish	13	>600

[*] From *State of the Environment in Asia and the Pacific, 1995* (ESCAP, ADB) Page 64.

[**] From IUCN, 1993. Published in *Global Environment Outlook* 1997 (UNEP).

The United Nations Convention on Biological Diversity, opened for signature during the 1992 Earth Summit, offers the best prospect for global protection of biodiversity. In Thailand, the cabinet approved the treaty on 15 July 1997, and it was awaiting ratification by the House of Representatives. It was supported by the Ministry of Science, Technology, and Environment, and the Ministry of Foreign Affairs, while the Ministry of Public Health and some non-governmental organisations expressed reservations about the treaty, fearing it would allow foreigners to exploit Thailand's indigenous knowledge, particularly concerning medicinal plants.[29]

Mangrove Forests

These forests, which support a multitude of biodiversity and are so important to coastal ecology, are fast disappearing from the Thai coast. Some 53 per cent of mangroves were destroyed in the 35 years since 1961. Mangroves provide a habitat for sea-birds, act as nurseries for large numbers of commercially important fish species, and offer protection against coastal erosion and storms. Yet, they are being lost at a rate faster than forests in mountain areas (another serious problem discussed more fully in Chapter 15).

The National Environment Board (NEB) in May 1997 approved an increased budget of 342 million baht, to be spent in 22 coastal provinces from 1999 to 2003, to rehabilitate mangrove forests and manage wetland areas. The budget would support the participation of provincial organisations.[30] The NEB was informed that the rate of destruction in the South was 26,711 *rai* (4,268 hectares) per year—from aquaculture development, logging, mining, community expansion, and the construction of boat piers and other infrastructure. Chonburi was the first coastal province to become devoid of mangroves.

Can the new budget be implemented effectively? Can it survive the drastic cuts in government expenditure required to remedy the 1997 financial crisis? Can it overcome the vested interests of so-called "development" supported by political influence?

Three months following the budget announcement, the vice president of the National Mangrove Resource Committee, Sanit Aksornkaew, said an adjustment in national mangrove management policy is needed to foster sustainable use of mangrove forest areas. Road-building and other construction projects were causing as much as 81 per cent of mangrove deforestation, especially in Chantaburi province, he said.[31]

Other experts have noted that the clearing of mangroves for intensive shrimp farming is not sustainable, since such farms pollute the land and must eventually be abandoned, leaving behind a degraded ecology. Such shrimp and prawn farms have become major sources of export earnings in many Asian countries, but at what cost? These monoculture farms replace an average of 283 species of finfish, 229 species of crustaceans, and 211 species of molluscs which occur naturally in mangrove forests.[32] Other threats to the existence of mangroves are housing and industrial developments, siltation, and highly polluted run-off from inland sources including untreated waste-water discharged by beach resorts and hotels.

In November 1996, the cabinet cancelled all logging and charcoal concessions in mangrove forests, and also approved a "rehabilitation" plan to improve ecological functioning of degraded mangrove forests, and allocated funds.[33] But that, apparently, is far from enough.

Other Marine Destruction

The *Four-Country Citizen's Report on the Environment, 1995*,[34] states:

> The Gulf of Thailand used to be known as one of the richest marine resources in the world. But today, it is a classic example of a dying marine ecosystem. The fishing grounds are overfished, coral reefs are in various degrees of degradation, and the mouths of estuaries are heavily silted. . . . As a result of the diminishing spawning grounds in mangrove areas, the fish catch has been declining.

Overfishing by large trawlers owned by large-scale investors is the most serious problem affecting offshore marine resources. Small-scale fishermen have incentives to conserve marine resources near their homes for long-term use, but the big investors rarely follow conservation practices because they can simply send their trawlers to a different location when one area is fished out. Such investors rely on political patronage to avoid observing regulations, such as the prohibition against trawlers operating within three kilometres of the coastline. They can simply go and encroach on protected areas.

These observations came at a seminar to discuss the crisis facing marine resources held in January 1997.[35] Participants suggested remedial measures such as stricter zoning, the use of subsidies, the imposition of fees, the use of public funds to "buy back" small trawlers from their owners, the abolition of factories which process undersized fish, and the mandatory use of wider-mesh fishing nets so that fry and other small fish are not caught. But the root cause of inaction, once again, was corrupt politics.

Solar Power

The *de facto* devaluation of the baht in July 1997 and the consequent need to curb oil imports made solar power generation a much more attractive option for rural Thailand. This so-called "alternative" source of power generation has not been given much support by the Thai government, one of the principal reasons being that the cost of generating power using solar cells (i.e., photovoltaic cells) was higher than conventional power generation. Emphasis has been placed on big-dam construction for hydro-electricity generation, and diesel-fuelled power generation—these two methods favouring big oil importers and construction companies. There are two major reasons to foster the large-scale use of solar power, especially in the Northeast and remote areas:

1. The large-scale manufacture of solar power units could benefit small-scale industry and create jobs in many provinces.
2. Both diesel-power and hydro-electric power generation have environmental costs, the former creating carbon dioxide pollution (contributing to global warming) and other noxious air pollution, and the latter destroying natural ecosystems and displacing populations through the need for large reservoirs.

India is set to become the world's largest solar power generator by 2010, by tapping the sunshine of the Thar desert, which covers 20,000 square kilometres in Rajasthan state. Using photovoltaic solar collectors and a new, experimental solar chimney collector, Rajasthan aims to generate 10,000 megawatts of power, enough to serve 16,000 domestic consumers of the state.[36]

Thailand is regarded as being fairly well endowed with solar radiation, and large-scale installation of solar panels on rooftops would make environmental sense. A solar water-heating industry has been established since the early 1980s, with collectors installed in hospitals, hotels, and private houses. By 1992, domestic production of solar collectors reached over 10,000 square metres per year.[37] A lot of research is currently going

341

into the improvement of design and materials (silicon wafers) used in solar energy generation. Photovoltaic cells produced only about 2.5 megawatts of power by the end of 1996, compared to Thailand's total energy demand during peak hours of more than 13,300 megawatts in 1996.[38]

Several developed countries subsidise the use of photovoltaic panels in individual homes for environmental reasons. But in Thailand, it is the conventional power sources that are subsidised through the extension of the national electricity grid to rural areas. The Electricity Generating Authority of Thailand has already conducted research which shows that, even at its present relatively high cost of generation, solar power in Thailand will generally be cheaper than diesel power for any village which uses 8,000 kilowatt-hours per year or less—roughly equal to the electricity used by about 20 houses without air conditioning.[39] It is especially cost-effective in remote areas.

Environmental Standards

One of the most encouraging developments by industry worldwide—and in Thailand—is the development of environmental standards and green labelling for products, giving environmentally-conscious consumers an opportunity to choose products which have been certified as meeting criteria for being environmentally friendly. The Thai Industrial Standards Institute, a government body, along with the Thailand Environment Institute, an NGO, began early in 1996 to promote the ISO 14000 environmental standards for industry. This followed the Standards Institute's earlier introduction of the more general ISO 9000 industrial standards.

Globally, the International Standards Organisation (ISO) is developing a set of standards and guidelines for environmental issues in five areas, including environmental labelling. The aim is to standardise the plethora of mandatory and voluntary labelling requirements that have been developed internationally. Work began in 1996 on the five areas, encompassing:

- general principles for all environmental labels (ISO 14020);
- guidelines for self-declared environmental claims (ISO 14021);
- symbols for use with self-declared environmental claims (ISO 14022);
- testing and verification procedures (ISO 14023); and
- third party accredited multiple criteria environmental labels (ISO 14024).[40]

Such eco-labelling, or green labelling, and the setting of national and international standards for products, could conceivably develop into a major system worldwide offering a significant boost to national and global environmental protection efforts. But initial efforts to establish and promote the ISO 14000 standard have become immersed in the stormy politics of global trade issues, especially the question of unfettered access to markets internationally. Many countries, especially developing ones, fear that such standards, if adopted internationally, may be used as discriminative trade barriers: *de facto* protectionism. The issue has become a major area of contention and negotiation within the committees of the World Trade Organisation (WTO), regarding how to achieve sustainable development.

The following quotation succinctly expresses the dilemma between trade and environment, hinging on the principle that consumers must pay the full environmental costs of creating industrial products and of disposing of leftover waste. The quotation comes from a United Nations briefing document circulated at the Rio de Janeiro Earth Summit:

> Internalising environmental costs has special implications for international trade. When the industrialised world imports products from developing countries at costs which do not reflect the destruction of their natural capital, this essentially exacts an environmental subsidy which impoverishes the developing countries' resource base and contributes to global environmental deterioration. At the same time, unilaterally imposed restrictions on imports to meet developed countries' requirements result in immediate and often critical damage to vulnerable developing economies. These dichotomies can only be resolved through international agreements which respect the interests of all parties and protect the integrity of the global environmental and developmental system.[41]

The *raison d'être* of eco-labelling is to show that an industrial enterprise has included certain environmental-protection costs, incurred during the production phase, into the price of the product. Dr. Chaiyod Bunyagidj, the director of Thailand Environment Institute's business and environment programme, said the ISO 14000 programme considers the environmental impact of a product in its entire life cycle, including production, consumption, and disposal. Products claiming to be "green" based on a single criterion such as power consumption are widely available on the market. But the ISO 14000 programme will take into account factors such as the consumption of material and energy, and emission of pollutants in the production process; energy consumption during use, and the recyclability and natural degradability of the product.[42]

In a 1997 WTO forum,[43] international NGOs noted that assistance to developing countries and transparency of standards in eco-labelling schemes were necessary for such schemes to succeed internationally. The NGOs called for:

- technical assistance and bilateral aid to allow developing-country producers to adapt to "greening" markets;
- longer transition periods for small- and medium-sized enterprises;
- independent certification of eco-labels;
- improved market access for developing countries in general; and
- greater transparency of "green" standards and technical regulations.

Some NGOs doubted that the ISO 14000 scheme could serve the interests of sustainable development, without changes in the ISO approach. One noted that the ISO 14000 drafters had objected to including environmental improvement as an objective. Of key importance was that national environmental laws themselves should be strong in the first place, and that industries in each country should meet national standards. But there was a feeling that efforts to launch the present scheme were just a first step in the harmonisation of standards internationally. They called for a better balancing of the objectives of trade facilitation and environmental improvement.

Some other problems they identified with the international approach to ISO 14000 were:

- a lack of participation by developing countries, public interest groups, and small- and medium-sized enterprises;
- domination by industry representatives of many committees and sub-committees; and
- the high costs of certification with ISO 14000.

But the development of more stringent ecological standards in commerce and industry is not a one-way street favouring the North over the South. Exporters in developing countries who are tuned into the trend towards stricter requirements in developed countries, can reap tidy profits. Case studies published in 1997 illustrate this. Organic farmers in the developing countries are leading the way (see Chapter 14), but major industrial enterprises are also succeeding, such as Century Textiles, one of India's largest companies. Century responded to the German ban on environmentally-unfriendly dyes by swiftly changing to cleaner alternatives. Within one year, Century had increased sales by over 10 per cent.[44]

In Thailand, the giant Siam Cement group has embraced the move towards meeting international environmental standards. Two of its companies—pulp subsidiary Siam Cellulose Co., and the Taluang cement plant—received ISO 14000 certificates in 1997, and the group was expecting 10 more of its companies to follow. The Siam Cement Group spent more than 2.4 billion baht from 1993 to 1997 installing pollution control equipment at its factories, according to its executive vice president. Siam Cellulose has installed air and waste-water control systems and re-uses waste from its production process.[45]

Meanwhile, the issue of barriers to free trade on environmental grounds continues apace, not only in a North-South context, but also in a North-North context. For example, the American pulp and paper industry and the federal government, in 1997, protested against the European Union's new eco-label for office paper products, claiming it was a "severe" trade barrier. The American Forest and Paper Association believed it would be difficult for any US producer to qualify for the eco-label, thus putting their exports at risk.

In the short term, the need is to build up credibility of eco-labels as transparent, truthful, based on sound science, and non-discriminatory, in the words of the US Council for International Business. What do consumers of the North make of all this? Many are sceptical, and find it difficult to distinguish environmental improvements from marketing hype, considering the proliferation of environmental claims and insignia for products. A survey in New Zealand revealed that only 5 per cent of consumers were willing to pay more for environmentally-certified products.[46] Much remains to be done.

Labelling is one way to promote changes n consumption and production patterns, but it cannot address the cverall need to reduce environmentally-unfriendly consumption. Other approaches such as environmental taxation are needed to ensure that consumers pay the full environmental cost of products. (This issue is discussed on a global basis in Chapter 3.) One such controversial proposal—an environmental tax on petroleum products—has met much resistance from oil-producing countries and from consumers. Such a tax could reduce consumption of petrol, and thus carbon dioxide pollution of the atmosphere, while the revenues generated could be used to support environmental goals such as massive reforestation, the introduction of alternative energy sources, or the funding of mass transit projects for cities. Environmental taxes can thus reduce environmental impacts while supporting environmentally-sound alternatives.

The Environmental NGOs

A positive, recent development benefiting the environment is the rising involvement and influence of non-governmental organisations, both in Thailand and globally. In the early 1980s, participation of the NGO movement in environmental conservation and development was barely discernible in Thailand. Fifteen years later, that had changed remarkably, with an estimated 150 NGOs active in the environment field alone. These environmental NGOs now hold an annual general meeting each December, have established network linkages, and publish a directory.[47]

In Thailand, as bureaucratic reform picks up momentum and the bloated, low-productivity government bureaucracy is downsized, expert consultants and NGOs can increasingly be expected to be engaged to carry out specific tasks and add a new dynamism to the development process. The 1992 Environment Act's new acceptance of NGOs provides official proof that they have a valuable and growing role to play.

By July 1996, there were 65 NGOs registered with the National Environment Board, and 10 NGO projects had been approved, worth a total of approximately 50 million baht, with another seven projects under consideration.

The approved projects were:
- promoting healthy villages and garbage disposal (three years, Songkhla);
- reforestation and rehabilitation of watersheds (Lampang);
- production of a book and journal on the environment for children;
- village foundation projects for reforestation and environmentally sustainable agriculture (Chaiyaphum, Songkhla);

- recycling aimed at students in some schools, and separation of paper from garbage;
- promotion of sustainable agriculture, using people's organisations (Maha Sarakam);
- rehabilitation of ecology of the Kong River, including development and reconstruction of watersheds (Khon Kaen);
- coastal conservation, including mangroves (Eastern Thailand);
- working with schools to organise environmental groups among children; and
- organising a network of villagers to promote sustainable agriculture and bringing in groups for information exchange (a special project worth 12 million baht, Northeast Thailand).

The Thailand Environment Institute (TEI), one of the largest NGOs with varied, high-level expertise, had cooperation with government agencies in several areas. The TEI's Dr. Chaiyod said the government was increasingly working through NGOs, thus allowing them to strengthen their capability. Additionally, NGOs (such as TEI) promoting environmental awareness amongst business found it easier than the government to liaise with companies. NGOs could also solve problems locally without bringing in people from the central government.

Global NGOs have also achieved full participation in international negotiations since the 1992 Rio Earth Summit. The International Institute for Sustainable Development underlined this in a bulletin reporting on the special session of the United Nations General Assembly (June 1997) to review the implementation of *Agenda 21*:

> The [preparatory meetings for the Rio Summit] saw the placement of UN security officers at every conference room door with instructions to keep NGOs out of informal consultations. Through the work of the Commission for Sustainable Development and the other conferences held since 1992, NGOs have made great strides in achieving access to and influence on the proceedings. [The June 1997 special session] marked a major milestone. For the first time NGOs and other major groups stood side by side with heads of state and government to deliver speeches to a special session of the General Assembly and were also allowed into ministerial-level consultations. . . .

The key role of NGOs was acknowledged in a meeting between NGOs and British prime minister, Tony Blair. Responding to [questions regarding] the strength of his commitments on climate change as outlined in his speech, Blair responded, "That was the easy part. Now you guys will have to get in behind us." This need to bring NGOs on board to keep up the pressure and help mobilise the public in readiness for far-reaching policy on climate change was also echoed in US President Bill Clinton's speech, with his announcement of a White House conference and stated belief that, "we must first convince the American people and the Congress that the climate change problem is real and immense."[48]

The NGO movement in Thailand is destined to grow, along with a greater participation of civil society in decision making and implementation. The government still limits the number of personnel of NGOs, and there is sometimes suspicion and confrontation between NGOs and governments. Kasem shared some of this suspicion, although he was also instrumental in bringing NGOs into the official development path:

> You find that there are good and bad NGOs. I prefer the good NGOs that have a positive approach, which point out the good and bad things to government, rather than NGOs going and instigating mobs and demonstrations. In Thailand, there are more bad than good. . . . There are many aspects of vested interest coming into the protests and demonstrations, rather than [such NGOs being] clearly motivated by environmental concerns. But this is a learning process. Because some get money from abroad, from international NGOs, they have to show performance—by what?—by instigating mobs and demonstrations because they might be seen on CNN the next day. I would like NGOs to be more constructive: don't give wrong information to the villagers or local people.

Conclusion

Environmental destruction has become so rampant in Thailand, especially in the cities, that the country desperately needs an attainable and sustainable vision of what a healthy environment should look like and how to achieve it.

Thailand's new Constitution is a beginning in establishing the people's fundamental rights to a healthy environment. Such fundamental rights need to be further elaborated. They would include the right to clean air, to clean water, to freedom from chemical contamination, and the right to green and open spaces in urban areas. In fact, such rights, along with the *ecological imperative* of stabilising the Earth's ecosystem, should be regarded as the foundation from which other human rights and individual freedoms arise. In a sustainable global economy, they would form the principles against which all development and money-making activities must be assessed.

It is high time that Thailand had a full-scale ministry of the environment, with the status of a Grade A ministry. It should have a legal division with powers to prosecute offenders against environmental legislation, perhaps through specialised courts, and to seek amendments to plans and projects to ensure environmental health and sustainability.

Decision making must integrate economic, social, and environmental factors at every level—not merely treating environmental protection and environmental impact assessments as mere formalities and window-dressings to cloak money-making activities that diminish environmental quality. The whole Thai development process needs to be monitored and evaluated on a regular and systematic basis. In the words of *Agenda 21*

> . . . the challenge is to achieve significant progress in the years ahead in meeting three fundamental objectives:
> - (a) to incorporate environmental costs in the decisions of producers and consumers, to reverse the tendency to treat the environment as a "free good" and to pass these costs on to other parts of society, other countries, or to future generations;
> - (b) to move more fully towards integration of social and environmental costs into economic activities, so that prices will appropriately reflect the relative scarcity and total value of resources and contribute towards the prevention of environmental degradation; and
> - (c) to include, wherever appropriate, the use of market principles in the framing of economic instruments and policies to pursue sustainable development.[49]

Chapter 14

Sustainable Agriculture: Thailand's Future

Thailand's 1997–99 economic crisis has highlighted the need for the kingdom to rediscover economic fundamentals. Especially, the country needs to link the social goal of uplifting its poor farmers to the strengthening and broadening of the national economy. The development of an efficient and sustainable agriculture, aiming to greatly increase output to provide for growing global food needs in the 21st Century, offers Thailand this dual opportunity.

Sustainability in agricultural practices is something that has been badly neglected in Thailand (and to a certain degree in other Asian countries) as the quest for immediate commercial gains has overridden concern for the health of the natural environment. The imperative of sustainability now calls for a badly needed ecological dimension to be incorporated into accelerated development of agriculture. In the short term, this calls for a huge effort to repair the damage done to the natural environment by massive deforestation and massive use of chemicals in agriculture.

With Thailand's rush over the past two decades to become a newly industrialised country—and in its placing of emphasis on the service sector to promote foreign exchange earners such as tourism—the agricultural sector has been neglected. Thailand has one of the largest areas of productive agricultural land in Asia, yet its productivity per hectare is one of the lowest. Farmers—especially in the Northeast—are mired in debt, have low educational levels, and are further disadvantaged through Thailand's convoluted and inequitable system of land ownership. All of these problems contributed to their pre-Crash drift to the cities, as farming offered them little hope.

Environmental problems and the growing gap between rich and poor in Thailand are also connected to chronic government neglect of the agricultural sector and of the wellbeing of poor farmers. A Bangkok-based United Nations consultant told me:

> After the devaluation of the baht [in 1997], most of the government's attention turned to financial reforms; now [in 1998] more attention is being given to the poor. Why has 70 per cent of the country—the rural areas—been marginalised in the last two decades?

Agricultural 'Second Wave'

Agriculture in Thailand must undergo a 'second wave' of development, in keeping with people-centred development, the new thrust of development emphasised in Thailand's Eighth Plan. There is a strong case to link farmers' development with much-needed reforestation—and to take long-term environmental sustainability as the starting point for all agricultural activities.

Thailand must now regard its small farmers as capital for the country's future. The challenge is to turn them into well-educated and efficient farmers, capable of responding to trends in the international market. Efficient farmers will add a new dimension to agriculture. This calls for the large-scale introduction of innovative and environmentally-friendly production techniques through education and government intervention, and for support in setting up new forms of cooperation, especially in commercial forestry.

This call for a new focus on poor farmers is supported by, among others, Dr. Ekkawit Na Thalang, an academic and former director-general of the Education Ministry's Department of General Education. He said:

> To decrease the gap [between rich and poor], we should realise that the future must be a world of communities. Farmers should not be made to run away from their farmland. Instead of putting all hope that national income comes from industry only, the state should give greater support to agriculture and agri-business. The state should refocus agricultural objectives to support agriculture in favour of communities and the environment. . . .

> People in rural areas should have their own system of higher
> education. They need to know more about management methods
> that can help them get a good income from their own agricultural
> productivity. They should be provided with choices to improve
> their livelihoods and to give [them] adequate bargaining power.[1]

I believe that the establishment of commercial tree plantations, to serve the dual purpose of establishing a large-scale wood industry and giving decent livelihoods to marginal or landless farmers, should be one of the major priorities. Other countries that have made large-scale investments in forest plantations have been able to create a sustainable resource base to satisfy their own needs for wood and wood products, and to boost export revenues.

There are sound reasons why a second wave of agricultural development to dramatically raise output makes good economic sense for Thailand's future. Some analysts predict that the demand for food in Asia will double in the next century as population increases, as increasingly affluent Asians consume more diverse food products, and as agricultural land in countries such as China shrinks because of spreading urbanisation. China is expected to become a net food importer on a large scale in the next century. The United Nations Environment Programme had this to say about food demand:

> Total global food demand is assumed to increase by more than
> 110 per cent by 2050. This would provide enough food to provide
> the world population with 3,000 calories per day. This increase,
> together with a trend towards more luxurious diets, means that
> although agricultural technology will improve yields, much more
> agricultural land will still be needed: 27 per cent more by 2015,
> and 42 per cent more by 2050.[2]

Thailand's agricultural sector has one of the lowest productivity levels in Asia, as can be seen from comparative rice yields among Asian countries in Table 14.1. Thailand's under-used potential is a significant factor in the country's opportunity to mount a second wave of agricultural development and thus strengthen the overall economy and society.

Table 14.2 shows the growth of GDP in Thailand's agricultural sector compared to growth of the total economy, between 1992–97. It can be

Table 14.1

Area, Production, and Yield of Rice in Major Rice Growing Countries in the Asian and Pacific Region, 1993 (FAO/RAPA 1994)[3]

	Area (,000 ha.)	Production (,000 tonnes)	Yield (kg/ha)
China	31,403	187,211	5,962
India	41,200	111,011	2,694
Indonesia	10,932	47,885	4,380
Bangladesh	10,900	28,000	2,569
Vietnam	6,466	22,300	3,449
THAILAND	8,972	19,090	2,128
Myanmar	5,794	17,434	3,009
Japan	2,139	9,793	4,578

Table 14.2

Percentage Growth in Thai Agricultural GDP Compared to Total Economy GDP (Real Economic Growth)

	1992	1993	1994p	1995e	1996e	1997e
Total economy	8.1	8.3	8.7	8.6	6.8	7.1
Agriculture	6.0	-1.9	5.5	3.0	3.0	3.6

p = provisional e = estimated Source: NESDB, 1997[4]

seen that growth in earnings from the agricultural sector has lagged behind the rest of the economy.

Thailand's economic strategy over several decades has been to extract surplus value from agriculture to fund industrial development and to make a pool of low-cost labour available for the growing number of factories.

Thus, the percentage share of agriculture within the gross domestic product (GDP) has declined from being the country's largest money-earner as the revenue generated from industries such as textiles and tourism has overtaken it.

Now, changing circumstances in the world economy call for a redirection of resources back into agriculture (including an emphasis on tree plantations) to realise agriculture's potential as a greater money earner. Human resource development for agriculture must be a priority, in keeping with the goals of Thailand's Eighth Plan. This means creating a nurturing environment to educate and uplift Thailand's subsistence farmers—a development which will eventually increase the resilience of the whole country. It has been estimated that 90 per cent of Thailand's 19 million farmers are subsistence farmers.[5]

What are the factors that have held back a move for massive rural development in Thailand, and thus significant improvements in quality of life that will serve to strengthen Thai society as a whole?

Land Reform

The failure to achieve meaningful land reform must rank as one of the major factors. Dr. Shalardchai Ramitanodh, an anthropology lecturer at Chiang Mai University, has said:

> The government should have initiated genuine land reform long ago, but through the failure to carry out such reform, tension has accumulated over the decades. . . .[6]

This tension can be seen in recent years in the rise of the Forum of the Poor, and the several mass migrations of its poor farmers to Bangkok to protest against a long list of grievances, prominent among which are land-rights disputes.

There are two important aspects to land reform in Thailand: what to do with the massive areas of degraded forest which have been occupied "illegally" by landless farmers; and how to reform the convoluted land-title system which favours the rich at the expense of the poor. An analysis of this latter question in The Nation reveals how Thailand's political culture and administrative practices, arising from old feudal traditions, reinforce this bias against the poor:

For a long time, the lack of proper land titles was not a big problem for the farmer. The local village community administered land rights without much need for documents or government intervention. The availability of so much empty land meant there was little competition over it. Over the last generation, all this has changed. The land frontier has closed. The village community is breaking down. Rapid commercialisation is changing the value of land, and heightening competition to control it.

Investors want to get control of land to develop golf courses, build factories, and establish plantations and resorts. They need a full title deed before they will risk their money. Land with a proper title now is worth many, many more times the value of property without a title. Converting land from titleless to properly-titled is one of the easiest ways in the kingdom to make a lot of money fast. . . . Local officials need to be persuaded to cooperate. In the absence of a land registry, the documentation is confusing. As with any obstacle courses, the only way to win is to cheat. . . . Powerful people can overcome the obstacles. They can get the cooperation of local officials by one means or another. They can gather up the documents and even create or adjust them if necessary. For little people, the obstacles are hard. The paperwork is tough for the barely literate. Local officials expect to be rewarded and will not cooperate when there is no prospect. . . .[7]

The crux of the matter is what to do with some 10.5 million ha. (66 million *rai*) of "degraded forest land" inhabited by some 10 to 12 million people without a title deed. This land is nominally "owned" by the Royal Forestry Department, although some of it since 1993 has been transferred to the Land Reform Department under the land reform programme initiated by the first Chuan Leekpai government.[8] Practically everyone agrees on the need to plant trees on this degraded forest land, but the issues of what kind of land rights to grant occupants and how to accomplish tree planting has been subjected to incessant political manoeuvring by a series of short-lived Thai governments.

The first Chuan government's land reform programme was praiseworthy, if only for the fact that it was an attempt to fulfil a long-standing need. However, following the Phuket land reform scandal of November 1994—when it was noticed that several wealthy landowners and business families (apparently enjoying political connections) were included among some 486 people scheduled to receive land—the Chuan government fell. The scandal once again revealed the permeation of the political patronage system in politics.

Another major issue regarding land use and forest conservation is how to treat the many villagers living in protected forest areas, and in ecologically sensitive areas such as watersheds. The establishment of community forests is seen as a solution, granting rights to village communities to live in and preserve their forests while benefiting in a sustainable way from products of the forest. This prescription, and the attempt to legislate for it in the Community Forest Bill, had become a subject of hot debate in Thailand as of 1997. (For a summary of the issues surrounding community forestry and related land reform, see Chapter 15.)

Entering the new millennium, the land reform situation still awaits resolution. The imperative of ecological sustainability requires that land reform, especially in the massive land area defined as "degraded forest land", be linked to forest preservation and to the growing of trees. It is now an accepted principle that tree plantations can serve environmental objectives as well as commercial needs: plantations can fulfill the need for wood and thus alleviate the pressure to exploit preserved, natural forests. But reforestation and plantation schemes need to be linked to the requirement of benefiting poor farmers (a social and quality-of-life imperative). It is possible to meet this requirement through the right combination of legislation, financial support, management training, and innovation of new forms of cooperation. Of course, following the controversy of the early 1990s regarding the suitability of eucalyptus trees for plantations, much care will also have to be taken to get an environmentally suitable mix of trees.

However, it is apparent that the will still does not exist within Thailand's patronage-based political system, nor is the bureaucracy properly equipped either in resources or in attitude to mount a massive commercially-oriented, tree-planting programme that will benefit villagers. Therein lies another challenge for political and bureaucratic reform, to launch this valuable and ecologically necessary component of a second wave of agricultural development.

The Rural Debt Crisis

Another factor holding back a move for massive rural development is the debt burden of farmers. This burden is a result of the structural inequities embedded in the rural society, the indifference of governments in addressing these inequities, and an exploitative mentality regarding money lending to small farmers.

Social activist Prof. Prawase Wasi, a major contributor to Thailand's Eighth Development Plan, sees a lot of suffering and social disruption in the rural areas—with the pervasive debt burden of farmers being one of the major factors. To a large extent, he blames the suffering on the practice of monocropping, the concentration of farmers on a single cash crop:

> Monocropping . . . leads to vast destruction of environment [because of the movement] from integrated farms into cheap monocrops: rice, tapioca, jute, sugar. Prices are very low. The farmers lose money in the final analysis; 80 per cent on the average are in debt, which they cannot pay back at 10 per cent interest per month. Villagers call this *nii amata*, immortal debt. They have to buy their food; they don't have enough to eat.[9]

Prof. Anuchart Puangsomlee, an advocate of alternative agriculture, in addition notes that

> . . . the most significant change in the past 50 years has been from self-sufficient localised production to agriculture for trade and export. In many ways this "modern agriculture" with its reliance on inputs such as chemicals, machinery, and seeds has failed and has had several negative impacts—poverty, debt, collapse of communities, ecological impacts, loss of genetic diversity, [a negative] effect on the health of producers and consumers.[10]

When a whole class of people—small farmers—falls into intractable debt which blocks aspirations for self-improvement, we must conclude that the system itself—not the participants in it—is flawed. Thus, the fundamentals of how agriculture is organised must be re-examined to remove the crushing debt burden of *nii amata*.

This is not just Thailand's problem, but is common to many developing countries as a result of the development model promoted for decades by the major global development and lending agencies, based upon the "Green Revolution". The model's failure is now being acknowledged in many quarters. At an International Conference on Food Security[11] in Penang in March 1999, participants were told:

> Since World War II, global development agencies, such as the Food and Agriculture Organisation (FAO) and the World Bank, have pushed a flawed development model. Southern countries were encouraged to increase agricultural production as a way of funding urban and industrial growth, with the object of shifting from an economy based on agriculture to one based on industry. Using chemical inputs and technologies transferred from the North, they were encouraged to focus on key agricultural commodities—goods that could bring the most money on the international market.
>
> Development agencies specifically encouraged adoption of large-scale, high-yielding, genetically uniform monocultures of cash crops, heavily dependent on off-farm inputs like chemical pesticides and fertilisers, "improved" (often hybrid) seeds, machinery, and irrigation. By contrast, traditional agriculture was viewed as "backward" or "primitive" and insufficiently productive. Traditional farmers were often viewed as ignorant, at best. But traditional agriculture was based on local knowledge and usually characterised by small fields containing polycultures of genetically diverse plants that are often used for multiple purposes and are usually very well suited to the local ecology.

The speaker was Dr. Michael Hansen, a research associate at the Consumer Policy Institute of the US-based Consumers' Union.[12] He noted that the agricultural "technology packages" were developed by scientists and government officials with virtually no input from farmers or rural communities. Hansen added:

> The Green Revolution . . . was initially touted as a success because of the dramatic increase in rice and wheat production in

Southeast Asia. However, by the early 1970s, its adverse effects were coming to the surface. Although yields had greatly increased, the channeling of aid to the "progressive" or better-off farmers and the need to purchase so many inputs led to concentrations of land and capital marginalisation of small farmers and a growing increase in the number of landless labourers. Particularly hard hit by the Green Revolution technologies were subsistence farmers raising food for their families on marginal, rain-fed land. Hunger, the basic problem the Green Revolution was supposed to address, did not disappear. Indeed, in many areas it grew worse.

The FAO has now acknowledged the failure of the Green Revolution paradigm, but the continued adoption of the paradigm has not diminished. This was pointed out by another participant at the food security conference, Nathaniel Don Marquez of the Manila-based Asian NGO Coalition for Agrarian Reform and Rural Development (ANGOC).[13] He noted:

The region's food production is firmly hinged on the Green Revolution framework. It is apparent that we have not departed from the idea of boosting production through the technological fix—a "package" of technologies bringing a high dependence on external inputs like agrochemicals, monocropping of high-yielding varieties (HYVs), and mechanisation and irrigation; and on the provision of credit, extension, and other support services. . . . Ironically, the very ingredients that made the Green Revolution an initial success opened up a Pandora's box—hefty hidden subsidies, both ecological and economic; and disastrous economic, social, ecological, and health consequences.

Thus, the Green Revolution paradigm has been good for the transnational corporations peddling pesticides, fertilisers, and high-yielding seeds, while contributing largely to the poverty, debt, and often malnutrition of Thailand and other developing countries. Additionally, ANGOC notes:

Increased yields realised by the Green Revolution have not accrued to farmers' incomes. Loans made for HYVs, irrigation, and mechanisation have trapped farmers in a cycle of indebtedness. . . . Diverse indigenous and traditional agricultural practices and knowledge developed over countless generations have given way to the simplified, standardised procedures of the Green Revolution. Traditional agriculture with its strong sense of community values has been overthrown by an individualised, cutthroat competitiveness. . . .

In many cases, legislation has forced producers to adopt the entire package of technologies promoted under the Green Revolution. . . . The social, environmental, and human health costs—when factored in—underscore the sad fact that modern agriculture has not benefited the very people who comprise the sector. . . . As a result, the already poor are left even more destitute than ever. In Thailand, 4.3 million farming families were buried in debt just several years after the adoption of HYVs. This grew to 5 million in 1990. In Isaan, the poor Northeast of Thailand, up to 85 per cent of the population earn less than they need to survive. In the Philippines, agriculture is deemed non-lucrative, as evidenced by half the rural families living below the poverty level.

Chemicals and Agriculture

As previously mentioned, a "second wave" of agricultural development must establish long-term environmental sustainability as the starting point for all agricultural activities, correcting the mistakes of the past.

Prof. Anuchart notes that the negative effects of "modern agriculture" have led, over the last 10 years

> . . . to a search for new methods, with the concept of "sustainable development" being adopted by both government and non-government sectors. Sustainable agriculture aims to promote greater integration and the renewal of ecosystems through low inputs, the avoidance or elimination of chemicals, and the use of appropriate technology. An accompanying change in philosophy often emphasises community self-reliance and learning through doing.[14]

Indeed, the need for sustainable, alternative agriculture gained official endorsement in the Thai government's Eighth Plan. It appears as one of 12 targets outlined in the section on Objectives and Targets:

> Increase awareness of sustainable alternative agricultural methods, and increase opportunities for their application.[15]

The Asian Development Bank and the Economic and Social Commission for Asia and the Pacific, in their joint report *State of the Environment in Asia and the Pacific, 1995*,[16] describe how a reliance on chemical pesticides and fertilisers began in Asia and the Pacific, and the negative results that their massive use has now caused:

> In the Asian and Pacific region, pesticides, along with chemical fertilisers, high-yielding seed varieties, and intensive agricultural practices, were the principal factor in the so-called Green Revolution. Heavily promoted by manufacturers, international aid agencies, and national governments, pesticide use was until recently considered the quickest path to food self-sufficiency. Application was encouraged through subsidies, tax incentives, and agricultural extension programmes. Consequently, pesticide use soared for a variety of crops, including cereals, cotton, sugarcane, and plantation crops. . . .
>
> Increased use of pesticides for the control of insect pests, weeds, and fungi threatens the life of many wildlife species in the region. In theory, pesticides are synthetically designed to be lethal to certain target organisms. However, in practice many other species of mammals, birds, fish, and insects are affected by them. This may disturb the natural prey-predator systems which are very effective agents of biological control [against] many pests. Ingestion of certain amounts of poisons may also reduce fertility rates of birds and other wildlife, resulting in a decrease in overall population of such species. . . . When a field is sprayed, only a very small portion of the pesticide reaches its target; the rest becomes an environmental contaminant. Even carefully applied pesticides can dissipate in the air as vapour, be carried by surface water run-off or leached through the soil into groundwater

reserves. Pesticide contamination of both surface and ground water, for example, by atrazine, has become increasingly common in recent years, endangering local water supplies and polluting aquatic systems. . . .

Table 14.3

Consumption of Pesticides in Selected Countries of Asia and the Pacific.[17]

Country	1975–77	1982–84
China	150,467	159,267
India	52,506	53,087
Indonesia	18,687	16,344
Japan	33,960	32,000
ROK	4,675	12,273
Myanmar	3,721	15,300
Philippines	3,547	4,415
THAILAND	13,120	22,289
Vietnam	1,693	883

Average annual pesticide use (metric tonnes of active ingredients) (Source: *World Resources 1992–93*.)

The report further indicates a dilemma facing Asia as increased agricultural growth is sought from increased fertiliser use:

Regional yields have been closely related to fertiliser application levels in the past. Until 1965, fertiliser had been estimated to be responsible for up to 10 per cent of the production increases in South and Southeast Asia (except Sri Lanka, where the application rate was already higher). By the 1980s, this contribution is estimated to have risen to between 24 and 64 per cent, with application levels in the region of 80–90 kg/ha.

Yet even during the eighties, diminishing returns could be discerned. In the developing countries of the region, mineral

fertiliser consumption increased by 6.4 per cent per annum during
1982–92, but cereal yields increased by only 2.1 per cent per
annum.[18]

The report warns that if allowed to rise to Japan's level of 400
kilogrammes/hectare, or New Zealand's level of 1,275 kg/ha, fertiliser
use is likely to have serious environmental implications for the region.
The average application of mineral fertilisers in the developing countries
of Asia and the Pacific reached 135 kg/ha by 1991, it said.

As well as environmental damage to soil and water, there are other
serious drawbacks to the use of chemicals, especially pesticides, in
agriculture. In Thailand, where pesticide poisoning is a reportable disease,
epidemiological surveillance reported 2,094 cases with no deaths in 1985,
while data collected from a variety of sources by the National
Environment Board gave a total of 4,046 cases with 289 deaths.[19] Run-
off of pesticide and fertiliser residues into rivers, in turn, ends up polluting
coastal areas.

Residues of highly toxic pesticides have been detected in many
agricultural products in Thailand. According to the World Health
Organisation, Thailand has been one of the biggest importers of the
world's most toxic pesticides known as the Dirty Dozen. These are aldrin/
dieldrin, chlordane, heptachlor, chlordimeform, 2,4,5-T (trichlorophenoxy
acid), ethylene dibromide (EDT), DDT, lindane, paraquat,
dibromochloropropane (DBCP), and pentachlorophenol (CPP).

Data published in the 1990 *State of the Environment in Asia and the
Pacific* (ESCAP), disclosed that organochlorine residues were identified
in 50.5 per cent of river and reservoir waters, 90.6 per cent of fish and
shellfish, and in 96.6 per cent of soil from agricultural fields.[20]

The Veterinarians Association of Thailand announced in 1994 that
the seven provinces using the most pesticides were Nakhon Sawan,
Pathum Thani, Kamphaneg Phet, Pitsanulok, Uttaradit, Sukhothai, and
Nakhon Pathom. Use in Loei was increasing rapidly.[21]

Alternative Agriculture

The previous sections of this chapter indicate that big changes are needed
in thinking about agriculture for the sake of the people's health, the health
of the environment, and the advancement of Thailand's poor farmers

and their quality of life. Individuals and groups have mounted their own attempts at sustainable, alternative agriculture, and efforts need to be made to replicate their efforts. *The Four Country Citizen's Report on the Environment* has documented examples of such activities in Thailand:[22]

> NGOs and people's groups have initiated campaigns to reduce the use of toxic chemicals in agriculture by using environmentally-friendly fertilisers and pesticides like the azadiracthin from neem trees. One project worth mentioning is the initiative of 500 farmers in Nakhon Si Thammarat. The farmers fertilise their rice plants with a combination of urea and organic fertiliser from blue algae. The result is a higher yield. In 11 villages of Kud-Chum district, Yasothon province, folks who call themselves Nature's Friends are proud of their organically grown rice. There is also a campaign to plant vegetables in screened houses. Although they are more expensive in the market than crops sprayed with chemicals, there is a growing demand for organically grown rice and vegetables. . . .

During the 1990s, there has been an upsurge in demand for chemical-free agricultural products in the developed world, and that trend was also beginning among educated and professional families in the developing world; for example, the rising middle class in Bangkok. A report by the International Institute for Environment and Development, *Unlocking Trade Opportunities: Case Studies of Export Success from Developing Countries*, noted that developing countries in the early 1990s were able to make $500 million per year in premiums from organic exports alone.

It is not just the small organic farmers who are cashing in on green markets. According to the report, farmers in Chile have recently increased exports of organically grown fruit by a factor of 400.[23]

Prof. Anuchart Puangsomlee has summarised different levels of the new agriculture[24] as:

- natural farming, or so-called "do-nothing" agriculture, emphasising ecological balance and eschewing chemicals;
- organic farming and integrated farming, emphasising self-sufficiency and production factors within the community to revive the ecosystem;

- natural agriculture, according to Mokichi Okda, with an emphasis on reviving the soil quality by using organic substances and no chemicals; and
- natural farming, according to the Kyusei method, improving the soil by using bacteria and no chemicals.

Prof. Anuchart notes that the first three methods are fairly similar, and farmers practising such agriculture have formed a Network of Alternative Agriculture. He lists the four main principles common to all three types:

1. Efficient use of resources within the farm, without outside inputs.
2. Emphasis on the importance of soil quality.
3. Prevention of pollution which can arise from farming—i.e., by not using any chemical fertilisers, pesticides or weed killers.
4. Emphasis on quality rather than quantity.

Prof. Anuchart is somewhat critical of sustainable agriculture as promoted by the government, which uses some chemicals and is still rooted in the business approach. He writes:

> Sustainable agriculture as promoted by the government is not so clear. Thus the words "sustainable agriculture" are used loosely, sometimes more in line with current fashion than in an integrated way. It does not eschew the use of chemicals, but merely cautions correct use. Increased production remains an aim, and market forces remain important. Thus, while farmers engaged in alternative agriculture will emphasise the ecosystem and self-sufficiency, those in government schemes retain business principles as their mainstay. . . .

Once again, the task for agriculture in the coming century is to remedy the neglect it has suffered. Practices that degrade the environment must be stopped and new approaches taken to uplift poor farmers. The challenge is to reinvigorate agriculture as a major money-earner while incorporating these two perspectives.

The United Nations Environment Programme attaches great importance to the development of eco-farming—sustainable agriculture that eschews chemicals and uses environmentally-friendly methods of cultivation—and has presented several Chinese eco-farming communities with a Global 500 Award for environmental achievement. In 1987, the 134-hectare Liuminying eco-farm at Zhangziying Village, some 40 kilometres outside Beijing, received such an award. Before 1982 the village planted only rice and wheat. Most of the straw waste was used as fuel. The village wanted to raise productivity by using only chemical fertilisers—about 250 tonnes per year. Such fertiliser use did increase crop yields, but it was costly and decreased fertility of the soil, said Zhang Kuicheng, the eco-farm's manager. He said:

> In order to utilise the raw materials rationally, we started to apply ecological farming. We made an overall plan for the village and began to raise animals, vegetables, and fruit. We re-use all the agricultural waste—rice straw, manure—to generate biogas.

As for chemical fertiliser use, Zhang indicated a small amount was used for rice cultivation, but not for other crops. It was possible to eliminate chemical fertilisers in the rice fields and use 100 per cent organic fertiliser—but the productivity would drop.

> The quantity drops, but the quality is better. If you use chemicals, each *mu* (1 ha. = 15 *mu*) produces 400–450 kilogrammes; with organic fertiliser, 350 kilogrammes. However, use of chemical fertiliser has been reduced from 250 tonnes for the whole eco-farm, down to 80 tonnes.

In some areas of Zhejiang province, farmers use an ancient system of stereo or multi-layered agriculture, which can achieve high yields without chemical fertiliser. For example, farmers grow gourds on racks over earthworm beds, with the luxuriant leaves influencing the micro-climate under the racks, making it more favourable to earthworm growth. Earthworm excrement can be applied as manure to paddy fields, where the yield of rice could reach over 1,000 kg per *mu*—or 15,000 kg per hectare.

Empowerment of Farmers

In keeping with the people-centred sustainable development model now gaining acceptance in Thailand, farmers need to be empowered by a

367

variety of means to uplift themselves. The World Food Summit of November 1996, convened by the FAO, emphasised in its Plan of Action that governments must be able to adopt the participatory approach with its stress on civil society organisations, NGOs, and women's participation.[25]

Michael Hansen, of the US-based Consumers' Union, notes that a movement towards truly sustainable agriculture and rural development (SARD) is now well under way in response to the problems associated with the Green Revolution. Especially important, he says, is the participatory approach:

> This requires that those involved in farming systems work to acknowledge that the rural community is a source of knowledge and that their participation is essential to success. Indigenous traditional knowledge needs to be respected and built upon, and the community needs to be involved in all stages of the development process—from identification of the farmers' needs and constraints, to the development of new technology to meet those needs, to the testing and adoption of that new technology.[26]

Another key to a sustainable agriculture approach is the use of agro-ecosytems analysis, says Hansen:

> The agro-ecological approach begins with an assumption that development efforts will use knowledge (both indigenous and scientific) to manage and improve existing agricultural ecosystems. Such an approach begins with research on the local ecosystem. Then, working with local farmers, who through generations of trial and error have often become the best repositories of information about agriculture and the local ecology, scientists can build on this knowledge to improve pest control and soil fertility. The agro-ecological approach tends to maximise on-farm inputs like green manures and biological pest controls, and to utilise small-scale, diverse cropping, while minimising chemical and other off-farm inputs.

The empowerment of farmers also means teaching them how to organise their farming communities to plan in a participatory way and how to build up their social and technical capacities. International organisations and NGOs have begun this approach already; for example, the farmer-centred, agricultural resource management (FARM) programme of the United Nations Development Programme (UNDP). It is an approach at the village level in several Asian countries to bring farmers to the centre of decision making and to make them responsible for their own development.[27] It uses natural resource management concerns as an entry point, and grounds action at the community level through the establishment of field sites. This approach encourages farmers to assume the ownership of responsibility to implement the decisions made. But, regarding farmers' empowerment, ANGOC warns[28] that there is still

> . . . an evident lack of emphasis on strengthening producers'
> organisations and on addressing their concerns such as agrarian
> reform and access to resources. A major case in point is legi-
> slation in relation to land tenure and land redistribution. While
> such reform has been enacted in many countries, its implemen-
> tation remains elusive. Many initiatives have failed to impact at
> the local level; political bigwigs have instigated opposition to
> further implementation in order to protect vested interests, and
> many national resource agencies have opposed such policy
> directions.

Globalisation and Sustainable Agriculture

Following the failure of the Green Revolution to achieve sustainable agriculture and alleviate rural poverty, attention has turned towards the next wave of technological "solutions" for agriculture being promoted by transnational corporations (TNCs) and their allies: that of biotechnology.

The debate about biotechnology, especially the genetic modification of food crops, had become intense by 1999. Many NGOs of the South have raised concerns that the genetic manipulation of seeds threatens biodiversity, cohesion of rural communities, and public health—as the companies that are promoting biotechnology are almost invariably pesticide- and herbicide-producing companies. At the Penang conference, ANGOC[29] had this to say:

369

Touted as the "new magic bullet", modern biotechnology, including genetic engineering, promises mini-miracles like earlier maturing crops, disease- and pest-resistant crops, "superior" animal breeds. It is feared, however, that compared to the first Green Revolution, the potential risks and negative impacts of the second one would be far more devastating. . . .

The spectre of a TNC "captive farmer market" is not far removed from reality—brought about by genetically engineered seeds that can withstand the very chemicals of the companies that produce them; seeds that cannot be replanted. Adding to this spectre is the push of the developed countries for the vertical integration of the agriculture industry. . . . Monopolies and transnationals have increasingly gained ground as the main players in agriculture with increasing business and profits at stake. A previously strong, self-reliant generation of producers has become several generations of a people disempowered and marginalised. Their rightful places as major players and stakeholders have yet to be reclaimed.

Another Asian NGO, the Forum for Protection of Public Interest, Kathmandu, had this to say:[30]

Large TNCs are coming to control the world's food chain, right from seed development, fertiliser and pesticide supply, to improved production techniques and retailing. With the help of the Trade Related Intellectual Property Rights (TRIPs) agreement, they are able to get patents on their inventions, living or otherwise, and monopolise the market. The biotechnology firms are the forerunners in this field, claiming that without their inventions being provided patent protection, the world cannot feed its growing population. However, shifting global food security into the hands of a few TNCs is extremely dangerous. An even more alarming fact is that most of them are enjoying monopoly protection through the TRIPs agreement. . . .

Hansen further notes the environmental risk:[31]

The most widely grown, genetically engineered crops, accounting for 99 per cent of the land under transgenic cultivation worldwide, are engineered for herbicide tolerance, insect resistance, and/or virus resistance. Each of these poses environmental risks. Herbicide-tolerant crops are varieties on which herbicides can be used to kill weeds, without killing the crop itself. These varieties encourage farmers to use more herbicides, which frequently pollute groundwater and can cause various other forms of ecological damage.

"Gene pollution" is especially problematic for the Southern countries, which are the centre of origin for many crops. In these areas, traditional crop varieties could become "polluted" with genes from the genetically engineered crops. In Thailand, the government decided to cancel field tests of Monsanto's Bt cotton in part in response to concerns raised that transgenes could flow from this cotton into some of the 16 plants in the cotton family, identified by the Institute of Traditional Thai Medicine, that traditional healers use as medicines. No research was being done to address or to test this concern. What can be done? The senior economist at the FAO Regional Office in Bangkok, T. C. Ti, offered these remarks in Penang:

> Governments of developing countries must strive individually and collectively in the next round of World Trade Organisation negotiations to protect the interests of the billions of small and subsistence farmers in Asia and the Pacific. At the same time, governments of developing countries should work together towards more favourable policies and programmes of the Consultative Group on International Agricultural Research (CGIAR). Strengthening the role of developing countries in the CGIAR would accelerate technology transfer for sustainable agriculture and food security. Governments must also pursue vigorously the protection and realisation of farmers' rights to genetic resources for sustainable agriculture and food security in the continuing negotiations on this important issue. . . .

The most immediately urgent task is mobilisation of manpower and investment capital for sustainable agriculture and rural development.

Chapter 15

Sustainable Forestry

More than ever—globally, regionally, and nationally—there is a compelling need to preserve existing forests, to regenerate lost natural forests, and to undertake massive tree plantations. The continuing, relentless destruction of forests worldwide has become a symbol of how humankind is recklessly undermining global ecological stability through its economic activities: whether such activities are for the survival of impoverished peoples, or whether they amount to money-making greed. This reckless destruction must be stopped.

Globally, at least two major environmental problems are daily being worsened by deforestation: climate change (including the greenhouse effect), and the loss of biodiversity. In addition, there are other serious impacts, recognised by such regional agencies such as the Asian Development Bank (ADB) and the Economic and Social Commission for Asia and the Pacific (ESCAP): reduced productivity of forest ecosystems, and severe water and wind erosion in catchment areas. The latter leads to an extensive loss of topsoil, a decline in soil fertility, poor microbial activity, frequent landslides, and sediment movements resulting in the siltation of reservoirs, water sources, and canals. Regionally (in this case, throughout mainland Southeast Asia), deforestation thus seems to be causing an intensification and increasing frequency of droughts and floods.[1]

And nationally, within Thailand itself, deforestation has additionally created chronic drought-prone areas in the Northeast, caused the drying up of water sources, and consequently soil loss on hillsides. In turn, as forests dwindle away, many species of plants and animals are increasingly coming under threat of extinction. Meanwhile, forest destruction goes on.

The ADB noted that in Asia, total forest area was reduced by 45 million hectares, or 9 per cent, between 1980–1990. This yearly average loss of 4.5 million hectares was more than double the annual replanting rate of 2.1 million hectares.[2] It further noted that fuelwood collection and slash-and-burn agriculture are as big, if not bigger, threats to Asia's tropical forests as logging. Communities remove 700 million cubic metres of timber a year from regional forests, or seven times more than loggers. The ADB declared that it would not finance any rural infrastructure or other public investment projects that contribute to the loss of forests. The ADB and ESCAP, in their survey, *State of the Environment in Asia and the Pacific, 1995* say:

> With a few notable exceptions (i.e. China, Japan, the Republic of Korea, New Zealand) forest cover has declined dramatically in the countries of the region during the past four decades. The countries with the highest deforestation rates by absolute area are: Indonesia, Thailand, Myanmar, Malaysia, India, and the Philippines.[3]

The answer to this grave problem is two-fold: sustainable forest management and reforestation, including the creation of tree plantations on a massive scale.

Thailand's Deforestation Dilemma

In 1961, Thailand's total forest area was recorded at 273,000 square kilometres, or roughly 53.2 per cent of the total land area. A report of the Royal Forestry Department (RFD) disclosed that in 1991, forested cover had dwindled to only 136,465 square. kilometres, about 26.6 per cent of Thailand's land area.[5] The situation in the Northeast was worse. In just 15 years to 1992, forest cover there declined from 50 per cent to 13 per cent, according to land profile surveys using the Geographic Information System (GIS). The surveys revealed severe soil erosion, soil fertility loss and salinity.[6]

As of 1999, natural forests continue to decline—despite a logging ban imposed in 1989, and despite the creation of forest and wildlife conservation reserves. Deforestation, including illegal logging facilitated by corrupt politicians and officials, continues to outstrip efforts at tree

Table 15.1

**Rates of Deforestation and Afforestation, 1981–1990
(FAO, 1993)[4]
Countries with annual deforestation above 300,000 ha:**

	Total forest land (1,000 ha)	Annual area of deforest.	% deforest.
India	51,729	399	0.6
Indonesia	109,549	1,212	1.1
Malaysia	17,583	396	2.0
Myanmar	28,856	401	1.3
Philippines	7,831	316	4.0
THAILAND	12,735	515	4.0

Plantations:	**Up to 1980 (1,000 ha)**	**1981–1990 (1,000 ha)**	**As % of forest land**
India	18,900	1,441.4	2.8
Indonesia	8,750	474.0	0.4
Malaysia	116	9.0	0.1
Myanmar	335	27.9	0.1
Philippines	290	-1.0	-0.3
THAILAND	756	42.0	0.3

planting. Thailand's Green World Foundation noted that in 1994 the rate of deforestation in Thailand remained at 160,000 hectares per year, with reforestation at between 16,000 to 48,000 ha. per year, regardless of the existence of various reforestation/afforestation programmes.[7] In January 1996, the then president of the Thailand Environment Institute, Dhira Phantumvanit, put the figure for deforestation at 240,000 ha. annually. He said it remained Thailand's most serious environmental problem, through lack of government action and lack of transparency.[8]

Why has Thailand not succeeded in reversing the trend towards greater deforestation, despite the well-documented harm to the environment and to the quality of life that it causes, and despite official commitments to reverse it? Thailand still has not been able to mount a massive programme for tree planting, whether for the regeneration of natural forests or for plantations.

The major issue over tree plantations has been, Who will benefit? Principles of rational and sustainable development call for Thailand to gear such economic activities towards uplifting the rural poor (as indicated in the previous chapter on sustainable agriculture and land reform) thereby serving both environmental and social concerns at the same time. But attempts at plantation agriculture have focused on "big business" and the dispensation of political influence, to the detriment of these important concerns. All kinds of abuses have been reported in big business's attempts at tree plantations, from grabbing land off villagers, to encroachment on forest and wildlife reserves, and to the neglect of other ecological considerations such as a proper mix of tree species.

A mass movement is needed for large-scale tree planting (other countries such as Indonesia[9] have done it), but it seems that Thailand's present political/bureaucratic structure and mindset are incapable of mounting a nationwide, mass-participatory programme for such activities. Politicians under the prevailing political patronage system would find it difficult to collect fees from such a programme; they could, on the other hand, collect fees from wealthy private operators seeking to obtain expanses of land to create large-scale plantations and to transform landless peasants into low-wage labourers.

Dr. Apichai Puntasen, an economics lecturer at Thammasat University, has documented how the target figure for forest cover in Thailand has been progressively reduced. The 1964 Reserved Forest Act called for total forest cover of 50 per cent. The target was reduced to 40 per cent in 1985, comprising 25 per cent economic forest and 15 per cent conservation forests:

> From 1910 until now, Thai forestry policy has . . . been reactive instead of pro-active. Targets for forest cover have been dictated by the rapidly declining forest area rather than by integrating targets into a true solution. . . . The RFD still sees local villagers as having no part to play in forest conservation. . . . Crucial to why forest laws are not enforced is the fact that the low wages and the support system for forestry officials is not commensurate with the work and danger involved in proper enforcement.[10]

The ADB/ESCAP environment report commented on the forestry policy revision of 1985:

> There is concern that it does not address the immediate needs of the country's forest resource situation, socio-economic conditions, and land-use patterns. This may be because its original focus was on the potential for economic exploitation of forest resources. It is therefore under review as part of the National Forestry Master Plan.
>
> The policy has led to strengthening of the system of national parks, wildlife sanctuaries, and forest parks, and promotion of community forestry programmes. Despite this, however, the area under forest cover declined and land lease arrangements were removed. The lack of an integrated national land- use policy dealing with both the agriculture and forestry sectors seems to be the greatest constraint.[11]

More recently, it seemed that the RFD might be changing its attitude. Addressing a seminar to commemorate the RFD's centenary year, 1996, director-general, Watana Kaeokamnerd said that a plan allocating 10 billion baht towards the protection of forests would be implemented by 2001. He said:

> It will encourage local people to participate in the prevention of forest destruction. It will also outline the management of clear borders surrounding conservation areas.

The budget would cover 37 projects in four areas: forest administration, conservation, promotion, and research. The plan would allow devastated areas to recover, said Watana. Operators of commercial plantations would be encouraged to plant fast-growing tree species to replace felled trees.[12]

But could the RFD really change? In 1994, the department began the five million *rai* (800,000 ha.) reforestation programme in honour of the King's Golden Jubilee. It was reported that some ,345 plots in national parks, wildlife sanctuaries, and national reserved forests in 59 provinces would be reforested, giving a total area of over 5 million *rai*—1.35 million in 1994, 1.65 million in 1995, and 2 million in 1996. In addition, trees would be planted along roads, rivers, and canals, as well as on government property, in temples, and in parks.[13]

A year later, journalist Paul Handley[14] examined the programme and wrote:

> It was only a couple of years ago, when some businessmen and politicians tried to capitalise on the "be green" trend, that something happened. Announcing the programme to reforest 5 million *rai* throughout the media, these businessmen tripped over each other to show who was more environmentally conscious, who was more public-spirited. But what happened? Basically, through greed, mismanagement, shortsightedness, and an overall lack of understanding of the reasons for the need to reforest, they created a mess out of the programme. . . . Today, the project is hovering quietly, embarrassingly, on the edge of total shutdown.
>
> Not only are the environmentalists unhappy, but so too are well-meaning businessmen who wanted to participate. . . . There is a desperate need for a reforestation campaign in Thailand. It can and should be done by mobilising the public, which was the ostensible basis for the abortive 5 million *rai* campaign. Reforestation by the people has been done elsewhere, and it can be done here. This one was just hijacked by self-serving businessmen, bureaucrats, and politicians.

Handley went on to examine in some detail the activities being advertised under the campaign, and concluded that the whole thing was a scam. One example:

> In one area of the Northeast . . . a company proposed to reforest an area of denuded national forest land long farmed by farmers without land title. They forced the farmers off of the land. Then, using saplings provided by the government, they planted the whole area in teak—which was not there before. They moved to claim ownership of the land under land reform, and then began marketing the areas to second-home investors as "buy your own

> forest plot and reap the benefits of selling teak trees in the future."
> All nicely subsidised by the government. . . .

> The most telling sign that [the 5 million *rai* scheme] was a scam
> was the money issue. The RFD declared that reforestation costs
> 3,000 baht a *rai*. That is an outrageous sum. Thai rice farmers do
> not even earn that much in gross income per *rai*. . . .

Reports abound of corruption and illegal activities concerning logging
and reforestation:

> In 1990, the Suan Kitti Reforestation Co. was caught destroying
> natural forest in order to increase the size of their eucalyptus
> plantations on leased, forest reserve land. Subsequently, the
> Chatichai administration prohibited the leasing of forest reserves
> to private investors. [The subsequent interim government of
> Anand Panyarachun] continued to severely restrict the practice.
> But this past 13 and 21 September 1993, the [Chuan Leekpai]
> cabinet agreed to allow private investors to operate commercial
> plantations on degraded forest reserve land and loosened the
> restrictions imposed under Anand.[15]

In another case:

> Many thousands of *rai* in Loei have been acquired since 1991 by
> an influential company to develop wine growing, other temperate
> crops, and a golf course. . . . All the land was in fact in reserved
> forest and had been made available to the company with the full
> knowledge of the provincial land department. Various officials
> were arrested in April 1994 and several have been suspended
> from active service. But because the company was regarded as
> an "important investor" in the province, the *Nor Sor* 3 land deeds
> would not be revoked.[16]

Again, could the RFD really change? To understand why illegal
logging and deforestation continue in Thailand, and why massive
reforestation cannot get started, it is best to understand the RFD in terms

of the political patronage system—a major theme of this book, which explains how there is much money to be made through the right connections in Thailand, and consequently how high standards of social development and environmental management cannot be attained. The RFD may be seen as an archetype of the patronage system in Thailand.

The Royal Forestry Department was 100 years old in 1996. Up until 1989, its function was to oversee and "manage" the exploitation of Thailand's forests. Huge logging concessions were awarded over the years; as ever, under the patronage system, "tea money" was always a factor. Because of the huge amounts of money to be made through logging (15 years ago, one mature teak log could bring one million baht), attempts at political infiltration of the RFD became the norm. This system of resource exploitation is so ingrained into the organisation that, even when its mission was changed to promote conservation rather than exploitation, the exploitation has merely continued in a covert way with protection of such operations guaranteed by political patrons.

This phenomenon has been well documented. The actors within Thailand's pervasive political patronage system commonly attempt to implant a covert, money-making operation on to any legitimate programme that can generate a substantial cash flow. (For a more detailed analysis of the patronage system, see Chapter 8.)

When the monetary spoils from patronage and corruption within government agencies become high, senior positions in those agencies are filled on the basis of tea money and political loyalties. Many allegations of this have been made about the RFD, where it has been said that the practice has spread also to the lower ranking positions. Belinda Stewart Cox, a long-time resident conservationist in Thailand, has written that lucrative senior posts in the conservation division of the RFD were said to be available for bribes of 5 million to 50 million baht.[17]

In an editorial to mark the 100th anniversary of the Royal Forestry Department, *The Nation* summed up the tragedy of Thailand's dwindling forests and the role of the RFD:

> Spurred on by its political masters, the RFD has looked for new ways to make money out of its fiefdom, whether it means leasing out land for plantations, granting permission for tourism and

development projects in national parks, or even replanting forests—a task at which it has largely failed. There are some good, young staffers who understand that the RFD needs a new vision and are trying to live up to it. Unfortunately, under the current system they are doomed to obscurity in low posts—their refusal to pay off the right people means they have little chance of promotion. . . .

For a while it was hoped that the increasing influence of the media and the environmental movement would help push the agency in the right direction. But the sacking in recent years of two of the RFD's most popular and effective sanctuary chiefs . . . shows just how much disdain the agency has for public opinion and competent management. . . .[18]

In mid-1997, yet another unlawful logging affair came to light: the massive Salween scandal at the Myanmar border. Teak logs were being illegally cut in the Salween National Park and the Salween Wildlife Sanctuary, whose two forests have a combined area of more than 100,000 *rai*, the largest growth of teak in Thailand. The trees were reportedly cut in Thailand, shipped across the Salween River to Myanmar to be stamped as having "Myanmar origin" and then "imported" by Thai companies through three customs checkpoints. A reporter for *The Nation* filed this report from Mae Hong Son:

Forestry officials here [on 15 May] said they will inevitably lose the battle against illegal logging along the Thai-Myanmar border as the operation involved influential people with vested interests. Udom Tarathitikorn, superintendent of the Salween Wildlife Sanctuary, said he found another 200 freshly-cut teak logs at Huay Kanompuk village in Mae Sariang district during an investigation via helicopter along the border a few weeks ago. But all the logs had disappeared when he returned last week. "The log transfer was incredibly fast [as the area is almost inaccessible, geographically and politically]. This means the timber traders are well connected with many influential groups in the province."[19]

The illegal activity had been reported to the Royal Forestry Department the previous year by a forestry officer. He claimed that many influential businessmen and officials were involved in the scam, including local police and Customs officers, Forestry Industry Office officials, district forestry officers, and village headmen in the district. The failures in 1997 and 1998 to have anyone prosecuted for the scam suggests that it was part of a political patronage system.

Protecting the Forests

The biggest single factor in protecting Thailand's forests is the need to remove the get-rich-quick mentality which still pervades agencies charged with protecting and regenerating forests, including the politicians that govern them, their business associates, and conniving bureaucrats.

Another major factor is the creation of large-scale tree plantations with landless farmers as major beneficiaries. Plantations have gained a bad name in Thailand because they have been associated with anti-social and anti-environmental practices such as land-grabbing, ignoring the plight of poor landless farmers, and monoculture of eucalyptus. On the other side, some conservationists have also scorned tree plantations as not being genuine reforestation: the need is to let natural forests regenerate, assisted by a small measure of positive human intervention, they say. This point of view has its merits. However, the question must be seen in a larger context: the need to provide sustainable livelihoods and secure land tenure for millions of poor farmers; the growing demand for wood and wood products nationally and globally; and the ecological benefits that large-scale plantations can provide.

The main ecological benefit of tree farms is that they take the pressure off natural forests as a source of raw material (wood). In addition, they act as carbon sinks—agents of absorption for carbon dioxide—thus helping to counteract the growing carbon dioxide pollution of the Earth's atmosphere and helping to mitigate the occurrence of global warming. And, while plantations cannot support the level of biodiversity of natural forests, they can (in some cases and if managed wisely) provide bridges between areas of natural forest that allow forest-dwelling animals to roam from one forest segment to another, particularly for breeding purposes. This is very helpful in cases where an animal species is becoming endangered through fragmentation and loss of its forest habitat.

Community Forests

Approaches now being debated in Thailand include the concepts of community forests and buffer zones.

Discussions about community forests go back more than a decade in Thailand. Finally, attempts to legislate a Community Forest Bill began in February 1996, when the Banharn cabinet's establishment of a drafting committee provided a meaningful focus for the differing points of view. A draft bill was approved by the cabinet in April, but it exposed a split within Thailand's environmental and development movement. The draft lapsed before it reached Parliament, due to the fall of the Banharn government in November 1996. However, it was revived in early 1997 by the Chavalit government.

It seems that Thailand may at last gain a community-based approach to preserving forests, although realism and vigilance is needed to make sure that the whole process of instituting village-based conservation is not sidetracked by commercial interests.

In July 1996, NGOs reached agreement that communities should be allowed to be established in all kinds of forests, except watersheds or pristine conservation areas, where only communities who had settled there before they were declared protected areas could live. But many so-called "hard-line" forestry officials were still insisting that conservation areas should be kept free from human activity. It was reported that NGOs agreed that community forests should be classified into three categories depending on their richness in biodiversity and other natural resources, with community activities differing in each category.[20]

What had been the major disagreement between the NGOs? *The Nation's* environment editor, James Fahn, characterised it as follows:

> On one side are the defenders of the present bill, a group we can call "the social scientists", made up largely of rural development groups along with anthropologists and other academics, active in the North. While concerned with protecting the forest, their first priority is to defend the rights of villagers. Calling for changes in the bill are the "natural scientists" or "conservationists", who are probably smaller in number but whose influence is growing. Made up largely of ecologists, biologists and wildlife experts, their first concern is to make sure

that some pristine forest remains to serve as vibrant watersheds and a habitat for biodiversity. . . .[21]

Dr. Oy Kanjanavanit, secretary-general of the Green World Foundation explained the rationale of the conservationists:

> The present draft bill grants rights to local communities to manage and utilise forest resources in all ecosystems, both in protected forests—national parks, wildlife sanctuaries, watershed areas—and economic forest reserves. Activities allowed include the felling of timber for local construction, hunting of unprotected species, and tending of livestock. Moreover, future expansion of community forest areas is permitted in all forest types. According to this law, "sustainability" will be guaranteed by the oversight of a local community forest committee appointed by the provincial governor, whose duty is to select suitable sites, make regulations, and evaluate the success or failure of the local management. The present draft bill, therefore, emphasises primarily support for human rights with only secondary priority given to preventive measures against environmental damage.
>
> However, there is an alternative treatment for the law, where a degree of ecological zoning and appropriate regulations are explicitly stated within a major clause of the law as a preventive measure. . . . We are, thus, proposing that different categories of community forests must first be recognised, each allowing varying degrees of human activities that are appropriate to different ecological units and areas of biodiversity. The basic idea is to ensure zoning. The reason is that the protected forests now contain much of the last remaining wild gene pool for future regeneration of degraded land elsewhere, so human activities within these areas generally need to be more restricted.[22]

Earlier, a representative of the Dhammanaat Foundation, which carries out watershed reforestation projects in the North, criticised the bill and said that despite its good intentions it will inevitably lead to further destruction of the forests, which everyone depends on to maintain the water supply in the dry season. Community forests should be allowed only outside conservation areas, said the representative. Villagers already occupy large areas of national parks, wildlife sanctuaries, and watershed areas, and existing supervisory committees have been unable to keep them from illegally expanding their land at the expense of the forests.[23]

Effective supervision is certainly needed, along with the development of a conservation ethic among villagers. But the problems do not end there. The *Bangkok Post* reported:

> The Huay Kaew villagers of Chiang Mai province have fought tooth and nail to keep their community forests from falling into the hands of powerful land speculators. In Nan province, the Silalaeng villagers are risking their lives patrolling their community forests to keep armed illegal loggers at bay. Some 400 community forests in the mountainous North, covering nearly two million *rai*, are increasingly under threat from illegal loggers, landless farmers, and land speculators. . . . Knowing that they are too weak to take on illegal loggers who are backed by big shots and big money, these conservation-minded villagers are appealing for support from the public for their forest preservation programmes. Calling themselves the Northern Farmers' Network, the villagers, who comprise Thai lowlanders and several hilltribes such as Karen and Hmong, aim to ordain [through a Buddhist ritual] 50 million trees in their community forests. . . .[24]

Apart from protection of existing forests, there are success stories about how degraded or denuded forest areas have had their ecological functions restored by dedicated individuals and NGOs. The founder of the Dhammanaat Foundation, *Ajaan* Pongsak, offers one such story from the mid-1980s, while he was the abbot of a forest *wat* (Buddhist temple). A reforestation project he began at that time has restored to their former pristine condition four headwaters of the Ping River whose levels had dropped drastically as a result of extensive clear-felling of forest cover.

Eleven major streams on a mountain some 70 kms southwest of Chiang Mai city were supplying water for the irrigation of *lamyai* orchards and for 11 villages before flowing into the Ping River. The mountain had been denuded by slash-and-burn activities of hilltribes who moved there in the 1970s. *Ajaan* Pongsak enlisted the help of villagers and government organisations and set up the Dhammanaat Foundation to try to prevent any further damage to the forest. . . . He began spreading the message, applying Buddhist *dhamma* (teaching) to educate villagers about the importance of preserving the forest. . . . To assure villagers of a year-round supply of water for their crops, he organised the construction of *muang faai* (small dams made from natural materials like bamboo) and small reservoirs along the Mae Soi valley. Said *Ajaan* Pongsak:

> These streams ran dry some years back. But this year (1995), even in the hot season, they were full of water.[25]

Thailand's senior official in charge of the environment, the then permanent secretary of the Ministry of Science, Technology, and Environment, Kasem Snidvongs, was asked for his views on forestry questions in July 1996:[26]

> If you talk about forestry, you can talk for ages. It's a management problem. I think the government is reluctant to make a policy that would lead to the control of forest encroachment. Political problems [are] sometimes detrimental to the environment. It's always the politicians who create more resource depletion.

> Talking about people in the forest, people encroaching on the forests, what can we do with them? How can we contain them? I think the question of removing them from the forest is something difficult to do. I think His Majesty [King Bhumipol] also indicates this. If they are in the forest, contain them. Help them cultivate, and make sure they do not cut down or burn down forest further. But removing them? In a very important case, a very important area, maybe you can remove them. But, when you remove them, you cannot find a better place for them to cultivate; you always remove them to a place where soil fertility is bad. So this problem of forest management is a big headache.

> I myself believe that what will be left for Thailand is the protected areas: national parks and wildlife sanctuaries. . . . If I were the government, I would put a lot of effort, money, [and] manpower towards protecting the protected areas—the national parks, the wildlife sanctuaries—and put a lot of money into research on

biodiversity [because it] is something which is important for our future.

The controversy over whether or not villagers could be trusted to live in and preserve forests has also become a key issue for land reform policy (See also the previous chapter). What rights should forest-dwelling villagers have over the land they occupy? The Chavalit government announced a controversial formula on 22 April 1997 at a cabinet meeting in Nakhon Ratchasima to solve rural land ownership problems.

Villagers who encroached on forest reserve land before 1954, when the current land code governing forests took effect, would be given non-transferable land title deeds while awaiting the designation of the land to be subject to the land reform programme. They would then get the standard land-reform deed, *Sor Por Kor* 4–01, which stipulates that the land may not be transferred but could be inherited. However, the land may be mortgaged with financial institutions.

Other decisions at the meeting indicated that forest areas marked by cabinet for conservation would have their status revoked if occupied by villagers, and *Sor Por Kor* 4–01 deeds would be issued. Forests designated by law for conservation would be surveyed and their status revoked. Sections would become forest reserves under strict protection but other areas would be allocated to villagers who would be given land rights documents.

Chavalit said the government must ensure people can live in forests and protect them, but some observers feared the measures could pose a serious threat to national forests and aggravate encroachment and land grabbing. Reporting the decision, *The Nation* quoted "forestry sources" who said the measures would result in many loopholes that could be exploited by unscrupulous landlords or speculators.[27]

Earlier, the Chavalit government announced that areas designated for land reform in 248 highly-populated districts nationwide were to have their status revoked. Poor people who could prove they had resided in such areas would be granted *Nor Sor* 3 or *Nor Sor* 4 documents, which allow recipients to sell the land. This move was popular among titleless villagers.[28]

Sor Por Kor 4–01 ownership documents were created under the 1993 Agricultural Land Reform Programme initiated by the first Chuan government. Land reform areas were announced in forest reserves and deteriorated forests. Eligible recipients must be poor, landless farmers and would be given no more than 100 *rai*. The land would still belong to the state.[29]

In May 1997, His Majesty the King showed his concern over the question of land rights and protection of forests, advising that forest-dwellers should be granted *Sor Thor Kor* documents which would allow them to make use of the land but not to sell, lease, or mortgage it. Use of the land could be transferred only by inheritance. *Sor Thor Kor* are issued by the Royal Forestry Department, while *Sor Por Kor* 4–01 are issued by the Land Reform Department for land in degraded forest reserves that were transferred from the RFD. An Agriculture Ministry inspector quoted His Majesty as saying there should be a cooperative or fund set up by the government to provide loans with low or no interest for the eligible villagers.[30]

In reflecting on the significance of these events, it should be kept in mind that Thailand has a major opportunity at this time to institute both sustainable forest management and large-scale, sustainable tree farming, as long as the state (the Royal Forestry Department) nominally owns Thailand's forests and the vast degraded forest lands.

The global trend regarding land ownership favours private ownership of land with full rights; a trend that is ideologically underpinned by the liberal, free-market-oriented model of popular democracy. However, this kind of land ownership makes it difficult to regulate land use, and especially to implement national forestry policies which specify ecologically-oriented land uses such as tree farming and conservation. Thailand's opportunity rests in the possibility of requiring recipients of land, through conditions linked to the issue of limited-use, non-transferable land deeds, to participate in tree farming and conservation schemes.

Following from this is the need for land-use planning that integrates forestry with other land uses. Planning beyond the 1990s means bottom-up planning, involving participation of all interested parties and stakeholders. This new approach is recognised in Thailand's Eighth Development Plan and the 1997 Constitution, instituting a new dimension to democracy where planning becomes a continuous process of dialogue between all stakeholders. Conventional top-down planning has largely failed in endeavours that also contain social objectives, such as forest management.

Just before this book went to press, the cabinet of the second Chuan government approved the Community Forest Bill in principle, on 5 October 1999. *The Nation* quoted cabinet spokesman Somchai Sahachairungruang, who said that the draft had been approved by the representative committee of the Assembly of the Poor, following a public hearing. Somchai related five points of the bill which he said answered issues under dispute regarding community forests:

1. The establishment of community forests in conservation areas will be allowed only on the part of those who can prove they have lived in and conserved the areas for at least five years. Community-forest establishment outside conservation areas is to be open to the general public.
2. The provincial community-forest committee would be the authority responsible for allowing the establishment of community forest areas.
3. A community forest will be managed by the committee for each area according to the master management plan of the provincial committee.
4. Authority to control community forest areas will rest with two committees—the policy-level panel, to be chaired by the agriculture minister, and the provincial-level committee to be chaired by the provincial governor.
5. The director general of the Royal Forestry Department will have sole authority to rescind designation as a community-forest area.

However, despite these points, the Northern Farmers' Network and the Northern Tribal People's Network accused the government of approving a draft which they said was the RFD's own and not the one which other interested groups had been party to, as the government claimed. . . .[31]

Buffer Zones

Another attempt to protect forests is the buffer zone concept. Dr. Apichai Puntasen, in 1994, noted that

> . . . results of research suggest that a buffer zone should be created around forests of some five kilometres. . . . Other reforestation

> programmes should also concentrate on this buffer zone. Land
> reform should deal with land rights certificates in land adjoining
> forests before others. In addition, public land in or next to villages
> bordering forest areas should be turned into community forests
> to act as a buffer zone and to provide forest products for the
> community. . . .[32]

The United Nations has supported the buffer zone concept in Thailand. At a conference[33] organised in October 1993, a project was outlined to conserve biodiversity by providing improved protection and management to four protected area complexes in Thailand. The first one to be considered was the Thung Yai Naresuan-Huai Kha Khaeng protected area complex. The approach utilises buffer zones by selecting particular areas, called integrated conservation and development sites, where many of the buffer zone activities would be concentrated.[34] The activities— such as reforestation, fruit tree production—would benefit buffer zone residents while preserving the protected areas, or at least keep people from harming the forest by providing alternative sources of income. The activities were expected to:

- improve people's awareness of the need for conservation;
- provide them with opportunities to seek new and better livelihoods;
- free them from the debt and poverty that forces many to hunt or log illegally; and
- give buffer zone residents opportunities to select their own paths of development in ways linked to conserving the protected forest areas. . . .

However, the proponents of the buffer zone concept stressed that the targeted areas were threatened from many sources, and no matter how successful the conservation buffer zone programme might be, it alone was not the sole answer to protecting wildlife sanctuaries and national parks. Chief among other requirements were political commitment and the enforcement of laws, education about conservation, and alternative income generating activities.

Since 1993, the buffer-zone strategy, simultaneously promoting both development and conservation, seems to be increasingly popular in Thailand, with the start of another half-dozen or so projects. For example, the Thailand Environment Institute has begun a buffer zone project outside

Phu Khiow Wildlife Sanctuary in Chaiyaphum province. The sanctuary contains the only forest left in the area, so local people often enter it to collect products, hunt wildlife, and cut down trees for both timber and fuel. A key component of the project is therefore to plant community forests which can provide these goods, on a now-degraded forest reserve on Phu Kratae, a small hill southeast of the sanctuary itself which used to provide water, timber, game, and other forest products. This arrangement is quite different from Huay Kha Khaeng, where the buffer zone will be in the form of a reforested strip of land in between the sanctuary and local villages.[35]

There are many ingredients needed to make buffer zones a success, especially cooperation between the various parties involved. Among the tools suggested for implementing the many project activities are formal compacts or contracts between the communities and the NGOs working with them, which are witnessed by leading government officials in the area. The setting up of conservation area advisory committees is also recommended.[36]

Dr. Apichai notes that at Phu Khiow the local women's groups have done most of the tree planting while teachers have taken it on themselves to educate children about the importance of preserving the forest.[37]

The International Situation

Thailand's attempts to come to grips with the vital questions of how to manage forests, how to reforest, and how to deal with villagers who depend on forests, are not taking place in isolation. Complex and difficult negotiations are going on internationally to institute the sustainable use of forests, and conclusions reached at that level will have an impact on Thai efforts.

Much work is currently being undertaken around the globe to measure and identify sustainability in forests through the development of criteria and indicators (C&I) of sustainable forest management (SFM), and related certification or accreditation schemes.[38] The idea is to promote global consumption of wood products taken only from sustainably-managed forests or plantations. This approach at eco-labelling would require further raising of environmental consciousness among the globe's commercial consumers, and a change of attitude among the big timber interests, represented by a handful of governments who control the great majority

391

Box 15.2
Sub-set of Criteria Common to CIFOR's Tropical Test Sites, 1996

The Centre for International Forestry Research (CIFOR) has undertaken work on the practical applications and social dimensions of C&I of sustainable forest management. Below is a "core" sub-set of C&I which emerged for the tropical sites and was also found to be widely applicable or adaptable to temperate forests.

Principle: Policy
Policy, Planning, and Institutional Framework are Conducive to Sustainable Forest Management
Criteria (number of indicators)
1. There is sustained and adequate funding for the management of forests (5)

Principle: Ecology
Maintenance of Ecosystem Integrity
Criteria
2. Ecosystem function is maintained (4)
3. Impacts to biodiversity of the forest ecosystem are minimised (4)
4. The capacity of the forest to regenerate naturally is ensured (2)

Principle: Social Environment
Forest Management Maintains Fair Intergenerational Access to Resources and Economic Benefits; Stakeholders, Including Forest Actors, Have a Voice in Forest Management
Criteria
5. Stakeholders/forest actors' tenure and use rights are secure (3)
6. Stakeholders/local populations participate in forest management (2)

Principle: Production of Goods and Services
Yield and Quality of Forest Goods and Services are Sustainable
Criteria
7. Management objectives are clearly and precisely described and documented (1)
8. A comprehensive forest management plan is available (4)
9. The management plan is effectively implemented (4)
10. An effective monitoring and control system audits management's conformity with planning (4).

Source: *Countdown: Forests '97*, Issue 2, 1996. International Institute for Sustainable Development.

of the global tropical timber trade. Logging interests in these countries are resisting such labelling schemes. However, members of the International Tropical Timber Organisation, which groups producer and consumer nations, have pledged by the year 2000 to trade only wood from sustainably managed forests,[39] giving a further boost to the eco-labelling concept.

Several parallel efforts by various organisations are being made to formulate C&I. The Centre for International Forestry Research (CIFOR),[40] based in Indonesia, is the first international organisation to undertake broad testing of a range of proposed C&Is (See Box 15.2).

It should be noted in criteria 5 and 6 of CIFOR that forest dwellers' land tenure and use rights of the forest must be secure; in addition, such stakeholders and local populations must have the right of participation in forest management. These requirements constitute another important international issue regarding forests—upholding the rights of forest dwellers. These rights are still being neglected in a number of developing countries where large-scale logging continues, and they have relevance to Thailand's attempts to institute sustainable forest management, considering that some quarters advocate removing forest dwellers from ecologically sensitive areas of forest. We should remember that the rights of forest dwellers were enshrined in the Forest Principles negotiated and adopted at the 1992 Rio Earth Summit, which state:

> Principle 2 (d): Governments should promote and provide opportunities for the participation of interested parties, including local communities and indigenous people, industries, labour, non-governmental organisations, and individuals, forest dwellers, and women, in the development, implementation, and planning of national forest policies.

> Principle 5 (a): National forest policies should recognise and duly support the identity, culture, and the rights of indigenous people, their communities, and other communities and forest dwellers. Appropriate conditions should be promoted for these groups to enable them to have an economic stake in forest use, perform economic activities, and achieve and maintain cultural identity and social organisation, as well as adequate levels of livelihood and wellbeing, through, *inter alia*, those land tenure arrangements

which serve as incentives for the sustainable management of forests.

The World Conservation Union, a major international NGO, set up a Working Group on Community Involvement in Forest Management. It has voiced a clear objective for decision makers in forest management:

The 21st Century challenge is to facilitate a devolution of greater authority to forest-based communities while minimising conflicts, and to support new partnerships among communities, government and the private sector to ensure the meeting of community needs, forest resource conservation, and sustainable use.[41]

The group draws a number of common conclusions from its diverse range of global experiences:
- Communities are increasingly concerned over forest degradation and growing resource scarcities.
- Community members often distrust forestry department staff and are fearful that large, private-sector timber interests will further degrade already threatened and eroding natural forest resources.
- Communities are increasingly organising and taking operational steps and political action to gain greater authority over local forest resources.
- Communities are building on traditional institutions and environmental values while integrating new planning skills and management practices in evolving forest protection systems.
- Forestry Departments are under growing political and financial pressures to involve communities in public forest management.
- National policies and programmes supporting community forest management initiatives are encouraging them to develop and spread.
- Community involvement in forest protection is leading to a stabilisation of degrading ecosystems, enabling natural regeneration.
- In many countries, community involvement is proving to be a cost-effective, socially just, and environmentally-sound approach to stabilising natural forests.

Mark Poffenburger and Roger D. Stone examined this cost effectiveness of the community approach, and found:

> Ironically, such grassroots efforts [as tropical Asian community forestry schemes], frequently require little or no outside capital or technical assistance. Yet, in places like Eastern India, they are achieving results where millions of dollars of external funding, along with the application of new technologies and policy instruments, have failed to dent the problem.[42]

Yet, the financing of sustainable forest management on a global basis is still a major, unresolved issue. The appropriate roles of the public, private, and civil sectors, as well as of rich and poor countries are under contention. Proposals for a global forestry fund have been raised. Another sought-after objective, an agreement to negotiate a global forestry convention, has also failed to get off the ground, although discussions continue. The International Institute for Sustainable Development (IISD) noted in February 1997 that:

> Nations and key sectors cannot yet agree on their respective rights and responsibilities in this important undertaking [of financing sustainable forest management]. For the time being, therefore, financing for SFM will come from a mix of public, private, and community sources, rather than from any single arena. . . . A range of governments and NGOs point out that local communities perform an important "community investment" function. Substantial case experience among NGOs worldwide shows that SFM can be supported by giving local communities greater decision-making control over forests, rather than by relying on external funds alone. . . .
>
> There was wide agreement among participants in a workshop of the Intergovernmental Panel on Forests (Pretoria, June 1996) that forests today are commonly undervalued around the world, and that a concerted effort must be made to capture the full value of forests in future policies.[43]

At the Pretoria workshop, recommendations for governments included the provision of incentives and the promotion of the use of appropriate technologies to support SFM, particularly to small enterprises, local communities, and forest owners. Incentives to other sectors must also be supportive of SFM. However, Jim MacNeill, the IISD chairman, told participants that:

> The Brundtland Commission [on environment and sustainable development] sampled over 20 countries, and in each we found that the forest industry attracted a wide variety of perverse subsidies, direct and indirect.

With the failure of governments to honour commitments made at Rio to direct increased financial resources into global sustainable development—including many governments' reluctance to spend large sums on SFM—private capital has become most influential in "developing" forests. McNeill noted that the ratio of public to private flows may be 1:5 or 1:6 and falling, although he regarded public flows as still very important:

> But we need to devote a great deal more attention to the huge and rising flows of private capital. It is these flows that will determine whether natural forests have a sustainable future or not. . . . What means are available to ensure that an ever-increasing proportion of private flows are invested in sustainable forestry?

This issue becomes even more important when we realise that, despite the current high level of destruction, pressures on forests globally continue to grow. A mid-1990s study into this question[44] foresaw steadily rising demands on forests—both for wood and non-wood products and services—as populations rise and conservation values become increasingly important. Particularly of relevance to Thailand, the authors advise intensifying forest management using plantations and other techniques, and improving the security of land tenure in order to reduce adverse effects on forests. Uncertain tenure is likely to increase short-term production and consumption and diminish long-term potential, they write.

The theme of plantations was taken up by the Intergovernmental Panel on Forests (IPF) in September 1996. New Zealand, which has built up a major export industry based on wood products harvested from sustainably-managed tree plantations, promoted the role of plantation forests in mitigating forest degradation and as an important element of SFM. (This view was supported by Australia, Chile, China, Japan, South Africa, and Uganda; Norway stressed the need for plantations to meet social, economic, and environmental conditions, including conservation of biodiversity.)[45]

The creation of sustainably managed tree plantations will bring large-scale benefits to economies of developing countries, especially as the timber trade moves towards the adoption of an internationally recognised voluntary code that stipulates sustainable management across a broad range of ecological and social issues. Ken Shirley, the executive director of the New Zealand Forest Owners' Association, has said:

> There is a huge benefit to be gained in getting recognition for plantation forestry as we practice it in New Zealand. Most of the world's commercial plantation forestry is concentrated in the Southern hemisphere and it is necessary to bring influential European and North American environmentalists to a greater understanding that "wood farming" can be undertaken sustainably, thereby offering protection to remaining areas of natural forest.[46]

The Forest Principles formulated at Rio de Janeiro support this view:

> Principle 6 (a): . . . the potential contribution of plantations of both indigenous and introduced species for the provision of both fuel and industrial wood should be recognised.

> Principle 6 (d): The role of planted forests and permanent agricultural crops as sustainable and environmentally-sound sources of renewable energy and industrial raw material should be recognised, enhanced, and promoted. Their contribution to the maintenance of ecological processes, to offsetting pressure on primary/old-growth forest, and to providing regional

employment and development with the adequate involvement of local inhabitants should be recognised and enhanced.

To conclude this section, and to underscore once again the absolute necessity to preserve forests, I would like to quote once again from Geoffrey Lean, a long-time, London-based environmental correspondent:

> Now, less than a quarter of the world's original forest remains, most of it gone during the past 50 years. Every week another 400,000 hectares disappear, and the rate of destruction has doubled over the past decade [1985–1995]. As trees fall, the Earth's precious topsoils are eroded away, its water supplies are disrupted, and its climate is beginning to change. . . . "Forests precede civilisation, deserts follow" runs the old saying. Uruk, the great Sumerian city state of Mesopotamian civilisation, is now a bump in the sand; its soils, which 4,000 years ago produced crop yields that compare with the American Mid-West today, were destroyed by deforestation. . . .
>
> At present, only a tiny proportion of the world's timber comes from . . . sustainable sources. But consumers in industrialised countries have shown that, providing they can identify it, they are willing to pay more, thus creating an incentive for conservation. . . .[47]

SECTION 5

THE URBAN CHALLENGE

Chapter 16

It's Time to Recognise an Urban Crisis in Thailand

Will Bangkok's woes never end? Traffic gridlock, air pollution, overcrowding, growing slum settlements, and forebodings of future water shortages lead one to think that the city, and the country, are facing an urban crisis. Can the governing authorities get a grip on the situation? Will they even acknowledge a crisis bigger than just Bangkok's traffic gridlock? The city's unresolved problems increasingly threaten Thailand's economic future, not to mention the health and sanity of the capital's population. Could things get much worse? Consider this:

In 1995, Bangkok had 55.7 per cent of Thailand's urban population of 11.8 million people, according to official estimates published by the United Nations in its *World Urbanization Prospects: The 1994 Revision*. Additionally, Thailand's total population is predicted to grow from 61 million in 1998 to around 70 million in 2020, according to estimates made in 1999.[1]

It is possible, therefore, that Thailand's urban population may double or nearly double in the 25 years between 1995 and 2020. The United Nations assumed in its 1994 calculations that rural Thailand would no longer be able to absorb the country's population growth, and that the rural population would remain the same or actually decline. The cities and towns would take all the new population growth as well as the net loss of people from the rural areas.

The population of the Bangkok urban agglomeration was estimated[2] at 6.7 million in 1995, and forecast to become 9.8 million in 2015. However, those estimates may be considerably on the low side. Figures published by the Bangkok Metropolitan Administration in 1996 gave a "best current estimate" of the mid-1995 BMA population at 7.9 million, and the corresponding population of the Bangkok Metropolitan Region at approximately 11 million.[3]

During the first half of the 1990s, the BMA population grew by around 200,000–235,000 each year, an annual rate of increase of just under 3 per cent, said the BMA. Following the 1997 economic downturn, there was a return of rural migrants to the countryside. But this would seem to be temporary. Unless a massive agricultural development is planned for Thailand in the 21st Century, it is likely that large-scale migration from the countryside to the cities will resume when the economy improves.

Can Thailand cope with a future upsurge of urban population? Will its politicians and administrators be able to end their eternal squabbling long enough to agree on a rational, sustainable approach to this immense challenge of urban development? Or will the present, unsustainable practices underlying Bangkok's chaotic growth continue, vastly compounding existing problems of overcrowding and pollution, leading to millions more city dwellers suffering from declining health, stress, and even despair?

Asia's Urban Transition

Thailand is not alone in this predicament. Asia as a whole is undergoing an urban transition in which 1.24 billion people are forecast to be added to its urban areas from 1995 to 2020—an increase of 103 per cent. Some 51 per cent of Asians would thus live in urban centres by 2020. As of 1995, some 34.6 per cent of Asians lived in urban centres. The proportion in 1970 was 23.4 per cent.

The urban transition for Southeast Asia looks even more dramatic. The region is forecast to add 190 million people to urban areas from 1995 to 2020—an increase of 117 per cent. Some 52 per cent of Southeast Asians would thus live in urban centres by 2020. As of 1995, some 33.7 per cent of Southeast Asians lived in urban centres. The proportion in 1970 was 20.4 per cent.

This historic social transformation was addressed in Bangkok in October 1993, at a Ministerial Conference on Urbanisation in Asia and the Pacific hosted by the Economic and Social Commission for Asia and the Pacific (ESCAP). The then executive secretary of ESCAP, Rafeeudin

Ahmed, told a press conference that action on cities had to be taken immediately to avoid very serious problems in the next decade:

> Mega-cities, unless managed efficiently, bring with them levels
> of environmental degradation which push to the limits their ability
> to sustain human life.

Governments, various agencies, NGOs, concerned individuals, and the media have to focus on the problem now, on an urgent basis, he said. Six years after that call, and three Thai governments later, very little had changed.

How to Use Land?

The question of how to use land is at the centre of Thailand's dilemma with its cities and towns. It also stirs controversy throughout the country. Land used wisely, with foresight, will set the foundations for improved health and sustainable economic growth far into the future. Present patterns of land use in Bangkok are definitely unsustainable. One thing is certain: government must intervene in the land development process to ensure sustainable development. Intervention means rational planning and its enforcement—something that has not mixed easily with Thailand's free-wheeling, individualistic culture. Rational planning needs a genuine and broad political commitment, and land-use policies need to be fair and not biased towards any particular group. The hurdle to be overcome is the reward-oriented, patronage system of Thai politics.

Up to now, Thai governments, apparently unwilling to challenge the narrowly-defined interests of the country's land-owning elite, have taken only token measures towards instituting effective city planning. The United States government sponsored an attempt at planning in 1959, when the Litchfield company was assigned to complete a preliminary survey before mapping out a city plan. Bangkok in those days was much smaller and there was little evidence of the economic dynamism of the 1990s, or of congestion and traffic jams.

A draft plan was produced in 1960, even before a city and town planning office was established in 1963 to implement it. But the new office had no strong political support and the plan was never acted upon. How much better would everyday life and business be today in Bangkok if rational planning policies had been given high political priority back then? Almost four decades later, Thailand still has no strong political commitment to city planning, although Thailand's coming urban transition makes it more necessary than ever. Meanwhile, the growth of Bangkok continues to surge outward, duplicating the same mistakes that have made central Bangkok so congested and unhealthy. A quantum leap of imagination and dedication to sustainable urban development is needed.

Cities Are for People

Cities are for people who must live and work there. But, strangely enough, this perspective has been lost in Bangkok. The city is notorious for its lack of open space, and lack of parks and public recreation facilities. There is more outside space available for cars and motorcycles (which manage to park in any empty space, even on the footpaths) than there is for people. Having lost this perspective, authorities have surrendered their mandate to make decisions on city development to the property market.

Who developed this city? asked Dr. Chamniern Paul Vorratnchaiphan, an urban planner and director of the Grassroots Action Programme at the Thailand Environment Institute:[4]

> It was the capitalists, the banks; not the government. The private
> sector is creating the city. It is really [determining] the land use,
> whether it is good or bad.

Thus, the free-wheeling property market was a very dynamic force in creating Thailand's bubble economy. The property boom was unregulated, with very little vision of where it was headed, until the bubble burst with disastrous consequences to the financial system and the economy. An additional tragedy to the economic one is that the undirected building boom concentrated high-rise offices and condominiums as close as possible to the commercial centre of Bangkok, with its severe lack of roads, bringing increased congestion of people and cars. By 1998, the empty shells of abandoned high-rise construction sites stood out like ghosts against the Bangkok skyline, concrete, high-rise monuments to folly. What remained was a degraded quality of city life, the legacy of a total lack of foresight.

A regulated and coordinated approach to property development, including proper financial supervision, could have lessened the 1996 plunge of the property sector. In fact, construction of high-rise buildings in Central Bangkok should have been banned years before, and development directed to outlying areas through rational planning of land use and transportation systems.

Why the rush to cram high-rise condominiums into the centre of Bangkok, pushing property prices sky-high and precipitating a property crash? Securities analyst Michael Stead blames authorities for failing to provide reasonably priced housing for its citizens:

> Because there was no decent mass transit system, people in
> Bangkok had two choices: live in the outer suburbs and spend
> two, three, or four hours per day commuting; or live in high-rise,
> high-priced condos in the city centre.[5]

Stead suspects there was a form of collusion at work: if a mass transit system had been developed, and residential land developed in the suburbs, property prices could not have risen so high. He noted that so many cabinet ministers had interests in the property market, either owning property companies or owning significant stakes in property companies or in banks. Thus, they had no incentive to develop mass transit to end the massive traffic jams of Greater Bangkok that forced many people to live in the centre.

The Traffic Dilemma

Bangkok is caught in a bind: traffic gridlock is paralysing the city, yet current policies and practices encourage the entry of more cars on to the road—policies such as low prices for petrol, the lowering of tax on auto imports, the construction of elevated highways . . . and the intensive mass media promotion of cars as sexy, prestigious, and "necessary", while healthier alternatives to cars remain unpromoted.

In the mid-1990s, we saw several piecemeal, stop-gap measures offered to ease the traffic situation, such as an (expensive) computer-controlled system for operating traffic lights, and the payment of monetary bonuses to traffic officers to "try harder" to enforce traffic regulations. Those measures failed. Measures that do not actually reduce the number of cars on the road cannot succeed in solving traffic gridlock. Computerised systems mainly bring benefits to the companies that import and install them, and to their political friends.

Other piecemeal measures, such as charging fees and attempting to ban cars from the centre, may offer some relief to the traffic problem. But, in effect, such measures are like trying to treat cancer by taking aspirin. Bangkok's traffic jams are basically a symptom of a broader disease. It's hard to ban a large number of vehicles from the central city when there are no ready alternatives to moving large numbers of people, and when business and government is concentrated in the centre.

The Tanayong "skytrain" project for the centre of Bangkok, due to become operational in December 1999, may ease travel for some, but it remained doubtful whether it could significantly ease the traffic gridlock. The construction of more elevated highways likewise eased travel to some destinations, but allowed more cars easier access into the centre of Bangkok. The city remained as congested and more polluted than ever.

Thai leaders seem to be unwilling to acknowledge that the traffic problem is just one dimension of a much larger problem: there is no comprehensive planning for urban development in Thailand. Since 1996, a rational solution has emerged in the form of the Bangkok Plan (outlined in subsequent chapters), but no one has so far showed the will to implement it. The current attempt to initiate mass transit schemes circling the Central Bangkok area should be seen as giving just a temporary relief to inner-city congestion, while town planning maps out whole new centres of rational growth outside central Bangkok. But this is not happening.

Planning efficient transportation requires a vision far into the future of what a healthy, efficient city should look like. I have concluded that no Thai government up to now has really wanted to solve the traffic problem. Solving this problem basically requires a painful decision to abandon *laissez-faire* transport policies and to tell newly affluent and high-status Thais what they cannot do. This goes against traditional Thai behaviour, and against the current political "wisdom" which says: don't do anything controversial or unpopular because it may threaten a major underlying objective of elected Thai governments, which is to create money-making opportunities for family and friends under the political patronage system. To break through this dual barrier, to progress, will need political leadership, courage, and determination.

Efficient public transportation and bicycles should replace the vast majority of cars. For those who "must" have cars, let them pay through the nose and subsidise public transport. Thai authorities would be well advised to study Singapore's policy. Singapore puts the highest tax on cars of perhaps any country. Its government decides how many cars should be allowed on its roads, taking into consideration the need to prevent traffic congestion and pollution, and therefore places a limit on the number of car licences that can be issued. Those wishing to run a car or other motorised vehicle must periodically bid in a national auction for a certificate of entitlement to obtain a vehicle licence. This, in effect, lets the free market determine who can own vehicle licences, and provides a major source of revenue for the government which may then be used for financing public transportation projects.

The Singapore government periodically announces the results of bidding for certificates of entitlement. Here are the minimum prices that affluent Singaporeans had to pay for their particular class of vehicle licence (1 Singapore dollar = about 18 baht, during the period):

	Dec 95	Jun 96	Dec 96
small cars	S$18,138	16,898	24,832
medium cars	30,528	44,498	47,764
big cars	55,008	47,010	53,360
luxury cars	56,400	46,200	51,008
motorcycles	4,202	2,860	3,150

The Singapore government, in pursuing its well-thought-out policy for public transportation, has set a goal that everyone in the city state should not have to walk more than 400 metres to gain access to some form of public transportation.

There is another area in which Singapore is leading the world in traffic control: the development of the electronic road pricing system (ERP). The system came into operation in 1998. It is based on the use of electronic devices known as in-vehicle units (IUs) mounted on the windscreen of every car. Drivers are charged electronically for driving their cars downtown at peak times—the more they drive, the more they pay. The IUs act as electronic identification of the vehicles and transmit and receive information to and from the antennae on ERP gantries which are located above major roads. The ERP charges are deducted from a smart card which the motorist has to insert into the IU when the vehicle is in use.[6]

There is a worldwide move towards ridding cities and towns of vehicle congestion and pollution. A Royal Commission was set up in Britain to make recommendations on traffic congestion, and announced its findings in October 1994 (according to a report by the British Broadcasting Corporation). To reduce the number of cars on the road and promote public transportation, the commission suggested doubling the price of petrol over 10 years, and halting the construction of new motorways, which only encourage more cars to enter on to the roads. This solution has also given rise in Britain to a popular movement to stop building new motorways, and to limit the number of cars allowed in towns and cities.

The above solutions might seem radical in Thailand, where the notion of "freedom" roughly equates with "do nothing" on the part of governments. But Thailand needs radical solutions before the present urban transport disaster turns into a mega-disaster. The kingdom needs to go beyond *ad hoc* and patronage-influenced solutions.

The Chinese Shophouse Syndrome

Thailand has to break the bad old habits of the past if it is to achieve sustainable development and a better quality of life. This means breaking free of the Chinese shophouse syndrome, which, by default, is still the main dynamic in urban growth throughout Thailand and especially Bangkok.

What is it?

Going back 60 years and earlier, the Chinese merchant class in Bangkok just built shophouses lining every major street, and adjoining side streets, without any space left open except for the grounds within *wats* (temples) and government offices. A new street, another 500 shophouses. . . . And so it went on, as every small businessman tried to acquire property as close to the commercial nerve centre as possible. They never saw a bigger picture of rational development beyond their own narrow, little strip of property. Environmental concerns were unheard-of in those days, and government likely did not even think about regulating such construction. Up to now, no one has seriously challenged this Chinese shophouse syndrome, which has been accepted as a natural, unstoppable growth phenomenon, just like an amoeba dividing into two.

Maximum Utilisation

Bangkok's most prominent bankers, in announcing their new high-rise developments during the bubble era, boasted about "maximum utilisation of land"—just like 60 years before. If we analyse this phrase, it includes: maximisation of profits from development, maximum obliteration of the natural environment, and maximum disregard for the mental and physical health of the population which must live and work in such overbuilt surroundings.

To be fair, property developers cannot take all the blame for this, although they failed to comprehend that they were participating in a large-scale environmental as well as financial disaster. The fault lies also with the political leadership, over a number of governments. It is absolutely the responsibility of the government (local and national) to create a framework in which ecologically-sound and sustainable development can take place. The irony of Thailand's situation is that the country has many well-educated experts, and Thailand is not poor by developing-country standards. But Thailand's political and administrative development are lagging woefully behind its economic development.

What approach can be followed from here? Urban planning—and dedicated implementation—that creates healthy, sustainable development for Thailand's cities must be given highest priority. Thailand must develop cities for people: environmentally-friendly, green cities. City governments and those of large towns must be given the powers to run their own affairs, and the people must be involved. Planning for new cities, such as the oft-proposed new capital and administrative centre, as well as for a Greater Bangkok, should incorporate all of these things.

Chapter 17

Thailand Must Establish a Framework for Healthy and Sustainable Urban Development

How will Thailand respond to the urban challenge of the 21st Century, when the number of people now living in towns and cities in the kingdom may double? Can politicians, officials, intellectuals, and property developers come together to cooperate on a framework for sustainable urban development? Or will the congestion and severe environmental degradation which characterise Bangkok become the standard in future for emerging cities and mega-cities?

Thailand has not yet succeeded in planning the environmentally-sustainable growth of any of its towns or cities. It needs to urgently strengthen its urban planning capacity and the administrative structures that will implement urban development plans. The 1996 Bangkok Plan deals with these issues, but it has been largely ignored. Much expertise exists in Thailand and internationally on how to develop large, ecologically-sound cities suited to Asian conditions. Can the politicians put aside political manoeuvring and self-interest long enough to set in motion a high-priority process to meet this challenge?

This chapter will outline some of the latest ecological thinking on healthy and sustainable urban development. Subsequent chapters will make suggestions on how to approach the administrative side of this massive undertaking. The major challenges for Thailand and Asia are:

- how to create healthy, efficient, green cities—not cities that undermine the health and limit the possibilities of their inhabitants;

- getting the transportation equation right—in a world whose cities
are already polluted, and which is facing global warming spurred
on by exhaust emissions from one billion petrol-burning vehicles;
and
- how to construct communities that will meet everyone's housing
and economic needs and preserve and enrich culture.

Cities will account for increasing shares of economic activity
throughout Asia, as the continent's urban transition progresses. The well-
planned and well-managed cities will become centres of commerce. Those
recognised as ecological and organisational disasters will in a large
measure be avoided by investors. We have already had a forewarning of
this, as Singapore rather than Bangkok was chosen as the site for the
headquarters of APEC (the Asia-Pacific Economic Cooperation forum).
More recently, Singapore has also become the preferred location for the
headquarters of transnational corporations doing business in Asia.

Compact Urban Clusters

In recent years, environmentalists have provided the lead on sustainable
urban development. Current thinking in planning for mega-cities is to
stress "compactness" rather than the urban sprawl that can be found in
so many Western cities. The key to future urban sanity lies in attention
to land use. Many authoritative sources stress this. Marcia Lowe pointed
out in a study for the Worldwatch Institute:

> All cities, whether surrounded by affluent suburbs or makeshift
> shantytowns, now need to plan land use far more carefully than
> in the past—before the developing world's urban crises turn into
> catastrophes, and the industrial world's problems become issues
> of survival.[1]

Rather than planning communities that compel each household to
rely on automobiles, the ecologically sound strategy of the future is to
reduce the need for cars as much as possible. The great majority of major
cities in the world are dominated by automobiles. New cities, especially,
have the opportunity through land-use planning to avoid this unhealthy
indulgence. Says Lowe:

> A city's land use defines its transport system more than any traffic
> planner or engineer can. The pattern of urban development
> dictates whether people can walk or cycle to work or whether
> they need to travel dozens of kilometres. . . . By failing to see
> land-use planning as a transport strategy, many of the world's
> cities have allowed the automobile to shape them.

Avoiding urban sprawl and opting for compactness is the answer.
This thinking leads to decentralised development, where the most
transport-efficient land-use pattern combines a dense, well-mixed
downtown with several outlying, compact centres of activity—clusters—
all linked by an extensive public transport system. This way, people can
walk, cycle, and take short public transport trips within a given area, and
can reach other areas via express bus or rapid light rail. Lowe additionally
notes that land-use planning as a transport strategy involves improving
the design of streets. A hierarchical street system is most efficient,
combining a finely meshed grid of small streets with slightly larger ones
and with a few main arterials.

Zoning for land use within and around cities is important, but urban
experts now also stress flexibility in zoning. Thus, emphasis is placed
on numerous clusters of compact settlements, where different styles and
densities of dwellings are mixed together in close proximity, while
allowing commercial and light industrial activities. Thus, high rise offices
and housing estates, along with various forms of low-rise housing
developments, both for high- and low-income populations, can be
integrated. Numerous small-scale and open green areas, and enclaves
where trees are planted are essential within each cluster.

Separating the clusters would be extensive green areas. Green belts,
parks, botanical gardens, bird sanctuaries, cycling paths surrounded by
greenery, and public sports grounds are all part of this eco-philosophy of
green urban development.

I find Lowe's study particularly enlightening for Thailand, and so
quote it at greater length:

> Antiquated zoning laws, in particular, need updating. In most
> industrial countries, planners have continued to segregate homes
> from jobs, shops, and other centres of activity long after the end
> of the heavy industrial period. . . . Unfortunately, most developing

413

countries have imported these compartmentalised zoning laws. Among the most serious repercussions are excessive distances between homes and jobs. . . . Many Asian cities were more dynamic and had greater internal variety before they adopted Western-style zoning. . . .

A more rational approach to zoning in both the developing and industrial worlds would be to integrate homes not only with workplaces, but with other amenities, so that they are easily accessible by walking, cycling, or public transport. Such reforms ideally would not hamper developers or impose uniformity, but instead would lift restrictions that inhibit mixed use and create unnaturally one-dimensional districts. Zoning laws need to be specific and carefully conceived, however; the real estate market, if left without controls, may fail to mix different land uses sufficiently. . . .

Many cities are linking stretches of verdant space along rivers, canals, or old rail lines into continuous paths for cycling, horseback riding, jogging, and walking. . . . The city of Leicester, England, is planning to convert an abandoned rail line into the Great Central Way, a car-free route that will bisect the entire city from north to south. . . .

There are some outstanding models for adopting land use as a transport strategy. These cities owe their success not only to carefully guided growth but also to systematic, coordinated investments in public transport, cycling, and walking. Portland, Oregon, for example, is a rapidly growing city of roughly 500,000 people within a metropolitan area of 1.3 million. Instead of giving in to ever-greater automobile dependence and sprawl, Portland has encircled itself with an urban growth boundary, an invisible line similar to England's green belts, beyond which new development is not allowed. Reinforced by zoning reforms, the Urban Growth Boundary allows Portland to grow quickly but compactly. In roughly two decades, Portland has successfully fended off sprawl and claimed valuable city space back from the automobile.

This perspective gained additional meaning in 1996, with the
publication of the book, *Home from Nowhere* by James Howard Kunstler.[2]
The suburbs that have blanketed the US in the decades since World War
II are not only irredeemably ugly, Kunstler says, but have shredded the
fabric of American life and are slowly bankrupting the nation.

> We've been engaged in a process for two generations of degrading
> the public realm of our towns and our cities and our
> neighbourhoods. The damage is now so tremendous that there's
> really some doubt we can continue to be a civilised society.

Kunstler blames America's decline and sprawl on the nation's slavish
devotion to the automobile and a planning establishment that designed
an expensive national infrastructure around the car. The average new car
now costs $20,000 and about $6,100 a year to keep on the road. But
those sums don't begin to cover the massive indirect costs of an auto-
based culture. . . . Few realise that the trashy and alienating environment
that resulted from the nation's post-World War II migration to the suburbs
is to blame for many of the country's current social and economic woes,
he says.

In highly-populated Asia, land will be less and less available for
American-style, middle-class urban sprawls, characterised by single
houses on plots of land. High-density, high-rise living will be a feature
of the upcoming mega-cities. But planned cities such as Singapore show
that high-density living can be combined with green, spacious landscapes.

Many Asian cities and towns, especially in Thailand, grew up with
the shophouse as the basic dwelling and business unit. This is a highly-
efficient unit from a family-business point of view, but if allowed to
proliferate without land-use controls, the Chinese shophouse syndrome
becomes an environmental and social disaster, as with the present
downtown Bangkok and its outward growth areas.

Blocks of shophouses can be designed in an environmentally-friendly
way, if they include ample green spaces, ample walkways and public
facilities, and do not predominate over a large area. For example, shophouses or townhouses should not be laid out monotonously row after row,
but should be grouped around open, green courtyards and parks, providing
a healthy spaciousness and opportunities for community development.
They should become components of the mooted mixed developments.

If planning goes ahead for a proposed New City as the administrative capital of Thailand, it will offer an opportunity to base urban development on the imperative of green, open space rather than on the creation of a concrete wasteland.

Preserving Street Culture

This perspective also means allowing street culture to flourish. It is one of the tragedies of overcrowded Bangkok that—in the absence of planning—parked motorcycles, pedestrians, and vendors increasingly must compete for space on the downtown's narrow footpaths. The vendors and food-stall operators are an important part of Thailand's market-oriented culture (albeit in need of greater food-safety control). Thousands of office workers and low-income workers in Bangkok eat at the cheap food stalls, which are usually stretched out along the footpath, often no more than a few metres from heavily-polluting traffic. Vendors have to breathe poisonous exhaust fumes for hours per day and then are harassed by the authorities when roadside congestion becomes unbearable.

The vendors and their low-income customers deserve a better deal. Sites for vendors and food stalls should be planned throughout the city. Small sections of parks, other green enclaves, and public spaces should be set aside at frequent intervals and a small licensing fee charged for supervision and maintenance of the sites.

Attention also needs to be given to these people in designing low-end accommodation. Research of the Economic and Social Commission for Asia and the Pacific (ESCAP) reinforces the Worldwatch Institute's recommendation for mixing of commercial and residential areas, and notes that the informal business sector works most effectively in such an environment. Thus, when new housing developments for the poor, especially high-rise developments, are brought on stream, they should allow for the storage of carts and other equipment required to carry on the vending, food-preparation, and other micro-enterprise activities of the poor.

Now we are beginning to visualise what an enlightened New City— a city for people—may look like. Yet to be discussed are the structures and the policies that will be needed to get there—if this shelved project ever goes ahead. If such a New City is well planned with the requisite infrastructure and economic opportunities, it will no doubt create a dynamic alternative to Bangkok.

416

Eastern Seaboard Corridor

But there is another high-growth area that has to be considered: the surging development on the outskirts of Bangkok, especially to the east of the metropolis, where an urban corridor to the eastern seaboard is well under formation. Thailand's weak attempts at urban planning have not been able to avoid the pitfalls of Central Bangkok's overcrowding and environmental degradation in these areas.

The same disastrous mistakes made in Central Bangkok are being repeated on the outskirts: development according to the Chinese shophouse syndrome, its associated "ribbon development" centred on roads like the Bangna-Trad highway, lack of adequate roads and lack of transportation planning. The same ecologically-friendly principles and approaches recommended for a New City should be simultaneously applied to this growing, Bangna-Trad urban corridor, which itself may become equal to a city.

A Last Chance for Bangkok?

After repeated failures and indifference, can Bangkok—and Thailand in general—enter the modern world of rational urban planning and management? In January 1996, Bangkok was given another chance through the publication of the initial draft of a new Bangkok Plan, commissioned by the Bangkok Metropolitan Administration (BMA) under Governor Krisda Arunvongse na Ayutthaya. The planning exercise employed consultants from the Massachusetts Institute of Technology in the USA, had inputs from 15 Thai government agencies, and was reviewed by European experts under aid provided by the European Union.

The Plan sets out rational steps, principles, and a framework to put Bangkok's growth on a healthy and sustainable path. It focuses on enlightened land-use policies, coordination of urban infrastructure development, and strengthening of urban administration. Much redefinition of the functions and powers of the BMA are called for, a key element of which is the creation of a Bangkok Development Authority as the city's development arm, with powers to carry out large-scale development and redevelopment schemes.

The necessity for such a powerful body is supported both within Thailand and internationally. For example, the National Economic and

417

Social Development Board (NESDB), in 1991, called for the establishment of a development committee for what it called the extended Bangkok metropolitan region. It recommended that the committee possess institutional responsibility for urban management in the extended metropolitan region, and that the membership composition should be at the highest policy level with the prime minister acting as chairman. Additionally, at ESCAP's Ministerial Conference on Urbanisation in Asia and the Pacific in 1993, the final declaration called for the establishment of an urban forum at the national level (and at local levels) specifically to ensure dialogue between all actors in urban development.

Thailand needs to put its best minds to work on the challenge of urbanisation, which may well be the next biggest challenge—apart from the macro economy and the need for a second wave of agricultural development—faced by the country over the next two decades or more.

Chapter 18

Politics and the Bangkok Plan

Who will support the Bangkok Plan, the best vision formulated in decades to reverse the sad decline of a once-charming city?

The Plan sets forth the prospect of managing the relentless growth of the Bangkok metropolis by designating five new metropolitan sub-centres outside Bangkok linked to the centre and to each other by integrated mass transit systems. It thus creates the long-term possibility of greatly reducing the number of vehicles—and traffic jams and vehicle pollution—in Greater Bangkok. It aims to create parks, open spaces, and efficient street designs, and to alleviate urban overcrowding, much to the relief of oppressed Bangkok residents. The Plan introduces a flexible system for regulation of land uses, recognising the mixed-use pattern that has grown up in Bangkok. It advocates zoning for high and low densities, with high-density, commercial-residential zones clustered around transportation hubs.

These are all rational approaches to avert increasing degradation of Bangkok and put its future growth on a healthy and sustainable path. But can the Plan survive Thailand's self-serving politics? Can it survive competition between government agencies? And can it overcome the individualistic Thai mentality and Thais' aversion to following regulations, which makes cooperation towards a common goal so difficult to achieve?

However, since 15 agencies have been involved, with committees bringing in the private sector, academics, and non-governmental agencies, the Plan could count on the backing of a number of stakeholders who are concerned with practical aspects, according to Dr. Utis Kaothien, director of the Urban Development Division of the National Economic and Social Development Board (NESDB).[1] He said, in a 1996 interview:

> We regard the Bangkok Plan as implementable. It is the first
> implementable plan for Bangkok. . . . The Plan causes no conflict
> with the NESDB; we have been providing feedback.

Thus, some academics and well-educated professionals in government
service occasionally speak about the need for planning. But political
leaders and would-be political leaders seem to have little to say about it.
The Bangkok Plan was not an issue during the Bangkok gubernatorial
election of 1996, nor was it an issue in the general election of that year.

In the Bangkok gubernatorial campaign, the only candidate to refer
to the need to implement the Bangkok Plan was the incumbent and
sponsor of the Plan, Krisda Arunvongse na Ayutthaya. However, he lost
the election. His successor, Bhichit Rattakul, as his four-year term was
ending, had made no apparent moves towards implementation. *The
Nation*, in a 1997 editorial, said:

> Bhichit has shied away from taking full responsibility to
> coordinate with state agencies as well as the Interior Ministry to
> resurrect a new town plan for Bangkok. . . . The governor would
> do well to take up the project to rehabilitate Bangkok that was
> initiated by his predecessor. . . . But Bhichit has chosen to ignore
> the project and so too the future of the city.[2]

Cabinet ministers of the Banharn government had nothing to say about
the Bangkok Plan; neither had any cabinet minister of the subsequent
Chavalit government. Then came the economic collapse, and attention
was diverted to economic survival. In the future, can comprehensive urban
planning, regarded by experts as the only rational way to solve Bangkok's
problems, fall victim once again to Thailand's factionalised political
culture and tangled lines of political authority between the central
government and the BMA?

The Challenge

As already mentioned, there has never been a successful example of
comprehensive urban planning in Thailand; the only possible exception
that comes to mind is the planning of the Rattanakosin Island, Bangkok's
original government complex, in the late 19th Century. This apathy to

rational planning is apparently reinforced by the money-oriented, political patronage system—by the perception that politicians or officials cannot support an initiative coming from another power group, unless rewards flow back to them.

On an individual level, we find an aversion among Thais towards working together, which requires putting aside differences to pursue a common goal. This is a hindrance to the setting up of a civil society, to promote popular input into the decision-making process and to promote independent civil action. Thais like to follow leaders, as opposed to working in groups through the principle of consensus; thus the concept of civil society has become associated with certain personalities.[3]

United Nations officials with long experience in Thailand have remarked on this difficulty in getting various groups to cooperate with each other. A senior health professional referred to the "vertical loyalties" that stymied attempts to promote horizontal collaboration between staff of different agencies. Another foreign expert, specialising in urban development, commented:

> There is not only a mess in the city; there is a problem with the attitudes of the experts: they don't communicate with each other, and there is a power struggle. They always want to reach through their own power network.

The same expert identified a related obstacle: whenever a new appointee comes into a high position, he is expected to start something new. If he simply follows his predecessor's plan, he is perceived as being weak.

But now that Bangkok's children (and the rest of us) are being poisoned by the air they breathe, can politicians, officials, and investors unite around a single plan, set aside their own egotism, and make it work for everybody? This writer's experience of Thailand has seen beautiful plans produced over the years for tourism developments in Patong Beach (Phuket), Pattaya, and Hua Hin. But they all failed because they had no political and financial support, and met with indifference from vested interests. The last attempt at planning for Bangkok in 1992 was unsuccessful because no one took its rules and implementation seriously, and no broad-based support was generated in favour of the plan.

Bangkok still has a chance, in the form of the Bangkok Plan. It may be the last chance to salvage a liveable environment in a city that otherwise could grow chaotically from 11 million to perhaps 20 million people in the coming decades. But there is a thread of optimism that this time Thailand can rise above past indifference. Said Thamarak Karnpisit, deputy secretary-general in charge of human resources at the NESDB:

> Thailand is fortunate in the sense that we always come up [and] change our concept when the time comes. . . . We are much more flexible and have been able to adjust ourselves to meet the realities of the situation.

Thamarak was speaking at an interview[4] in 1996 to discuss Thailand's Eighth Development Plan. Thamarak was not directly involved with the Bangkok Plan, but said that if it has participation, it can be implemented:

> You must have political commitment. This means not just from politicians, but participation [so that the Plan] is backed up by a lot of people, a lot of partners in the society. It is a management process in the society, not just a matter of having a blueprint or getting the money. . . . The planning concept has to change from top-down to a participatory type—this is the meaning of "people-centred".

Who Will Support the Bangkok Plan?

The key point is, this plan does not "belong" to any political party, nor to the BMA, nor to its initiator, former governor Krisda. It belongs to all those people who genuinely want to make Bangkok a better city and are prepared to make a contribution, big or small, to make it happen. It offers everyone—the politicians, administrators, businessmen, and NGOs—the opportunity to exercise their management skills to generate popular support for the goals of the Plan at local level. But it will need a big effort to quickly raise up the management capacity of the administrative system; and administrative reforms and decentralisation of authority are needed. Proponents of the Plan see its present form as a vision rather than an actual plan as such. Dr. Ksemsan Suwarnarat, then deputy director-general of the Policy and Planning Department of the BMA, said:[5]

It needs implementation processes. The link is missing how to realise this plan. There are certain mechanisms [but] the people's will is not integrated well.

Dr. Chamniern Paul Vorratnchaiphan, an urban planner and director of the Grassroots Action Programme at the Thailand Environment Institute, agreed. He saw implementation as a question of management reform bringing together the various sectors, and especially promoting people's participation. He commented:[6]

> The management ability [for implementation] is so limited—to coordinate related agencies, to enforce rules and regulations, to translate the master plan [vision] into specific plans.

In his view, specific plans can be elaborated at the various localities—the metropolitan sub-centres—with participation from the people, officials, town planners, and the private sector in partnership. To achieve this, more decentralisation of authority is needed:

> We need a new approach; there is now a lot of conflict. Local residents claim that the Plan does not take their needs into account.

Under the present system, the overall plans and all the specific plans have to be approved by the cabinet. This is wrong, Chamniern said:

> Local authorities should be able to take the initiative, to play more of a role. Now, local authorities in general do not have enough power to decide; it is with the directors of the government agencies.

The BMA's Ksemsan agreed:

> To follow this Plan, there must be important changes in the organisational, structural, and implementation programmes of the BMA.

But will the central government devolve more power to the BMA? Ksemsan added:

> It depends on how we prove that we can be effective. With the
> [Tanayong] electric train project [and] the sewerage project, we
> are far ahead of the central government . . . because we got some
> support from certain central government officials. . . . Presently,
> BMA officials are not so well prepared [for more power]. But a
> quick evolution is possible. If we try to be strategic, we can put
> the few right people we have into the right spot of the development
> strategy. If we want to realise this suburban centre development
> plan we should make a choice of appropriate people to be district
> directors—BMA officials, but the right ones. The governor can
> empower them as representatives to implement the Plan. The
> nucleus of such a development can be constructed based on
> BMA's budget and resources.

Ksemsan believes that strategic planning can lead the way, dealing
first with essential elements. Not everyone believes the Plan is realistic,
but our duty as officials is to produce a compromise, he said.

It seems that while there is need to compromise in management
approaches and strategies, and with people's wishes in local communities,
the overall principles and objectives of the Bangkok Plan should not be
watered down. Early priority should be given to integrated mass transit
schemes. What is needed is agreement among the different groups in
local societies about the shape of their communities, and on acceptable
means of compensation for land acquisition, change of land use, and
how to operate mechanisms such as land swaps. Private sector cooperation
and partnership will be crucial. According to Chamniern, part of the
reason for failure of the 1992 Plan for Bangkok was non-compliance of
private land developers with land-use regulations:

> The private developers did not care about the city plan. They
> looked at the Plan and said, "No, I will go my own way." That is
> why we have a mess, going in all directions. We have to ask the
> private sector: If you want to make money, do you also want to
> have traffic jams and pollution—the side effects of your own
> development at present?

They cannot make more money under these conditions; rather, they
lose money, said Chamniern. However, he added:

The private sector is [now] becoming more willing to discuss things, like the polluter-pays principle, after resisting it at first. They see things are getting so bad, that something must be done. Now, [instead] they ask, how much do we have to pay? If we can bring these people together, we can succeed with planning.

In order to have the people accept planning, they have to be informed. They can accept it. In Germany, I saw mobile units of students going out to explain to the public. The municipality hires the students. . . . It is a part of their study. This is the time now. No matter how late it is, we have to employ land-use planning in the development process. Even ordinary people realise this now.

NGOs have an important role to play, as they did in formulating Thailand's Eighth Development Plan:

About 3,000 people were organised to participate in drawing up the Eighth Plan—they had hundreds of meetings to discuss different topics. We can transfer this kind of participation to urban development. It is up to the BMA to invite them.

Chamniern listed three major points for BMA officials:
1. They have to set up a very good structure.
2. They have to set up a good process.
3. The emphasis must be on a vision, with people to come together to express objectives.

The NESDB's Thamarak had this to say about participation:

This participatory technique in planning has to be promoted. It requires various partnerships. Government, the private sector, NGOs—all have to participate. The bureaucratic system has to change its attitude. An holistic approach is needed to coordinate within the same area. Every department would retain its functional responsibility, but share the same efforts and goals without duplication.

This requires moving from a committee approach to teamwork. Emphasis would be on process, through multi-disciplinary and multi-sectoral teams.

> Attempts in the past failed because there was no process. Everybody has to commit themselves. If there is no commitment, how can you have action? Bottom-up planning is not easy for government officials. We have to reorient our officers. They have to change from being administrators to being good managers. The day has gone for top-down planning; it does not work.

People's Power

The Bangkok Plan must be raised up from its present obscurity to become a highly-visible framework and agenda which can accommodate a wide range of progressive innovations to make Bangkok a healthy city. The general public has a role to play—especially the professional groups of Bangkok. It may take a display of people's power to convince the politicians and administrators to act in concert.

Professional associations and NGOs—whether in finance, industry, architecture, engineering, property development, the health sector, and many others—need to study the Plan and make their voices heard. They need to place consideration of the Plan on the agenda of their meetings. They need to speak in many voices directly to the politicians, officials, and developers and urge them to grasp this last chance for Bangkok. Such an outpouring of people's power can compel the system to take action.

Chapter 19

What the Bangkok Plan Will Do

Most of Bangkok's millions of residents complain about the city's traffic jams and the air pollution. There is not a lot of awareness about what comprehensive urban planning can achieve; there has been so little of it, and it is an alien concept within Thai culture.

So, what will the Bangkok Plan do? Will it get rid of the traffic jams, the pollution, and the overcrowding?

The following sequence offers a simplified answer. There can be:

- no end to traffic jams (and pollution) until vehicle numbers are reduced;
- no reduction in vehicle numbers until efficient mass transit schemes are in place;
- no efficient mass transit schemes built without a clear idea of where communities will live and work in the future; and
- no possibility of creating healthy, sustainable living and working communities until rational land-use planning and basic infrastructure development take place.

The Plan provides a far-sighted vision and the mechanics for achieving a healthy, efficient future for Bangkok. It focuses on the BMA as the responsible agency, and calls for institutional changes to the BMA to greatly increase its capacity and expertise. The authors of the Plan emphasise:

> If the Bangkok Plan is to be more than simply a vision of a possible future, these critical changes in powers and procedures need to be made. They will provide the tools to make the Plan a

reality, and move Bangkok quickly into the world of modern development management.

The overall Bangkok Plan contains a strategic Urban Development Plan, whose principles call for officials and participants to:
- create a system of metropolitan sub-centres;
- encourage the highest density development in areas accessible by mass transit;
- establish higher standards for infrastructure;
- increase housing opportunities in inner-city areas, where improved housing opportunities must be provided for Bangkok's poor; and
- encourage mixed development, by mixing employment, commercial, service, and residential uses.

The logic of this approach is further described:

> The Urban Development Plan is a strategic plan: it focuses upon the essential areas for public initiative and control, while leaving much of the city to be guided by private decision making. Bangkok is a large and dynamic city, and the public sector must choose carefully those areas where it wishes to influence private actions to achieve important public purposes.

In the words of the Bangkok Plan, here are some of the main proposals:
- Creation of a Bangkok Development Authority. Projects of the Plan cannot be carried out by staff of the BMA working within the framework of current governmental rules, staff appointment procedures, salary scales, and contracting and procurement requirements. Organisations managing such projects require a degree of independence not possible as a governmental line agency, including the capacity to raise capital and redeploy revenues without having these pass through normal budgeting procedures.

    The authority would have a mandate to conduct feasibility studies, make plans, acquire land, install infrastructure, construct public facilities, etc . . . and to borrow money or raise capital for development projects from the government or from private sources. It would thus have powers to carry out large-scale development and redevelopment schemes. A revolving capital fund would be created to enable the authority to initiate development schemes. In addition, the commissioning of infrastructure for the Greater Bangkok areas would go to an independent company, beyond ministerial control.

- Creation of a BMA Planning Board is called for, with powers to approve special-use permits, exceptions from land-use controls for large projects, detailed special area plans, specific plans, and land readjustment schemes. The Plan also calls for decentralising power over land sub-division approval from the Ministry of the Interior to the new planning board.

- Creation of five urban sub-centres is proposed, to become new growth poles on the rapidly developing fringe of the Bangkok metropolitan area—Lat Krabang, Taling Chan, Bang Khun Thian, Min Buri, and Lam Lukka—with Lat Krabang chosen as the first to be developed, as a model. Their purpose is to help balance the locations of jobs and housing, thereby reducing the need to commute long distances. They seek to draw commercial, office, and light industrial uses, as well as high-density housing into a planned complex, rather than allowing it to spread aimlessly along arterial roads and expressways. The centres have a second important aim: demonstrating a higher quality environment that can be obtained through planned development. Achieving this will depend upon public agencies coordinating delivery to private development of key facilities and services—road improvements, parks and open spaces, municipal services, schools and health facilities.

A key factor in the successful development of the Lat Krabang sub-centre as a prototype will be an early announcement of the government's intention to decentralise a block of ministry employees to the sub-centre. It will also be critical to indicate the intention to extend mass transit service to the sub-centre at an early date. The Lat Krabang area should be designated a special development area, and the proposed Bangkok Development Authority should take the lead in establishing the project, working closely with the NESDB and other agencies who can be persuaded to join the effort to construct the centre. It will primarily be a public-private joint venture.

Encouraging new employment opportunities in the metropolitan sub-centres will help people to live and work in close proximity. Broad decentralisation of employment closest to the proposed metropolitan sub-centres is advocated as an urgent priority of the Plan. Special efforts will be needed to convert sites to public ownership for mixed-income housing projects.

- Existing by-laws will need to be reviewed. A number should be repealed and others converted into special area regulations.
- Park land must be acquired or set aside in advance of development before it becomes prohibitively expensive.
- Cooperation from the Department of Town and Country Planning will be required. Particularly, it is important that areas zoned for agricultural use on the western side of the city be maintained as agricultural land.

The Bangkok Plan advocates an improved development guidance system:

> If the development plan is to achieve its important objectives, a much more effective development guidance system must be put in place. Current land-use controls make fine-grained distinctions between uses, but are often not followed. There is no effective control over the intensity of development, or over building heights in most land-use districts. Sub-division control and development standards are often not synchronised.

Policies under this development guidance system call for decision makers to:

- separate incompatible uses by defining a system of permissible uses;
- allow considerable flexibility for mixing compatible uses;
- ensure adequate open space, setbacks, pedestrian ways, and parking space with new standards for development;
- establish environmental standards for small-scale manufacturing where mixing of uses is permitted;
- prescribe a maximum density of development for all sites, related to infrastructure capacity;

- reward developments that serve a public purpose through a density bonus system;
- maintain and strengthen contextual regulations for conservation areas of the city; and
- define priority areas for planned development.

In addition, the Plan proposes a strategy to help overcome Bangkok's perennial flooding problems: combining floodwater retention ponds with public parks wherever possible—thereby giving greater impetus to efforts to acquire land for the much-needed creation of new parks.

The Bangkok Plan may not be perfect, and is still subject to popular review and amendment. But changes should be aimed at facilitating implementation of its basic principles and goals, not at diluting them. For example, the Plan envisages doubling the amount of parkland available per capita. It could well increase the amount five-fold but still be far behind other major cities such as London. Administrators should consider introducing measures such as taxes and penalties to prevent property speculation—presently a favourite enrichment practice of people who have political connections.

Politicians may wince when they see that cabinet ministers are being asked to give up their power to control infrastructure development for Bangkok. Undoubtedly, such financial power is a mainstay of the political patronage system. But who can deny that Bangkok, and the nation, will benefit from having a technical body—working transparently according to a coordinated plan—commission infrastructure for the city?

Let's not forget the uncoordinated mess that "unusually rich" cabinet ministers made out of mass transit projects during the Chatichai administration (1988–91). That same lack of vision about infrastructure development still persisted in 1999.

Empowering the Bangkok Metropolitan Administration

A major theme of this section of the book is that the political will for comprehensive urban planning in Thailand has yet to materialise. Attempts have been made to plan for the outward growth of Bangkok, but legislation, administrative structures, and personnel are lacking. To make matters worse, the BMA is involved in perpetual jurisdictional

431

competition with the government over infrastructure development for Bangkok, and the various government departments and agencies find it difficult to coordinate among themselves. As the Bangkok Plan summary states:

> The problems of providing infrastructure services to Bangkok's growing population have been exacerbated by government agencies' historic lack of the capital and institutional capacity to coordinate even basic infrastructure, such as sewerage treatment, in a timely way.

The Plan, in effect, recommends that the BMA be given full power. Although the Bangkok governor is elected by the people of Bangkok, he still serves under the interior minister, who has no direct responsibility to Bangkok voters. This is anti-democratic, and a severe political anomaly. Agencies of the central government—also with no direct responsibility to Bangkok voters—have power over infrastructural development and over the administration of utilities in Bangkok. A case could be made for transferring all the central government agencies (or their units) which deal solely with Greater Bangkok, to BMA control.

Bangkok governor, Bhichit Rattakul, shortly after his 1996 election, told the Foreign Correspondents Club of Thailand:[1]

> We have to coordinate with 17 government agencies: water, electricity authority of Bangkok, traffic, mass transit, elevated expressway, housing authority. . . . I have to be very careful to deal with these agencies. You cannot make a quarrel, you cannot [talk] down to any one of those guys. If you don't agree with them, you are in bad shape. We beg them sometimes; sometimes we ask them politely. . . .

This is not the way to run a rapidly-growing mega-city of 11 million people.

Let's take a closer look at the mess which has resulted from the attempt to initiate four mass transit systems in Bangkok since 1988. Decisions were made by small groups of people behind closed doors. Terrible mistakes were made through lack of coordination and transparency. Since the process began during the government of Chatichai Choonhavan, practically every new government has reopened and revised what had gone before.

Attempts to realise two of the four mass-transit schemes have already failed. The other two schemes, the Tanayong light rail scheme and the Hualamphong-Huay Kwang subway scheme, merely circle Central Bangkok. They were both based on obsolete planning ideas for Bangkok which were more than 25 years old, with no reference to future urban growth. They are examples of infrastructure following development rather than leading it.

Additionally, these attempts at introducing mass transit systems still fall into the serious problem of large-scale projects being designed in isolation without reference to a comprehensive, forward-looking plan for Bangkok. According to Kraisak Choonhavan, advisor to BMA Governor Bhichit, central government ministers never consult the BMA when elevated highways or mass transit projects are proposed:

> Even though [the projects] are built on BMA land, they just [take a] cabinet decision, sign the contracts, and there they go. They leave all the problems to us.[2]

This misguided, uncoordinated infrastructure development cannot continue. A single, powerful, decision-making body for the development of Bangkok must replace this *ad hoc*, patronage-based system. The Bangkok Plan, as already outlined in previous pages, has proposed new bodies with new powers for the BMA which would accommodate a transfer of powers from the central government: a Bangkok Development Authority, a BMA Planning Board, and an independent company to commission infrastructure for the Greater Bangkok area.

Among these bodies, the proposed Bangkok Development Authority offers the best prospect of becoming the powerful, decision-making body for Bangkok that would incorporate democratic principles that have been talked about in Thailand and incorporated into the 1997 Constitution (but not yet wholeheartedly accepted by Thailand's power brokers) such as:
- transparency in decision making;
- broad consultation among affected parties; and
- people's participation.

The other two bodies could be offshoots of the authority.

Meetings of the authority would be conducted openly. Proposals would be sought from qualified people and be subject to review by the public and NGOs, and especially by expert panels set up for the purpose. The country's most talented professionals should be employed in actual planning or at least in advisory and evaluative capacities. And where expertise is lacking, technical assistance should be requested from United Nations specialised agencies, or foreign consultants employed. All plans and proposals for Bangkok development would be tabled in the authority for all to see. In addition, various sectors which may potentially be in conflict with the planning process, such as landowners and property developers, would be encouraged to collaborate with planners and financial authorities over how to implement sustainable land use.

In fact, all Thailand's towns and cities need such a body, and a Bangkok Development Authority could ultimately set standards for the rest of Thailand's urban development. Its leader should be one of the country's most respected administrators possessing a strong commitment to environmentally-sound and sustainable development.

The planning of Bangkok is a technical question, calling for a technical body of highly-qualified professionals. It is not a political question. Politics enters the scene when the mandate for the body is set up and when its methods of operation are defined, and when consensus is needed among local communities and developers. Political influence beyond that point is not needed—and, indeed, is destructive, as political factions manoeuvring for financial advantage have often shown in the past.

Governments come and go regularly in Thailand, but plans for sustainable urban development are not something that can be revised for financial or political gain every time the government changes.

Contributing to the tragedy of Bangkok is the fact that politicians at the national level have been reluctant to effectively decentralise political power. The BMA is much weaker than city governments in many other countries. It seems indecent and self-seeking that ministers of the central government should be so obsessed with controlling the development of Bangkok, right down to the issue of traffic control. These things are jobs for an elected city government with full responsibility. Town planners and administrators the world over recognise that towns and cities need their own elected administrations to take the great share of responsibility for their own development. Thailand is severely lagging behind in this respect.

The Economic and Social Commission for Asia and the Pacific (ESCAP) took up this theme in its report, *State of Urbanisation in Asia and the Pacific, 1993*:

> Implementation of economic development strategies at the local level, of course, requires that local governments have significant authority over at least some of the important development tools—such as land-use regulation, prioritisation of local capital budgets, and budget authority to set up special development funds.

Local Government Finance

Local government financial structures in Asia are under pressure and are failing to grow to meet the challenges of urban population growth, at a time when urban incomes are rising, ESCAP noted. Thailand displays the same trends, as almost the entire increase in local revenues during 1979–81, for example, was neutralised by population increase and inflation.

There have been no noticeable changes in the resource-raising powers and responsibilities of urban local bodies in the Asian countries. They continue to depend heavily on tax revenues, without exploiting the large non-tax revenue potentials, said ESCAP. One of the first steps a national government can take towards enhancing the capacity of local governments is to support local authorities in generating their own revenue sources, such as through sales and property taxes.

Infrastructure Is Crucial

Another crucial element in Thailand's future urban development will be the provision of basic infrastructure to precede actual development of land. The inability to provide infrastructure before property development has been an important factor leading to the chaotic growth of Bangkok. This is one of the main problems that the Bangkok Plan attempts to address, and has been recognised for many years.

In a 1990 interview with *The Nation*, Dr. Krisda Arunvongse na Ayutthaya—then the deputy Bangkok governor (civil works)—lamented that Thai city planners were way out of step with other cities, and unable to keep up with private developers:

435

Sometimes it seems those developers are the city planners themselves because they have total freedom to select the least cumbersome site for their new developments. What we are doing is running after them trying to cope with infrastructure demand in each newly-developed area. No one takes collective responsibility for the buildings and the traffic jams they produce. City planners cannot map out any plan in advance as they are unable to predict or control the behaviour of real estate developers.

ESCAP's report confirmed Krisda's observation:

Part of the congestion problem in Bangkok is due to uncontrolled private land development, which has allowed developers to install only the limited access roads needed by their developments, while leaving the city without the possibility of through roads, which cannot traverse the tangle of individual development projects. From this perspective, Bangkok's congestion (as well as its environmental degradation) illustrates some of the consequences of the functioning of an unrestricted market. Furthermore, due to a number of internal and external factors, it is very unlikely that the market alone could create regulatory mechanisms to minimise its own negative impacts on the society at large.

Little has changed since Krisda's 1990 remarks and ESCAP's 1993 report. Forging a working relationship between planners and property developers is a challenge that could be met by a Bangkok Development Authority. At the same time, large-scale expansion of capacity for provision of infrastructure should be undertaken.

Designing Urban Clusters

How to implement the urban development concept of numerous clusters of compact and mixed settlements, while integrating all-important green spaces and recreational areas, will need further cooperation from these major players. One approach may be initially to design "modules". For example, architects, developers, environment officials, and others may cooperate to draw up plans for small-scale model developments combining different forms of housing, with the integration of green spaces and community facilities.

Thus, shophouse and townhouse developments could face onto large parks and other public areas. Another example could be how to distribute high-rises according to certain densities, mixed with low-rise commercial buildings, and incorporating green areas, vehicle-free pedestrian malls, and bicycle lanes. Creativity may prevail, as long as certain necessary principles are observed for ecological, social, and transport purposes.

Greater Powers for Land Acquisition

City administrators must exercise greater authority over land acquisition as well as land use. How to acquire land, and how to ensure that the supply of new land and infrastructure continues to meet demand, will be crucial. Related to these concerns are the efficient use of land and keeping land prices down.

One reason for inefficient use of land, the experts say, is that urban regulations and various forms of specifications have tended to work against more flexible and more appropriate site designs. The dilemma here is that many of these regulations, norms, and standards—such as the ratio of saleable land to land for public use (roads, schools, health centres, public parks, etc.), minimum size of plots and density standards—are devised to enhance the environment. Marcia Lowe of the Worldwatch Institute writes:

> Municipalities can enhance the supply of affordable housing by replacing exclusionary regulations with controls that promote a variety of housing types. . . . If communities learn to focus on controlling the pattern of growth rather than its amount or pace, they can avoid adopting restrictions that inadvertently worsen problems such as traffic congestion and the lack of affordable housing. . . .[3]

It seems to me that the call for more flexible regulations should not be misconstrued as a mandate to downgrade environmental concerns, especially the creation of a green, low-pollution urban environment. This will become even more important in this dawning age of the Asian mega-city.

The Land Institute Foundation has noted several points to keep the rise in land prices closely aligned with the land's true economic value:[4]

- Most importantly, the political, institutional, and financial constraints that contribute to delays in servicing urban land should be addressed.
- Increase the availability of alternative investments [so as not to inflate the property market].
- Reduce the level of risk associated with land development by increasing the quantity and quality of information available to investors, and by taking steps to streamline and shorten the land development process.
- Reduce the transaction costs of land transfer by further streamlining the process and eliminating "unofficial" costs.

The argument in favour of land taxation gains more strength if the concept of public capturing of "unearned increments" or "windfall gains" in land value is pressed, said the foundation. For a land tax on unearned increments or a vacant-land tax to be most effective in reducing land price, increases in the tax receipts should be allocated to financing infrastructure provision, thus increasing the supply of serviced land towards a balance with its demand, it said.

ESCAP, in its report on urbanisation, agreed with the latter:

> Land increment taxes can be used as a special form of property tax . . . on the increase in land values resulting from public investment. Alternatively, the government may require landowners to pay a one-time capital installation fee to recover the cost of water and road extension.

On this point, the Bangkok Plan makes a similar recommendation that the BMA be given the authority to institute a system of betterment charges to recover costs of infrastructure. The ESCAP report also recommended that authorities should levy tax on the capital values of properties rather than their rental values, to mop up the appreciation that frequently takes place in the capital values of properties. Here are some additional strategies and principles towards enlightened land use also mentioned in the ESCAP report:

- Provision of basic infrastructure, such as roads and utilities, should precede actual site development, as a means to keep land prices down, and to guide development. Thailand's provision of road and water networks to cities and towns has lagged far behind demand. It will require a major effort in the coming decades. ESCAP notes that infrastructure provision is the most effective tool that governments possess for expanding land supply. It transforms land in new development zones from a raw state, suitable only for temporary squatting, to land where permanent housing and business facilities can be built. Conversely, a breakdown in infrastructure installation can stall land development, precipitating land and housing price increases, and intensifying the growth of squatter areas.

The provision of infrastructure by government can be linked to revenue generation or to the obtaining of land, through agreements with land owners. For example, through land readjustment schemes, the two parties agree to bring public infrastructure to a new development zone and to have private landowners pay for the public costs of investment by transferring to the government private land whose market value (after infrastructure investment) equals the public investment costs.

- Land pooling, land banks, and land swaps, already applied to some degree in Thailand, should be explored on a large scale. ESCAP notes that land banking, through which the government buys and keeps land out of the market by setting it aside for a variety of future uses, including exchange with developers for land elsewhere in the city, can also provide land for low-income households and communities. This has been attempted in Bangkok where the National Housing Authority began purchasing land ahead of development in the 1970s, making an estimated 25 to 67 per cent savings over market prices which began to prevail in the early 1980s, said ESCAP.

- Land reform, aimed at giving secure land tenure to urban residents and especially encouraging the poor to invest in their own houses, neighbourhoods, and communities will lead to improved environments and enlarged life space for the inhabitants of the city, ESCAP noted. However, Asian governments up to now generally have proved unable or unwilling to devise urban land policies that provide access to land and guarantee rights of tenure to the poor.

Tools that may be included in such reform are land inheritance and transfer laws that counter trends toward land accumulation by large land-owning families through the generations, and limits on the size of land holdings, among other things.

According to ESCAP's report, Thai government policy towards slums and housing—which has included slum clearance, land sharing, resettlement, and low cost housing—has been unable to effectively counter the effects on the poor of the massive land redevelopment by the private sector over the previous decade in Bangkok. The government would avoid confronting the broader issue of land concentration and would, instead, yield ever-decreasing areas of public space as a means of mediating the conflict between the rich and the poor in the city. This situation apparently still prevailed in 1999.

The conversion of large amounts of land from agriculture to urban development needs to be debated. Up to now, the Thai government has tended to place priority on conservation of agricultural land. Of course, agriculture will remain important to the country, but its future lies in higher, environmentally-sustainable productivity. Some tracts of agricultural land should be deliberately integrated into expanding urban areas to provide green space and relief from intensive residential and commercial development nearby. The Bangkok Plan has already called for conservation of agricultural land on the western side of the Bangkok metropolis.

So much for the crucial question of land acquisition, as a prerequisite for sustainable land use. However, there are many other important issues of urban development which have not been raised here, such as how to approach urban poverty and the mushrooming of large-scale squatter settlements. Other environmental issues concern provision of safe water, sanitation, drainage, hazardous and solid waste management, and sustainable energy use.

A last point needs to be made: Thailand has experienced a property market crash which bankrupted many developers as well as finance companies. It will take many years before they can pick up the pieces. Now is the time to begin planning a new system to guide urban development. Developers who suffered from the Crash should also welcome an opportunity to put the whole sector on a rational and sustainable basis, through participation in a Bangkok Development Authority and a master plan.

Chapter 20

The Developing World Can Create Eco-friendly Cities

Thailand's future cities don't have to be overbuilt pollution traps dominated by concrete and cars and devoid of green, open space. There are examples of city governments in the developing world that have consciously planned, and then developed, people-friendly, green cities. Close neighbour Singapore, and Maringá in Southern Brazil, are two such cities which feel proud enough of their achievement to present it to the rest of the world.

The Singapore Green Plan

Singapore is probably the most environmentally-conscious city in Asia. In the city's Green Plan, published in 1992, the government declares its intention to make Singapore a model Green City by the year 2000. It envisaged a city with high standards of public health and a quality environment; one which is conducive to gracious living with clean air, clean land, clean water, and a quiet living environment, says the Plan.

The Plan summarises the city state's approach to dealing with potential environmental problems faced by all cities: Singapore has a daily refuse collection system; the policy for solid waste management is to incinerate all incinerable wastes that are not recyclable, re-usable or recoverable. All incineration plants are fitted with flue gas cleaning devices. Singapore also aims for a less wasteful society by encouraging waste minimisation. All waste-water is collected and treated before discharge. Energy in the form of bio-gas is recovered at all the treatment works.

In the field of environmental planning and control, the impacts of all developments on the environment are assessed and considered before each development is allowed to proceed. Land has been zoned under the Singapore Master Plan for residential, recreational, and other uses since the 1950s. Singapore's land-use planning approach also ensures the compatible use of adjoining land parcels. The impact of a development on the surrounding environment is carefully assessed.

Singapore is committed to introducing stricter emission standards to stabilise the emission of sulphur dioxide, nitrogen oxides, carbon dioxide, and particulate matter, as its industry continues to grow. The Green Plan proclaims the use of bicycles as one of the most energy-efficient and cleanest means of transportation. Consequently, the government is planning extensive networks of cycling tracks to link mass rapid transit and bus stations, commercial centres, and neighbourhood centres to nearby residential areas for commuting purposes.

The Green Plan declares that the physical environment should not suffer because of strong economic growth and rapid urbanisation. . . . Despite urbanisation and limited land availability in Singapore, large tracts continue to be committed for conservation of the natural environment. Some 2,000 hectares of land, or about 3 per cent of the island's current total land area, have been set aside for nature reserves. As Singapore's reclamation of land from the sea continues, the setting aside of land for nature conservation will bring this total up to 5 per cent. Singapore plans to increase its population from three million to four million people, and will continue to balance land allocated for development with land set aside for green areas and open spaces.

As far as possible, areas of ecological merit, including forests and swamps and some marine environments will be conserved. Some of these areas can be integrated with developments, for example as nature parks, says the Green Plan. In selecting areas for conservation, one of the objectives will be to conserve the diversity of Singapore's flora and fauna and protect their natural habitats. Major parks and green areas will be linked by continuous green trails.

In 1993, following up on its Green Plan, the government produced an Action Plan for a Green Singapore. The government recognised that "a pro-active population" that will conscientiously keep the environment clean, is the way to proceed. Singapore will have to move away from punitive measures to discourage pollutive practices and have in their place environmentally-friendly attitudes in its people, says the Green Plan.

The Maringá Example

At the 1992 Earth Summit and Global Forum in Rio de Janeiro, Brazil, authorities of Maringá mounted a display to show how they had designed a green city that gave first priority to the health and wellbeing of the population. At that time, Maringá was a city of 240,000 people with a metropolitan area of 340 square kilometres in Southern Brazil. The city boasts five major public parks and 85 public gardens. One of the major aims of the city government was to create "a green intensity of life in the city," wrote Mayor Ricardo Barros, who runs his administration along the lines of a company to achieve efficiency in serving the public. Said Barros:

> The city has a significant ratio of 22 metres of green space per inhabitant, and it is proud of its arbourisation (tree-planting), parks, forests, and quality of life, one of the best in Brazil.

Maringá remains a green city despite having the highest number of vehicles per inhabitant in Brazil. It has 1.5 million square metres of parks and forest reserves. Maringá was born in a forest and was founded officially in 1947, says the city's publicity booklet. Its planners strove to maintain the forest reserves, create wide avenues and an efficient road system. Master architect Jorge de Macedo Viera designed the city with three large parks in its downtown area, which are still preserved today, despite Maringá's rapid urban growth. Large-scale tree planting programmes were started from the beginning.

By 1992, Maringá's growth had exceeded its originally-planned boundaries, and formed a metropolitan region with three other cities. A green belt surrounds the whole region, limiting the expansion of the urban trap, as the officials refer to it. The municipal administration created laws especially to protect the environment, and any new urban development must gain approval according to those laws. There are so many tall trees along the avenues of Maringá, says the booklet, that a unique problem arose: the night-time street lighting was obscured. The city opted for a unique solution by lowering the whole lighting system below the canopy of its urban "forest".

The administration has also given priority to creating the possibility of mass community participation in sports. Nine sports centres are maintained, serving over 20,000 people of all ages. Mayor Barros said he had strived to develop a city administration that is responsive to the needs of development. He created the post of city manager, thus separating political functions from administrative ones, giving more time to the mayor to guide city development policy at a high level, and to keep in touch with the people's wishes.

A large degree of self-government was given to municipalities in Brazil's 1988 Constitution; the four municipalities of the Maringá area took advantage of this to harmonise their planning policies in the Metroplan. This harmonisation allowed for the institution of the green belt of environmental preservation around the perimeter of the whole metropolitan region of Maringá. The city is located in a highly-productive economic region, and the administration says there are no slums in the city. Low-cost, self-help housing for needy families is assisted through a municipal dwelling fund, maintained by levying a tax on property speculation.

Singapore and Maringá show that cities can be pleasant, healthy places to live, even in the developing world—if government leaders accept their responsibility towards the people.

Notes

Chapter 1
Thailand Discovers the Meaning of Sustainability

1   Bangkok Bank website, 15 Jan 99.
2   An updated figure offered by economist and former deputy prime minister Virabongsa Ramangkura, *The Nation*, 29 Jul 99.
3   *The Nation*, 18 Jan 99.
4   Analysis on the World Bank web site, Jan 99.
5   Interview with Kasem Snidvongs, 11 Jul 96.
6   *The Nation*, 28 Sep 96, quoting Pisan Manoleehakul, the president of Thai Farmers Bank Research Centre.
7   *The Economist*, 15 Nov 97, quoting Michael Pinto-Duschinsky, an expert on political financing in Britain.
8   This delicious term (I do not know where it originated) has surfaced to indicate a class of people, including politicians and their broad-based group of adherents, whose major purpose is to extract money from the public coffers through any means possible, including corruption and theft. It is related to the term kleptomania, defined by the Oxford Dictionary as *an irrisistible tendency to steal*.
9   *Bangkok Post*, 14 Nov 96.
10   During a conversation at the Foreign Correspondents Club of Thailand, 27 Aug 97.
11   *Summary of the Eighth National Economic and Social Development Plan (1997–2001)*, National Economic and Social Development Board, Bangkok. English version, 33 pages.
12   Ibid. Section 4.1.
13   Ibid. Section 3.1.

Chapter 2
Stepping Back From Global Disaster

1   The nuclear winter phenomenon leapt dramatically to public attention in October 1983 at a meeting in Washington DC, when a group of five American scientists, including astronomer Carl Sagan of Cornell University, and known by its acronym TTAPS, unveiled

445

various scenarios of nuclear war, predicting a plunge of temperature of tens of degrees Celsius within a month of a nuclear exchange of 5,000 megatons.

2   Fred Sai in *Our Planet*, the magazine of the United Nations Environment Programme (UNEP).

3   At The Korea Environmental Technology Research Institute, Seoul, 30 Aug–1 Sep 95.

4   In *Our Planet*, the magazine of the United Nations Environment Programme, Vol. 7 No. 6, 1996.

5   Which resulted from a merger of the Business Council for Sustainable Development, and the Industry Council for the Environment, in 1994.

6   From *The State of the Environment, 1972–1992*. United Nations Environment Programme (UNEP).

7   UNEP's *Global Environment Outlook* (press overview). Page 9.

8   The foreword to *The State of the Environment in Asia and the Pacific, 1995*. ESCAP, Bangkok.

9   *Human Development Report, 1996*. United Nations Development Programme. Page 56.

10   *The Nation*, 3 Mar 96, by James Fahn and Nantiya Tangwisutijit.

11   In its *Earth Negotiations Bulletin*, Vol. 5 No. 88, 30 Jun 97.

12   *The Progress of Nations, 1998*. The United Nations Childrens Fund.

13   *Human Development Report, 1996*. United Nations Development Programme. Page 45.

14   *How Much is Enough?* Alan Durning, Worldwatch Institute, 1992. Pages 38–41. Also quoting Michael Argyle, *The Psychology of Happiness; Tibor Scitovsky, The Joyless Economy* (New York. Oxford University Press, 1976).

15   Ibid. Page 107.

16   The greenhouse effect theorises that the burning of fossil fuels such as oil, coal, and gas raises the level of carbon dioxide (CO_2) in the atmosphere, thus trapping heat from the sun and thus causing global warming.

17   CNN, 20 Jan 99.

18   Reuters news agency, London. Published in *The Nation*, Bangkok, 3 Oct 97.

19   Environment editor for *The Nation*, Bangkok, 22 Dec 97.

20   Reproduced in *The Nation*, 21 Dec 97.

21   *The Economist*, 13 Dec 97.

22   Reuters, London, 6 Nov 98.

23   Reuters, Buenos Aires, 10 Nov 98. Quoting a report of the Paris-based International Energy Agency.

24   Reuters, United Nations, 12 Nov 98.

25   Reuters, in *The Nation*, 12 Dec 97.

26   According to a report jointly issued by the World Bank and the Chinese Government,

and reported in the *Far Eastern Economic Review*, 13 Apr 95.

27 *The Daily Express*, London. Reprinted in *The Nation*, 5 Oct 97.

28 *The Economist*, 15 Mar 97.

29 *Worldpaper*, Oct 97, by Karen Fox. Published with *The Nation*, Bangkok.

30 *World Urbanization Prospects: The 1994 Revision*. United Nations, New York, 1995.

31 Kalle Lasn, director of the Vancouver-based Media Foundation, one of the event's backers, quoted by Reuters news agency and published in the *Bangkok Post*, 29 Nov 96.

32 *How Much is Enough?* by Alan Durning, Worldwatch Institute, 1992. Page 149.

SECTION 1
STRIVING FOR SUSTAINABLE ECONOMICS

Chapter 3
Global Ecology and the Crisis of Free-market Economics

1 Reuters, in *The Nation*, 10 Oct 98.

2 Reuters, in *The Nation*, 7 Oct 98.

3 Reuters, in *The Nation*, 8 Oct 98.

4 *The Nation*, 15 Oct 98, by Pana Janviroj.

5 CNN BizAsia, 4 Nov 98. Richard Newfarmer, World Bank East Asia economist.

6 Bangkok Bank website, 15 Jan 99.

7 According to Harvard economist Dani Rodrik, quoted by *Newsday* and reproduced in *The Nation*, 17 Dec 1997.

8 *The Economist*, 20 Feb 99.

9 *The Nation*, 2 Dec 97.

10 *The Nation*, 7 Aug 97.

11 *The Nation*, 22 Sep 98.

12 Mark Daniell, managing director of Bain and Co., Singpaore, at the World Economic Forum, Singapore. Reported in *The Nation*, 15 Oct 98.

13 David Llewellyn of Loughborough University, United Kingdom, reported in *The Nation*, 3 Nov 97.

14 *Quality of the Environment in Japan, 1995. Towards an Affluent and Beautiful Global Civilisation*. Environment Agency, government of Japan, Tokyo.

15 *Earth Negotiations Bulletin*, International Institute for Sustainable Development, 30 Dec 97.

16 *The Economist*, 12 Sep 98.

17 Originally published in the *Baltimore Sun*, republished in *The Nation*, 29 Sept 98.

Chapter 4

Politics and Thailand's Financial Crisis

[1] *The Nation*, 16 Aug 97.

[2] *Responding to the Thai Economic Crisis*, by Ammar Siamwalla and Orapin Sobchokchai, Thailand Development Research Institute; prepared for the United Nations Development Programme, 22 May 98.

[3] Quoted in the text of US Federal Reserve chairman, Alan Greenspan's testimony to the House Banking and Financial Services Committee, November 1997. *The Nation*, 14 Nov 97.

[4] All quotations and page numbers from the Nukul Report, given below, are taken from the English Translation of the report by the *The Nation* Multimedia Group, 1998.

[5] Nukul Report. Page 19.

[6] *Responding to the Thai Economic Crisis*. TDRI, 1998.

[7] *The Nation*, 5 Nov 97.

[8] Nukul Report, Page 43.

[9] Ibid. Page 44.

[10] Ibid. Page 47.

[11] Ibid. Page 48.

[12] Ibid. Pages 64–66.

[13] Ibid. Pages 70 and 80.

[14] Ibid. Page 90.

[15] Ibid. Page 91.

[16] *The Nation*, 12 Nov 97.

[17] *The Nation*, 6 May 98.

[18] *The Nation*, 1–2 Jan 98.

[19] *The Worldpaper*, Oct 97, with *The Nation. Asia's Wounded Tigers*, by Andrew Hilton.

[20] TDRI, ibid.

[21] In an interview, 28 Aug 97.

[22] The Nukul Report. Page 153.

[23] *The Economist*, 15 Nov 97.

[24] *The Nation*, 25 Aug 98.

[25] *The Nation*, 28 Nov 97.

[26] *The Nation*, 1–2 Jan 98.

[27] *The Nation*, 6 Aug 97.

[28] TDRI, ibid.

[29] *The Nation*, 26 Nov 97.

[30] *The Nation*, 7 Aug 97.

[31] *The Nation*, 7 Aug 97. Thanong Khantong and Vatchara Charoonsantikul.

[32] TDRI, ibid.

33   *The Nation*, 11 Aug 97.

34   *The Nation*, 31 Aug 98.

35   *The Nation*, 25 Aug 98.

36   *The Nation*, 25 Sep 97.

37   *The Nation*, 15 Oct 98.

38   *The Nation*, 14 Oct 98.

39   *The Nation*, 25 Aug 98.

40   *The Nation*, 2 Oct 97.

41   *The Nation*, 2 July 98.

42   *The Nation*, 16 May 98.

43   *The Worldpaper*, Oct 97, with *The Nation. Asia's Wounded Tigers*, by Andrew Hilton.

44   *The Nation*, 22 Jun 97.

45   *The Nation*, 11 Aug 96.

46   *The Nation*, 6 Aug 97.

47   *The Nation*, 5 May 98.

48   *The Nation*, 21 Oct 97.

49   *The Nation*, 28 Oct 97.

50   *The Nation*, 13 Oct 97.

51   He later returned to the post, following the collapse of the Chavalit government.

52   *The Nation*, 28 Oct 97.

53   *The Nation*, 10 Dec 97.

54   *The Economist*, 20 Dec 97.

55   *The Economist*, 15 Nov 97.

56   *The Nation*, 28 Nov 97. Banthoon Lamsam, president of the Thai Farmers Bank.

57   *The Nation*, 25 Sep 98.

58   *The Nation*, 23 Sep 97.

59   *Responding to the Thai Economic Crisis*, ibid., 1998.

60   Pana Janviroj, in *The Nation*, 20 Oct 97.

61   Ibid.

62   Ibid.

63   Reported in *The Nation*, 14 Sep 97.

64   AP-Dow Jones, reported in *The Nation*, 24 Aug 97.

65   *The Nation*, 4 May 98.

66   *The Nation*, 23 Mar 97.

67   *The Nation*, 2 Sep 97. This observation was offered at a Thammasat University seminar by lecturer Rangsan Thanapornpan.

68   *The Economist*, 11 Oct 97.

69   *The Nation*, 4 Sep 97.

70 At the Foreign Correspondents' Club of Thailand, 27 Aug 97.

71 The Nukul Report. Page 169.

72 *The Nation*, 12 Nov 97.

73 *The Nation*, 4 Mar 98.

74 The Nukul Report. Page 170.

75 Ibid. Page 171.

76 Ibid. Page 169.

77 Ibid. Pages 140–142.

78 Ibid. Page 163.

79 Ibid. Pages 159–160.

80 *The Nation*, 30 Jul 97.

81 The Nukul Report, Page 166.

82 *The Nation*, 10 Dec 97.

83 *The Nation*, 26 Nov 97.

84 The Nukul Report, Page 163.

85 Ibid. Page 158.

86 Ibid. Page 8.

87 Ibid. Page 125.

88 Ibid. Page 126.

89 *Asiaweek*, 31 Jul 98.

90 Ibid.

91 The Nukul Report, Page 128.

92 *Asiaweek*, 31 Jul 98.

93 *The Nation*, 27 Dec 97.

94 *The Nation*, 10 Jul 96. From a special report of seven articles published between 2–17 Jul 96, by Thanong Khanthong.

95 *The Nation*, 27 Jun 96.

96 *Asiaweek*, 31 Jul 98.

97 *The Nation*, 10 Jul 96. From a special report of seven articles published between 2–17 Jul 96, by Thanong Khanthong.

98 Ibid., 13 Jul 96.

99 The Nukul Report. Page 134.

100 Ibid. Page 129.

101 *The Nation*, 25 and 31 Aug 98.

102 *The Nation*, 18 Jan 99.

103 *The Nation*, 8 Feb 99. Finance Minister Tarrin said at the recent no-confidence debate that the growth rate in 1997 was actually -0.5 per cent, and in 1998 was -8 per cent. Former deputy prime minister, Virabongsa Ramangkura later revised the 1998 figure to

-9.4 per cent (*The Nation*, 29 Jul 99). The Bangkok Bank had earlier given the GDP figure for 1996 as 4.692 trillion baht.

[104] *The Nation*, 10 Aug 98.

[105] *The Nation*, 5 Aug 97.

[106] *The Nation*, 7 Aug 97.

[107] *The Nation*, 9 Aug 97.

[108] *The Nation*, 11 Nov 98.

[109] *The Nation*, 14 Nov 98.

[110] *The Nation*, 6 May 98.

Chapter 5
Transparency and Accountability:
The New Zealand Experience

[1] Interviewed at the State Services Commission, Wellington, 3 Nov 95.

[2] In an article in *Forbes Magazine*, 6 Nov 95. Reported by the New Zealand Press Association in *The Dominion*, Wellington, 1 Nov 95.

[3] *New Zealand's Reformed State Sector*. State Services Commission, Wellington, 1994. Page 3.

[4] Information is this section is largely taken from the *Fiscal Responsibility Act 1994: An Explanation*. The Treasury, Wellington, September 1995.

[5] *New Zealand's Reformed State Sector*. Page 13.

SECTION 2
REFORMING THAILAND'S DESTRUCTIVE POLITICS

Chapter 6
The 1997 People's Power Constitution

[1] At the Foreign Correspondents' Club of Thailand, 27 Aug 97.

[2] Ibid.

[3] Much of the following material describing the Constitution is excerpted from an unofficial translation of the charter published in *The Nation* during September and October 1997, and from *What the People will Get from the [Draft] Constitution*, a booklet prepared by the Constitution Drafting Assembly's Public Relations Committee, and serialised in four parts in *The Nation*, 18–25 Aug 97.

[4] *The Nation*, 6 Jan 96.

[5] *Bangkok Post*, 23 Nov 95.

[6] *The Nation*, 6 Jan 96.

[7] *The Nation*, 23 Jun 96.

[8] *Bangkok Post*, 16 Dec 96.

[9] *The Nation*, 27 Dec 96.

[10] *The Nation*, 28 Sept 97.

[11] *The Nation*, 25 Feb 97.

[12] *The Nation*, 29 Apr 97.

[13] *The Nation*, 13 May 97.

[14] *The Nation*, 3 Jun 97.

[15] *The Nation*, 3 Jun 97.

[16] *The Nation*, 17 Jun 97.

[17] *The Nation*, 18 Jun 97.

[18] *The Nation*, 16 Jul 97.

[19] *The Nation*, 17 Jul 97.

[20] *Bangkok Post*, 17 Jul 97.

[21] *The Nation*, 2 Aug 97.

[22] Related to me during an interview in August 1992 with Dr. Suchit Bunbongkarn, Chulalongkorn Faculty of Political Science.

[23] *The Nation*, 19 Mar 97.

[24] *The Nation*, 10 Apr 97.

[25] *The Nation*, 10 Apr 97.

[26] *The Nation*, 13 May 97.

[27] *The Nation*, 22 Dec 97.

[28] Reported by Duangkamol Chotana in *The Nation*, 26 Aug 96.

[29] *The Nation*, 2 May 97.

[30] *The Nation*, 10 Nov 97.

[31] *The Nation*, 22 Dec 97.

[32] Ibid.

[33] *The Nation*, 20 Nov 97.

[34] *The Nation*, 31 Dec 97.

[35] *Bangkok Post*, 11 Jul 98.

[36] *The Nation*, 10 Oct 99.

[37] *The Nation*, 29 Feb 96.

Chapter 7
The Failure of Money Politics

[1] *The Nation*, 21 Nov 96:

[2] *25 Years of The Nation*, 1 Jul 96. An additional 13 people were missing and 300 injured in the massacre.

[3] *The Nation*, 20 Aug 97.

[4] *The Nation*, 1 Jun 97.

[5] *Corruption and Democracy in Thailand*, by Pasuk Phongpaichit and Sungsidh Piriyarangsan. The Political Economy Centre, Faculty of Economics, Chulalongkorn University, Bangkok. 1994.

[6] *Thailand's Boom!* by Pasuk Phongpaichit and Chris Baker. 1996. Silkworm Books. Page 221.

[7] Michael Blackman, director of research at the Castle Group, a Jakarta-based investment research company, in the *Asian Wall Street Journal*, 3 Sep 96.

[8] *The Nation*, 17 Aug 96.

[9] *25 Years of The Nation*, 1 Jul 96.

[10] *Waltzing With a Dictator*, Raymond Bonner, Times Books, New York. 1987.

[11] *The Nation*, 24 Jul 92.

[12] See the "circle of life" scheme drawn by *The Nation*, 9 May 96, to illustrate the allegations against Suchart.

[13] *The Nation*, 30 Jul 96.

[14] *The Nation's* review of 1996, 29 Dec 96.

[15] Entered the cabinet during a reshuffle.

[16] *The Nation*, 23 Nov 96.

[17] *The Nation*, 18 Nov 96.

[18] Commentary in the daily *Thai Rath*, reproduced in *The Nation*, 8 Nov 96.

[19] *The Nation*, 21 Nov 96.

[20] *The Nation*, 5 Oct 95.

[21] NAMFREL was set up with the help of US government funds and officials prior to the election of 1951, to mount a mass publicity campaign urging people to vote and for clean elections.

[22] *The Nation*, 8 Oct 96.

[23] Ibid.

[24] *The Nation*, 14 Jan 96.

Chapter 8
Thailand's Culture of Patronage and Corruption

[1] *The Nation*, 11 Aug 96.

[2] *The Nation*, by Thanong Khanthong, 23 Sep 96.

[3] *The Nation*, 28 Oct 97.

[4] Ibid.

[5] Reviewed by Pasuk and Sungsidh. Ibid.

[6] Ibid.

[7] Ibid.

8 Ibid.

9 Ibid. Page 7.

10 Ibid. Page 5.

11 Ibid. Page 131.

12 Ibid., *Thailand's Boom!* page 89.

13 Ibid. Page 180.

14 *Bangkok Post*, 30 Jul 92.

15 Pasuk and Sungsidh. Page 149.

16 Pasuk and Sungsidh. Page 178.

17 Related to me in a conversation with Dr. Tongtong Chandransu, Chulalongkorn University Law School, 20 Aug 92.

18 Pasuk and Sungsidh. Page 39.

19 Pasuk and Sungsidh. Pages 27, 116, and 117.

20 *The Nation*, 17 Feb 96.

21 *The Nation*, 19 May 96.

22 *The Nation*, 26 Aug 96.

23 *The Nation*, May 96.

24 *The Nation*, 26 and 27 Jun 96.

25 *The Nation*, 23 Jun 96.

26 *The Nation*, 30 Jul 97.

27 *The Nation*, 4 Mar 97.

28 Ibid.

29 *Bangkok Post*, 11 Jul 98.

30 *The Nation*, 6 Nov 98.

31 *The Nation*, 18 Aug 98.

32 AP, Riyadh, in *The Nation*, 14 Jun 95.

33 *The Nation*, 8 Jan 98.

SECTION 3
QUALITY OF LIFE OR GROWTH WITHOUT DEVELOPMENT?

Chapter 9
Defining a New Quality of Life

1 In its 1993 publication, *The Progress of Nations*.

2 See table of GDP, 1990–98, in the next chapter.

3 *25 Years of The Nation*, supplement to *The Nation*, 1 Jul 96. Page 48. *The Race to Consume,* by Pravit Rojanaphruk and Patcharee Luenguthai.

4   Ibid. Page 50. *Consumerism's Dilemma*.

5   During an interview, Nov 94.

6   In *The Nation*, 12 Mar 95.

7   In the Seventh Plan (1992–96).

8   *The Economist*, 16 Aug 97.

9   *The Nation*, 18 Oct 97.

10 *The Nation*, 11 Oct 97.

11 During an interview, Dec 94. Dr. Suvit emphasised he was speaking not as a UN official, but as the head of several non-governmental organisations in Thailand.

12 Originally published in *The Straits Times* (Singapore) and reported in the *Asian Mass Communications Bulletin*, Singapore, Nov–Dec 1997.

13 *The Nation*, 31 Dec 97.

14 *The Nation* , 8 Aug 98. Third part of a report of *The Nation* forum.

15 *The Nation*, 11 May 95.

16 United Press International, in *The Jakarta Post*, 28 Jun 95.

17 *How Much is Enough?* by Alan Durning. The Worldwatch Institute. 1992. Page 120.

18 *Human Development Report, 1998*. Page 64.

19 Ibid. Page 63.

Chapter 10
How We Measure Progress Affects the Quality of Life

1   As of July, 1999. 1990–96 figures from Bangkok Bank; 1997 figures from the finance minister; 1998 figure from economist Virabongsa Ramangkura.

2   Conducted at the NESDB, 1995.

Chapter 11
From Socrates to *Status Sickness*

1   A profile obtained in 1995 from the Centre for Non-Communicable Diseases Control, Ministry of Public Health, Bangkok.

2   Figures quoted from the Interior Ministry's Local Administration Department in *The Nation*, 14 Oct 95. Dr. Akom reported in Oct 96.

3   *The 1995 Situation of Non-Communicable Diseases in Thailand* (the National Commission on NCD Prevention and Control), published by the Department of Medical Services, Ministry of Public Health, Jul 95.

4   *The Nation*, 14 Aug 96.

5   *Survey of the Behaviour Risks to Non-Communicable Diseases, 1995* (MOPH).

6   In an interview, Jan 95.

7   In an interview, Nov 94.

8   *Bangkok Post*, 20 Sep 94.

9   *Bangkok Post*, 4 Jul 94.

10 *The Nation*, 6 Feb 95.

11 *The Nation*, 12 Mar 95.

12 *The Nation*, 14 Aug 96.

13 Ibid.

14 *Manila Standard*, 8 Nov 94.

15 *The Nation*, 27 Nov 94.

16 *The Nation*, 12 Mar 95.

17 *The Nation*, 13 Feb 96.

Chapter 12
Go Fast, Make a Big Noise

1   ESCAP, 1993.

2   See *Motor Vehicle Air Pollution*, edited by David Mage and Olivier Zali, World Health Organisation, Division of Environmental Health, Geneva. 1992. And *State of the Environment in Asia and the Pacific, 1995*, Economic and Social Commission for Asia and the Pacific, and the Asian Development Bank. Chapters 6 and 12.

3   BBC World Service news broadcast, 15 Mar 96.

4   During a conversation at the Foreign Correspondents Club of Thailand, 24 Jul 96. Kraisak was accompanying Bangkok governor, Bhichai Rattakul as an advisor.

5   During an interview, 11 Jul 96.

SECTION 4
PROTECTING AND ENHANCING THE ENVIRONMENT

Chapter 13
Legislating for the Environment

1   Economic and Social Commission for Asia and the Pacific (ESCAP), 1993.

2   *State of the Environment in Asia and the Pacific, 1995*. ESCAP, Asian Development Bank (UN, NY, 1995). Page 308. Information extracted from the Thai report to the 1992 Earth Summit, and Birk 1993).

3   *State of the Environment in Asia and the Pacific, 1995*. Page 477.

4   *The Nation*, 21 Mar 97.

5   *The Nation*, 12 Jan 97.

6   *The Nation*, 26 Nov 96. Attributed to a student leader at a student demonstration against the project in Chiang Mai.

7   *The Nation*, 20 Nov 96.

[8] Krungthep Turakit, 2 Aug 94. Quoted in *The State of the Thai Environment, 1995*. United Nations Environment Programme and the Green World Foundation. Page 274. The Kaeng Sua Ten Dam.

[9] *The Nation*, 7 Dec 96.

[10] *The Nation*, 26 Nov 96.

[11] *The Nation*, 23 Nov 96.

[12] *The Nation*, 19 Feb 97.

[13] *The Nation*, 12 Feb 97.

[14] *The Nation*, 15 Mar 96. Sirithan was speaking at the Environmex Conference, March 1996.

[15] *The Nation*, 15 Mar 96. Sirithan.

[16] *The Nation*, 12 Nov 96. According to a senior environmental official.

[17] *The Nation*, 28 Nov 96. Thien Mekanontachai, director general of the Industrial Works Department.

[18] *Agenda 21, Chapter 20: Environmentally-Sound Management of Hazardous Wastes Including Prevention of Illegal International Traffic in Hazardous Wastes.*

[19] Source: US-ASEAN Council for Business & Technology, quoted in *The Four-Country Citizens' Report on the Environment, 1995.*

[20] *The Nation*, 28 Nov 96. Thien Mekanontachai, director general of the Industrial Works Department.

[21] Ibid.

[22] *The Nation*, 28 Mar 97. By Kamol Sukin.

[23] *The Manager* newspaper, 26 Jul 94. Quoted in *The State of the Environment in Asia and the Pacific, 1995*. Page 292.

[24] Ibid. Page 363.

[25] *Global Environmental Outlook*, United Nations Environment Programme (First edition). 1997.

[26] *Guide to the content of Agenda 21*, prepared by the UNCED Secretariat. 1992.

[27] *Agenda 21, Chapter 15. Conservation of Biological Diversity.*

[28] *Global Environment Outlook*, United Nations Environment Programme (UNEP). 1997. Page 48. Quoting World Resources Institute (WRI), UNEP and World Conservation Union (IUCN). 1992.

[29] *The Nation*, 23 Aug 96.

[30] *The Nation*, 25 May 97.

[31] *The Nation*, 2 Aug 97.

[32] *The State of the Environment in Asia and the Pacific, 1995*. Page 126.

[33] *The Nation*, 20 Nov 96.

[34] *The Four-Country Citizens' Report on the Environment, 1995*. Pages 37–38.

35 *The Nation*, 4 Jan 97.

36 Reuters, March 1996.

37 Newsletter of the Regional Energy Resources Information Centre, Bangkok. Vol. 15 No. 3, Sep 92.

38 *The Nation*, 21 Mar 97. According to Prof Krissanapong Kirtikara, dean of Industrial Engineering at the King Mongkut's Institute of Technology.

39 *The Nation*, 21 Mar 97.

40 *Export News*, Christchurch, New Zealand, 18 Mar 96.

41 In a document, *Guide to the Content of Agenda 21*.

42 *Bangkok Post*, 6 Apr 96.

43 WTO Symposium on Trade, Environment, and Sustainable Development. 20–21 May 97, in Geneva. Reported in *Sustainable Developments*, a publication of the International Institute for Sustainable Development, Vol. 5 No. 1, 26 May 97.

44 In the report, *Unlocking Trade Opportunities: Case Studies of Export Success from Developing Countries*, by the International Institute for Environment and Development.

45 *The Nation*, 15 Jul 97.

46 *Export News*, Christchurch, New Zealand, 12 May 97.

47 Dr. Chaiyod Bunyagidj, the director of the Thailand Environment Institute's business and environment programme. Apr 96.

48 *Earth Negotiations Bulletin*, Vol. 5 No. 88, 30 Jun 97.

49 *Agenda 21, Chapter 8: Integrating Environment and Development in Decision Making.* Paragraph 8.31.

Chapter 14
Sustainable Agriculture: Thailand's Future

1 *25 Years of The Nation*, 1 Jul 96. Page 72.

2 *Global Environment Outlook, 1997* (press overview) Page 15. United Nations Environment Programme.

3 Reprinted as table 9.3 in *The State of the Environment in Asia and the Pacific, 1995*. Economic and Social Commission for Asia and the Pacific, Asian Development Bank. United Nations, New York. 1995.

4 *The Thai Economy in 1996 and Prospect in 1997* (NESDB). Presented at a Press Conference, 27 Jan 97. Table 1: Thailand Key Economic Indicators.

5 According to Associate Professor Somphob Manarungsan of Chulalongkorn's Faculty of Economics, quoted on Page 70 of *25 Years of The Nation*, a supplement to *The Nation*, 1 Jul 96.

6 Ibid. Page 70. *Sitting On a Powder Keg*, by Pravit Rojanaphruk.

7 *The Nation*, 11 May 96. *Thai Politicians and Land-grabbers*, by "Chang Noi".

8   Some 200,000 rai was distributed nationwide in 1994. *The State of the Thai Environment, 1995*. UNEP, Green World Foundation (Bangkok). Page 281.

9   Interview with Dr. Prawase Wasi, 18 Jan 95.

10 *The State of the Thai Environment, 1995*. Page 278. *Alternative Agriculture*.

11 Held by Consumers International, Regional Office for Asia and the Pacific, 5–7 March 1999, on the theme of "Sustainable Food Security: The Agenda for the Millennium".

12 His paper was entitled, *Biotechnology, Intellectual Property Rights, and Food Security*.

13 In his paper, *National Policy on Food Security in Asia and the Pacific: Prospects and Challenges*.

14 Ibid.

15 *Summary of the Eighth National Economic and Social Development Plan (1997–2001)*. National Economic and Social Development Board.

16 *The State of the Environment in Asia and the Pacific, 1995*. Chapter 9, *Agriculture*. Page 230.

17 Ibid. Table 9.12. Page 230.

18 Ibid. Page 231. *Chemical Fertilisers and Agricultural Growth: A Dilemma for Asia and the Pacific*. Information sourced to FAO/RAPA, 1994.

19 ADB/ESCAP. Ibid. Chapter 16, *Human Health*. Page 425. Quoting the World Health Organisation, 1990.

20 *Four-Country Citizens' Report on the Environment, 1995*. Published by the Asia-Pacific Forum of Environmental Journalists, Philippine Environmental Journalists Inc., Rockefeller Brothers Fund. Page 48.

21 *Matichon* newspaper, 26 Jul 94. Quoted in *The State of the Thai Environment, 1995*. Page 292.

22 Ibid. Page 49.

23 Reported in the bulletin of Asian Mass Communication and Information Centre, Singapore, Jul–Aug 97.

24 Ibid. UNEP/Green World Foundation. Page 278.

25 T.C. Ti, senior economist, Food and Agriculture Organisation Regional Office for Asia and the Pacific, Bangkok. Speaking at the International Conference on Food Security, Penang, 1999.

26 Op. cit.

27 See Bishan Singh, "People Empowerment For Regional, National, and Community Household Food Security: Case Study of the FARM Programme", presented at the International Conference on Food Security, Penang, 1999.

28 Op. cit.

29 Op. cit.

30 *Hungry Backyards: Impacts of Globalisation on Food Security*, by Ratnakar Adhikari.

Circulated at the Penang meeting.

31   Op. cit.

Chapter 15
Sustainable Forestry

1   This observation awaits confirmation by scientifically-obtained data.

2   News release, 6 Mar 94, announcing approval of the ADB's new forestry policy.

3   *The State of the Environment in Asia and the Pacific, 1995*, ESCAP, Asian Development Bank. UN. New York. 1995. Chapter 2, *Forests*. Page 32.

4   Quoted in *The State of the Environment in Asia and the Pacific, 1995*. Table 2.3. Page 33.

5   Calculated from data published in the *Four-Country Citizens' Report on the Environment, 1995*. The Asia-Pacific Forum of Environmental Journalists, Philippine Environmental Journalists Inc., Rockefeller Brothers Fund. Page 39.

6   *The Nation*, 5 Jan 93.

7   *The State of the Thai Environment, 1995*. UNEP, Green World Foundation (Bangkok). Page 281.

8   *Bangkok Post*, 27 Jan 96.

9   In 1991, Indonesia inaugurated its first Industrial Plantation Forest, requiring 300,000 ha. in South Sumatra to be planted with rapidly growing trees. Some 67,000 slash-and-burn farming families were given a permanent job, a house, and a one-hectare farm for commercial crops. (The author has no recent information regarding evaluation of this project.)

10   *The State of the Thai Environment, 1995*. Pages 285–286. *The Forest Crisis and Future Solutions*.

11   Ibid. ADB/ESCAP. Page 44.

12   *The Nation*, 13 Dec 96.

13   *Matichon* newspaper, 7 Feb 94. Reported in *The State of the Thai Environment, 1995*. Page 283.

14   *The Nation*, 3 Feb 95.

15   Reported in *The Nation*, Sep 93.

16   *Matichon* newspaper, 20–21 Feb 94. Reported in *The State of the Thai Environment, 1995*. Page 282.

17   *The Nation*, 23 Sep 96.

18   *The Nation*, 13 Sep 96.

19   *The Nation*, 16 May 97.

20   *The Nation*, 20 Aug 96.

21   *The Nation*, 12 Sep 96.

22   *The Nation*, 30 Jun 96. Letter: Community Forest Bill.

²³ *The Nation*, 3 May 96.

²⁴ *Bangkok Post*, 14 Jan 97. By Kulcharee Tansubhapol.

²⁵ *The Nation*, 13 Nov 95, with material from the newsletter of the Foundation.

²⁶ At an interview conducted at the ministry, 11 Jul 96.

²⁷ *The Nation*, 23 Apr 97.

²⁸ Ibid.

²⁹ *The Nation*, 19 Apr 97. The scheme was introduced by a cabinet resolution, 4 May 93.

³⁰ *The Nation*, 15 May 97.

³¹ *The Nation*, 6 Oct 99.

³² *The State of the Thai Environment, 1995*. Pages 286–7.

³³ Consultative Conference on the Conservation Forest Area Protection, Management and Development Project—21–22 Oct 93.

³⁴ The following account of this approach comes from the paper, *Conservation Buffer Zone Management*, by Charles Mehl, Chulalongkorn University. 1993.

³⁵ *The Nation*, 2 Feb 97. *Conservation Buffer Zones*, by James Fahn.

³⁶ Mehl. op. cit.

³⁷ Ibid.

³⁸ Elaborated in *Countdown Forests 97*, a publication of the International Institute for Sustainable Development (IISD), Issue 2, Sep 96. The IISD was established in 1990 with continuing financial support from Environment Canada and the province of Manitoba. It also receives revenue from foundations, private sector, and other sources.

³⁹ Dispatch of Agence France-Presse, Jakarta. Published in *The Nation*, 22 Jan 96.

⁴⁰ Its initiative is independent but internationally funded as part of the Consultative Group on International Agricultural Research (CGIAR) network.

⁴¹ *Countdown Forests 97*, Issue 4, Feb 97.

⁴² *Hidden Faces in the Forest: A Twenty-First Century Challenge for Tropical Asia*, Mark Poffenburger and Roger D. Stone. In *SAIS Review*, Winter–Spring 1996. Quoted in *Countdown Forests 97*, Issue 4, Feb 97.

⁴³ *Countdown Forests 97*, Issue 3, Feb 97.

⁴⁴ *The Long-Term Trends and Prospects in World Supply and Demand for Wood*, coordinated by the European Forestry Institute and the Norwegian Forest Research Institute, with the added involvement of a range of international experts. Excerpts reported in *Countdown Forests 97*, Issue 7, Feb 97.

⁴⁵ Report on the Third Session of the CSD, Earth Negotiations Bulletin, Vol. 13 No. 25, 23 Sep 96.

⁴⁶ *Export News* (NZ), 5 Feb 96.

⁴⁷ *The World Paper*, Boston, USA, Feb 95.

SECTION 5
THE URBAN CHALLENGE

Chapter 16
It's Time to Recognise an Urban Crisis in Thailand

[1] Population projections made in the early 1990s were being revised downwards, for Thailand and globally, as of 1999. This is because many of the better-off developing countries, including Thailand, were experiencing a faster-than-expected decline in their fertility rates.

[2] The 1998 Revision, Population Division of the UN Department of Economic and Social Affairs.

[3] Source: MVA Asia Ltd, et al. *Bangkok's mid-1995 Population* (Working Paper D6), Bangkok: OCMRT, Jul 95 (as quoted in the The Bangkok Plan, Discussion Draft, Jan 96). The precise current population is difficult to pin down because of the divergence between census and registration figures.

[4] During an interview, 27 Apr 96.

[5] Interviewed on 28 Aug 97.

[6] Information provided by the Vehicle and Transit Licensing Division, Land Transport Authority, Singapore.

Chapter 17
Thailand Must Establish a Framework for Healthy and Sustainable Urban Development

[1] *Shaping Cities*, by Marcia Lowe, published in the Worldwatch Institute's *The State of the World, 1992*.

[2] Reviewed in the *Bangkok Post*, 12 Nov 96.

Chapter 18
Politics and the Bangkok Plan

[1] Telephone interview 2 May 1996.

[2] *The Nation*, 23 Jan 97.

[3] *The Nation*, 21 Nov 96. *In search of a Civil Society*.

[4] During an interview, 1 May 96, at the NESDB, Bangkok.

[5] During an interview, 20 Mar 96.

[6] During an interview, 27 Apr 96.

Chapter 19
What the Bangkok Plan Will Do

1   At a panel discussion, Foreign Correspondents Club of Thailand, 24 Jul 96.

2   Ibid.

3   *Shaping Cities*, by Marcia Lowe, published in the Worldwatch Institute's *The State of the World, 1992*.

4   In a report serialised in *The Nation*, Feb 1990.

About the Author

John Laird has spent more than 23 years in Asia and Africa working variously as a foreign correspondent, a United Nations official, and as a writer and consultant specialising in sustainable development. He was born in Lancashire, England in 1946, received most of his early education in Canada, and graduated with specialties in philosophy and political science from the University of Auckland, New Zealand in 1973. He became a New Zealand citizen in 1976.

As a journalist, he has covered such headline-making events as the attempted military coup in Thailand in 1981, the fall of the Marcos regime in the Philippines in 1986, the Rio de Janeiro Earth Summit of 1992, and the process of Cambodian peacemaking and reconciliation leading up to the UN-supervised election of 1993. Most recently, his interest has turned to the question of promoting sustainable lifestyles and the need to harness politics, economics, and the mass media to bring about sustainable consumption that does not threaten the diversity and balance of the global ecology. John Laird lives in Hua Hin, Thailand with his wife Joselyn.